THE REPUBLICAN COMMAND

THE
REPUBLICAN
COMMAND
1897-1913

Horace Samuel Merrill
and
Marion Galbraith Merrill

THE UNIVERSITY PRESS OF KENTUCKY
1971

ISBN: 0–8131–1245–1

Library of Congress Catalog Card Number: 76–147852

Copyright © 1971 by The University Press of Kentucky

A statewide cooperative scholarly publishing agency serving Berea College, Centre College of Kentucky, Eastern Kentucky University, Kentucky State College, Morehead State University, Murray State University, University of Kentucky, University of Louisville, and Western Kentucky University.

Editorial and Sales Offices: Lexington, Kentucky 40506

To Sam Merrill's graduate students at the University of Maryland who for a quarter of a century have made our search for historical truth a joyous undertaking

Contents

Preface

Our concern with the unnecessary suffering, waste, and danger which legislative inadequacy perpetuates in our society prompted us to make this study. We decided to examine the dominant political leadership in an important era in our nation's history in order that we might better assess the reasons why political leaders take so long—or even refuse—to provide much-needed and long overdue legislation. We chose the Republican era from 1897 to 1913. In those years the party had before it both the opportunity and the need to modernize its policies. We have focused our attention primarily on the tariff, currency, trusts, and the plight of Negroes, because they were fundamental matters upon which party leaders had built Republican strength and with which voters continued to associate the party.

During the early stages of our work on this study, we employed the word conservative to characterize the outlook and performance of the coterie of politicians who made up the Republican top leadership in the era. Theodore Roosevelt, however, seemed to us in some ways an exception to the general rule; he manifestly showed more inclination than his colleagues in the group to modernize the Republican party. We also recognized that, to a lesser degree, some of the other top leaders on rare occasions seemed tempted to experiment with new approaches to the problems of the twentieth century. Never, however, did we find it possible to devise an accurate scale to measure the variations in their conservatism. We therefore decided that any reader desirous of labels for these men as individuals in terms of "conservative," "progressive," "liberal," or whatnot would do well to employ his own criteria. We do suggest, however, that, irrespective of the individual beliefs and efforts of the members of the Republican high command, the overall result of their collective effort for the era was both very limited in scope and very conservative in tenor.

Acknowledgments

THE AUTHORS of this book have been the recipients of a great deal of help, both directly and indirectly, as a result of the scholarly work of others. They wish to thank all those who helped them. They give special thanks to Frank Freidel of Harvard University, Louis R. Harlan of the University of Maryland, Richard Lowitt of the University of Kentucky, and Gerald D. McKnight of the University of Maryland, all of whom read the manuscript and gave generously of their time and insight to improve it.

Miss Kate M. Stewart of the Manuscript Division of the Library of Congress gave counsel and advice on manuscript materials. Other librarians and library officials provided help and hospitality beyond the call of duty at the Library of Congress; Iowa State Department of History and Archives, Des Moines; the Baker Library, Harvard University; the Massachusetts Historical Society Library, Boston; Columbia University Library, New York; and the Connecticut State Library, Hartford. Herbert Collins of the Smithsonian Institution helped immeasurably in the research on campaign buttons and pictures relating to Theodore Roosevelt and Booker T. Washington.

Mr. Merrill is grateful to the Guggenheim Foundation and to the University of Maryland's General Research Board for their generous financial support during the research period of this study.

Mrs. Merrill acknowledges a lifelong debt to Mrs. Lila Fisher Woodbury of Concord, Vermont, and to Osman P. Hatch of Lebanon, New Hampshire. She attributes much of her desire to collaborate in this book to the patience of these exceptional teachers in a two-room school in Passumpsic, Vermont, more than forty years ago, where "they led a little girl gently by the hand into the magical world of books and free inquiry."

THE REPUBLICAN COMMAND

"The truth about it is that nearly all of the older
politicians are like a bunch of belated travellers
who have come to catch a train and stand on a platform
waiting for it when as a matter of fact the train has
passed on a long while ago. Their watches are bad,
that is all."

ALBERT J. BEVERIDGE, 1906

INTRODUCTION:
A REPUBLICAN ERA
1897-1913

O N M A R C H 3, 1913, the day before the Republican party
relinquished the remnants of its control over the national
government to the Democratic party, an editorial entitled "Rocks
that Wrecked a Party" appeared in the *New York World*. The
pitfalls the writer reviewed constitute a warning to leaders of
any party at any time. "Sixteen years ago," the editorial reminded its readers, "with William McKinley at its head, the
Republican party was restored to power. It has been supreme in
all departments of government during that time except for the
last two years in the House of Representatives." Compared with
the Democratic party, moreover, the Republican party had been
impressively popular with the voters. "It carried four national
elections by tremendous pluralities. It polled in 1908 for William H. Taft the greatest vote ever thrown for a Presidential
candidate." But, the editorial pointed out, the Republican party
"goes out of office to-morrow a third party, its candidate the
choice of but two small States, its ranks broken, its leaders im-
placably hostile to each other." To the *World*, "reduced to the
fewest terms . . . the fate of the Republican party may be
attributed to privilege, plutocracy, and personal government.
These are the rocks on which it went to pieces." In conclusion,
the *World* warned that "The forces that have humiliated the
Republicans in spite of much good service will unfailingly undo
the Democrats, if given the upper hand."

The reasons for the Republican party's reliance on "privilege, plutocracy, and personal government" were rooted in the past. The party leaders insisted upon carrying into the twentieth century outmoded practices and precepts that, in the less complex nineteenth century, had brought individual Republican leaders great rewards. They kept in their own hands decisions that, in a democratic society, belonged with all voters at the polls, all delegates at conventions, all members of Congress, and all members of congressional committees. They distrusted the democratic process. They feared the political consequences of efforts to reform the tariff, the currency, and trusts, or to relieve the plight of southern Negroes.

Between 1897 and 1913, eight Republicans—three presidents and five members of Congress—jealously watched over the Republican party and the national government, and sat on the lid of threats from below. Five of these eight were on hand at the outset; the others came forward as replacements or additions to this power elite. With one of them always occupying the White House and others of them always in charge of legislative matters in Congress, they commanded the key official posts of national power. The president's position as chief of the Republican party and the close relations others in the group maintained with various powerful interests also gave the leadership great power in the party's presidential nominating conventions.

At the beginning, in 1897, President William McKinley and a coterie of senators, called "The Four," constituted the top command. The Four were Nelson W. Aldrich of Rhode Island, Orville H. Platt of Connecticut, William B. Allison of Iowa, and John C. Spooner of Wisconsin. In September 1901, the assassination of McKinley brought Theodore Roosevelt into the presidency. In March 1903, an assertive House of Representatives contributed Speaker Joseph G. Cannon of Illinois to the group. As time passed, retirements and deaths altered the number: Platt died in 1905, Spooner left in 1907, and Allison died in 1908; William Howard Taft replaced Roosevelt following the 1908 election; Aldrich retired in 1911; Cannon and Taft met with election defeats in 1912.

No other Republicans wielded the great power over policy,

legislation, nominations, and appointments that these eight possessed. Others had to be content to serve as aides, administrators, and advisers. Among these were Mark Hanna, Elihu Root, Henry Cabot Lodge, Philander C. Knox, and Booker T. Washington. For a time, Taft also served as an aide and administrator.

The leaders in command at the turn of the century had earlier helped mold the party into a highly disciplined, proudly partisan, professional organization. They valued party regularity, control over key committees in Congress and over campaign funds, and the skillful use of patronage. They also kept constantly in mind the importance of the historic Republican alliances. Partnership between the party command and business interests provided much of the means to meet the high cost of party maintenance. The regional alliance between the East and the Middle West delivered sufficient votes to sustain Republican power in the national capital. The early twentieth century leaders continued to champion the protective tariff, a gold standard for the currency, and at least nominal opposition to monopoly. They reminded the voters of the glorious humanitarian and patriotic crusade the party had once led to free the slaves and preserve the Union. The party's broad appeal was based on this distinguished past.

The personalities of the eight top leaders contributed significantly to the Republican party's return to power in 1897 and to its continuation in power until 1913. Their limitations also largely accounted for some of the Republican inadequacies under their leadership. They possessed qualities that fitted them for political command. Until late in the era, they stood out as the ablest tacticians in the party. In 1897 and 1898 they showed better understanding of the tariff issue and the Cuban crisis than did the majority of Republicans in Congress, although even here they bowed to public opinion. They worked well together. When one of the eight showed an inclination to support a proposal that appeared likely to disturb party equanimity, the others discouraged him. This was true, for example, of the proposals to create a tariff commission, to establish a more flexible currency system, to modify the trust policy, to enforce Negro voting rights, and to stop lynchings. Except on rare occasions, political expediency immobilized the leadership or weakened legislation.

The relatively bland, unorganized political milieu of the era was one reason why the Republican command produced very little legislation on basic domestic problems. Relatively little organized pressure existed for national reform. Since the 1890s the Democratic party had been divided into two hostile camps, the Grover Cleveland Bourbon phalanx and the William Jennings Bryan reform element, neither able to take decisive action. It resumed substantial strength (and in 1910 captured control of the House of Representatives) only after the Republican party had become hopelessly divided. Most of the other protest against the old order was at local and state levels or in relatively small, nonpartisan organizations.

Perhaps it was not accidental that the most effective state-level protests came from Republicans in the home states of Senators William B. Allison of Iowa and John C. Spooner of Wisconsin. The "Iowa Idea," whose sponsors felt that Congress could destroy offending trusts by lowering tariff duties on goods produced under monopoly conditions, was so popular for a short time that it constituted a serious threat to national Republican unity.

Robert M. LaFollette and his "Wisconsin Idea" also threatened the national command and placed Senator Spooner in a most precarious position. LaFollette challenged the alliance in Wisconsin between political bosses and big business. His success led to the destruction of Spooner's state machine and ultimately of his tenure in the Senate. But the national implications of the "Wisconsin Idea" constituted an even greater warning. If LaFollette could persuade a sufficient number of voters to favor the application of his plan to the national government, the existing national big business-Republican alliance would be in serious danger.

The "Iowa Idea" and the "Wisconsin Idea" failed to mount sufficient strength nationally to have more than a mild impact on the Republican command. President Roosevelt took a firm and effective stand against the "Iowa Idea," and its leading sponsors eventually abandoned the scheme. LaFollette carried the "Wisconsin Idea" with him when he entered the Senate in 1906, but the Republican command prevented him from playing a major role at the national level, rejecting him because of his defiant manner, his scorn of their nineteenth century attitudes, and the challenge he presented to big business.

In their actual legislative performance, the Republican leaders almost ignored the Negro problem and administered but superficial attention and patchwork legislation to the tariff, trust, and banking-currency questions. Their self-imposed isolation from popular need and human deprivation made it easy for them to confine their legislative efforts to the demands of their associates in the Republican-business partnership. Thus the legislation that emerged on the tariff, trusts, and banking-currency mainly established business-endorsed codes, governmental administrative services, and governmental referees for intrabusiness contests. These measures afforded incidental benefits to the general public, but the party command could have served the nation much better had it performed with less elitism and more democracy. The leaders should have served a broader constituency which included wage earners, farmers, and the poverty-stricken. Meanwhile, only less powerful politicians, mostly on the local, state, and regional levels, listened to these unhappy citizens and engaged in progressive reform.

By the time the Taft administration assumed office, the determined protesters in Congress had sufficient strength to embarrass the Republican high command—though not to destroy it. They did, however, initiate the movement that finally brought the McKinley-Roosevelt-Taft era to a close. Some of those recalcitrants were members of the now reviving Democratic party; others were Republican insurgents, such as Wisconsin's LaFollette, Iowa's Albert Cummins and Jonathan P. Dolliver, and Nebraska's George W. Norris.

The party had slowly disintegrated during these sixteen years of Republican power because Republican leaders neglected the party's heritage of humane goals and responsible policies, failed to sustain its once highly effective alliances, esprit de corps, and discipline, and at the same time seemed unable to attract to the party any notable group of imaginative and resourceful young men who could launch a new national program. In terms of basic national needs, there now seemed to be little promise in this fragmented party. The most the Republicans could hope for in the foreseeable future was a return to power through Democratic failure.

I

REPUBLICAN RETURN TO POWER
1897-1898

A NEW POLITICAL ERA began in March 1897 when William McKinley was inaugurated president. In the nation's capital and among the majority of Republicans back home, there was impressive agreement that the American experiment had succeeded and that our political, economic, and social institutions, grown to maturity, should be left alone except for minor repairs. Party leaders agreed that it would be wise politics to proclaim their devotion to the protective tariff, to sound currency, and to the flag, with an occasional frown at monopolies, corruption, and lynching of Negroes. Most Republican voters seemed content with the "tried and true" power alliances that had prevailed in the party since Reconstruction days—the accommodation between business and politics and the regional rapprochement between the East and the Middle West. These partnerships satisfied a loose collection of interested groups, none of which fully understood or sympathized with the fears and aspirations of the other parties to the arrangement but all of which found cooperation mutually advantageous. Briefly, however, six recalcitrant Silver Republicans posed a threat to party harmony, for they held the balance of power in the Senate on certain issues, but by the end of 1898 their power had evaporated. It appeared, meanwhile, that it would be a long, long time, if ever, before the Democratic party could again threaten the Republican power. Moreover, with definite signs of recovery from the protracted depression of the 1890s, Republican leaders saw no reason to hurry ill-conceived reform measures through Congress. At the same time, they were serious-minded professional politicians, so politically adroit that they managed to emerge with new strength after capitulating to public demand for an ill-advised war with Spain.

President McKinley held the center of attention. The Republican leadership could count on his consideration for their interests. He was ornamental enough to provide the party with an aura of dignified respectability and was politically sophisticated enough to contribute to the smooth operation of the Republican organization. His public personality made a deep and lasting impression on his party and the nation. In photographs, McKinley appeared the unbending, immovable guardian of all the solemn virtues of the solid citizen—equal, as an emblem of Republicanism, to the GOP elephant. Many came to regard Republicanism and McKinley as identical.

The discerning recognized McKinley as essentially a decent, unpretentious, professional politician, committed to his party and the nation. His lack of zeal and imagination troubled very few, for most believed he would have sufficient courage and independence to make sound decisions if any crisis should arise.

The new president's eloquence and his persuasive manner spread goodwill. Robert M. LaFollette, who had served in the House of Representatives as a young man at the feet of the veteran McKinley, remembered with "peculiar admiration and affection" McKinley's effectiveness as a public servant. "McKinley drew men to him by the charm, courtliness, and kindliness of his manner." He was a "magnetic speaker," with a "clear, bell-like quality voice, with a thrill in it." He spoke with both dignity and freedom of action. "The pupils of his eyes would dilate until they were almost black, and his face, naturally without much color, would become almost like marble—a strong face and a noble head." In Congress his conciliatory manner was an asset.[1]

McKinley succeeded equally well off-stage. In the difficult realm of person to person politics he was a skillful professional. He appeared indeed to be more modest than most politicians.

---

[1] Robert M. LaFollette, *Autobiography: A Personal Narrative of Political Experiences*, 92–93.

He appealed to both professionals and nonprofessionals. Naturally gregarious, he had moved easily from a joiner of clubs to the president of clubs. He was at home holding office; it made little difference whether it was an office in the Knights of Pythias in Canton, Ohio, or president of the United States.[2] He also enjoyed telling yarns as he visited with friends and puffed at his cigar. One evening he told his secretary, George B. Cortelyou, with amusement about the time he had discussed with Senator Nathan B. Scott of West Virginia a judgeship vacancy. Scott had declared that he wanted "someone for Judge who won't gag every time Lincoln's name is mentioned." McKinley chuckled to recall that Scott had feared the president was about to appoint a Democrat to the post.[3]

McKinley was tactful. According to fellow Congressman LaFollette, "He never had a harsh word for a harsh word, but rather a kindly appeal: 'Come now, let us put the personal element aside and consider the principle involved.' "[4] He looked so very disconsolate whenever he had to refuse a request for a job that one not knowing him well might easily conclude that McKinley despised the patronage chore. An unsuccessful applicant, according to Senator William Mason of Illinois, felt sorry for McKinley because of the expression of pain on his face when he refused the request. McKinley ended the anger of one rejected applicant by a gift of a carnation for his wife. If it was an important person the president had to rebuff, an invitation to lunch sometimes followed the news. "The President was such a gracious host and I enjoyed myself so much at his table," Senator Edward O. Wolcott of Colorado recalled, "I almost forgot I had been turned down."[5] But of course not all persons accepted disappointment gracefully. After McKinley's onetime congressional colleague John S. Wise of Virginia failed to obtain an expected appointment, he characterized McKinley as "exceedingly ambitious" and "selfish." "His natural inclination to weaker friends," said Wise, "was kindly, and when he might assist them without danger to himself he did so with a show of great gener-

[2] Margaret Leech, *In the Days of McKinley*, 11, 69.
[3] George B. Cortelyou, diary, 22 June 1901, William McKinley Papers, Addenda.
[4] LaFollette, *Autobiography*, 93.
[5] Leech, *McKinley*, 134–35.

osity." But, Wise continued, "when doing so called on him to imperil any selfish interest he did not hesitate to leave them in the lurch."[6] McKinley handled his detractors so skillfully, however, that he had remarkably few enemies. After he had been in the presidency a few years, the *New York Times* editorialized, "Very much greater men have made, and would make, far less successful Presidents. Perhaps his most useful accomplishment is in knowing how to meet an attack in such manner that the man who wants to quarrel with him feels as if he had 'fallen into a bank of roses.' "[7]

There were several professional politicians in the country with records equal or superior to McKinley's, but he had the good fortune to acquire some especially useful aides. In 1896, by being more conspicuously identified than most politicians with Republican high tariff policy, he was in the minds of many worried, depression-ridden voters a symbol of the good old days of economic security and progress. His undistinguished record of a term in the Ohio governorship and a decade in the national House of Representatives went unnoticed as Republican political managers concentrated on the statesmanship of McKinley's tariff record. The fact that his opponent, William Jennings Bryan, likewise had an undistinguished record helped the Republican effort. With high tariff as the prime symbol of Republican regularity, it was easy for frightened Republican voters to look upon McKinley as wise and sound on all matters. Gold-standard Republicans knew that McKinley would abandon his silver inflation position if the party leadership so decreed because he was so conspicuously a traditional Republican regular. So in the 1896 campaign the slogan was "McKinley, Protection, and Prosperity."

Also fortunate was the fact that McKinley's early political experience was in Ohio. There he had learned how to gather votes in the large and politically critical Ohio Valley. There the East, West, and South merged, and there agriculture, commerce, and manufacturing formed a conglomerate of farm, town, and city voters, each group a significant power. There McKinley had built a reputation for friendliness toward varied groups, includ-

[6] John S. Wise, *Recollections of Thirteen Presidents*, 226–29.
[7] *New York Times*, 8 May 1901.

ing even currency inflationists and labor unions. Most fortunate of all was the appeal McKinley's personality and record had for fellow Ohioan Mark Hanna. Until Hanna generously aided McKinley with his enthusiasm, organizational skill, and bulging bank roll, McKinley remained on the political fringes. It was Hanna who spelled political success for McKinley.

Any political organization looking for a candidate to promote could have picked McKinley. It so happened, however, that Hanna was a political organization centered in one explosively animated and wealth-laden personality. This one-man promotional committee advertised McKinley, as Theodore Roosevelt later remarked, "as if he were a patent medicine." An energetic, likeable, generous, sometimes indiscreet businessman, Hanna shone as a promoter, especially when he was deeply interested in the product he sold. McKinley was such a product. The uncomplicated and somewhat boorish Hanna felt genuine deference and admiration for the more gentle, conventional, and scrupulous McKinley. Together Hanna and McKinley constituted an effective vote-getting team.[8]

Hanna saw nothing wrong in government favors to businessmen and jobseekers. His occasional indiscretion when distributing rewards worried McKinley, who took pains to disassociate himself from that feature of Hanna's activities. Charles G. Dawes, who served as an intermediary between Hanna and McKinley when election campaigns were on, observed that at times Hanna would complain bitterly because McKinley was "always unwilling to allow the Government's attitude upon any essential matter of department business to be affected by political considerations," but despite his "disappointment at what he termed McKinley's lack of cooperation, he would faithfully labor to do the best he could under the circumstances."[9]

In one of his rare demonstrations of hard-headed determination, McKinley saw to it that the governor of Ohio appointed Hanna to the Senate seat which John Sherman vacated in 1897 upon entering the cabinet. As a freshman senator, Hanna could not hope to achieve the influence held by some of the more

[8] Leech, *McKinley*, 68–69, 139–40.
[9] Charles G. Dawes, *A Journal of the McKinley Years*, 365.

seasoned members, but his closeness to McKinley, his proven usefulness as a campaign money raiser, and his acquaintances in the numerous local and state party organizations gave him status much beyond that of most newcomers to the Senate.[10]

On inauguration day all the factors that had contributed to the election of McKinley for the presidency were very much on display in the audience and among the participating dignitaries. Republican regularity and Republican tradition were there—top hats, beards, countless serious faces, and not a little complacency. An air of superiority was conspicuous among the congressmen, senators, Supreme Court justices, visiting officials, and especially the cabinet.

Political orthodoxy appeared almost in caricature in the McKinley cabinet. Collectively it was aged, conventional, and parochial. Six of the eight members were over sixty. There was some uncertainty in the land as to their physical fitness, but nobody questioned their political-economic soundness. With a cabinet possessing such a patina of age, people of substance felt confident that the past would continue to serve the future. Politically most of the cabinet were thoroughly committed to Republican orthodoxy. Since before the Civil War, Secretary of State John Sherman, now seventy-four years old, had worked conspicuously in Ohio and in national politics. Three—Secretary of the Navy John D. Long, Secretary of Agriculture James Wilson, and Attorney General Joseph McKenna—had served in the House of Representatives with McKinley. Secretary of the Interior Cornelius N. Bliss was treasurer of the Republican National Committee; Postmaster General James A. Gary had been instrumental in delivering Maryland's electoral votes to McKinley; Secretary of War Russell A. Alger was a former governor of Michigan and twice his state's favorite son at Republican national conventions. Only Secretary of the Treasury Lyman J. Gage was a relative outsider, having been a Bourbon Democrat until Bryanism captured the Democratic organization.

For an equally long time, members of the cabinet had been on friendly terms with important business leaders. Since the Civil War, no politician unfriendly toward business had acquired

[10] Leech, McKinley, 138–40.

a cabinet post and no one conspicuously sympathetic to the demands of labor unions and farmers had entered the club. While his immediate predecessor Grover Cleveland had a proclivity for filling cabinet posts with fellow business-oriented lawyers, McKinley showed a preference for self-made businessmen. Alger was a Michigan lumber king, associated with the Diamond Match trust; Gage was a Chicago bank president; Bliss of New York and Gary of Baltimore were textile magnates. Within two years the advanced age and inefficiency of most of the cabinet resulted in the resignation of all but Gage, Long, and Wilson. Two of the replacements were notable: John Hay, ambassador to Great Britain, replaced William R. Day, who had earlier replaced Sherman; Elihu Root, a New York corporation lawyer, replaced Alger.[11] Oldtimers in the party could take comfort in the continued presence of familiar faces, but they were an annoyance to younger men in the party, such as Assistant Secretary of the Navy Theodore Roosevelt. McKinley's aide Cortelyou wrote in his diary one Sunday in the spring of 1898 that Secretary of the Navy Long "is not so sure-footed as his friends would have us believe; he hesitates, questions too much, seems hampered by too great conservatism and oftentimes seems to be in the position of a surgeon who fails of the end desired in an operation" because of "lack of 'nerve' and decision at the critical moment."[12] Nevertheless, Long was about to "lead" his navy into war against the Spanish armada, and Mark Hanna was soon to urge that the administration endorse him for the vice-presidency in the 1900 election, to stop Roosevelt.[13] Meanwhile, nobody in high political circles expected that the cabinet would exert substantial influence or power on important matters of policy. William Howard Taft hoped, however, that the presence of Theodore Roosevelt in the junior cabinet would inject "some live blood . . . into a body whose pulse" did not "seem to be strong or distinct."[14]

The Supreme Court and Congress were also essentially cus-

[11] *Ibid.*, 110.

[12] Cortelyou, diary, 15 May 1898.

[13] George B. Cortelyou memorandums, 19, 20 June 1900, McKinley Papers, Addenda; Dawes, *Journal*, 232, 233.

[14] Taft to Henry Cabot Lodge, 4 March 1897, Lodge Papers.

todians of the political-economic-social blueprint that the Republicans had drafted during and after the Civil War and Reconstruction era. All branches of the government looked more to the past than to the future. In fact the Court and Congress were even more opposed to change than the executive branch. For two decades the Supreme Court had not budged from its fear that state and federal governments might through anti-property and social reform legislation violate the American tradition of laissez-faire. Recently the Court had rescued railroads from regulation-minded state legislatures, saved monopolist manufacturers from unfriendly persons who declared them to be subject to the Sherman Act, and protected the well-to-do from the burden of a federal income tax. In 1896 the Court had "solved" the gravest public problem of the century by declaring that "equal but separate" treatment of Negroes was constitutional. In so doing, it declared racial segregation legally permissible in tax-supported institutions.

Since the time of Lincoln, the most important Republican political activity had centered in Congress, and in 1897 both the new president and Congressional leaders were clearly prepared to continue that practice. It was equally apparent, however, that the center of power was now in the Senate rather than in the House. Several Republican senators controlled the organizations in their home states that selected House members, making the latter subject to their will. House members, moreover, were well aware that within the Senate there was a small group of leaders who had superior access to campaign fund contributions and exceptional influence over patronage. A newsman champion of the party hierarchy, Louis A. Coolidge, observed in 1901 that "For twenty years the Senate has been gaining on the House. It has seized one advantage after another until it has things about its own way."[15] (But a little later, when

---

[15] Henry L. Higginson to Henry Cabot Lodge, 13 December 1896, and Lodge to Higginson, 12, 15, 31 January, 3 February 1898, Henry L. Higginson Papers; *Washington Post*, 28 February, 9, 12 March 1897; *New York Times*, 10, 22, 25 March 1897, 10 November 1898; Louis A. Coolidge, "Senator Aldrich, the Most Influential Man in Congress," *Ainslee's Magazine* 8 (December 1901): 406; see also Nathaniel W. Stephenson, *Nelson W. Aldrich; A Leader in American Politics*, 163.
The numerical situation in the Senate was slightly fluid and uncertain. The

Uncle Joe Cannon replaced the more tractable David B. Henderson as Speaker, the House again asserted its independence.)

In 1897—and until after the November 1898 elections—the regular Republicans nevertheless lacked complete control in the Senate. The six western Silver Republicans, who had refused to support their party's national ticket in 1896, now held the balance of power in the Senate on some issues. Although they did not attempt to form a coalition with the Democrats and Populists to organize the Senate, they did secure some concessions. They managed to obtain strategically important committee assignments, to influence greatly the rate schedules in the 1897 Dingley tariff, and to keep alive the prospects of an increase in silver-backed currency. The regular Republicans recognized that public disapproval of their performance could easily bring defeat in the 1898 elections, weakening still further their position in the Senate. The outcries for war against Spain greatly increased their anxiety.

Four men in the Senate soon emerged with great power and by 1899 were very much in command. "The Four," as they came to be called, were Nelson W. Aldrich of Rhode Island, William B. Allison of Iowa, Orville H. Platt of Connecticut, and John C. Spooner of Wisconsin. These men had both superior ability and close ties with powerful economic interests. They were hardworking, knowledgeable, experienced, professional politicians. The *Philadelphia Press* observed that "Mr. Platt's unerring sagacity marked him for leadership as clearly as Mr. Aldrich's robust strength and Mr. Allison's unfailing equipoise and Mr. Spooner's combined penetration and forensic power marked them for the foremost rank."[16] Albert J. Beveridge, who became

---

World Almanac stated that in 1897 there were forty-six Republicans, thirty-four Democrats, and ten others (five Populists, two Silver Party, and three Independents). The *New York Tribune Almanac* stated there were forty-eight Republicans, thirty-four Democrats, eight others (five Populists, two Silver Republicans, and one Independent). Both almanacs reported twenty-nine Silver Democrats. This compilation is in the Biographer's Notes, Nelson W. Aldrich Papers. On 22 June 1898, W. F. Sutton reported to President McKinley that there were then forty-three Republicans, thirty-five Democrats, six Silver Republicans, four Populists, one Independent, and one vacancy (Oregon); in McKinley Papers.

[16] *Philadelphia Press*, 22 April 1905, quoted in Louis A. Coolidge, *An Old-Fashioned Senator: Orville H. Platt of Connecticut*, 633; see also Louis Brownlow, *Passion for Politics: The Autobiography of Louis Brownlow*, 1: 394, 396.

a U. S. senator in 1899, later recalled that a marvelous combination, composed of Aldrich as manager, Allison as conciliator and adjuster, Spooner as floor leader and debater, and Platt as designer and builder, dominated the Senate.[17]

The Four educated each other, helped each other, protected each other from making errors of commission and omission. It was for them a very happy, rewarding companionship, affording them collectively much more power than any of them could have possessed individually. The Four arrived at their collective decisions through frequent informal conferences among themselves, often held in Platt's simple but comfortable apartment. Political expediency and protocol led them to consult with and use the talents of such seasoned colleagues as Senator Eugene Hale of Maine, and Senator George F. Hoar of Massachusetts, but these relationships never involved any serious power struggles.

On any matter of importance, they politely conferred with the president before formally presenting their collective decision to the Senate. Trustworthy Mark Hanna frequently served as liaison man between the Four and McKinley. This was especially common in matters of patronage and political tactics.

When dealing with the Senate, the Four worked primarily through the key standing committees, all of which they controlled. One of them served as chairman of a given committee and the others as members. For quite some time, for example, all four served simultaneously on the Finance Committee. Allison, who headed the Appropriations Committee, was also chairman of the Republican caucus and its Steering Committee and thereby made the committee assignments.[18] After the 1898 election assured them of dominance in the Senate, the Four made the decisions, when they chose, for the Republican caucuses. All this was for the Four a most convenient arrangement. They ruled as they pleased and wielded the rubber stamps they appropriated from the committee rooms. New York's Thomas C. Platt expressed an attitude typical of the lesser senators. In 1899 he wrote to Allison, "I consider the interests of the Gov-

---

[17] Claude G. Bowers, *Beveridge and the Progressive Era*, 138.
[18] See David J. Rothman, *Politics and Power: The United States Senate, 1869–1901*, 43–61; "Real Rulers of the Nation," *Cincinnati Enquirer*, 19 February 1903.

ernment as embodied in you and Senator Aldrich. What you say goes. Kindly keep me posted as to what you do, so that I may not go astray."[19]

There were some guidelines to follow in committee assignments, such as geographical distribution and seniority. For Allison and his cohorts these mainly afforded useful excuses for making certain assignments, since they could make exceptions whenever their wisdom so decreed. Brave would be the Republican who would complain when Spooner in 1897 became a member of the Appropriations Committee, although he was little more than a freshman senator. He had served one term in the Senate earlier but had been absent from it for six years. His ability and his loyalty to powerful economic interests netted him the post.

The individual and collective ability of the Four brought them very useful connections with powerful forces; besides dominating their home state party organizations, they had great regional and national power. Regionally, they represented the two largest and richest wings of the Republican party, the East and the Middle West. They spoke for an awesome array of contributors stationed in the citadels of investment banking, commercial banking, railroad corporations, and manufacturing corporations. They had close affiliation with seasoned and entrenched leaders both inside and outside the Washington political community and with numerous party bosses. Fellow senators were very much aware that the Four had influence with political campaign contributors in addition to their other valuable political assets. The Four were able to extend helping hands to fellow senators when elections came around.

Because it was so apparent that the power of the Four transcended control by traditional Senate machinery, their colleagues and outsiders came to view them as more than just presiding chairmen of committees. The Four were chieftains of a vast but viable political superstructure which changed with the strength of each individual member as he grew older and with shifts in his political constituency. Among the Four, Aldrich became so obviously dominant that colleagues and political observers came

[19] 26 July 1899, William B. Allison Papers.

increasingly to refer to him as "the Republican leader in the Senate."[20]

As time passed the most vulnerable spot in the armor of the Senate Four was their belief in the small role of the federal government. Along with most of the lesser leaders, they failed to realize that individual or even community and state action alone was incapable of satisfying the requirements of the newly maturing nation. The growth of urban-industrial society, with its largeness, complexity, and lack of order and discipline, often made necessary the application of higher authority. Only the federal government could possibly supply that need. Some people, most notably preachers, educators, and editors, were returning to the humanitarianism of the mid-nineteenth century. They felt that only through federal action could the country rid itself of racial cruelty as expressed in lynchings, burnings, and disfranchisement. While the failure of the Senate Four and other leaders to concern themselves with the gradually emerging demands for more positive federal participation in society constituted no danger of revolution or even immediate loss of power, that limitation did corrode the Republican party enough to dull its luster. Thus dulled, it could not remain in power indefinitely.

Although they worked well together, the Four possessed such strong and attractive personalities and power that they never faced the danger of losing their individual identities. In fact they were thought of mainly as individuals. There was much disagreement as to just how much power each one possessed, how worthy one or the other might be of public support, but everyone agreed that as individuals they were forceful and shrewd. By 1897 each of them had attained marked success in law, business, or politics, and each already had a distinguished reputation. They were narrow in their outlook, parochial in their thinking, limited in their humanity, but they possessed strong personalities, active minds, innate shrewdness, and knowl-

[20] See Orison S. Marden, ed., *Little Visits with Great Americans*, 521; *Men and Women of America: A Biographical Dictionary of Contemporaries* (New York, 1910), 21; David S. Barry, *Forty Years in Washington*, 160; George H. Haynes, *The Senate of the United States: Its History and Practice*, 1:490. There was no official Senate majority leader until much later. The first time the *World Almanac* used that term was in its 1946 edition, p. 686, when it designated Alben W. Barkley as the majority leader.

edge in matters that were useful to their ambitions for power.

The fifty-five-year-old Aldrich had acquired his exceptional power by successfully combining two careers, business and politics. By the time the Republicans returned to control of the national government in 1897, he was the political spokesman for the business-political partnership that had existed for three post-Civil War decades. Aldrich had emerged from the post-Civil War industrial upsurge a wealthy, influential man. His preparation for a business career had begun with a job as store clerk in the drab Rhode Island mill town where he was born. At seventeen, upon completion of a common school education, he entered the business world in earnest as an employee in a Providence wholesale grocery concern. After four months of Civil War soldiering, most of them spent in a hospital recovering from the effects of bad drinking water, young Aldrich was back at his job. Soon he was a junior partner in the firm, and by the time he married the wealthy Abby Chapman in 1866, it was clear that he had the qualities necessary for success in business. In a few years he became president of a local bank and president of the local Board of Trade.[21] From there his business activities gradually expanded to include large investments in street railway, banking, steel, sugar, and tobacco operations.[22] In 1901 Louis A. Coolidge reported in *Ainslee's Magazine* that when Aldrich had first come to Washington twenty years earlier he had been comparatively poor but that he had since become several times a millionaire. "The foundation of his fortune," this ardent Aldrich admirer added, "was laid in consolidating the street railways of Providence, which he still controls."[23]

Aldrich acquired his greatest wealth after he had been in politics several years, his first real stroke of fortune coming in the early 1890s while serving his second term in the U. S. Senate. Marsden J. Perry, president of the Union Trust Company of Providence, who was involved in numerous enterprises including the traction business in Rhode Island and Massachusetts, later

[21] Stephenson, *Aldrich,* 7–8, 32–35, 55–56.
[22] See Bernard M. Baruch to Aldrich, 7 June 1909, W. H. Stayton to Aldrich, 22 June 1909, and a list entitled "Accounts with J. P. Morgan and Company, 1909–1915," all in box 50, Biographer's Notes, Aldrich Papers.
[23] Coolidge, "Senator Aldrich," 412.

related that one evening in the spring of 1892 Aldrich had come to him with the lament that he could no longer remain in the Senate because his income was too low to support his growing family. Perry recalled that Aldrich alleged his income to be but the 6 percent return he had on his capital of $60,000. He seemingly, and understandably, made no mention of his wealthy wife's income. Perry thereupon welcomed Aldrich into association with him in the traction business, then netting fortunes for entrepreneurs in cities over the land. Aldrich was a useful man to have in the Senate and his influence in the Rhode Island political-business world was substantial. On January 7, 1893, he made a contract with a Providence bank to purchase its holdings in the Union Railroad Company of that city and in the Pawtucket Street Railway. On the same day, four men, Aldrich, Perry, John E. Searles, and William G. Roelker, implemented the contract. Searles advanced the necessary $100,000 for the down payment on the stock, and for it received two-fifths share in the new company they were organizing. The other three each received one-fifth share, for which they paid no cash but provided influence and services.[24] Aldrich was on his way financially and he remained in the Senate. He eventually became associated with the financial and industrial giants of Wall Street, especially J. P. Morgan, whom in many ways he resembled. Both were interested in large-scale business, European travel, collecting art masterpieces, and conspicuous display. Both were imperious. Aldrich and Morgan developed an increased mutual interest after the panic of 1907, when the members of the Republican-business alliance finally concluded that they should utilize the government to help obtain a workable currency system.

From the outset of his political career in the late 1870s, Aldrich acquired a position in Rhode Island politics that relieved him of political chores and continuous concern over reelection. The state Republican machine was there to handle any challengers to his power. When Aldrich first entered politics and until 1885, Senator Henry B. Anthony doubled as state Republican boss. Most of the work, however, Anthony delegated to nearly blind

[24] Marsden J. Perry memorandum; "General Outline of Senator Aldrich's Career, Prepared by [David S.] Barry" (hereafter cited as Barry, "Aldrich's Career"), both in box 50, Biographer's Notes, Aldrich Papers.

Charles R. Brayton, and it was the shrewd Brayton who recruited young Aldrich into active state politics and served his cause for many ensuing years.

Brayton became boss in 1885 upon the death of Anthony and thereby increased his usefulness to Aldrich. Their association was typical of the era's widespread sordidness. Not only did the business-political partnership prevent other business interests from having effective political representation, but it embraced insolence toward the nonwealthy and downright thievery. Money was the keystone of the system. Brayton collected large sums from persons he served. Aldrich contributed money for his political advancement and protection; businessmen gladly paid for favorable legislation and prevention of unfavorable legislation; people of property willingly paid for government practices that were efficient and limited enough to keep tax rates small. Aldrich and other businessmen contributed generously to help elect office seekers of their choice.

In the distribution of funds, Brayton obtained especially good bargains in his deals with members of the state legislature. That body operated under a constitution which afforded the heavily populated urban centers little representation and the relatively sparsely populated rural counties large representation. The city of Providence, with 40 percent of the state's population, had but one state senator out of thirty-seven. Brayton concentrated his money and patronage on rural bosses and machines in order to control the legislature. On election day voters in the rural areas found that their votes constituted a lucrative "cash crop." That a poorly apportioned legislature in the nation's smallest state selected one of the most powerful political figures in the land angered a growing portion of the nation's citizenry.[25]

The handsome Aldrich had unusual charm. His large, dark brown eyes were arresting. They had a penetrating, analytical quality that seemed to pierce deeply, with some friendliness. All the movements of this tall, well-proportioned, dignified, and graceful figure seemed to bespeak power. On the Senate floor,

[25] Stephenson, *Aldrich,* 3–40; Sidney A. Sherman, "Relation of State to Municipalities in Rhode Island," *Annals of American Academy of Political and Social Science* 17 (May 1901): 472–74; Chester Lloyd Jones, "The Rotten Boroughs of New England," *North American Review* 197 (April 1913): 489.

he did not bother with oratorical display but relied upon his charm, his commanding appearance, his superior mind, his ability to speak forthrightly, and his exceptional memory for details. He could recite tariff schedules with great speed and assurance. Often, rather than address the Senate as a whole, he moved about, sitting now with one colleague, now with another. In a sense, however, he was almost too strong a personality. His forcefulness caused many people to regard him as arrogant.

When colleagues in the Senate defied his will, Aldrich occasionally became furious and retaliated with destructive force. This was especially apparent in the closing years of his senatorial career when the equally furious Insurgent Republicans attacked him. But he normally controlled his emotions and chose to make concessions to opponents rather than engage in protracted and disruptive battle. He usually knew when it was wise to retreat a little in order to avoid complete defeat. The *New York Tribune*'s Washington correspondent, George G. Hill, felt that Aldrich "was unlike [Secretary of the Treasury] Leslie M. Shaw and [House Speaker] Joseph G. Cannon, who did not vision the inevitable, and preferred to be blown down by a storm rather than to stand by and let it sweep past." To Hill, "This was a marked characteristic of his, and one of the secrets of his immense influence."[26]

Because he lacked insight into the problems of wage earners and farmers, Aldrich had an inadequate understanding of how other people might react to issues. He operated on the assumption that the public was untrustworthy, excitable, and fickle; hence any wave of anger from that source would soon subside. In fact, he avoided contact with the public. He made few public appearances, confined his newspaper reading to a hasty morning perusal of one paper, and ignored complaints and pleas that at times came in great quantity by mail. He did not even bother to have his secretaries acknowledge for him the receipt of such letters.[27]

Aldrich associated with people who were useful to his political purposes or personalities that attracted him. Miss Josephine

[26] George G. Hill memorandum, box 50, Biographer's Notes, Aldrich Papers.
[27] See Barry, "Aldrich's Career," box 50, Biographer's Notes, ibid.

Patten, a family friend, reported that a close friendship existed between nonchurchman Aldrich and Cardinal James Gibbon. "It was because of his love for the Cardinal," she stated, "that he contributed and obtained funds from friends to aid the Cardinal in meeting the deficit resting upon his shoulders for the Catholic University of America." Too, Aldrich regularly attended the cardinal's annual dinners in Washington.[28]

Indifference to public opinion was as common in the Republican hierarchy as in the Bourbon element of the Democratic party, but with Aldrich indifference was more obvious than with most of his associates. This limitation contributed much to his eventual undoing. After Allison and Spooner left the Senate and no longer forced him to consider the Middle West, Aldrich antagonized that vitally important Republican area. He failed to grasp the depth and intensity of anger among the voters of the Middle West and the West and misunderstood their champions in the Senate. He considered the Republican Insurgents insincere and regarded some of them as demagogues. He looked upon LaFollette as the most insincere and most dangerous, albeit brilliant, of the lot, but the Wisconsin crusader for his part gave every indication that he believed Aldrich was sincere, although misguided.[29]

Aldrich embraced a simple, direct philosophy concerning the role of government. He believed that business and government should combine to run the country. Within that framework he was convinced that business should play the leading role. Government should serve business and exercise great restraint on those who tried to use government to harness the power of business. On one occasion, in the course of a Senate debate on a food inspection proposal, Aldrich asked, "Are we going to take up the question as to what a man shall eat and what a man shall drink, and put him under severe penalties if he is eating or drinking something different from what the chemists of the Agricultural Department think it is desirable for him to eat or drink?"[30]

[28] Josephine Patten memorandum, box 48, Biographer's Notes, ibid.
[29] A. B. Shelton, Josephine Patten, John W. Dwight, George E. Roberts, Mrs. John D. Rockefeller, Jr., memorandums, boxes 48–50, Biographer's Notes, ibid.
[30] U. S., *Congressional Record*, 58 Cong., 3 sess., 1904, 39, part 1:263.

It was apparent that his love of power was the motivating force in Aldrich's political career and that several factors combined to afford him this power. His own personality, temperament, reputation, seniority in office, money, and connections with people who chose him as a vehicle to obtain their ends were all valuable assets. He was a "man of action and arrangements."[31] The amount of money at his command and the uses to which he put it were especially striking. The latter ranged from the purchase of newspapers in Kansas to aid in the reelection of high tariff advocate Senator Charles Curtis, to supplying money to the campaign of Charles H. Grosvenor of Ohio, a high tariff member of the House of Representatives. Sometimes Aldrich worked directly with candidates who welcomed help; sometimes he worked through other individuals or agencies. One very useful colleague in such work was Senator W. Murray Crane of Massachusetts, a wealthy high tariff protectionist. In the case of Grosvenor, Aldrich worked through the Republican House election committee. The grateful Ohioan wrote to Aldrich on October 25, 1902, "Again I am under obligations to you. I have a letter from the Congressional Committee . . . with a contribution of two thousand ($2,000.00) to my campaign. I will pull through all right and hope to have a complimentary majority. I thank you very much."[32]

From the outset of his senatorial career and until the Panic of 1907 brought the currency question to the fore, Aldrich was more deeply involved in the tariff issue than in any other question, first as the most active member of the Finance Committee and, after 1897, as chairman of this committee. At times, on matters aiding business Aldrich was able to command a significant following among Republicans and Democrats alike. He early made common cause with high protectionist Arthur Pue Gorman, Democratic senator from Maryland. A story circulated in the 1880s and later that a wit in the Senate press gallery, seeing Aldrich and Gorman sitting side by side on a sofa in

[31] Mark Sullivan, *The Education of an American,* 264. See also O. O. Stealey, *130 Pen Pictures of Live Men,* 25–30.

[32] Box 48, Biographer's Notes, Aldrich Papers; see also: Charles Curtis to Aldrich, 13 October 1909; Aldrich to Curtis, 22 October 1909; Aldrich to Porter J. McCumber, 22 October 1909—all in Aldrich Papers.

the rear of the chamber, remarked, "The Senate is in session!"[33] Aldrich and the Democratic "sugar senators" from Louisiana had much in common. One episode that greatly amused the Senate during the debate on the sugar schedule in the Payne-Aldrich Tariff concerned Senator Samuel D. McEnery of Louisiana. The deaf McEnery came up to Aldrich, held his hand behind his ear and shouted, "If I don't vote right, Senator, you'll understand it's because I don't hear what it is you want."[34] By 1901, an apologist for the Republican-business alliance, Louis A. Coolidge, asserted in an article entitled "Senator Aldrich, the Most Influential Man in Congress," that "the great industries of the country have learned to look upon him as their special representative." The admiring Coolidge added, "And, after all, the great mass of really important legislation has to do with business."[35]

Aldrich served in the Senate until 1911, outlasting the other members of the powerful Four in that body. He thus had to rely during his later years on a weaker team; in particular, Aldrich relied on high tariff Senators W. Murray Crane of Massachusetts, Reed Smoot of Utah, Charles Curtis of Kansas, and Eugene Hale of Maine.

Orville H. Platt, in contrast to the Wall Street-oriented Aldrich, typified the more staid, industrial New Englander. Platt was interested in Yankee tinkerers and entrepreneurs who had become manufacturers, large or small. He carried with him into his Washington career a devotion to the ordered way of life he knew in his home city, Hartford, Connecticut, in contrast to Aldrich's enthusiasm for the newer finance capitalism which had its chief headquarters in Wall Street. But Platt, like Aldrich, operated from a political base of rural rotten boroughs. In 1901, a constitutional amendment modernized the state senate, but the state house of representatives remained far removed from popular control. As late as 1910, for example, New Haven, with a population of 133,605, had two representatives in the

[33] "Lincoln," *Boston Transcript*, reprinted in *Providence Tribune*, 17 June 1909, clipping, Aldrich Papers.
[34] Senator Moses Clapp memorandum, box 50, Biographer's Notes, Aldrich Papers.
[35] Coolidge, "Senator Aldrich," 406.

house, while the town of Warren, with a population of 412, had one.[36]

In 1897 Platt was seventy, a highly respected veteran of almost two decades in the Senate. One of the Senate freshmen of that year, Albert J. Beveridge, later recalled that Platt was over "six feet tall, slender, bony," the John Marshall and Abraham Lincoln type. In appearance "he reminded one of what the greatest of the Hebrew prophets must have looked like; his head was very noble, his features grave, composed, determined, and full of character; his eyes uncommonly large, deep brown in color, and fathomless; his forehead was high, broad, intellectual, and commanding." Beveridge added, "One could not look at him without repeating Milton's immortal lines, 'On his brow deliberation sat, and public care.' "[37] Theodore Roosevelt, early in his presidency, remarked to Platt's son, "Your father is the whitest man I know!"[38]

Platt had entered the Senate in 1879 after a brief and undistinguished apprenticeship in the Connecticut legislature. Seniority, soundness, sagacity, integrity, and hard work brought to him steady advancement in the Senate. He built a reputation as a specialist, a constructive lawmaker in such exacting fields as copyrights, Indian policy, and the tariff. Now, in 1897, as a member of key committees and a sagacious veteran, Platt was clearly a man of importance. While senator, he chose to live simply with Mrs. Platt in their Washington apartment and in their summer camp at Long Lake in the Adirondacks. A man of modest means, when he ran short of funds he earned a little during the summer by writing articles for magazines.[39] On one occasion, replying to a request for a loan of one hundred dollars, Platt wrote, "I would be glad to lend it to you if I could possibly do so, but I have not had in all my life one hundred dollars ahead."[40] He would have been better off financially if he had not allowed his Wall Street friend John H. Flagg to speculate for him in the stock market on the eve of the Spanish American

[36] Jones, "Rotten Boroughs," 489.
[37] Quoted in Bowers, *Beveridge*, 138–39.
[38] Quoted in Coolidge, *Platt*, 595.
[39] Ibid., 1–133 passim; Bowers, *Beveridge*, 139.
[40] Platt to Austin Brainard, 10 February 1904, in Orville H. Platt Papers.

War. Flagg, to whom Platt sent hourly telegraphic reports as the hour of decision approached, bet on a stock market collapse when war was declared. Instead, stock prices went up.[41]

After his death in 1905 at seventy-eight, a number of Connecticut manufacturers and J. P. Morgan contributed a thousand dollars each to provide an annuity to Platt's financially insecure widow.[42] He had served that group well, with honesty and a sincere belief in the efficacy of the high tariff and government aid to business. Modestly he even admitted that currency and the trust issue were beyond the depth of his understanding. He relied for counsel on his old friend Flagg, who numbered Standard Oil among his legal clients.[43] The problems and aspirations of fellow Republicans in the Middle West and beyond were as far beyond his ken as they were to his fellow easterner Aldrich, who said upon Platt's death that he "was all in all the best man I ever knew."[44]

William B. Allison of Iowa was the most influential senator from the crucially important Middle West in the business-government coalition. In 1897 he was chairman of the Republican caucus, the Steering Committee, and the Appropriation Committee, and a member of the Finance Committee. The coalition needed a politician par excellence from this awesomely large agricultural region and Allison was such a man; he was a politician's politician. He needed to be responsive because, unlike Aldrich and Platt, he was constantly confronted by the possibility of a voter revolt in Iowa. It might be a rebellion within the Republican party that threatened to unseat the current leadership, or a voter switch that would sweep the Democrats into power. Iowa voters, like those in many states outside New England and the South, were markedly fickle. Back in the mid-1880s, Iowa's Republican Congressman Jonathan P. Dolliver had cockily proclaimed that his state "would go Democratic when hell went Methodist."[45] In 1889 Iowa went Democratic.

[41] Flagg to Platt, 11, 19 February, 28, 30 March, 2 April 1898, Platt Papers.
[42] Isaac Ullman memorandum, box 49, Biographer's Notes, Aldrich Papers.
[43] Platt to Flagg, 7 November 1899, 29 July 1903, Platt Papers.
[44] Quoted in Coolidge, *Platt*, 599.
[45] Quoted in Cyrenus Cole, *I Remember, I Remember: A Book of Recollections*, 176.

The grangers, populists, prohibitionists, nativists, currency inflationists, and antimonopolists, or a combination of them, were
at times more influential in such states as Iowa than was loyalty
to a political leader or party or faction.

Over the course of several decades Iowa Republican leaders
had concentrated much effort on improving their expertise and
organization in order to withstand the periodic explosive anger
of agrarian voters. The Iowa leaders, with Allison the most
powerful, worked together like members of a secret fraternal
order to obtain and sustain a close alliance with executives of
the railroads that traversed the state. Despite the outcries of
rural shippers, the absence of any major manufacturing enterprises in Iowa left the way clear for a very firm alliance between
the politicians and railroad interests. The alliance did make
minor concessions to rural shippers and diverted their attention
to tariff reform.

In 1897, Allison, then sixty-eight years of age, had been in
Congress for thirty-three years, ten in the House and twenty-
three in the Senate, and during that time he had never lost an
election. Even more impressive, after making common cause
with the business-political partnership that characterized the
Republican national hierarchy, Allison never found it necessary
to abandon that group. He had helped shape the partnership; he
was a major participant in it. His success as a nationally influential politician rested largely on his invariably shrewd and
consistent application in Iowa and in Washington of the Republican party's national image. By concentrating on the national party's Civil War triumph in preserving the nation and
freeing the slaves and on the party's identification with the
industrial revolution, Allison afforded Iowa Republicans emotional and economic identification with a great tradition that
they believed embraced patriotism, humanitarianism, and economic progress.

In the Senate, previous to 1897, the currency question, expressed through greenbackism and later through free silver, had
caused Allison his greatest difficulty with his Iowa constituents.
He solved that problem—or rather postponed its solution—by
appearing to obtain for them a large measure of what they

wanted. The Bland-Allison Act of 1878, for example, which he helped fashion and which modestly increased the supply of currency, saved face for politicians committed to inflation and subdued the fears of persons fearful of change. In the same spirit he voted for the compromise Sherman Silver Purchase Act of 1890. These measures brought peace of mind to Allison's friends in the business-political partnership. They were grateful to him for his actions and admired him for his skill in sitting on the lid of discontent in the farm belt. His defense of the protective tariff likewise contributed to his high standing in the hierarchy.

In the difficult role of inducing rural Iowa to embrace the national business-political partnership, Allison operated with impressive equipoise. He never made a false step politically. He moved with such cautious surety that it was widely said that he could walk on eggs from Des Moines to Washington without breaking one of them, or the length of a piano keyboard without making a sound, or glide across the Senate floor in wooden shoes making no more noise than a fly on the ceiling. He managed to keep from Iowa voters the full extent of his alliance with railroad companies. Had the voters been fully aware of the facts, many of them would have felt that the real capital city of Iowa was not Des Moines but railroad headquarters Chicago.[46]

The alliance between the Allison-dominated Republicans and the railroads operated through Joseph W. Blythe, chief counsel for the Chicago, Burlington, and Quincy Railroad Company, and Judge Nathaniel M. Hubbard, counsel for the Chicago and Northwestern Railroad. On one occasion, in the course of preparation for the 1898 off-year elections, the chairman of the Iowa Republican State Committee, C. T. Hancock, beseeched Allison to help him obtain campaign funds from Chicagoan Marvin Hughitt, president of the Chicago and Northwestern Railroad. Hancock urged Allison to go to Chicago for the purpose and to "see Mr. Hughitt, as he is such a personal friend of yours." If Allison could not go to Chicago, then it would be helpful if he would at least write to Hughitt about the matter. The discreet

[46] See Leland L. Sage, *William Boyd Allison: A Study in Practical Politics*, 1–268 passim.

Allison refused to do either.[47] Allison's ties with Charles E. Perkins, president of the Chicago, Burlington, and Quincy Railroad were close. One knowledgeable lobbyist informed Boston financier Henry L. Higginson that Allison's "most trusted friend is Mr. Perkins."[48]

All the while Allison carried with him an approachable manner, quiet charm, and an aura of safeness. Iowa folk liked to call him the "Sage of Dubuque." Despite his fondness for the companionship of his eastern friends in Washington, his constituents chose to think of him as a favorite son, a great power in Washington, and a contender for the 1892 and 1896 Republican presidential nominations. By the time he died in 1908 at seventy-nine, however, Iowa voters had come to look with more favor on such Insurgents as Jonathan P. Dolliver and Albert S. Cummins.

The other midwestern member of the Four, Wisconsin's Senator John C. Spooner, was eminently qualified for leadership in the Senate. He was gifted with superior legal knowledge, acumen in formulating legislation, and forensic skill in senatorial debate. On constitutional questions he was the most brilliant and persuasive member of the Senate. Former Judge William Howard Taft in 1901 wrote from his post as commissioner of the Philippine Islands, "I have the warmest friendship for Spooner, and have often told him he ought to be president, and have prophesied that he would be. He is, I believe, the best man in the Senate."[49] Spooner's ability made it unnecessary for him to acquire seniority in order to accede to power. In 1897 he was a relative newcomer, having entered the Senate in 1885, lost his seat to Democrat William F. Vilas in 1891, and been elected again in 1897. Aldrich, Allison, and Platt quickly took him into their fold.[50]

Attorney Spooner was especially useful to Aldrich, who was

---

[47] Hancock to Allison, 30 September, 5 October 1898, Allison Papers.

[48] Hugh H. Hanna to Higginson, 4 January 1901, Higginson Papers.

[49] Quoted from Taft to Amos P. Wilder in Wilder to Spooner, 22 June 1901, John C. Spooner Papers.

[50] See Dorothy Ganfield Fowler, *John Coit Spooner: Defender of Presidents*, 3–222 passim; Joseph Benson Foraker, *Notes of a Busy Life*, 2:10; Leech, *McKinley*, 483.

untrained in law and temperamentally impatient with legal restraints. Aldrich needed not only legal guidance, but guidance forcefully presented. Sometimes, one Washington correspondent reported, an observer might discover upon entering Spooner's committee room that books were scattered everywhere on the floor where the senator had tossed them. "If then asked what had happened, Spooner would be likely to reply, 'Oh, I have been trying to get some law into Aldrich.' "[51]

Spooner was gifted with both the tongue and the pen. On the floor and in the galleries of the Senate there was invariably an anticipatory stirring when the Wisconsin solon arose to debate a measure. There, as elsewhere, the short, energetic Spooner spoke extemporaneously and with rapierlike thrusts at his opponents. He was so nimble witted and logical, so full of information, that many people considered him the best debater in the Senate. His unruly hair seemed to go in all directions at once, but not so his mind and tongue. His general appearance and spirited manner reminded observers of how they supposed Stephen A. Douglas had been. His talent at drafting compromise legislation led another newsman to remark that time and again Spooner demonstrated "his ability to get two diametrically opposite questions into one harmonious whole." Spooner also, in contrast to the senators who specialized, had a broad range of interests and knowledge.[52]

Spooner's political background was—and threatened to continue to be—more stormy than that of his cohorts, Aldrich, Allison, and Platt. His excessive pride, stubbornness, and irritable nature invited trouble. Moreover, he was closely identified with the cynical, unsavory Wisconsin Republican hierarchy. When he first became a senator, his first significant political office, he was a protegé of millionaire Senator Philetus Sawyer. Sawyer had found young Spooner very capable as a railroad

[51] George G. Hill memorandum, box 48, Biographer's Notes, Aldrich Papers.
[52] "Real Rulers of the Nation," *Cincinnati Enquirer,* 19 February 1903; Walter Wellman, "Spooner of Wisconsin: A Sketch of the Present Leader of the Senate," *Review of Reviews* 26 (August 1902): 167–70; Edward G. Lowry, *Washington Close-Ups: Intimate Views of Some Public Figures,* 21; *Boston Herald,* 14 June 1901; *Brooklyn Daily Eagle,* 14 June 1901, clipping, Spooner Papers; James E. Watson, *As I Knew Them: Memoirs of James E. Watson,* 59.

lawyer, railroad lobbyist, and stump speaker. His work as a lawyer and lobbyist at the state capital had helped Sawyer acquire choice timberlands. Spooner and Sawyer were closely allied with Milwaukee's Henry C. Payne, a lobbyist, a street railroad and electricity entrepreneur, and an astute political manager.[53] Spooner had connections with Sawyer, Payne, and other exploiters and machine-type politicians, but because of his brilliance and prestige as a lawyer, his effectiveness on the political hustings, and his disinterest in mere political manipulation, the public tended to assume that he was morally superior to his compatriots. Many voters also took pride in Spooner as the Senate's most fervent spokesman for the southern Negro.

It was unfortunate that Spooner made himself beholden to Sawyer and his cohorts. They had obtained special privileges from the state legislature for their business interests, shockingly gerrymandered election districts, diverted the interest on state treasury funds to their party's coffers, and spent unduly large sums to nominate and elect their chosen candidates. Finally, in the election of 1890, those excesses, plus the unpopularity of a Republican-sponsored anti-parochial-school law, the McKinley tariff, and hard times in general, resulted in their temporary loss of the state government. In 1891 Democrat William F. Vilas replaced Spooner in the Senate.[54] In the 1890s, moreover, the practices of the Sawyer-Payne Republican machine brought Robert M. LaFollette and his Insurgent Republicans into prominence.

Although LaFollette publicly attacked the Sawyer-Payne cabal, he carefully refrained from directly criticizing Spooner. But, much to Spooner's mounting fury, LaFollette's relentless war of attrition on Spooner's cohorts eventually isolated Spooner and ultimately destroyed his power. Faced with defeat, he resigned from the Senate in 1907.[55] He became a conspicuous

[53] Richard Nelson Current, *Pine Logs and Politics: A Life of Philetus Sawyer, 1816–1900*, 134, 138, 140–42, 145, 179, 187–93, 200–216, 226, 236–39, 255, 270–75, 287–89; Robert S. Maxwell, *LaFollette and the Rise of the Progressives in Wisconsin*, 10, 11.

[54] Horace Samuel Merrill, *William Freeman Vilas, Doctrinaire Democrat*, 151–88 passim.

[55] Belle Case LaFollette and Fola LaFollette, *Robert M. LaFollette*, 1:154–55, 156.

New York corporation lawyer and lived in that city until his death in 1919.[56]

In 1897 the Republican leaders had a policy blueprint already at hand. They all liked it and did not intend to alter it. This blueprint was thoroughly Republican, and was designed to satisfy the requirements of the business-Republican alliance and the Republican East and Middle West. It was in essence the cumulative record of the Republican party's past experiences, promises, and achievements. It was a guide to the future and hence well suited to the tastes of the 1897 custodians of the status quo. The main items on the blueprint—and actually the only ones of longterm concern—were high tariff rates, a sound currency system, concern for southern Negroes, and only nominal government control of business. With this blueprint, it appeared to them that the East-Middle West alliance and the political-business combination would thrive.

Protectionist tariff policy was like manna from heaven. It netted so very much power at so little expenditure of energy. Protectionism almost sold itself. Back in the 1850s, the northern Whigs had carried the protectionist policy with them into the emergent Republican party, and its popularity had grown apace. As the Civil War and Reconstruction absorbed less attention and as industrialization accelerated, Republican leaders focused increasing attention on protectionism. It had great appeal to producers with goods to sell, be they manufacturers, miners, lumbermen, or farmers, and to wage earners in those enterprises. It also appealed to voters who had complete confidence in the judgment of Republican political and business leaders. The plausibility of protectionist arguments, the force of the protectionist tradition in the party, and the pronouncements of party spokesmen constituted a powerful force.

The Republicans concentrated their greatest protectionist salesmanship on the industrialists and farmers of their two major bailiwicks, the East and the Middle West. In both places they managed without difficulty to indoctrinate and keep indoctrinated their patrons, as Mark Hanna discovered when gathering

[56] Fowler, *Spooner*, 371–91.

campaign funds. He found it especially lucrative to "fry out the fat cats" of the tariff-protected industries, leaving it unnecessary to collect funds from the less affluent protectionist farmers. Commentator "Lincoln," writing in the *Boston Transcript*, attempted to assess the power that tariff makers possessed: "The position of favor distributor under the American protective tariff," he said, "is one of a degree of power that might well make princes and kings and shahs and czars green with envy." In fact, "A little lifting of a tariff here and a lowering of another there may throw millions of dollars in or out of a few pockets." Senator Julius Caesar Burrows from lumber-rich Michigan reported to the president of a lumbermen's association an episode that transpired in the course of his friendly efforts on behalf of that industry. Burrows, a member of the conference committee on the Dingley tariff bill, said a group of lumbermen, working around a table during the final stages, paused in their deliberations to learn how they were coming out. Their mathematics revealed that "for the men there assembled" it appeared that "it made a difference of 6½ million dollars to have the higher rate prevail."[57]

Republican politicians found it quite easy to convince farmers, whose votes were of vital concern to the Republican party, that their economic security and progress depended upon high tariff rates on the products they raised. The farmers even accepted this assertion when their product proved to be part of a surplus that poured into an uncontrolled market. In such a case, it was their own overproduction rather than foreign imports that caused the low prices. But it was so much easier to blame their plight on foreigners, especially when respectable and respected Republican politicians presented them with word-pictures of fleets of ships laden with farm goods, produced by cheap labor, to be dumped on American shores. In actuality, however, the amount of farm produce imported from abroad was too small to glut the market. Senator Aldrich later recalled in a letter to President Taft that Senator Robert M. LaFollette was the first Republican leader to admit that "the farmers could be fooled

[57] Reprinted in *Providence Tribune*, 17 June 1909, clipping, Aldrich Papers.

by the imposition of high duties on farm products in which there could be no competition." Aldrich added that in his own opinion "the only argument legitimately made why farmers should support the protective policy is that it afforded them, by the encouragement of manufactures and other industries than agriculture, a profitable domestic market for their products—a market which cannot in the nature of things be found elsewhere."[58] Aldrich stopped there, without explaining what protectionism could do, and often did do, to raise prices unduly on manufactured goods which farmers had to buy.

Whatever satisfaction a high protective tariff brought to the Republican leaders, tariff-making was a legislative nightmare. Seasoned Republicans were aware of the serious political dangers inherent in tariff-making, the measures Congress enacted often being so badly drawn as to cause political revolt. In the process of tariff-making, raw material producers battled with processors and both became involved in arguments with vote-conscious politicians representing antitariff consumers. Tariff makers and the public were prone to judge proposed rates in terms of past rates; but past rates were so largely based on guesswork and deals that they were an inadequate measure of anything. Even if tariff makers conscientiously attempted to determine equitable rates, they were frustrated because no really adequate statistics existed on which to determine rates. Businessmen were more than hesitant to provide the tariff makers with reliable statistics. Tariff makers had to arrive at a rough estimate of the comparative costs of foreign and domestic producers, largely guessing at wage levels and costs of raw materials. Whatever tariff makers could theoretically learn from statistics, political deals and pressures, not statistics, prevailed before a tariff bill could become a law. During the struggle, businessmen kept up a din calling for quick action on the grounds that the existing uncertainty over the new rates was ruinous to their businesses. As astute politicians, the tariff makers were well aware not only of the unsatisfactory nature of tariff-making but also of the inevitability of an unsatisfactory

[58] 17 February 1911, William Howard Taft Papers.

end product. They knew that they should sponsor a measure to transfer the process from Congress to a nonpartisan commission of experts. But very few of them publicly acknowledged this as Spooner did in 1897.[59] In 1901 and after, Theodore Roosevelt also suggested a tariff commission as a way out of the morass,[60] and Taft favored it, too.

The Republican position on the currency question reflected the same friendliness toward the political-business alliance in the party. This policy was intended to protect the public from ruinous inflation by having all currency redeemable in gold at the national treasury. Republicans referred to the result as "sound" currency.

The 1897 Republican currency policy had its origins partly in party tradition and partly in the Bourbon element of the Democratic party. During the three decades following the Civil War, the currency system was manifestly gravely inadequate but neither party possessed the ability or will to go beyond inadequate patchwork remedies. During each economic crisis of the era, the currency issue came to the fore in politics; finally in the 1890s it became the dominant issue. Fear and anger took command, driving politicians toward unrealistic positions on the issue.

In 1896 the Republican party inherited a windfall. A Democrat occupied the White House and he was unable to stem the depression-fed tide of currency reform agitation. The Democratic party split. Grover Cleveland Bourbons clung tenaciously and blindly to a rigid gold currency policy and William Jennings Bryan Silverites clung just as tenaciously to the free silver panacea. Republicans capitalized on the situation. They achieved control of the national government and appropriated the Bourbon "sound" currency policy. Economically it was a bad policy, but in 1897, with prosperity on its way, the Republican hierarchy faced no immediate political crisis. In fact, the 1896 election victory and the return of good times afforded the Re-

[59] *Boston Herald,* 9 July 1897; Clifford Folger to Spooner, 13 July 1897, Spooner Papers.

[60] *Boston Globe,* 1 May 1901; Roosevelt to Spooner, 30 September 1901, in Elting E. Morison, ed., *The Letters of Theodore Roosevelt,* 3:155 (hereafter cited as Morison, *Letters*); *Milwaukee Journal,* 2 October 1902.

publicans an opportunity to boast of their "sound" currency policy. Meanwhile, they quietly paid homage to retired Democrat Cleveland.

On the question of federal control of "business," which was the commonly used designation for "big business" when federal policy was being discussed, Republican policy in 1897 was uncertain and limited. Sympathies and performance favored the business interests, which in turn favored a minimum amount of governmental interference with private enterprise. But there were some clear differences of opinion both within and outside the business world over what constituted an acceptable minimum of government interference.

No event in the nation's history had forced the leadership of the Republican party to take a position on business control beyond a few general declarations and vague legislative actions. Two of those gestures, which both Republicans and Democrats had sponsored, nevertheless contained some promise of a sophisticated approach to this increasingly complex problem. In 1887 Congress had passed the Interstate Commerce Act and in 1890 the Sherman Act, but by 1897 neglect, confusion, legalistic hair-splitting, apathy, and "special pleading" had conspired to render these laws almost moribund.

Numerous complications existed. The question of jurisdiction between the state and federal governments and between the legislative, executive, and judicial branches of government complicated the matter, as did widespread confusion over definitions of interstate and intrastate commerce, and of "combinations in restraint of trade" and competition. Some people used the word trust as a substitute for the word monopoly, while others used it simply to designate any big business, which might or might not be monopolistic. This state of confusion was convenient for politicians and monopolists. Many people considered bigness in business a grave threat, regardless of the presence of monopoly, and hence a matter for governmental concern. So there was a tendency for the concerned public to lump all their anger and fears together into one generalized protest against what they called the "trust" menace.

Republican party leaders obtained their dominant position of

1897 through more than their record and position on economic matters. Their identification with the movement to liberate and lift the nation's largest segment of downtrodden citizens, the Negroes of the South, had contributed much to the establishment of the Republican party and remained an important source of loyalty and unity. The Civil War victory provided Republican orators for many years with a very effective rallying call. Detractors called it "waving the bloody shirt." The passage of time and the economic depression of the 1890s markedly reduced this emotional appeal, but in 1897 there remained enough war veterans, humanitarians, and shrewd politicians to keep the matter before the voters. Negro disfranchisement and lynching fanned the embers. Republicans occasionally referred to President McKinley as Major McKinley, veteran officer of the War of the Rebellion. But McKinley and his colleagues confined their interest in the subject to mere rhetoric and petty political concessions to Negroes.

Republicans continued to implement the agreement they had made back in 1877 with southern Democrats to permit the southern whites to handle the situation as they saw fit. They thought it would be unwise for "outsiders" to interfere, at least directly, with the way southern whites, Booker T. Washington, and the courts were dealing with the mounting number of Negro lynchings, the recently augmented Jim Crowism, and the recent wave of Negro disfranchisement.[61] In 1900 the *New York Tribune,* which consistently followed the Republican blueprint, editorialized that the race question in the South was truly deplorable, but that the solution lay outside the province of the North and also beyond the efforts of the southern politician. "It must be done by the sober, intelligent Southern people who wish to use neither the negro nor the prejudice against the negro for ulterior purposes."[62]

For several years some Republicans, including a few party leaders, had refused to accept the finality of the 1877 agreement, but they too lost hope that their party would again champion

[61] Thomas Robert Cripps, "The Lily White Republicans: The Negro, the Party, and the South in the Progressive Era" (Ph.D. dissertation, University of Maryland, 1967), 48–53.
[62] 8 April 1900.

the cause of justice for the Negro. Spooner was one of the last to surrender.[63] Back in 1887, in a letter about Negro suffrage, he had stated that the position of the Republican party "should not be a cowardly one. We should not allow ourselves to be deterred from a fearless and persistent discharge of duty in this respect, either by the commercial spirit of some of our own people, or by the senseless cry of 'bloody shirt' which the Democrats hurl at us."[64] But soon the failure of his party colleagues to unite behind the "Force Bill" of 1890, designed to obtain southern compliance with the Fifteenth Amendment, and their continued lack of determination to enforce Negro rights in general, caused Spooner to abandon the fight. In 1893 he wrote to Iowa's James S. Clarkson, fellow champion of the cause, that "the interest of the Republicans of the United States in an honest ballot, in maintaining the rights of citizenship, and in holding sacred the pledge of Abraham Lincoln's proclamation to the colored men is dead, or in a slumber too deep for us to arouse."[65]

There was, nevertheless, a small group of southern Negro Republicans in a position to harvest special advantages from the Republican return to power. They attended the 1896 national convention and dutifully followed Mark Hanna's advice to vote for McKinley. They were important at the convention because the number of delegates from a given state was based on the population of the state. It mattered not whether they had the freedom to vote in elections. Since the early 1890s, Hanna had cultivated assiduously the Negroes of the South. He had paid their expenses to presidential nominating conventions, and now he and McKinley were prepared to pass out numerous small patronage plums.[66]

The Republican party in 1897, with public support and seasoned leadership, was in an enviable position to achieve increased prestige and power. Having weathered the devastating depression of the 1890s, the leaders now saw little reason to

---

[63] Stanley P. Hirshson, *Farewell to the Bloody Shirt,* 141, 154, 223, 249, 252–53; Fowler, *Spooner,* 133–37.

[64] Spooner to Joseph Ulman, 5 December 1887, Spooner Papers.

[65] 16 April 1893, quoted in Hirshson, *Bloody Shirt,* 249.

[66] Cripps, "Lily White Republicans," 11–16, 21–34.

modify policies that had worked to their advantage in the past. Soon, however, the requirements of a rapidly expanding economy and the needs of a large number of voters who had been left out of the mainstream of prosperity would necessitate some modernization of party policies. It remained to be seen whether or not the cautious Republican leadership would recognize these complexities and meet these needs in the new era ahead.

II

SPECIAL INTERESTS AND WARMONGERS DISRUPT THE LEADERSHIP 1897-1898

C ONTESTS IN THE SENATE over the Dingley tariff bill in 1897 and the Cuban crisis in 1898 caused the Republican command to make concessions that did violence to their personal convictions and to their pride. But despite these concessions they operated with such consummate political skill that they emerged with enhanced power. Because they were professional politicians with responsibilities to their party followers, it was understandable that they bowed to political expediency. Nevertheless, it was regrettable that they lacked sufficient will and ability to prevent enactment of what they knew to be a disgraceful tariff measure and to prevent a deplorable war with Spain.

The 1896 Republican platform and Republican orators had promised the voters enactment of a new tariff measure at the earliest opportunity. Shortly after inauguration day, Congress convened in special session to carry out this promise.[1] It behooved the Republicans to enact a new tariff law before prosperity and progress came back in full bloom with a Democratic tariff still in force. The outcome, however, did not altogether please congressional leaders. Special interest demands forced through the Dingley Tariff, a measure so shockingly high that it testified to the failure of the Four to impose the moderation they considered politically wise and economically sound.

The bill started out as a moderate measure in the House, and moderation characterized its initial treatment in the Senate. Aldrich, as chairman of the Senate Finance Committee, was in charge of the work, although Allison, Platt, and Spooner worked closely with him. In fact, before the contest ended, illness forced Aldrich to the sidelines and Allison took his place.

The Four began their assignment with the clear intention, stated both publicly and privately, of obtaining only moderate rate changes. Aldrich even suggested to Henry C. Frick that the current duty on steel was excessive.[2] They felt no impelling pressure to do otherwise and were cognizant of the political risks in conspicuously high rates. They knew all too well the disastrous results of the McKinley Tariff. Many political analysts believed that it had contributed considerably to Spooner's defeat in the 1890 election.[3] When Aldrich opened the debate in the Senate he reminded his colleagues that during the 1896 election campaign it had been "thoroughly understood throughout the country . . . that if the Republican party should again be entrusted with power no extreme tariff legislation would follow." He emphasized that the "cause of protection" should not be "burdened by the imposition of duties which are unreasonable and excessive." Aldrich felt that the "industrial conditions in this country with a very few exceptions do not demand a return to the rates imposed by the Act of 1890."[4]

The Four were unable, however, to control the six so-called western Silver Republican senators and some agrarian-oriented Gold Republicans and Populists.[5] Among the unreliable Gold Republicans was Senator John M. Thurston, "a beet sugar apostate" from Nebraska, who had been chairman of the 1896 Republican National Convention that nominated McKinley. These western senators demanded higher duties on the products of

---

[1] New York Times, 4 November 1896; Harold U. Faulkner, The Decline of Laissez Faire, 1897–1917, 59–60.

[2] 29 March 1897, cited in George Harvey, Henry C. Frick, 295.

[3] Horace Samuel Merrill, Bourbon Democracy of the Middle West, 1865–1896, 209.

[4] Quoted in Nathaniel W. Stephenson, Nelson W. Aldrich: A Leader in American Politics, 142.

[5] The six Silver Republicans were Henry M. Teller (Colorado), Richard F. Pettigrew (South Dakota), Lee Mantle (Montana), Frank J. Cannon (Utah), William M. Stewart (Nevada), and John P. Jones (Nevada).

their constituencies than Aldrich and his Finance Committee planned to allow. More than loyalty to their constituencies was involved. They resented the Republican power structure and were determined to defeat, distract, and discredit that group as much as possible. Clearly they even hoped that their recalcitrance would force the Republican high command to make concessions to them on the currency question.

The first indication of trouble came when the Finance Committee's rate schedule reached the floor of the Senate for debate. There the unexpected happened. Missouri Democrat George G. Vest moved to cut the duty on anvils by a quarter of a cent. The motion carried. It happened to be the first day of Aldrich's illness, so Allison was in charge, with Platt trying to keep the Senate Republicans in line. When the vote on the anvil rate went against the party, there was "a hearty laugh." Allison "looked puzzled, but said he would not call for the yeas and nays."[6]

It soon became apparent, as Horace Taft reported to his brother, that "The Wild Western Senators are on top" and "the Tariff seems more of a grab than the McKinley bill."[7] When the majority of the Finance Committee refused to submit to Thurston's demands for higher rates on sugar, he threatened to unite with the Democrats and Republican Silverites to obtain his goal, and he won his point. In order to obtain Republican unity, Aldrich and his cohorts allowed the Republican caucus to make the decisions on the various schedules. With the ultimate fate of tariff-making now in the hands of the party caucus, rather than the Finance Committee alone, each and every Republican senator was subject to the direct pressure of lobbyists. In order to have at least a nominal face-saving role in tariff-making, Finance Committee members then felt obliged to make concessions to the lobbyists. Log-rolling and pressure politics took over.[8]

[6] *New York Times,* 3 June 1897.
[7] Horace Taft to William Howard Taft, 18 June 1897, Taft Papers.
[8] Spooner to H. L. Humphrey, 9 April 1897, and Walter Wellman in *Chicago Times-Herald,* 27 May 1897, clipping, Spooner Papers; Horace Taft to Taft, 18 June 1897, Taft Papers; H. D. Tichenor to Grenville M. Dodge, 22 June 1908 (reporting on George C. Tichenor's work on the Dingley bill in 1897), Grenville M. Dodge Papers; *New York Times,* 21 February, 9 June 1897; Claude G. Bowers,

In addition, certain producers were able to use the reciprocal trade clause in the Dingley bill as leverage for higher rates. Congress had included this clause in the bill as a gesture to foreign trade enthusiasts. Producers whose goods were subject to possible lower tariff duties under the reciprocal plan sought and obtained a means to protect themselves from the disadvantages that could result from implementation of the plan. At their behest Congress put an additional 20 percent rate increase on those goods in question; this afforded the petitioners an extra protective cushion for their goods should the government arrange with a foreign nation to reduce the duty on any of them.[9] This rate increase proved to be unnecessary. Although President McKinley, through John A. Kasson, conscientiously negotiated seventeen reciprocity treaties and submitted them to the Senate for ratification, that body permanently pigeonholed all of them. The 20 percent extra duties, nevertheless, remained.[10]

The Dingley bill clearly distressed the Senate leaders both before and during its enactment, but pride and political considerations caused them to refrain from direct public declarations of their feelings. During the debate on the measure, Aldrich growled at callers who came to his apartment at the Arlington Hotel, where indigestion confined him while the logrolling was going on. He recovered in time to vote for the final draft of the bill and thereby demonstrate his dedication to party unity.[11] Spooner was so disgusted with the lengthy four-month performance that even before its final passage he introduced into the Senate a resolution calling for the creation of a tariff

Beveridge and the Progressive Era, 70; Stephenson, *Aldrich*, 142–43; Edward Stanwood, *American Tariff Controversies in the Nineteenth Century* 2:388–89; William Dana Orcutt, *Burrows of Michigan and the Republican Party*, 104–05; Frank W. Taussig, *Tariff History of the United States*, 323–24.

[9] See *Washington Post*, 22 September 1902; John Ball Osborne, "Expansion through Reciprocity," in Robert M. LaFollette, ed., *The Making of America*, 2:382; U. S., Tariff Commission, *Reciprocity and Commercial Treaties* (Washington, D. C., Government Printing Office, 1919), 202–03.

[10] Margaret Leech, *In the Days of McKinley*, 141–42; Sage, *Allison*, 295; H. Wayne Morgan, *William McKinley and His America*, 280–81.

[11] *New York Times*, 3 June 1897; Henry Cabot Lodge to Aldrich, 9 June 1897, Aldrich Papers; S. N. D. North to William Whitman, 10 June 1897, box 49, Biographer's Notes, Aldrich Papers; Stephenson, *Aldrich*, 144–45.

commission to review rates.[12] In this he was ahead of his time.

The Dingley Tariff remained on the statute books for twelve years as an embarrassment to the Republican party. Even such high protectionists as Senator Burrows of Michigan later stated that if a party back in 1890 or 1894 had been responsible for passing such a bad tariff measure, that party would have been defeated at the polls. The returning good times in 1897, however, caused the public to greet the afront with relative indifference.[13] Less than a week after passage of the Dingley Tariff, railroad president Melville E. Ingalls, in a lengthy statement to the *New York Sun* on the economic and political situation, did not even mention the tariff. He had just taken a ten-day, 2,500-mile trip of inquiry into the Middle West during which he interviewed citizens of varied political and economic persuasions. Ingalls found hopefulness at every turn. "Perhaps," he said, "I can illustrate the feeling of the people of the Middle West by telling a story." He related a conversation with an Ohio "dyed-in-the-wool Democrat, of the free silver stamp." After stating that the economic prospect "might be a heap worse," that crops were good, that it appeared that "wheat would go to pretty nigh a dollar a bushel," this Silverite confessed his bewilderment over it all. "I don't quite understand, but things seem to have been on the mend ever since McKinley was elected." But Ingalls thought he himself understood! He told the *Sun* reporter that the mounting price of wheat was attributable to a crop shortage abroad. "The wheat fields of India are as a desert. Russia's crop is away below the average, England, France, Turkey, Austria, and the Danubian provinces are short of wheat, and the locusts have dropped down on the wheat fields of Argentina." As the price of wheat rose, interest in the free silver panacea declined, he declared. Ingalls further observed, "The sober second thought of the people is asserting itself." The people see that "neither the isms of agitators . . . nor the theories of professors . . . can put a dollar into an empty pocket," that "all the money in the world

[12] W. E. Gardner to Spooner, 2 May 1897; Spooner to C. F. Freeman, 14 May; Elihu Coleman to Spooner, 5 June; Spooner to Henry Fink, 12 June; Spooner to Henry C. Payne, 22 June; *Boston Herald*, 9 July 1897, clipping; Clifford Folger to Spooner, 13 July 1897—all in Spooner Papers.
[13] Orcutt, *Burrows*, 104–05.

cannot be produced by laws, but by labor," that "prosperity comes not by talk but by the natural laws of trade and commerce, and they have concluded that those laws are now making things come their way." Perhaps Ingalls failed to mention the Dingley Tariff because the measure was clearly not a "natural law."[14]

McKinley also avoided public discussion of the Dingley Tariff. Three months after its passage, when addressing a dinner of the Commercial Club of Cincinnati, he pleaded for "reciprocity of trade" but made no mention of the Dingley Tariff. A few months later he told the Commercial Club of Boston, "We have quit discussing the tariff and have turned our attention to getting trade wherever it can be found."[15]

In addition to the difficulties Republican leaders confronted with the tariff issue, in 1897 and 1898 they faced a disruptive situation, outside the normal stream of political events, which they were ill prepared to handle.[16] Anger in America at Spanish mistreatment of her Cuban subjects brought on unreasoned sentimentality, misguided humanitarianism, and crude sword rattling. The party command deserved sympathy, for, as educator Horace Taft observed, "The Jingo sentiment brings to the front all that is vulgar and bad among us."[17] By early 1898 the clamor for war with Spain reached a climax, and a three-month war ensued.

As the nation moved toward war, President McKinley and the Four, along with such colleagues as Speaker of the House Thomas B. Reed and Senator Mark Hanna, wanted to stem

[14] New York Sun, 30 July 1897, clipping, McKinley Papers.

[15] McKinley's address was summarized in "The Bulletin of the American Iron and Steel Association," 10 November 1901. A copy of this bulletin was sent to Aldrich with a note attached, by an unidentified person, stating, "This is where the trouble began." It is filed under the date 10 November 1901 in the Aldrich Papers. See also Cincinnati Commercial Tribune, 31 October 1897; Boston Herald, 18 February 1899.

[16] Inexplicably, in the following books by authorities on the reasons for the United States' going to war with Spain, there are either but passing references to or no mention whatsoever of the views and actions of the Senate Four and Mark Hanna: Walter LaFeber, The New Empire: An Interpretation of American Expansion, 1860–1898, 326–417; Leech, McKinley, 172–89; Walter Millis, The Martial Spirit: A Study of Our War with Spain, 71–145; H. Wayne Morgan, America's Road to Empire: The War with Spain and Overseas Expansion, 19–63; Julius W. Pratt, Expansionists of 1898: The Acquisition of Hawaii and the Spanish Islands, 230–78.

[17] Horace Taft to Taft, 18 June 1897, Taft Papers.

the emotional tide. They distinctly did not want war, which seemed to them a dangerous and costly venture into the unknown. They saw nothing in the Cuban situation to justify such extremism. Moreover, as men well acquainted with the operations and trends in business, they did not regard war as a reasonable device to facilitate economic expansion.

As politicians at the head of their party, however, they approached the war issue very cautiously. For a time they brushed aside reports of politicians that the party would be defeated in the 1898 election if it failed to support war. But eventually, as the majority of their party and the public moved toward war, they knew well that they were in danger of losing command of the situation and their desire for party unity took precedence over their better judgment on the issue.

Following the February 15 sinking of the *Maine*, tension mounted precipitously. The party leadership had special cause for alarm when Senators Redfield Proctor of Vermont and William Mason of Illinois, normally loyal to the party hierarchy, fervently proclaimed their support of the prowar element. On March 17, the influential Proctor delivered his blow and thereby deserted his party's leadership. He was among a group of Congressmen recently returned from a visit to Cuba, and it was in the course of his report on the horrors he had witnessed there that he called for armed intervention. Proctor had been a staunch McKinley friend and supporter and had received in return much patronage. Speaker Reed, who worked closely with McKinley to prevent war, was so surprised and infuriated at the performance that he sarcastically attributed it to Proctor's lucrative marble empire. "A war will make a large market for gravestones,"[18] he commented.

Mason was a longtime friend of McKinley's, but when a naval board report reached Congress on March 20 which afforded an opportunity to blame the *Maine* disaster on Spain, Mason led a Senate stampede toward war. When he announced he favored war, a demonstration broke out on the Senate floor that proved almost impossible for Vice-President Garret A. Hobart to quell.[19]

[18] Leech, *McKinley*, 172.
[19] Ibid., 175–78.

Platt, who was the most antiwar of the Four, wired that day to his friend Flagg in Wall Street, "Sentiment for immediate action is growing stronger in Congress and more difficult to hold in check." Flagg then sold his own "dividend-paying" stocks.[20] Henry Cabot Lodge, in answer to persistent antiwar letters from fellow Bostonian Henry L. Higginson, declared that if the incumbent Republicans refrained from war the Bryanites would win control in the 1900 election.[21]

A New York friend of Mark Hanna's was in Washington a few days after the Senate heard the naval board's appraisal of the *Maine* explosion. He recorded in his diary that in the course of a Sunday visit with Hanna the "burden of his talk was the danger of war and he was extremely outspoken." According to the diary, Hanna said that "he and Senator O. H. Platt of Connecticut were the only two Senators who were absolutely and unqualifiedly opposed to war under all circumstances and that Senators Spooner and Aldrich came near to the point but did not quite reach it." Hanna "spoke bitterly of the scoundrels of the Cuban Junta who were simply trying to sell Cuban bonds" upon the strength and intentions of the United States. Hence, Hanna insisted, if this nation "intervened at all, annexation of Cuba was the only proper thing." Sometime during the conversation, Platt came in and "confirmed everything" Hanna had said.[22] On the same weekend, Spooner answered a friend's frantic telegram saying, "Apparently Congress cannot keep its head" and seems about to "let loose the dogs of war." Spooner believed that the president, "if let alone," could negotiate a peaceful settlement. "The situation," Spooner concluded, "is one calculated to make a man distrust our system a little bit."[23]

In early April, the discouraged McKinley prepared a message to Congress asking for authority to intervene in Cuba with armed force if necessary to secure peace and stable government.

[20] Quoted in John H. Flagg to Platt, 28 March 1898; Flagg to Platt, 20 March 1898, Platt Papers.

[21] Higginson to Lodge, 19 February, 8 March, 4, 11, 14, 21 April 1898, Lodge Papers; Lodge to Higginson, 4, 16 April 1898, Higginson Papers.

[22] Diary entry concerning visit with Mark Hanna on Sunday, 3 April 1898, Frederick W. Holls Papers, Columbia University, but used here from copy in box 49, Biographer's Notes, Aldrich Papers.

[23] Spooner to Herbert B. Turner, 2 April 1898, Spooner Papers.

In this expression of his policy of "neutral intervention," he said nothing of independence for Cuba or of retaliation for the *Maine* episode. The message reached Congress on April 9.[24]

That evening a tired and resentful Spooner wrote to his son Willet that he had "entertained nothing but contempt, pending this sensitive and delicate diplomatic correspondence and negotiation, for the Masons and the Proctors and Co.," who, "in order to draw attention to themselves, and gain for their utterances a publicity which under no other circumstances could they attain, have stirred up our people and embarrassed the President in his negotiations." But, continued Spooner, now that diplomacy has failed, "I am for armed intervention." In both the economic and the political sense he clearly had come to believe that war was the least costly course. The situation in Cuba, he said, "shocks our humanity, disturbs our trade, destroys our ships and sailors, costs us millions in enforcing our foreign enlistments act, keeps us upon a quasi war footing, and imperils our peace." Spooner ended his letter by saying, "I am tired, very tired, of this public life and its burdens, and I sigh for home, the companionship of my boys, my books, my horses, my friends, and what it seems to me since I reached manhood I never have had—peace."[25] And on April 25 the Senate closed ranks, voting without a dissent for the act declaring that a state of war existed. "I think," Spooner informed an old friend on May 2, that "possibly the President could have worked out the business without war, but the current was too strong, the demagogues too numerous, the fall elections too near." He added, "probably it had to come."[26] In a feeble explanation for his change of heart, Spooner stated that if the war "could have been forced upon us three months ago, by the Billy Masons & Co., what stress we would have been in."[27]

[24] Leech, *McKinley*, 186–87.

[25] 9 April 1898, Spooner Papers; see also Spooner to J. V. Quarles, 14 March, to John G. Gregory, 14 March, to H. H. Porter (telegram), 29 March, to Herbert B. Turner, 2, 7 April, to Edward Scofield, 2 April, to Orsamus Cole, 9 April, to Andrew J. Aikens, 9 April, to J. H. Palmer, 9 April, to John H. Knight, 23 April, to Edward W. Keyes, 23 April, to E. E. Bryant, 23 April, to Frank G. Bigelow, 9 March, 27 April 1898—all in Spooner Papers.

[26] Spooner to C. W. Porter, 2 May 1898, ibid.

[27] Spooner to Frank G. Bigelow, 17 May 1898, ibid.

Allison, as usual less volatile than Spooner, was nevertheless just as unhappy, and the reports that reached him from Iowa afforded him no solace. His nephew, a young Dubuque lawyer, reported that in his area there was a "great deal of unrest," with many people feeling that "the President should have plunged ahead." He observed that "Almost all seem to be anxious for war. Most of the younger men want to go." He emphasized that unrest was general, and "not merely among hot heads." Hence, "unless something comes to divert attention it may cost some Republican offices."[28]

Platt was even more discouraged with the drift of affairs, and the letters he received almost daily from his intimate friend Flagg afforded him no cheer. Flagg, a lawyer for Standard Oil and a Wall Street stockmarket investor, predicted financial calamity if war came. He doubtless would have been in a still greater frenzy without the telegrams Platt sent him, sometimes several per day "during market hours," reporting on events during the crisis. He had requested Platt's flood of information for investment purposes.[29]

Meanwhile, the Senate warmongers, employing the *Maine* episode in particular, pushed the nation relentlessly toward war. They overpowered the Four, passing resolutions that were tantamount to a declaration of war. A state of war existed by April 21, and its legal formality was declared on April 25. For several weeks the antiwar senators and their supporters had been swallowing one bitter pill of defeat after another, wondering where it would all end. However, McKinley and the Four very carefully avoided making personal attacks in public on warmongering Republican colleagues. During the final days of debate before war came, they exhibited a conciliatory mood toward their prowar colleagues. At one point, in a Senate address, Aldrich remarked that he did "not mean to suggest that Senators who have arrived at a different conclusion are not controlled by patriotic motives."[30] At no time, however, did the

---

[28] William B. Allison, Jr., to Allison, 14 April 1898, Allison Papers. See also Sage, *Allison*, 271–72.

[29] John H. Flagg to Platt, 11, 19 February, 28, 30 March, 2 April 1898, Platt Papers; see also Louis A. Coolidge, *An Old-Fashioned Senator: Orville H. Platt of Connecticut*, 260–83.

[30] Quoted in Stephenson, *Aldrich*, 158.

top leaders show signs of deliberately accommodating individuals who sought war for economic gain. If in private correspondence or in conversations they even considered making concessions to such individuals, they and persons close to them were markedly successful in hiding or destroying all evidence to that effect.

Despite the almost frenzied anger and the doubts about the future that were apparent in their private communications among themselves and their amateurish foreign diplomacy, the party leadership emerged from the war crisis with increased political strength. At every stage both McKinley and the Senate Four displayed impressive political acumen as they retreated into acceptance of war as the only feasible course. If McKinley and the Four had been a little more familiar with the art of diplomacy and had applied themselves to its practice with the astuteness with which they approached Congress on the matter, they might well have prevented the outbreak of war. The president possessed sufficient courage, but he lacked the will to break out of the narrow circle of professional politics and copy-book officialdom. He was, however, quick to protect his constitutional prerogative to conduct foreign relations himself rather than permit aggressive senators to assume command, but he was clumsy in his diplomacy.[31]

McKinley profited from the popularity of the conflict. With his sincerity and calmness, he seemed to bring maturity to the military crusade. He delivered platitudinous addresses in his melodious voice. Republican newsmen dared to suggest that the nation had found another Lincoln, another great war leader. McKinley even escaped the odium of the shocking ineptitude of his subordinates, both military and civilian, who conducted the war effort. He had such a benign, innocent manner that people felt sorry for him, rather than criticizing him for the chaos. In a period of childlike emotionalism, McKinley seemed steadfast and sympathetic.[32]

In looking beyond the war to the future, the Republican

---

[31] On McKinley protecting his prerogatives see Paul S. Holbo, "Presidential Leadership in Foreign Affairs: William McKinley and the Turpie-Foraker Amendment," *American Historical Review* 72 (July 1967): 1321–35.

[32] Leech, *McKinley*, 228–29.

leadership foresaw a new era and cautiously accommodated themselves to it. Earlier, Aldrich, McKinley, and a few others had sensed the need for and the advantages of increased American foreign trade and investment. The Spanish-American War stimulated more awareness of these prospects. Early in the war Spooner wrote to a friend that, "It looks as if events . . . forced us away forever from the traditions which we have regarded as of so much consequence."[33]

When the war ended, the Republican leadership, and most especially the Senate Four, quickly, ably, and enthusiastically applied their talents to the problems and opportunities that the military victory brought to the nation. The conflict turned out to be less disruptive than they had anticipated and the prospect for national economic expansion much greater than they had foreseen. Victory afforded a fortuitous outlet for surplus goods and surplus capital to invest, both inevitable results of prosperity and rapid industrialization. These opportunities were advantageous to the Republican-business alliance.

Platt and Spooner applied their superior legal talents to the thorny problem of the constitutional relationship between the United States and its newly acquired island territories. Spooner's name became associated with a measure which replaced military with civil control of the Philippines. Platt's name adorned the famous Platt Amendment, which in effect made Cuba a semi-protectorate of the United States. Aldrich, as a member of the Cuba Committee, was influential in determining economic relations with that island.[34] An incidental example of the close cooperation of the leaders occurred when Spooner had to make an unscheduled visit to his home at the time the Republican caucus was bringing to a close its discussion of the Porto Rican bill. Platt, who had left for one of his numerous visitations to Cuba, had asked Spooner to deliver his vote. Spooner, in turn, asked Allison to act for both Platt and himself. He also asked Allison to attach to the bill one amendment making it possible for some friends of Spooner's to construct a manufacturing plant

---

[33] Spooner to Frank G. Bigelow, 17 May 1898, Spooner Papers; Leech, *McKinley*, 229–30.

[34] Coolidge, *Platt*, 284–383 passim; Dorothy Ganfield Fowler, *John Coit Spooner: Defender of Presidents*, 223–52; Stephenson, *Aldrich*, 161.

on a particular tract along the shore of Porto Rico. He said they were already there and waiting for Congress to act.[35]

While the Four concentrated on the economic and legal details involved in bringing the former Spanish-owned islands under United States control, McKinley as usual kept a close watch on public sentiment and went along with it. After he finally decided to support annexation of the Philippines, he had the good fortune to interview the General Missionary Committee of the Methodist Episcopal Church, an ardent expansionist group. "Hold a moment longer," McKinley said to them as they began to troop out. "Not quite yet, Gentlemen! Before you go I would like to say just a word about the Philippine business." He told them of his difficulties in making up his mind on whether or not to advocate annexation. "I walked the floor of the White House night after night until midnight," he said; "and I am not ashamed to tell you, gentlemen, that I went down on my knees and prayed Almighty God for light and guidance more than one night. And one night late it came to me this way—I don't know how it was, but it came . . . that there was nothing left for us to do but take them all, and to educate the Filipinos, and uplift them and civilize and Christianize them, and by God's grace do the very best we could by them, as our fellow-men for whom Christ also died. And then I went to bed, and slept soundly, and the next morning I sent for the chief engineer of the War Department (our map-maker), and I told him to put the Philippines on the map of the United States, and there they are, and there they will stay while I am President."[36]

The Republican command was now thoroughly in control of the party and of the national government. Thanks to the return of prosperity, to victory in war, and to their own political acumen, the Republican leadership was in an awesomely enviable position of great political power. Seemingly McKinley and the Senate Four could speedily implement the party blueprint to which they were so attached, of which they were so proud, and for which they were so grateful. With such power, they could

[35] Spooner to Allison, 24, 26 March 1900, Allison Papers.
[36] Quoted in Leech, *McKinley*, 344–45.

modernize the currency-banking system, modernize the government's policy on control of big business, modernize the tariff policy, and make amends for their party's abandonment of the Negroes after having held out to them promises of decent treatment.

III

SHREWD GESTURES ON CURRENCY AND TRUST PROBLEMS 1897-1900

BOTH CURRENCY AND TRUST PROBLEMS haunted the McKinley administration. The party leadership so adroitly handled the issues, however, that party unity remained intact. McKinley and the Senate Four accomplished this by making gestures that had more sales value than substance. The half-measures they induced Congress to enact satisfied their Republican constituents but, in actuality, merely postponed adequate reform. After much cautious maneuvering, Congress passed an innocuous currency measure and, on the trust problem, created an investigative commission. The election victory of 1900 gave testament to the skill of the party leadership.

The currency question was so complex and divisive that, despite the fact that currency had been the only issue in the campaign of 1896, the party leaders postponed any action whatsoever until political pressures forced them to enact the 1900 Gold Standard Act, a frail gesture toward currency reform. They refused even to sponsor a government commission to study the problem. Good times made it possible for them to delay action. "As for currency," Horace Taft observed in the fall of 1897, "the policy of the Republicans seems to be that of the man who couldn't fix his leaky roof in the rain and who wouldn't fix it in good weather because then it didn't need it." But, "we shall catch it . . . when hard times strike us."[1] Early in 1897 the administration did, however, explore with France and England the possibility of an international bimetallism treaty. When this move to comply with an 1896 platform promise collapsed early in 1897, the Republican leadership seemed indifferent.[2]

Concerned businessmen and economists, meanwhile, discussed the currency problem and various possible solutions. The debate revolved mainly around the merits and defects of assets currency, which was designed to provide elasticity.[3] The term "assets currency" seemed to be incomprehensible to laymen, which doubtless helped explain why some citizens retreated from their earlier interest in the currency issue. The term was not as graphic as "silver" or "gold," which people saw, handled, and used from day to day. Assets currency was not based on gold, silver, or United States government bonds, but on commercial paper in the possession of banks. Commercial paper consisted of such valuable and marketable assets as municipal bonds, promissory notes, mortgages, and clearing house certificates. Silver, gold, and government bonds constituted a relatively static base upon which to issue currency. With commercial paper added to this list, authorized persons could from time to time issue more currency to facilitate business or could withdraw it when inflation threatened. Hence, the addition of commercial paper would effect a more flexible currency system, albeit a dangerous one, some believed.

Though it was relatively easy for members of the business community to see the advantages of assets currency, they found it impossible to reach agreement on who should control the system and how much discretion should be used in its application. Love of power, greed, and genuine concern for the national economy combined to prevent a consensus. Heated battles en-

[1] Horace Taft to Taft, 23 September 1897, Taft Papers.

[2] *New York Times*, 1, 4 March 1897; William E. Chandler to Allison, 4 July, 15 August 1897, Allison Papers; Leon Burr Richardson, *William E. Chandler, Republican*, 551–75; Leland L. Sage, *William Boyd Allison: A Study in Practical Politics*, 270–71; Nathaniel W. Stephenson, *Nelson W. Aldrich: A Leader in American Politics*, 140–41; Margaret Leech, *In the Days of McKinley*, 143–44; H. Wayne Morgan, *William McKinley and His America*, 282–87.

[3] Assets currency is defined and discussed in Robert H. Wiebe, *Businessmen and Reform: A Study of the Progressive Movement*, 13, 62, 66.

sued. Failure of bankers and businessmen to resolve these bitter differences afforded politicians an excuse for inaction.

Large Wall Street bankers were the most hesitant to accept the assets currency plan. Most of them felt no need for such reform, which, moreover, would certainly be at their expense. Public suspicion of Wall Street inhibited Congress to such an extent that, even if it wished to do so, Congress would not dare to place control of an assets currency system in Wall Street hands. Some large city banks outside Wall Street, however, especially in Chicago, found the proposal attractive. The move would wrest some power from Wall Street and at the same time replace independent small banks with branch banks. Financial authorities generally agreed that, aside from the government, only large, highly professionalized city banks were in the position to make trustworthy decisions on the issuance of assets currency, and that only they possessed the necessary sound assets. They could distribute and withdraw the currency through the branches they would establish in the small cities and towns. Fear of that development caused the smaller independent banks of those communities to join forces with Wall Street banks to block the scheme.

The town and small city bankers had great prestige among the voters of their communities. They also had numerical power in the American Bankers Association. In the final analysis, Republican politicians needed to be at least as aware of their views as of those of the large city financiers. With them, Bryan would have obtained a much larger vote in the 1896 "battle of the standards." It was clearly not a safe time for bold political action on the currency issue.

Meanwhile, various individuals and groups worked diligently and ably to keep the cause of currency reform alive. Charles N. Fowler, a New Jersey congressman, was the most notable advocate among those consistently, persistently, and deeply interested. Elected to Congress in 1894, Fowler in 1897 launched a personal crusade for a government-controlled assets currency system and remained with it during his ensuing seven terms. In 1897 he delivered a comprehensive address in the House on assets currency. It was later printed into a 130-page pamphlet, which was widely read. Fowler saw as a major obstacle to his goal the traditional conflict between the advocates of government control and private banker control of currency issuance. He said in his speech to Congress, "the establishment of a system of currency responsive to the requirements of trade—involves the struggle of the future, that struggle of bank issues against Government issues which Mr. Bryan but recently announced had scarcely begun."[4]

Large, influential Chicago bankers leaned toward the assets currency approach. They had valuable allies in such important newspapers as the *Chicago Times-Herald* and the *Chicago Tribune*. Three Chicago bankers held important federal posts— Secretary of the Treasury Lyman J. Gage, Director of the Mint George E. Roberts, and Comptroller of the Currency Charles G. Dawes.[5]

The Indianapolis Currency Convention which carried on an active campaign had its beginnings in 1897 in Indianapolis and soon attracted national interest as it sponsored affiliated organizations elsewhere. The founder and director was Hugh H. Hanna of Indianapolis, an entrepreneur who had founded the Atlas Engine Works and helped start the Peoples' Gas Company of his city. The goal of the convention was to achieve an assets currency system, to explore possible means to mobilize bank reserves to meet financial crises, and to defend the gold standard.[6]

Initially, the Indianapolis Currency Convention approached McKinley and Gage. Herman H. Kohlsaat, aggressive editor of the *Chicago Times-Herald*, served as a spokesman for the convention. On August 11, 1897, Kohlsaat wrote McKinley that the executive committee of the Indianapolis Convention had decided that McKinley and Gage "should be consulted before

[4] *New York Tribune*, 30 May 1900. See also: *New York Times*, 4 March 1897; H. W. Goodwin to Spooner, 28 December 1896, 26 April 1897, and Frank G. Bigelow to Spooner, 6 May 1897, Spooner Papers; Charles A. Conant to Henry L. Higginson, 10 March 1897, Higginson Papers; Farmer's Loan and Trust Company, Sioux City, Iowa, to Allison, 25 March 1897, and *Burlington Hawk-Eye,* Iowa, 6 January 1898, clipping, Allison Papers.
[5] Charles G. Dawes, *A Journal of the McKinley Years,* 203, 204, 206, 207; Wiebe, *Businessmen and Reform,* 63; George E. Roberts to Allison, 18 May 1899, Allison Papers. Roberts was also politically influential in his native Iowa.
[6] *New York Tribune,* 8 April 1900; Wiebe, *Businessmen and Reform,* 62.

any action is taken" and had therefore established a select committee to discuss the situation with them.[7]

Efforts to make McKinley into an active currency reformer came to naught. Until 1900, he said little on the currency subject in his public pronouncements and he never advocated a plan of real value. Secretary Gage did prepare an assets currency proposal,[8] but most people fixed their attention on the Senate Four, who, like McKinley, never formulated a comprehensive plan.

As interest in assets currency mounted, the Four became increasingly unhappy. The opportunity and the responsibility for legislative action rested primarily with them, and they had no intention of leaving the matter to Fowler and others in the House of Representatives, to President McKinley, or to Secretary Gage. The Four wanted no one, including themselves, to take any action whatsoever. They decided at the outset to count on time and prosperity to quiet the reformers.[9] At one point Allison suggested to Aldrich that it might be wise to hold their next Finance Committee meeting in Washington. "You and I," he said, "could have a talk also with the President and with Secretary Gage, which would at least be a courtesy to them, and probably we might secure some valuable information."[10]

Aldrich was uncompromising in his determination to maintain the existing great power of Wall Street bankers. Fellow easterner Platt clearly leaned in the same direction, but he employed the elusive device of pleading ignorance on the subject, even when he was deeply involved in policy-making conferences on it.[11] Aldrich and Platt could afford to be relatively silent on the issue. They and their Wall Street cohorts were in command and the currently rising prosperity worked to their advantage. Allison and Spooner experienced more difficulties than their eastern cohorts in explaining why the Four took no action.

Spooner became a member of the Senate Finance Committee in 1899. Caught between two diametrically opposed forces in

[7] McKinley Papers.
[8] Wiebe, *Businessmen and Reform*, 62.
[9] Allison to Aldrich, 11 September 1898, 13 May 1899, Aldrich Papers. See also Joseph Walker (chairman, House Committee on Banking and Currency) to McKinley, 22 November 1897, McKinley Papers.
[10] 11 May 1899, Aldrich Papers.
[11] Platt to John H. Flagg, 29 July 1903, Platt Papers.

his constituency, the small bankers and the big city bankers, he felt obliged to dodge the assets currency issue. Banker Andrew J. Frame of Wisconsin was the nationally recognized spokesman of the small bankers on this issue. This group was afraid, and with good reason, that a monetary system embracing assets currency would result in the destruction of small banks. As president and cashier of the Waukesha National Bank, Frame envisaged the disappearance of his own bank under such a system. If small banks issued assets currency, he believed, they would ultimately collapse because the assets upon which they would issue the notes would be so poor.[12] He called this populistic and explosively pointed out to Spooner how awful it would be to allow the "wild-cats of the west . . . to issue currency based upon such assets as are held by the little one horse country banks" which consisted of "chattel mortgages, secured on lean cows, cadaverous horses, broken down wagons, uncertain crops and various other things too numerous to mention." He also shuddered at the alternative and pointed out to Spooner that in all other nations where such currency existed, the banks "are large, strong, well managed, central institutions, with branches located in the smaller towns."[13]

On the other hand, a good friend of Spooner's, Frank G. Bigelow, president of the First National Bank of Milwaukee, was one of the nation's leading advocates of assets currency. He told Spooner, in the course of his comments on H. H. Hanna's monetary views, that an assets currency system would operate "directly and forcibly to the benefit of the more underdeveloped sections of the country. It will serve to awaken in them industry, enterprise and the easier exchange of goods."[14] He wrote Spooner that although it "will take time to educate the country into a feeling of security with assets currency," the trial must come sometime.[15] Spooner in reply praised Bigelow for his sound cautionary advice to assets currency champion H. H. Hanna, and added that he himself thought Hanna was a "fine looking

[12] Wiebe, *Businessmen and Reform*, 63–64.
[13] Frame to Spooner, 27 May 1898, Spooner Papers.
[14] Bigelow to Spooner, 18 January 1897, ibid. Bigelow was later imprisoned for embezzlement.
[15] Ibid.

gentleman. He seems [however] to have damned little sense of policy or judgment as to what can and cannot be accomplished."[16]

Allison was also a center of attention in the currency question, and it made him most uncomfortable. His long record of service in currency legislation, reaching back to passage of the Bland-Allison Act of 1878, and his influential position as a senior member of the Senate Finance Committee made him a pivotal figure. Furthermore, Allison's reputation for reasonableness and willingness to compromise made him more approachable than the adamant, often arrogant Finance Committee chairman, Aldrich. The leaders of the Indianapolis Monetary Convention, however, made it a point to keep Aldrich informed of their views.[17]

The Chicago-based assets currency advocates exerted enough pressure on Allison to keep him constantly embarrassed and on the defensive, but not worried enough to demand even a minor concession on assets currency from Aldrich. The Chicagoans lacked sufficient power to undermine Allison in Iowa because assets currency was unpopular there. Iowa was a region of small bankers and it seemed obvious to them that assets currency would bring Chicago branch banks into the state.

At the outset, Allison made one of his rare mistakes in public relations. He invited criticism when he told an Associated Press inquirer that the nation would get along well "if we do not get any currency legislation." Thereupon, Kohlsaat employed his *Chicago Times-Herald* to castigate Allison for his "do nothing policy." News of the episode spread widely, but finally, as Kohlsaat reported to McKinley, the senator relented and "We let him say he was misquoted."[18]

Later in 1897 Allison and *Chicago Tribune* publisher Joseph Medill exchanged views on the problem. Medill allegedly had no plan of his own, but drew Allison's attention to the assets currency plan that fellow Chicagoan Gage had submitted to

---

[16] Spooner to Bigelow, 3 June 1898, Spooner Papers.

[17] Charles A. Conant (secretary, Executive Committee of the Indianapolis Monetary Convention of the Boards of Trade, Chambers of Commerce, and Commercial Bodies, Washington, D. C.) to Aldrich, 10 May 1899, Aldrich Papers.

[18] 25 December 1897, McKinley Papers. On December 18 McKinley had written Kohlsaat, "I do not believe he [Allison] gave the interview which has been imputed to him." (Ibid.)

McKinley. Allison expressed emphatic disagreement with the Gage plan and regret that the secretary had made it public before he presented it to Congress in "the regular way." Allison also carefully explained to Medill that the Silverites possessed sufficient strength on the Finance Committee and in Congress to prevent passage of a satisfactory currency measure. However, he added, "We may secure a majority in the Senate in the next Congress." Allison then launched upon a defense of the present system and praised Grover Cleveland for "forcing his political associates to vote for repeal" of the Sherman Silver Act. Allison rambled on, suggesting that no other act of Cleveland's was so beneficial, unless it was his handling of the Pullman strike.[19]

Shortly before and just after the 1898 election, Allison was still confident that his "do-nothing" policy was the safest approach. He wrote Aldrich that "The more I see, the less I am inclined to do much work in the direction of reform of the currency." But he did express a desire to visit Aldrich in Rhode Island to "talk matters over."[20] Five months after the election, however, Allison bestirred himself enough to suggest to Aldrich that the committee might do well to discuss the currency issue. "This matter is now in such shape," he said, "and is being followed up by the press, so that I think we should take action, at least so far as to consider the question." Nevertheless, he felt that the committee "should come to no final resolution until near the meeting of Congress, or at least until sometime during the fall." He remarked that a House committee was already working on the subject.[21]

Meanwhile, evidence mounted that the regular Republican politicians felt no immediate need to make more of a gesture to their constituents than a reaffirmation of the gold standard.[22]

[19] Allison to Medill, 13, 22 November 1897, and Medill to Allison, 17 November 1897, Allison Papers.
[20] 11 September 1898, Aldrich Papers. See also Allison to Leslie M. Shaw, 29 November 1898, Allison Papers.
[21] 11, 13 May 1899, Aldrich Papers.
[22] John Luchsinger to Spooner, 8 December 1897, Spooner Papers; Whitelaw Reid to William E. Dodge, 4 June 1898, Whitelaw Reid Papers; *Muscatine* (Iowa) *Daily Journal*, 18 December 1897, clippings, and letters to Allison from S. S. Farwell, 22 November, W. T. Rigley, 25 November, Leslie M. Shaw, 26 November, William D. Washburn, 28 November, Charles E. Perkins, 29 December 1898,

Even the Indianapolis Monetary Convention relinquished its crusade for assets currency. It concentrated instead on the more popular movement to remove the last vestiges of silver from the currency system.[23]

The Chicago assets currency group retreated reluctantly but with good grace. Gage and Roberts saw that Aldrich and his Senate cohorts controlled McKinley on the subject, despite the president's former identification with currency reform. They hoped, however, almost to the end of 1899, to persuade the Four to accept at least a weak compromise measure, but their efforts came to naught.

In the spring of 1899, Director of the Mint Roberts in a letter to Allison presented his views with an eloquence and sophistication that put to shame the performance of the Four. He was "decidedly of the opinion that we will never have a perfect currency system until we have either a great central bank of issue or a system which binds our present national banks together in a national clearing house and permits the issue of their notes upon their general assets." Roberts conceded, however, that the public was not ready for such a system and that "even the bankers themselves fail to comprehend the advantages" that a "bank note currency would yield." Meanwhile, he insisted, "the country ought to be immediately provided with the facilities for an emergency issue of notes."[24]

In the fall, Comptroller Dawes became aware that Gage had retreated. On October 30, 1899, the two discussed the weak gold currency plan that Gage had prepared for McKinley. Dawes recorded in his journal that Gage also discussed "the principles underlying bank asset currency" but did not recommend any specific plan. Dawes added "that one will be submitted to Congress which he [Gage] hopes may be found practicable."[25] Dawes thereupon attempted to formulate an

George E. Roberts, 18 May 1899, and John A. Stewart, 1 February 1900—all in Allison Papers; Edward Wolcott to Aldrich, 16 May 1899, and Charles W. Fairbanks to Aldrich, 7 June 1899, Aldrich Papers; *New York Tribune*, 7, 11, 12 December 1898.

[23] *New York Tribune*, 8 April 1900; Wiebe, *Businessmen and Reform*, 62.
[24] 18 May 1899, Allison Papers.
[25] Dawes, *Journal*, 203.

acceptable compromise plan but in the end experienced complete defeat of his efforts.[26]

With the convening of Congress in December 1899, the Republican leaders had a choice opportunity to enact currency legislation. For the first time since 1883, non-Silverite Republicans were in unquestioned control of both houses of Congress, but they had no intention of being accused of overexertion. The friendly *New York Tribune* reported that the "unusually settled and orderly political conditions under which the new Congress takes up the burden of legislation were clearly reflected in the tameness and quietude which marked the opening ceremonies in both houses." This Republican paper further stated that both houses "could hardly fail to come together in any other spirit than that of easy going acquiescence in the rather listless and colorless role forced upon them by the exigencies or accidents of National politics." The *Tribune* felt obliged to predict that the current Congress "will probably be remembered more for the mistakes it has avoided than for the amount and importance of the legislation which it succeeded in getting through."[27]

The Republican leadership found it easy to do very little. Allison and Aldrich produced and Congress enacted the Gold Standard Act, which reaffirmed the gold standard, slightly increased the currency supply, and made possible an increase in the number of national banks. McKinley signed it on March 14, 1900.[28] With more optimism than realism, Senator Chauncey Depew of New York said the new law "ended a monetary controversy in this country which began a hundred years ago, when Jefferson and Hamilton were arrayed on opposite sides in the great battle of the standards, which was to last a century."[29]

While Republican leaders dealt with questions of the tariff and the currency, an increasing number of their constituents asked them to enact legislation that would ensure firmer control over big business. Between 1899 and 1902, seventy-nine very large trusts emerged. Railroad consolidations continued at a rapid pace. In little more than a year, beginning in mid-

[26] Ibid., 203–11, 218.

[27] 5, 12, 18 December 1899.

[28] Henry Cabot Lodge to Henry L. Higginson, 22 April 1910, Higginson Papers; *New York Tribune*, 6, 7, 15 March 1900.

[29] *New York Tribune*, 8 June 1900.

1899, large companies absorbed an additional eighth of the railroad mileage of the nation.[30] In 1901, J. P. Morgan organized the giant United States Steel Corporation. Frenzied speculation took place in new enterprises and in already established enterprises. As exploitive, monopolistic practices mounted, public fear and anger also grew. The public, moreover, could not rely on the courts to handle the problem. The 1895 Knight Case, with its restrictive definition of the power of the federal government over interstate commerce, had narrowed the application of the Sherman Antitrust Law.

The situation in the railroad industry was especially critical. Since 1887, the federal government had experimented with at least a modicum of regulation, but the situation had deteriorated to the edge of anarchy. From 1896 through 1898, the Supreme Court precipitated much of the trouble through a series of decisions which destroyed what little national railroad rate regulation existed. The decisions left the Interstate Commerce Commission powerless over rates and prevented the railroads themselves from controlling rates by getting together in a pooling system.[31] Amid the anarchy, discriminatory rate-making prevailed, through rebates or other forms of favoritism, and threatened to grow apace. Railroad mergers increasingly placed rate-making in the hands of a few powerful railroads. Such mergers increased concern among smaller railroads still in service, among shippers, and among buyers of goods transported by railroads, leading them to welcome legislative relief.

As the evils of monopoly spread, newspapers poured forth a flood of editorials and reports on the subject. The Republican and business-oriented *New York Tribune* accounts evidenced a concern that went far beyond mere partisanship. *Tribune* editorials reflected a recognition that current practices by trusts would lead many of them into bankruptcy, which in turn would cause serious "injury to banks and other businesses."[32]

The Senate Four found themselves in an uncomfortable posi-

[30] Harold U. Faulkner, *The Decline of Laissez Faire, 1897–1917*, 37, 191; G. Wallace Chessman, *Governor Theodore Roosevelt: The Albany Apprenticeship, 1898–1900*, 158–60.

[31] Gabriel Kolko, *Railroads and Regulation, 1877–1916*, 80–86; James W. Neilson, *Shelby M. Cullom, Prairie State Republican*, 206.

[32] 11 January, 23 February, 11 April 1900.

tion on the railroad question; the middle western branch of the party faced revolt unless the national leaders agreed upon a plan of legislative action. The threat of insurgency happened to be strongest in Iowa and Wisconsin, making both Allison and Spooner vulnerable, since each had strong ties with railroads.

Railroad attorneys and lobbyists had for many decades infiltrated both the Republican and the Democratic state organizations of the Middle West. Allison, however, had succeeded in giving the appearance of indifference to the railroad interests, although it was general knowledge that he exhibited no enmity toward them. He was no populist. His status as elder statesman in the national party, in addition to his always cautious performance, protected him from seeming to be a tool of the railroads. In the offing, however, were signs of political insurgency in Iowa. An able and ambitious lawyer, Albert B. Cummins, who had railroad connections himself, was making a serious bid for leadership in the Iowa Republican party. He was interested in the trust and tariff issues in particular. Allison and his cohorts were watching him with uneasiness.[33]

Spooner did not appear to be a mere tool of the railroad interests. His apparent lack of guile partially protected him from this charge, but it was general knowledge that he was friendly toward railroad interests. He had been a conspicuously successful railroad attorney and lobbyist. He had close relations with such important figures as Frances Lynde Stetson, general counsel for the Northern Pacific, and Marvin Hughitt, president of the Chicago and Northwestern.[34]

Even while in the United States Senate, Spooner saw to it that railroad-sponsored bills received friendly treatment in the Wisconsin legislature. In achieving that end, he and his asso-

[33] C. T. Hancock (chairman, Iowa Rebublican State Committee) to Allison, 30 September, 5 October 1898, 12, 15 January 1900, Allison Papers; Sage, *Allison*, 260, 261, 264, 276–7.

[34] See, for example: J. W. Kendrick to Spooner, 26 January 1897, 1, 18 November 1898; H. H. Porter to Spooner, 31 March, 12 April, 2 May 1897; Spooner to Porter, 8 April, 3 May 1897; Spooner to Thomas Wilson, 18 March 1897; Edwin White to Spooner, 1 April 1897; Spooner to Marvin Hughitt, 2 April 1897; Hughitt to Spooner, 21 March 1900; Spooner to C. W. Bunn, 8 April 1897; C. H. Coster to Spooner, 10 August 1897; Henry C. Payne to Spooner, 23 August 1898; George R. Peck to Spooner, 16 September 1898; Edward W. Keyes to Spooner, 20 February 1899; Stuyvesant Fish to Spooner, 2 May 1900—all in Spooner Papers.

ciates did all they could to avoid antagonizing populists and other antirailroad agitators.[35]

Because railroad executives concentrated especially great pressure on Spooner, some powerful shippers did likewise. Two Milwaukee shipping groups disagreed with each other on the question of federal regulation of railroad rates. The big brewers wanted no changes in their very satisfactory current arrangements with the railroads. An association of smaller business operators, however, insisted that the railroads grossly mistreated them. The spokesman for the disgruntled shippers, Edward P. Bacon, a Milwaukee grain commission merchant, was extremely aggressive. Beginning in 1898, Bacon berated Spooner without mercy to support the Cullom rate-regulation bill.[36] He was a pioneer in the new movement of organized shipper protest, and Spooner was simply one of the first targets. In 1899 Bacon founded the League of National Associations, the first important small-shipper organization.[37] Spooner took no positive steps on behalf of the shippers beyond vaguely discussing with them prospects of Interstate Commerce Committee action on the subject.[38] Eventually more shippers organized, including the cattlemen of Iowa.

The Senate Four kept the shipper protest from getting out of hand. They faced no serious difficulties with the House or the president. In fact, McKinley showed no interest whatsoever in the issue. All the Four needed to do was to control the Interstate Commerce Committee, which they easily did.[39] The chair-

[35] On one occasion Stetson wrote from New York to Spooner the suggestion that "it might be well if the proposed amendment to Section 1788" be submitted to the legislature in manuscript form "so as to avoid the suspicion resulting from the appearance of so formal (and perhaps formidable) a document." He also wondered if Spooner cared to communicate with "any representative of the Democrats, as well as with your own Republican members" before the introduction of the bill. (23 November 1898, Spooner Papers.)

[36] Letters to Spooner from: Edward P. Bacon, 15, 16 March 1898, 8 September, 5 December 1899, 24, 27 February, 17 May, 2 June 1900, 2 December 1901, Robert H. Eliot, 25 February 1899, 11 June 1900, Charles Schlogel, 1 March 1900, J. J. Kereny, 7 March 1900, A. Murowsky, 22 March 1900, Fred Pabst, 2 April 1900, R. Calvert, 31 January 1901—all in Spooner Papers.

[37] Kolko, *Railroads and Regulation*, 93.

[38] Spooner to Bacon, 15 May 1898, and Spooner to Robert H. Eliot, 9 July 1900, 9 March 1901, Spooner Papers.

[39] Robert H. Eliot to Spooner, 11 June 1900, and Spooner to Eliot, 9 July 1900, Spooner Papers; Kolko, *Railroads and Regulation*, 89.

man of the committee was venerable Shelby M. Cullom, whose inclination was to aid shippers through federal regulation of railroad rates. But his advanced years discouraged him from action of any sort. The committee, moreover, was rife with prorailroad senators. Aldrich was on it, as well as such close allies of the railroads as Stephen B. Elkins of West Virginia and John H. Gear of Iowa. Gear was a brother-in-law of Joseph W. Blythe, general solicitor of the Chicago, Burlington, and Quincy Railroad and a close political ally of Allison.[40]

The committee saw to it that no railroad bill reached the Senate floor. The railroads were popular enough with the committee to prevent action on the Cullom bill but too unpopular with the public to make it politically advisable for the committee to legalize railroad pooling arrangements on rate schedules. The basic rate problem remained.

It was unthinkable to expect that the political leadership of the country could long avoid legislative action on the railroad problem. In 1903, with passage of the antirebate Elkins Act, Congress made a gesture to the demands of smaller shippers and smaller railroads, but this solved nothing. The measure proved to be unsatisfactory.[41]

On the broader question of the trusts, Congress in 1898 wisely established the Industrial Commission. Important among the duties of this commission was the task of investigating "the growing concentration of economic power." The nineteen-member commission, Republican dominated, of course, included neither top party leaders nor top intellectuals. Except for Senator Boies Penrose of Pennsylvania, the members were conscientious men. The hard-working committee chairman, Senator James H. Kyle of South Dakota, an educator and Congregational minister, at times showed signs of political independence, but not enough to worry the party hierarchy.[42]

In the spring if 1900, before the national party convention, the commission issued a preliminary report recommending some mild reforms. It called for legislation to force businesses, es-

[40] Neilson, Cullom, 206–08.
[41] See Kolko, Railroads and Regulation, 95, 98–102, 116–17.
[42] Leech, McKinley, 545–46.

pecially trusts, to reveal to the public significant information about their finances. The commission also recommended that Congress give the Interstate Commerce Commission increased authority to combat railroad rate discrimination. The report afforded political campaigners a modicum of material to insert in their speeches and the promise that there would be more to come when the final report of the commission became available. Some politicians also put antitrust bills into the legislative hopper, but they died a quick death.[43]

Among the top Republican leaders, Platt of Connecticut showed more than passing interest in the trust problem. For many years he had watched small New England factories grow, and now he saw the finance capitalists of New York and Boston move in with their holding company and merger blueprints. This take-over disturbed him, and the Republican book of rules failed to instruct him on just how to improve the situation.

In the fall of 1899, while preparing a speech on trusts to a Republican club in Connecticut, Platt called upon his old friend Flagg for help. Flagg, as a Wall Street lawyer in the employ of the Rockefellers, was close to the subject but professed to be in a quandary. He agreed with Platt that the article in the current issue of *Scribner's Magazine,* entitled "The Formation and Control of Trusts," was inconclusive. The author, Arthur T. Hadley, president of Yale, was a supposed expert on the subject. Flagg said that "most of the academic discussions were inconclusive —were drivel and rot." Unable to supply Platt with a suitable bibliography on the subject, Flagg nevertheless had some thoughts of his own. He reviewed for his friend the story of the evolution of industrialism. He considered the result inevitable, necessary, and desirable, even though it embraced some evils. "If some method could be devised to prevent fictitious capitalization and the floating of watered stock upon an innocent public a great incentive would be removed to form industrial organizations solely to benefit promoters."

Flagg did not know what method to employ. He was "anxious to see" what Platt concluded. "It is an important and

[43] Ibid.; Gabriel Kolko, *The Triumph of Conservatism: A Reinterpretation of American History, 1900–1916,* 28, 63–64, 132.

difficult subject," he added. He felt it was "especially difficult" to find a remedy for "acknowledged abuses," and was "made more so by conflicting jurisdictions between state and federal authority." Perhaps, he said, "some Constitutional amendment will be the way out of it, but that is not only remote but will be most difficult to attain." Meanwhile, "the prevailing discussions . . . will do much good" and "in the end some course will be evolved to meet evils that in reality—not in fancy—exist."[44]

In the speech Platt delivered, which indicated his acceptance of the inevitability and desirability of trusts, he emphasized the importance of moderation. He told the ancient fable of the two knights who approached a beautiful shield from opposite sides; upon reaching it one declared that it was made of gold and the other said it was made of silver. That began an argument which in turn led to a fight. After both were nearly killed they came to the conclusion that there were two sides to the shield, one silver and the other gold. So it was, thought Platt, with the trust question—there were two sides to it. People should not kill each other over the matter. In fact, he believed people of "the present day" were too prejudiced, and those who could not get rich wanted to keep all others from getting rich. He pointed out that people were living on a better scale than they had been thirty years previously and that everyone benefitted from the trusts, not just the rich. Platt counseled against making the matter of trusts a political issue "until someone thinks he has discovered . . . a proper method of regulation without injury." He believed that in the absence of a proposed remedy worthy of serious consideration, discussion of the trust problem would remain on the level of dangerous demagoguery.[45]

The other members of the hierarchy did even less than Platt about the overall trust problem. Aldrich, as was his custom when dealing with the public, remained silent. But so did Allison, Spooner, and President McKinley. Although in March 1899 McKinley confided to Dawes his intention to launch a movement

[44] Flagg to Platt, 31 January, 7 November, 18 December 1899, Platt Papers. See also Arthur T. Hadley, "The Formation and Control of Trusts," *Scribner's Magazine* 26 (November 1899): 604–10.

[45] *New Haven Evening Register*, 10 November 1899; Louis A. Coolidge, *An Old-Fashioned Senator: Orville H. Platt of Connecticut*, 441.

for trust restriction, he somehow never got around to it. The subject was too complicated for McKinley in both its political and its economic implications; there being no Republican dogma on the matter on which to lean, McKinley was unable to do more than issue platitudes. He permitted the 1900 Republican platform to contain the vaguest possible statement on trusts and seemingly welcomed Hanna's decision to assign to vice-presidential candidate Roosevelt the task of handling the 1900 campaign oratory on trusts.[46]

Two lesser Republican politicians, Roosevelt and Insurgent Robert M. LaFollette, showed a more lively and enlightened interest in the trust problem than did members of the command. Roosevelt was most conspicuous. His record as governor of New York indicated his active interest in the question. As he reached out for national political prominence, he used the trust issue in his speeches.[47] In the summer of 1899 he wrote editor Kohlsaat in Chicago, "How about trusts?" He went on to emphasize his belief that "there will be a good deal of importance to the trust matter in the next campaign." He feared that if the party failed to have "some consistent policy to advocate, . . . multitudes will follow the crank who advocates an absurd policy."[48] In like vein he wrote to Henry Cabot Lodge. After stating that the "agitation against trusts is taking an always firmer hold," he emphasized that the antitrust movement was politically more dangerous to the Republican party in the East than elsewhere. He clearly feared that the Democrats had found in the trust issue a cause much more promising to capitalize on than in the free-silver crusade.[49]

While party leaders grappled with the problem, public discussion of the trusts mounted. In September 1899, the Civic Federation of Chicago sponsored a widely publicized Conference on Trusts. In New York in 1900, Cooper Union sponsored a People's Institute Conference on Trusts at which economist John Bates Clark of Columbia University was one of the im-

[46] Dawes, *Journal*, 185–86, 205; Leech, *McKinley*, 547–48, 576; Herbert D. Croly, *Marcus Alonzo Hanna: His Life and Work*, 306–07, 327–28.
[47] Chessman, *Roosevelt*, 162.
[48] 7 August 1899, Morison, *Letters*, 2: 1045.
[49] 10 August 1899, ibid., 1048.

portant speakers. In what the *New York Tribune* termed a "gently satirical speech," Clark told the audience that "The people of this country are not in the least decided whether trusts are good or bad; don't know exactly whether they raise prices or lower prices; are not precisely certain whether they increase or decrease wages; are not altogether sure whether they do quite the right things by their competitors or not, and yet in the face of all these doubts it is a curious fact that we agree thoroughly on just one fact, and that is, we must have legislation that will smash them." Turning to the role of politicians and parties, Clark said that although "such an admission would be the frozen truth," they do not dare admit that they themselves "don't know whether trusts are good or bad." The politicians simply employ the cry "smash the trusts" because it seems to be the only politically acceptable approach. Meanwhile, Clark insisted, "We are still in the guessing period" as to what to do about trusts.[50]

Soon the 1900 election campaign diverted the attention of political leaders from the less pressing matters of party policy, but little about it exhilarated the "old hands" in any of the political camps. Before and during the Republican convention, however, some political jockeying went on that revealed much about President McKinley and some of the party managers. This maneuvering revolved largely around Mark Hanna, with McKinley quietly injecting his will when events called for a steady hand.

A disagreement over southern representation in the 1900 convention epitomized the personality clashes and struggle for power that characterized the party managers and also served as a reminder of the sorry state of traditional Republican humanitarian policy on the plight of the southern Negro. This difference of opinion showed that party leaders focused their attention on the Negro only as a bearer of valuable votes at the national nominating convention. Since the early 1890s Mark Hanna, as agent for McKinley, had been currying the favor of southern Negro Republicans. The election of McKinley brought to the McKinley-Hanna alliance a supply of patronage which

[50] *New York Tribune,* 23 February 1900.

assured both of them popularity in southern Republican en-
claves. Not only did this afford them an unjustified amount of
power in a supposedly democratically operated organization, but
it perpetuated an unhealthy situation in southern Republican
organizations. A large number of unworthy office-holding political hacks, both white and Negro, who were beholden to
McKinley, became delegates to national nominating conventions. In this role they held and exercised for McKinley a disproportionately large amount of power, inasmuch as the overall
number of delegates to a convention depended on population
statistics rather than on the number of registered voters. Recent
Negro disfranchisement laws and unofficial intimidation of
Negroes prevented most Negroes in the South from voting, but
they were counted as members of the population.

Wisconsin's Henry C. Payne, vice-chairman of the Republican
National Committee, and Pennsylvania's Matthew Quay attempted, albeit unsuccessfully, to use the southern delegation
question as a means to reduce Hanna's power. With Payne taking
the initiative, they launched a movement to change the convention rules in such a manner as to reduce the number of southern
delegates. Normally McKinley righteously stood aside from such
embarrassing situations and allowed the bluff, often indiscreet
Hanna to reap the whirlwind. But this time the president was
unable to ignore completely Payne's insistent demand. In the
evening of December 15, 1899, the day before the National
Committee was to meet, McKinley went into action to quiet
Payne. He called Payne and three powerful Ohio political
leaders into the cabinet room to discuss the pros and cons of
the proposed reform. McKinley was well prepared. He was suave
and ingratiating but too dignified to appear the "oily" politician
he really was on that occasion. McKinley's secretary, the wor-
shipful and naive Cortelyou, was present and at midnight wrote
in his diary that "As usual the President was in favor of the
fullest discussion and a fair hearing of both sides; he could not
allow his own personality to play a part in the matter; said he
was simply a member of the party and must not be regarded as
desiring to influence a decision one way or the other." Cortelyou
even seemed to accept McKinley's statement that until a few

days previously he had favored the change, but, as Cortelyou recorded it, "communications had come to him from many colored men in the north and today Bishop Arnett had spoken to him so strongly on the subject that he now doubted its expediency." According to Cortelyou, the president feared such a change might endanger the election outcome in Ohio, Kentucky, Indiana, and maybe elsewhere, where the Negro vote was substantial. His fellow Ohioans present spoke in the same vein.[51]

Payne was unable to withstand the pressure, and upon his capitulation, the president as usual administered "soothing syrup" and absolved himself from the disciplinary action. As Cortelyou admiringly recorded it, "The President told Mr. Payne that it seemed to him that one of the important considerations was that it must not hurt him—Payne—; that whatever was done there must be no embarrassment attached to him—Payne." To this implied "let's-keep-it-in-the-family" admonition, McKinley added, according to Cortelyou, that "he would not allow himself to be put in the position of saying to the Committee what they should do on this or any other proposition."[52]

The next threat to the Hanna-McKinley "rotten borough" of southern Republicans came during the June 1900 presidential convention in Philadelphia. This time Quay took over. The Pennsylvania boss introduced a resolution to enact the Payne reform. The resolution at once became involved in Hanna's opposition to the movement to nominate the young Theodore Roosevelt for the vice-presidency. Payne and Quay favored Roosevelt. McKinley and most of his admirers felt that it would be wise to "follow the crowd," but Hanna proposed that the administration sponsor colorless old Secretary of the Navy Long, who had been Roosevelt's superior before the Spanish American War. McKinley in effect ordered Hanna to surrender, which he did. Quay, pleased with this success, withdrew his resolution on southern delegation reform. Thus the convention ended on a note of harmony.[53]

---

[51] George B. Cortelyou, diary, 15 December 1899, McKinley Papers, Addenda.
[52] Ibid.
[53] Cortelyou memorandums of long distance telephone conversations between

In the campaign, the Republican hierarchy delegated as many chores as it could to three able professionals: responsible presidential candidate McKinley, vice-presidential candidate Roosevelt, and experienced Chairman of the Republican National Committee Hanna. The Democrats countered with golden orator Bryan as presidential candidate and Adlai E. Stevenson of Illinois, a mild vice-presidential candidate. Voters, markedly prosperous and apathetic, paid little attention to party platforms or issues. There were, nevertheless, a few interesting events. When, for example, the delegates to the Democratic National Convention arrived in Kansas City, the keeper of the morgue of that metropolis placed on his building a banner with the legend "Welcome."[54] But in general it was a dull summer and autumn. In August, Roosevelt wrote to his friend Henry Cabot Lodge that the "apathy of which you speak is very marked here" in New York state. "There is not the slightest enthusiasm for Bryan but there is no enthusiasm for us and there seems to be no fear of Bryan."[55] Lodge reported to historian James Ford Rhodes, "I have never known a Presidential campaign so quiet."[56]

Public interest did quicken, however, toward the end of the campaign. Fear spread that Bryan might repeal the current prosperity. Charles Taft later reported to his brother William Howard Taft, whom McKinley had put in charge of civilian affairs in the far off Philippines, that the "business interests of the country . . . took hold of the matter" when Republicans became worried. "Bryan's more recent speeches," Taft explained, "indicated the clear demagogue. They frightened business men." Bryan arrayed classes against each other "and took advantage of every little opportunity to incite the lowest instincts in man. If he could have carried out what he preached he would have brought about revolution."[57]

Cortelyou, at White House, and Charles Dick (17 June 1900), Charles G. Dawes (19, 20 June 1900), and George W. Perkins (20, 21 June 1900), all in Philadelphia, McKinley Papers, Addenda; Dawes, *Journal,* 232–34, 235; Leech, *McKinley,* 536–42; Croly, *Hanna,* 308–18.

[54] Charles Taft to Taft, 7 July 1900, Taft Papers.
[55] 22 August 1900, Roosevelt Papers.
[56] 6 August 1900, Lodge Papers.
[57] 6 December 1900, Taft Papers.

As usual, business fears were exaggerated and far from ubiquitous. Early in the campaign, betting in the New York financial district on the outcome was two to one on McKinley. By the close of the campaign it was five to one. The *New York Tribune* estimated that an aggregate of $1,500,000 was wagered in the financial district.[58] Meanwhile, enterprising Mark Hanna experienced no difficulty in raising a huge campaign war chest, more than five times that of the Democrats. The result: Republican voters dutifully turned out, in as large numbers as in 1896, to reelect McKinley, their great war leader, empire builder, and "advance agent of prosperity," but most especially to retain their "full dinner pails." The score was, in round numbers, 7,220,000 for McKinley, to 6,359,000 for Bryan.[59] Next day the *Tribune* rejoiced that "most thoughtful Republicans here" felt the victory meant that "While no backward steps will be taken anywhere, no crude or undigested measures will be framed or recommended."[60]

[58] 8 November 1900.
[59] Croly, *Hanna*, 322–27; Paolo E. Coletta, *William Jennings Bryan: Political Evangelist, 1860–1908*, 283.
[60] 9 November 1900.

IV

OPPORTUNITIES AND
DANGERS EMERGE
1900-1901

IN THE NINE MONTHS between the sweeping Republican victory of 1900 and the assassination of President McKinley, the top leaders showed no real desire to inaugurate a new program or to improve the old one. They believed the current system made possible the current prosperity. McKinley, however, suggested that means were available to the party to foster ever greater prosperity, and Vice-President Theodore Roosevelt, together with some lesser lights in the party, talked about modernizing the party's economic policies. They left it to the future and to Congress, however, to formulate actual proposals. McKinley was hesitant to challenge the Senate Four and used as an excuse for his timidity the division of powers implicit in the federal Constitution.

Although the institutions within American society were becoming larger, more complex, and thus more in need of governmental control, the entrenched Republican congressional leaders continued to ignore this need and their party's conventional role. Such troubles seemed to them to be purely of individual, local, or state concern. They chose to operate on the assumption that the plight of the poor, the prevalence of corrupt political machines, the exploitation of labor, and the continued subjugation of Negroes lay beyond their jurisdiction. Moreover, within the realm of their acknowledged responsibilities, they had no legislative plans of note, believing that they had for the time being disposed of the tariff, currency, and trust issues.

The leaders in the East were entirely complacent and found time for relaxation after the election results indicated their worth in the eyes of the public. The aging Platt and his wife spent the summer of 1901 in their modest summer cottage. Aldrich remained in his palatial mansion, helping prepare for the wedding of his daughter Abby and John D. Rockefeller, Jr.[1]

In the Middle West, however, Spooner and Allison had to contend with irritating state political contests. The situation was fraught with danger for them and the party organization in general. Spooner had to deal with Governor Robert M. LaFollette, and Allison had to accommodate himself to Albert B. Cummins.

Although national events and personalities kept it in the background for the time being, Spooner and his Wisconsin cohorts faced one of the most ominous threats to the national Republican hierarchy since the 1896 victory. Only the simultaneous insurgency that Allison faced in neighboring Iowa approached it as an indication of troublous times ahead. Insurgent LaFollette had won the governorship in 1900 and, worse luck, he had done it by means of a protracted and relentless attack on the Wisconsin segment of the Republican-business partnership. If such could happen in one strongly Republican state, it could happen in other states.

The goal of the newly elected LaFollette was to drive the Republican-business partnership, the Stalwart element, from its powerful position in the Wisconsin state government and return the state to the people as a whole. He believed that the Republican-business partnership embraced special privilege and thievery at the expense of the general citizenry. LaFollette believed the people, restored to power, could obtain honest taxation and control of corporations.

LaFollette's program was attractive to the increasing number of citizens who felt that the spread of industrialization and urbanization was robbing them of their small-community-oriented way of life. LaFollette not only attacked exploitation and corruption but struck out at the corporate structure itself. He

[1] Nathaniel W. Stephenson, *Nelson W. Aldrich: A Leader in American Politics,* 173.

disregarded small enterprise inefficiency, exploitation of employees, and overcharges, and leveled a Jeffersonian attack on the new bigness. In speeches at county fairs and other rural gatherings, LaFollette decried the growth of corporations and claimed "they have practically acquired dominion over the business world." He asserted that "the individual as a business factor is disappearing" and that "gathered in corporate employ, men become mere cogs in the wheels of complicated mechanism." The corporation was "reducing men to mere numbers."[2]

Conducting his crusade in stages, LaFollette in 1901 used his first year as governor to consolidate his political organization and to seek enactment of two important measures, a primary election law and a law to increase state taxation of railroads. He failed to obtain passage of either that year, but his efforts did much to popularize further his insurgency against the Wisconsin Republican-business partnership.

Spooner became increasingly convinced that LaFollette was determined to get his Senate seat for the 1903–1909 term. He viewed LaFollette as a vicious, scheming, power-hungry demagogue, and wrote one Wisconsin Republican, "Mr. LaFollette is a malignant enemy of mine, and I have no doubt whatever that if his candidacy were successful, and the party machinery were turned over to him, he would use it to his uttermost to work out his revenges."[3] Spooner believed that if LaFollette obtained enactment of a direct primary law, he would thereby have the means to capture control of the legislature in the next election and thence the coveted United States senatorship. He apparently assumed that LaFollette would be too impatient to wait until 1905, when he could more easily obtain the seat currently occupied by colorless Joseph V. Quarles. Spooner had placed Quarles in the Senate and the latter took his orders from Spooner. Actually, however, LaFollette gave no indication that he aimed to replace Spooner in the Senate.

There was little within Spooner's power to blunt the edge of LaFollette's conquering sword, unless he endorsed the primary

[2] Roger Spooner to Spooner, 27, 28 August 1897, and clippings, including *Chicago Record*, dateline Waukesha, Wisconsin, 27 August, Spooner Papers.

[3] Spooner to J. H. Healy, 8 June 1900, Spooner Papers.

election bill and economic reform designed to tax and regulate corporations. Spooner, however, was too much a part of the Republican-business partnership to disentangle himself from this long-standing arrangement. All he could do was to hope that LaFollette would fail. He did, nevertheless, favor the pursuit of a better ordered society, as his interest in the establishment of a tariff commission of experts showed, but he would not condone doing it at the expense of business or of the Republican-business partnership.

LaFollette refrained from leveling any direct attack on Spooner. He shrewdly went to great lengths to avoid a public confrontation with the popular and powerful senator, and instead reserved his stinging barbs for the more vulnerable machine politicians and the financial manipulators who officiated over the Wisconsin Stalwart Republican organization. Henry C. Payne and Charles Pfister were the chief recipients of the LaFollette onslaught. They were wealthy men with positions of power in both public utilities and politics in Milwaukee, and they found those interests harmonized well. Payne was also a highly successful political manager on the state and national levels; currently, for example, he was vice-chairman of the National Republican Committee. Pfister, although a bungling politician, worked much and spent much for the Stalwart cause. One of his contributions was his purchase in 1901 of the previously hostile leading newspaper of the state, the *Milwaukee Sentinel*.[4] Before that purchase, Payne had on one occasion reported to Spooner that "To be subjected day after day to the malicious spleen and vindictive malice of the 'Sentinel'. . . is almost more than I can bear."[5] Payne and the other Stalwarts were therefore overjoyed when Pfister came to the rescue. Payne told Spooner that while "the situation as to the future of the party is difficult to forecast," the control of the *Sentinel* "will be almost the determining factor."[6] Pfister also contributed to the purchase of at least one northern Wisconsin newspaper.[7] His

---

[4] Pfister to Spooner, 19 February 1901, Spooner Papers; Russel B. Nye, *Midwestern Progressive Politics: A Historical Study of Its Origins and Development, 1870–1958*, 199.

[5] 22 February 1900, Spooner Papers.

[6] 7 February 1901, and Spooner to Payne, 11 February 1901, Spooner Papers.

generosity seemed boundless. Spooner's son Willet reported from Milwaukee that the "situation is very encouraging. Pfister has practically placed his account at the disposal of the counties which need" political aid.[8] Meanwhile, Pfister became the state party chairman.

Publicly, Spooner pretended to be above and outside the party strife in Wisconsin. As early as July 1900, after it had become apparent that LaFollette was to become governor, Spooner announced that because of his wife's health he was "unalterably determined not to be a candidate for reelection" at the expiration of his term in 1903. But he privately exhorted his Wisconsin political associates to fight LaFollette, helped with the purchase of at least one newspaper ($1,500) and aided Pfister with political material in the *Milwaukee Sentinel*. By inconspicuous means, he showed antagonism not only toward LaFollette personally but also toward the primary election bill and the taxation of railroads bill.[9] But Spooner's efforts were small. He could not cast aside much of his past.

While the entrapped Spooner publicly withdrew from the fray and fumed and fussed to his friends, Allison labored to maintain the domination of his so-called Regency in Iowa, which the ambitious and popular insurgent Albert B. Cummins threatened to shatter. It was fortunate that Allison's inclination and experience led him in the direction of compromise rather than a head-on attack, because Cummins was well prepared for a direct fight. The handsome, tall, personable Cummins had accumulated a substantial following among the Iowa voters and his record and connections in business and professional circles tended to neutralize the strength of Allison's powerful Republican-business Regency.

Cummins, as the *New York Tribune* noted, was not only "the leading attorney of the State,"[10] but in good standing with in-

---

[7] Solon Perrin to Spooner, 6 March 1900; Payne to Spooner, 10 May 1900, Spooner Papers.

[8] 19 June 1902, Spooner Papers.

[9] Payne to Spooner, 10 May 1900, 14 February 1901; Payne to Henry Fink, 4 June 1900; Spooner to Payne, 11 February 1901; Charles Pfister to Spooner, 19 February 1901; Spooner to Pfister, 10 December 1901—all in Spooner Papers.

[10] 4 August 1901.

fluential businessmen and lawyers in Chicago and Iowa. These men helped him directly and constituted evidence that Cummins was no populist, no dangerous demagogue. Cummins quietly enlisted the support of businessmen and lawyers not already definitely allied with Allison, as were railroad attorney and political boss Joseph W. Blythe, and his brother-in-law John H. Gear. He approached, among others, Will H. Blodgett of the Wabash Railroad, Vice-President Robert Mather of the Chicago, Rock Island, and Pacific Railway, and attorney Carroll Wright of the same road.

In a letter to Mather in the spring of 1897, Cummins made clear his intention to utilize his connections with the business world. After referring to Gear's campaign to seek reelection to the Senate and his own intention to bid for that position, Cummins said that in his campaign he intended "to neutralize" Gear's effort "so far as I can." To that end, "I want you and Carroll Wright to take up the fight for me and occupy toward my contest the same relation that J. W. Blythe occupies towards Gear's." Several months later, in the course of his attempt to maintain friendly relations with businessmen, Cummins even reached out to DeKalb, Illinois, for support.[11] In a letter to Isaac M. Ellwood, a barbed wire manufacturer of that city, Cummins complained that "someone has attempted to create the impression that I am distinctly hostile to railway and corporate interests." He thought that to be "extraordinary, in view of the fact that I have been attempting to defend their interests throughout nearly the whole of my professional life." Cummins pointed out, "I have been continuously the attorney for nearly all the railways that enter Des Moines, for the water company, the electric light company, insurance companies, etc."[12]

Despite Cummins's impressive strength, the Allison group controlled the legislature and hence in 1900 returned the seventy-five-year-old Gear to his Senate seat. Thereupon the state's most influential and largest Republican newspaper, the *Des Moines Register*, stated that Cummins faced Joseph W. Blythe and the

---

[11] Albert B. Cummins to Robert Mather, 23 April 1897, Albert B. Cummins Papers.

[12] 24 December 1898; see also W. E. Odell to Cummins, 28 November 1902, Cummins Papers.

Chicago, Burlington, and Quincy Railroad Company, "a railroad with millions backing the biggest 'boss' the state ever knew."[13] The *Register*, Cummins, and people in general refrained from direct attacks on the venerable Allison, the "Sage of Dubuque," but they were well aware of the nature of that railroad and of the other business connections of Allison's Regency.

But the stop-Cummins movement was short lived. In July 1901, the dottering Gear died, and the Allison Regency faced a predicament. It must either arouse the ire of Cummins again or accept this difficult man into the fold. Allison and his cohorts risked the consequences of Cummins's resentment. They instructed Governor Leslie M. Shaw to appoint the relatively unknown Jonathan P. Dolliver, an Allison protegé, to the Senate vacancy. Cummins was more than a little irritated, but, like LaFollette in Wisconsin, he carefully avoided criticizing the state's most honored statesman. By late summer 1901, however, Cummins had so much strength that there was no denying his bid for high office. In the fall election, he became governor, and Allison's Regency began a definite and irrevocable decline.[14]

This defeat had significant implications for the national leadership. Cummins not only had successfully challenged Allison, but had also challenged the national party policy itself by largely ignoring dangerous state issues. Taking advantage of the anti-big-business, anti-eastern feeling in small-farm and small-town Iowa, he leveled his attack on Washington and Wall Street. He advocated tariff reciprocity and the Iowa Idea, a scheme that called for the elimination of tariff protection on those industries where monopoly, rather than competition, determined the selling price.[15]

The Iowa Idea was an attractive device for gathering votes in a rural area where there were no large manufacturers to worry about but where there were many farmers and also friendly railroads. It appealed to many Republicans because it promised tariff reform without relinquishment of their cherished protec-

<hr />

[13] 19 January 1900, quoted in Leland L. Sage, *William Boyd Allison: A Study in Practical Politics*, 277.
[14] Sage, *Allison*, 276–79, 282–83; J. W. Blythe to Allison, 28 June 1901, Allison Papers.
[15] *Iowa State Journal* (Des Moines), 8 August 1901; Sage, *Allison*, 282.

tionist credo. When the Bryan Democrats cried, "The tariff is the mother of trusts," Republican voters feared it was a Democratic slogan to move the nation into a "free trade" position.

Attractive as it was among rural voters, the Iowa Idea contained fatal economic weaknesses and fatal political defects on the national level. More sophisticated reformers, such as Theodore Roosevelt, believed that the nation should approach the trust problem on a selective basis. The government, they held, should retain and regulate the good trusts and break up the exploitive ones. The Iowa Idea was indiscriminate. Moreover, it did not touch products such as coal which it was not feasible to import. Politically, any advocate of the plan could not hope to attract support in areas where manufacturing was important; employers and wage earners alike would reject it. But it remained a dangerous threat to the Republican party, for conceivably it could constitute an attractive rallying point for the hosts of rural voters, traditionally Republican but resentful of the great influence of the manufacturers in the party.

Allison's close political connections with the high protectionists in the alliances that sustained national Republican unity and his close identity with the 1897 Dingley Act made it difficult for him to accommodate himself to the Cummins tide. If challenged, he would have been hard pressed to demonstrate that the tariff plank in the Iowa state Republican platform conformed to his views. It contained an endorsement of both the Iowa Idea and reciprocity.[16] Unlike Spooner, however, the shrewd Allison managed to save face. He used various political tricks to cover up his chagrin and at the same time fulfill his duty to national party unity. On the Iowa Idea, he took advantage of the ambiguous phrasing of the plank to be equally vague in his interpretation of it. On reciprocity, he was faced with the cold fact that the Senate had buried the reciprocity treaties which the administration had negotiated. Allison blandly commented that the Senate had a responsibility at least to vote on the treaties,[17] but in actuality he had failed to exercise his great power to bring them to a vote.

[16] Sage, *Allison*, 282.
[17] Sage, *Allison*, 294–95; Allison to Joseph Wharton, 21 November 1901, Allison Papers.

Cummins's August 1901 success in Iowa attracted national attention. New York newspapers that failed even to make note of the more localized Spooner-LaFollette conflict paid close heed to the Allison-Cummins contest. The nomination of Cummins, the *New York Tribune* announced, "made a transference of power within the organization in Iowa from an older to a newer set of State leaders." This Republican paper added that Cummins, who had worked ten years to achieve power, would have no trouble winning in the November general election, for Iowa was as sure a "Republican State as either Vermont or Pennsylvania."[18] "Boss" Blythe, who had earlier shuddered at the thought of a Cummins victory and predicted to Allison the "disintegration of the Republican organization in the State" if Cummins won,[19] came to accept the change. He wrote to Allison that the "blunders of the Democratic State Convention seem to have made everything easy for us."[20] In November Cummins won easily.

Meanwhile, on the national stage President McKinley and the youthful Vice-President Roosevelt went about the country spreading goodwill but wisely avoided involvement in Wisconsin and Iowa battles. They made no public appearances in those states and kept away from Ohio, where the newly elected mayor of Cleveland, Thomas L. Johnson, was pointing the way toward municipal reform and was an annoyance to Mark Hanna and other important Ohio Republicans. McKinley and Roosevelt reminded citizens that the Republican party was responsible for their "full dinner pails" and predicted that the same party would provide even greater prosperity. McKinley spoke of the great opportunities for foreign trade and investment and Roosevelt touched on the specific problems of tariff revision and monopoly. Clearly Roosevelt had his eye on the 1904 election.

In April and May, in the course of a trip through the South and to the Pacific, and then in September at Buffalo, the genial McKinley engaged in speech-making on the glories of American economic well-being and progress. The *New York Evening Post* hopefully editorialized at length about the supposed purpose of

---

[18] 9 August 1901.
[19] Joseph W. Blythe to Allison, 8 June 1901, Allison Papers.
[20] 3 September 1901, ibid.

McKinley's journey. "He is bent," it asserted, "on preparing the people, and especially his own party, for a great change in the commercial and fiscal policy of the United States," which the *Post* called his New Departure. The *Washington Post* thought there was "some reason in that explanation of the President's journey."[21] No one, however, seemed to know the specific content of this New Departure.

McKinley's speeches, it turned out, constituted something short of a New Departure, although he said enough on a few occasions to worry the high protectionists. In an editorial entitled "McKinley's 'Free Trade' Bias," the *Boston Globe* observed, "[McKinley] having no reelection to figure for and having the new policy of expansion instead of protective tariffs in view, now talks in a vein that he would once have characterized as full of 'free trade virus.' "[22] McKinley's speeches, however, were primarily "chamber of commerce" lectures on the place of the nation in the current expansion of international trade and investment, along with a few hints on how the nation could maintain and further increase its trade through tariff reduction and subsidies to shipbuilders. On the tariff, he confined his remarks to a reminder that ultimately the nation would require a reciprocity program, although he said nothing of the Kasson treaties that were gathering dust in the Senate pigeonholes. McKinley had long endorsed the reciprocity idea. In 1897 in Cincinnati, in 1899 in Boston, and in both his inaugural addresses, the president had called for reciprocity.

In his speeches, McKinley avoided direct reference to subsidies to the shipbuilding industry, doubtless because the Senate Four lacked a consensus on that subject, though it was Mark Hanna's pet prescription for trade expansion.[23] However, in a speech at Memphis, Tennessee, the president noted how useful subsidies had been to the development of our railroads.[24] What

---

[21] *New York Evening Post*, 1 May 1901; *Washington Post*, 4 May 1901.
[22] 3 May 1901.
[23] Hanna to McKinley, 15 November 1900, McKinley Papers; William F. Vilas to Spooner, 17 February 1901, Spooner to Emil Baensch, 18 February 1901, Spooner to A. J. Cheney, 31 March 1902—all in Spooner Papers; Harvey Polster, "Mark Hanna and the Republican Hierarchy, 1897–1904" (master's thesis, University of Maryland, 1964), 17–43; Margaret Leech, *In the Days of McKinley*, 575–76.

he said left little doubt, the *San Francisco Chronicle* editorialized, that what he "had specifically in mind was assistance to our shipping interests."[25] This assistance would not be a startling new departure, for the Republicans had always been friendly toward schemes to subsidize business.

A stroke of misfortune greatly deflated the impact of McKinley's spring tour. The illness of Mrs. McKinley forced him to cut short his trip. He had to return to Washington and the speeches he was unable to deliver to audiences in the Middle West ended up in the White House file. They dealt with foreign economic expansion and carried such titles as "The North West and Middle West in Foreign Trade," "The Mississippi Valley and Latin American Trade," and "The Recent Growth of Our Trade." In each of these addresses, McKinley emphasized the suddenness and great extent of the upsurge in American exportation of both goods and capital. He asserted that "From the dependent position of debtor nation, we have risen, with startling suddenness, to that of the creditor nation of the world." He reported that "Three of the foremost European governments . . . have found it necessary to come to New York for important loans."[26]

It was trade in goods, however, that most intrigued McKinley. To him "the story of our suddenly acquired eminence in foreign trade, as told by our consular officers reporting from every corner of the globe, reads like a romance, and it is, in truth, a picture to warm the heart of every American." He pointed out that during the "last calendar year, our exports amounted to one and a half billion dollars, or but 350 million less than those of Great Britain." A major factor in the increase was our growth in manufacturing, he said.[27]

Looking into the future, McKinley sketched the good and bad prospects. "As our industries produce more and more largely for foreign markets," he observed, "they will need less and less to rely upon profits from the home market, and a gradual lowering

[24] *New York Times*, 1 May 1901; *Washington Post*, 1 May 1901.
[25] 2 May 1901.
[26] See McKinley speeches prepared for delivery on April–May 1901 western trip, box 250, McKinley Papers.
[27] Ibid.

of prices of manufactured goods will probably follow. . . . We cannot hope always to sell everything and buy little or nothing." And, he said, "we must not expect that the rest of the world will tamely submit to a one-sided bargain."[28]

Back home in Canton, Ohio, McKinley carefully prepared his forthcoming address for the Pan American Exposition in Buffalo. He instructed the second assistant secretary of state, Alvey A. Adee, to send him pamphlets on trade relations and in particular the publication of the Bureau of American Republics.[29] In early September, the president journeyed to Buffalo and picked up where he had left off with his earlier, interrupted goodwill tour. The Pan American Exposition provided a fine opportunity to exude goodwill, optimism, and an enthusiasm for increased foreign commerce. He reminded his Buffalo audience of the role of tariff reciprocity in the nation's expanding economy. Restating what he had written in a previous speech, the president said, "We must not repose in fancied security that we can forever sell everything and buy little or nothing." Unless America relaxed its policy, he said, retaliation would surely come. He further pointed out that "isolation is no longer possible or desirable. . . . God and man have linked the nations together. . . . The period of exclusiveness is past."[30] Next day, on September 6, he was fatally shot, and on September 14 he died.

At the time McKinley was touring through the South and to the west coast, other important Republicans were converging on Boston to speak on April 30 at a dinner of the Home Market Club. Vice-President Roosevelt was the principal speaker, and the Bay State's two United States senators, venerable George F. Hoar and aristocratic Henry Cabot Lodge, also spoke. It was a gala occasion, with the "Bay state's best known and most-loved sons, . . . and with Boston's fairest daughters in the galleries as spectators." Roosevelt with "his hands in his pockets" evoked "rounds of applause for his patriotic utterances and his common sense," said the *Boston Globe*. Senator Hoar, the *Globe* added, "was very witty," spoke in behalf of protection and "referred to

[28] Ibid.
[29] George B. Cortelyou memorandum, box 49, Biographer's Notes, Aldrich Papers.
[30] James D. Richardson, *A Compilation of the Messages and Papers of the Presidents*, 13:6618–22.

the President as a man with an 'illustrious and spotless name.' "[31]

The speeches of Hoar's close friends Lodge and Roosevelt reflected the nation's concern over the tariff. Lodge defensively proclaimed that "We have had now since 1816 a protective policy. There have been lapses, but never an entire departure from it. Under protection we have had good times and bad but we have never lapsed from the protective policy without having bad times." He referred to the nation's recent momentous overseas economic expansion. "The United States from being a country of borrowers has become a country of lenders, . . . and we have entered the foreign markets. We wish to enlarge them." To this end he urged construction of an Isthmian canal, favored a subsidized merchant marine, and endorsed an open door into China. He cautiously hinted at reciprocity, going no farther toward its advocacy than to suggest, "When it comes to the question of reciprocity with our rivals, then we want a reciprocity that is reciprocal." He then became vague but left the impression that he was suspicious of the goodwill of other nations in reciprocity agreements.[32]

Roosevelt was committed to protection, but instead of sidestepping the question of rate reform as a means of fostering foreign trade, the vice-president admitted, "There may have to be changes in detail to suit the shifting national needs" but we shall always require duties "at least equivalent to the difference in the labor cost here and abroad." He also inferred a liking for a tariff commission by adding that "I almost venture to hope for the arrival of the day when the tariff shall be treated less as a matter for party controversy than for scientific discussion and administrative application."[33] In his addresses during the summer, Roosevelt "substantially followed" a course Senator Spooner had previously outlined for him. Spooner was an advocate of scientific rate-making through a commission of experts.[34]

In a letter to his friend Taft during the summer, when everything was "at slack water politically," Roosevelt lucidly summa-

[31] 1 May 1901; *Washington Post,* 2 May 1901.
[32] *Boston Globe,* 1 May 1901.
[33] Ibid.
[34] Roosevelt to Spooner, 30 September 1901, Morison, *Letters,* 3:155; see also W. Barda to Roosevelt, 21 March 1901, Theodore Roosevelt Papers; *Milwaukee Journal,* 2 October 1901.

rized his feelings about the tariff. "The protective tariff," he said, "has vindicated itself in a most astonishing way, but our own people now acknowledge—or at least some of them do—that in some way or shape the reciprocal principle should be introduced in our tariff dealings with other nations." The cautious politician in him was apparent at that point, for he added that "when we admit that there should be any change in the tariff the inevitable result is to strengthen those who agitate for a disruption of the tariff. It is not easy to make any change in the tariff without opening the door for all sorts of changes." Apparently he disapproved of "all sorts of changes." He went on to lament, "Personally I should think that the nation would understand the need of continuity and steadiness of tariff policy as far more important than all else."[35]

In early September Roosevelt invaded the Middle West armed with a major speech on the trust question. Allison had invited him to speak in Iowa at a Grand Army of the Republic meeting, but the politically astute Roosevelt avoided the explosive situation in that state. He wanted to be on good terms with both the powerful Allison and the rising Cummins.[36] Instead, he delivered his address in Minneapolis, skirting also Wisconsin and thus avoiding the Spooner-LaFollette party battle.

In Minneapolis, Roosevelt told an enthusiastic audience about the nation's great accomplishments and the trust problem. He also said a little about the tariff. "In the long run, one of our prime needs is stability and continuity of economic policy; and yet, through treaty or by direct legislation, it may at least in certain cases become advantageous to supplement our present policy by a system of reciprocal benefit and obligation."[37] Soon he would have his chance to foster such legislation for within a few days he became president of the United States.

[35] 15 July 1901, Morison, *Letters*, 3:122.

[36] Roosevelt to William Allen White, 27 August 1901, and Roosevelt to Cummins, 7 September 1901, Morison, *Letters*, 3:137, 140.

[37] *Minneapolis Journal*, 2 September 1901, clipping in Spooner Papers. The Reform Club, meanwhile, increased its demands for tariff revision. See, for example, the form letter dated 23 May 1901, by Calvin Tompkins, chairman of the Committee on Tariff Reform, of the Reform Club, in Henry L. Higginson Papers.

V

ROOSEVELT INVIGORATES
THE PARTY
1901-1902

ROOSEVELT'S ACCESSION to the presidency automatically elevated him to the status of party chieftain. As such, he had to work with Aldrich, Platt, Allison, and Spooner, who continued in the top command. The new president and the Senate Four, being intelligent, seasoned professional politicians, quickly accommodated themselves to each other's needs. Hence the work of running the government and the party proceeded as smoothly as in the McKinley years. Roosevelt recruited some new men to aid him politically and to help modernize and expand the activities of the executive branch, but he never attempted to destroy the power of the Senate Four. Moderation and caution prevailed.

Despite some surface indications to the contrary, the new leadership continued to give the party's usual high priority to the seemingly endless demands of industrialism. Although Roosevelt himself indicated uneasiness over the excesses of business power, he and his associates made no determined effort to divorce their party from its accommodation to business interests. This partnership had weathered such troublous times as the depression of the 1890s, and it seemed unlikely that it would fall apart during the good times that followed. It was also apparent that the leaders had no intention of disrupting the long-standing geographical alliance of eastern and middle western Republicanism as personified in the Senate Four.

From the outset Roosevelt was very much in the center of the stage. The early months of his administration constituted a crucial time for the young, ambitious president, so much was at stake for him. No grave governmental crisis diverted Roosevelt from the purely political work required to secure for himself the 1904 presidential nomination. He worked with zest and skill to attain his goal. To that end, he immediately attempted to acquire able and influential associates and to restore the party's strength in the South. At the outset Roosevelt wisely cultivated the Senate Four and tried to prevent Mark Hanna from controlling convention delegates. Through his appointments he managed to serve both causes at the same time—pleasing the Four and undermining the power of Hanna.

The Senate Four, though mourning the loss of McKinley, took satisfaction in his replacement. They could not fail to conclude that Roosevelt recognized and respected their roles as the leaders of Congress; everything in his past political record afforded evidence that he would do so. They were, indeed, very fortunate to have the services of this popular, politically deft, and seasoned recruit, though they doubtless found it difficult and at times impossible to admit this even to themselves. Roosevelt's record showed that he understood the rules that governed professional politics. They were well aware of his marked popularity with the voters, especially in the crucial Middle West and West. In November 1901, Charles G. Dawes wrote to Cortelyou, "Everybody is for him out here in Illinois; and will be so. Whenever they want to hurt somebody politically out here they start a report that he is against Roosevelt—just as they used to in McKinley's day when he was strong."[1] Although the Four found it difficult to accustom themselves to Roosevelt's unorthodox personality, his wide-ranging enthusiasms, his swift pace, and his colossal ego, they nevertheless knew that these traits were a political asset to themselves and to the party.

The older leaders were well aware that Roosevelt had long since passed the test of party regularity. As far back as 1884, he had fought off the temptation to join the anti-Blaine Mugwumps who supported Democrat Cleveland for the presidency, and he had learned how to work with the business segment of the

[1] 3 November 1901, George B. Cortelyou Papers.

Republican-business partnership. They knew that Roosevelt had also learned how to work within the party organization with such questionable bosses as Thomas C. Platt. During the 1900 election campaign and after he had become vice-president, he had been the leadership's most effective public persuader. As vice-president, he had presided briefly over the Senate and in so doing had learned at least a little about its operation and personnel. It was inconceivable that either Roosevelt or the Four would break the political rules and their own political habits to go their separate ways. The Four may have anticipated some difficulty in holding him in leash once he won the 1904 election, but such men as Aldrich, Platt, Allison, and Spooner were not of the type to quiver in the face of such a challenge. To help them control Roosevelt, they had at hand the Senate and they were well aware of their own awesome power.

Roosevelt performed with wisdom and correctness as he assumed the duties of the presidency. In accordance with the tradition of vice-presidents who suddenly become president through accident, Roosevelt announced that he would continue the policies of his predecessor and retain his predecessor's cabinet. Six weeks later William Howard Taft, out in Manila, received from his brother Henry a perceptive report on Roosevelt. New York lawyer Henry, who was the same age as Roosevelt and was acquainted with him, observed from his office in Wall Street, "The accession of Roosevelt came without disturbance, and the country seems to stand back of him very well." Looking into the future, Henry anticipated a successful administration. "Of course his impulsiveness leads him into errors sometimes, but in the long run he appeals strongly to the people for his uprightness and honesty." Thus "it seems to be thought that he will be a strong candidate for a renomination." Henry Taft also believed that Roosevelt would get along well enough with the party leaders in Washington, being "amenable to reason, particularly from those who are placed in the position of his official advisers."[2]

Roosevelt had not been president long when he approached the Four for advice, particularly with reference to his anticipated

---

[2] 8 November 1901, Taft Papers.

inclusion of matters relating to the tariff and the trusts in his forthcoming year-end message to Congress. To Allison he wrote, "I shall want to see you before I write my message, because there are two or three points upon which I do not desire to touch until after consultation with you."[3] To Aldrich, Platt, and Spooner, he wrote in the same vein.[4] But he added in his Spooner letter that he supposed it was "hardly necessary for me to say that during the coming three years I hope to keep in closest touch with you and to profit by your advice in the future as I have profited by it in the past."[5] In July, while still vice-president, Roosevelt had indicated to Taft sufficiently high regard for Spooner to look upon him as a worthy presidential prospect.[6] In mid-October, Spooner was able to report to a Wisconsin friend and political cohort, "My relation to the new administration is cordial and intimate."[7]

The Four as a group were clearly not fully prepared with unified advice when Roosevelt initially approached them for suggestions. In late October, following a conversation with Roosevelt in Farmington, Connecticut, the uneasy Platt wrote to Aldrich, "I thought if I could have met you before I saw him that we could talk up the situation a little and we might perhaps talk along the same lines with him." Platt added that he wanted to see friend Aldrich anyhow, "for there are a good many matters ahead of us that are likely to be embarrassing I think, and I have not had a soul to talk to about them all summer."[8]

The summer of 1901 had not been a good one for meetings of the Four. It was for them a season of retreat from national affairs. Allison and Spooner had matters to attend to in their home states, and Aldrich was absorbed in the wedding of his daughter. Not until fall, after Roosevelt had been president for a few weeks, did Aldrich appear to be politically concerned. His old friend Thomas B. Reed, ex-Speaker of the House, finally

---

[3] 27 September 1901, Allison Papers.
[4] Roosevelt to Aldrich, 30 September 1901, Roosevelt Papers; Louis A. Coolidge, *An Old-Fashioned Senator: Orville H. Platt of Connecticut*, 445, 511–13.
[5] 30 September 1901, Morison, *Letters*, 3:155.
[6] 15 July 1901, ibid., 121.
[7] Spooner to John M. Whitehead, 15 October 1901, Spooner Papers.
[8] 26 October 1901, Aldrich Papers.

jogged him a bit. In October Reed visited the Aldrich home, wedding gift in hand.[9] Later, in mid-November, he wrote Aldrich from New York, "A good many people here are in a tremor lest the Anti Trust and Reciprocity cry may have a loud echo in the [December annual] message. That would be unfortunate for a time at least. Fear hits harder than disaster."[10]

Roosevelt's conversations with the Four and others, however, soon led him to conclude that the tariff and trust questions had become so explosive he had better tread softly. Platt and Aldrich in particular favored his giving no encouragement whatsoever to the crusaders for change. When Roosevelt sought Platt's advice on a specific antitrust proposal, Platt replied that he feared the courts would declare it unconstitutional. But he added, characteristically, "It is a question that requires careful study—more careful than I have yet been able to give it."[11] Aldrich counselled the president against calling for tariff revision. Roosevelt responded with a "Hearty thanks for your letter. I will follow exactly the course outlined therein and in my conversation with you." He added, "I hate to be a nuisance, but . . . I should much like to submit my whole message to you for a last looking over of certain parts."[12]

Roosevelt's message turned out to be mild indeed. He skirted the matter of tariff reform and dealt cautiously with the trust issue. The response in Wall Street was a notable rise in the price of stocks.[13]

Successfully calming whatever apprehensions existed among Republican leaders and voters, the new president recruited the services of some able advisers, administrators, and political managers. He sought to improve the quality of governmental administration, to broaden the base of the Republican party to include the South, to shore up the shaky middle western political organizations of Spooner and Allison, and in general to ensure his own 1904 nomination. The types of men he selected under-

---

[9] Nathaniel W. Stephenson, *Nelson W. Aldrich: A Leader in American Politics,* 173.

[10] 19 November 1901, Aldrich Papers.

[11] Platt to Roosevelt, 13 November 1901, quoted in Coolidge, *Platt,* 445.

[12] 18 November 1901, Morison, *Letters,* 3:199–200.

[13] Stephenson, *Aldrich,* 183.

scored the cautious approach to traditional Republican attitudes, policies, and arrangements he had exhibited as governor of New York.

Elihu Root's new prominence in the high command clearly indicated Roosevelt's intention to retain the Republican-business partnership. Root was a remarkably successful corporation lawyer who had contributed yeoman service to the Republican party. He had been an adviser to Governor Roosevelt and in 1899 had become President McKinley's secretary of war. Roosevelt retained Root in that cabinet post until, in 1905, he made him secretary of state. In 1909 Root became a United States senator from New York, a post which he held until 1915. Roosevelt—and for ample reason—frequently referred to Root as the most valuable member of his cabinet.

The same qualities that earned for Root a place of eminence as a corporation lawyer earned him prominence in government. His acutely analytical, orderly mind and persuasive manner were very useful whenever there was need for organizational changes from small operations to large operations. Thus in an era of great corporate growth in business and great governmental expansion, Root was in great demand.

Though Root had grown up in central upstate New York, where his father, "Cube" Root, taught mathematics at Hamilton College, he had made the transition from small town living with ease. In New York and in Washington, he transferred his own experience onto large canvases. In the 1890s he responded to a request of the Havemeyers by recommending the legal formula that made possible the great Sugar Trust. This trust soon controlled 98 percent of the nation's sugar production. He also applied his great legal talent to help William C. Whitney and Thomas Fortune Ryan form the New York traction syndicate.[14] His work in Washington, modernizing the nation's colonial system and its army command, was additional evidence that both big business and big government required and were beginning to use men who understood how to organize efficiently for bigness.

Though Root's keen mind, retentive memory, great industry,

[14] Richard W. Leopold, *Elihu Root and the Conservative Tradition*, 15–17.

and attractive personality carried him from small-town Clinton to New York City, he brought with him an insufficient sense of social responsibility to meet fully the challenge of bigness. While Root helped businessmen form giant monopolies that had the power to wrest special privileges from unprincipled politicians and to exploit countless citizens through overcharges, he showed no inclination to involve himself in efforts to check these excesses. Root conceded that it should be unlawful for corporations to issue bogus stock, but his much greater concern for the "rights of individuals" caused him to shun any thoroughly comprehensive legal restraints on corporations.

When engaged in a project that involved the implementation of change, Root accepted the challenge as long as it was limited to organizational change. He admitted privately that his approach as a lawyer was too limited, too much confined to the concern of clients at the expense of the public good. In 1906, when anti-big-business feeling was at a high pitch, Root wrote, "The pure lawyer seldom concerns himself about the broad aspects of public policy. . . . Lawyers are almost always conservative. Through insisting upon the maintenance of legal rules, they become instinctively opposed to change."[15] Roosevelt, untrained in law himself and occasionally attracted to unrealistic schemes, found in Root a safe anchor.

Roosevelt also had ties with William Howard Taft, though until 1904 Taft remained as an adviser almost exclusively through an exchange of letters. The two had known each other in Washington during the Harrison administration, when Roosevelt was a Civil Service commissioner and Taft was solicitor general.[16] In January 1899, after a month in office as governor, Roosevelt wrote to the genial 320-pound Taft, then a circuit court judge, "The thing I should most like would be to have someone here just like yourself to advise with. Elihu Root comes nearest to it. He has given me a great deal of his time and his advice has been as wise as it was disinterested."[17] Shortly

[15] Ibid., 18.

[16] Roosevelt to Taft, 19 August 1891, Morison, *Letters*, 1:258; Nicholas Murray Butler to George W. Wickersham, 13 February 1925, Elihu Root Papers; Taft to Mark Sullivan, 18 July 1926, Mark Sullivan Papers.

[17] Roosevelt to Taft, 31 January 1899, Morison, *Letters*, 2:1140.

after this, Taft became head of the commission to govern the Philippine Islands, where he remained until 1904.

Taft's record, views, and character cemented his relationship with Roosevelt into a rewarding friendship. Taft was obviously successful as an administrator and a judge. Roosevelt believed that he was capable of commanding the highest office in either the executive or judicial branch of government. As a solicitor general involved in patronage distribution or a judge dealing with corporations he was shocked whenever he confronted cheap, greedy, inhumane practices, and he seemed to be more interested in using governmental power to combat injustice to the ordinary man than were Root or the Four.

Taft, however, shared with all the men in the party leadership a fear that reform might endanger the rights of individuals and even alter the Constitution. He once complained to his brother Horace that Oliver Wendell Holmes, Jr., belonged to that group of justices that "proceeds as if the American Constitution were as malleable as the British Constitution."[18] In 1902, in the course of one of his long letters to Roosevelt, Taft expressed his confidence that the president had acquired sufficient influence over the people to enable him "to guide the feeling against trusts and the abuses of accumulated capital, in such a way as to remedy its evils without a destruction of those principles of private property and freedom of contract that are at the base of material and therefore of spiritual and intellectual progress."[19] Taft shared Roosevelt's concern for humanity and was very useful to him in expressing this concern to the voters. He was also an efficient, legalistic, cautious administrator.

Roosevelt's closest friend was Henry Cabot Lodge, ten years his senior, whose contribution to the ruling group was chiefly through this intimacy with Roosevelt. The friendship had begun back in the early 1880s when Roosevelt was an apprentice professional New York politician and Lodge was a more seasoned politician in Massachusetts. Roosevelt once wrote to Lodge that "I can't help writing you, for . . . there are only one or two people in the world, outside my own family, whom

[18] 13 September 1922, Taft Papers.
[19] 9 November 1902, ibid.

I deem friends or for whom I really care."[20] Even though he had served ably in the Washington community since 1887, first as a member of the House, and after 1893 as a senator, Lodge had accumulated no conspicuous influence in Congress. But people respected him. He had a superior mind, intellectual sophistication, cultural interests, and commitment to administrative reform, to national defense, and to everything Republican. But few people felt close to Lodge. Outside his home and away from his few close friends, he had a suspicious, haughty, supercilious manner as unpleasant as his drooping eyelids. Roosevelt, nevertheless, understood Lodge. He was able to overlook his idiosyncrasies and recognize his high-mindedness, loyalty, and frankness. He could relax with Lodge and even seemed to appreciate Lodge's occasional scoldings.[21]

In addition to these major figures in his entourage, Roosevelt recruited some less prominent but more professionally political men to help him prevent Hanna from controlling the 1904 Republican convention. These choices reflected Roosevelt's high degree of political acumen and demonstrated his instinct for finding uniquely able, useful people. By chance, or perhaps somewhat by design, he recruited some politicians who could assist him in more than one important way. Some of them, as they helped reduce the power of Hanna, could further the president's good relations with the Four. Some could consolidate his strength in the traditional East-Middle West heartland of the party and at the same time extend his political strength into the South.

In mid-December 1901 Roosevelt appointed Wisconsin's Henry C. Payne to the postmaster generalship. It was a move clearly designed to bolster the beleaguered Spooner and at the same time help the president reduce Hanna's power. Payne was an old machine-type politician. With this appointment, Roosevelt in effect endorsed the Spooner-Payne Stalwarts rather than the LaFollette Insurgents. Aside from his role in the intraparty power struggle in Wisconsin, there was nothing in the appoint-

[20] Quoted in William Henry Harbaugh, *Power and Responsibility: The Life and Times of Theodore Roosevelt*, 72.

[21] Ibid., 71–73; John A. Garraty, *Henry Cabot Lodge: A Biography*, 61, 84–87, 176, 178 n, 196, 258, 265, 281–82, 291–93.

ment of Payne that disturbed political observers. To most people it seemed to be a relatively routine matter. Most metropolitan newspaper comment on the Payne appointment was uninspired. It was normal for such a man to be in that post. The papers noted Payne's support of Roosevelt in 1900, that he was an able machine politician, vice-chairman of the Republican National Committee, and a successful business executive.[22] The *New York World*, however, after initially making no complaint, next day made more of the matter than did its more orthodox competitors. Cognizant of the Wisconsin situation, it editorialized, "It would be difficult to conceive of a man whose character and conduct are more absolutely at war with the ideals Mr. Roosevelt professes and which the people believe him to cherish." The appointment, the *World* concluded, "will shock" the Middle West and, "as the people of the rest of the country grasp its apparent significance it will amaze and gravely disappoint them."[23] The *World* story aroused the interest of the editor-in-chief of the *New York Times*, who telegraphed to Roosevelt for information. The president replied that "They say he [Payne] is a corporation man and a politician; but this is merely another way of saying that he has been a successful businessman and has devoted himself to political work without holding office."[24] Roosevelt's explanation to his newspaper friend Joseph B. Bishop was more explicit. "I have carefully gone into the Payne matter. The lobbyist-at-Washington business," Roosevelt insisted, "I have been able to investigate thoroughly. . . . Senator Spooner says there is nothing whatever in the accusations about Payne's alleged manipulations, political and otherwise, in Wisconsin."[25] He was overlooking Spooner's bias in the matter.

The fact that Roosevelt relied so much on Spooner's opinion of Payne and so readily brushed aside the complaints of LaFollete sympathizers underscored the new president's determined loy-

---

[22] *New York Times,* 18, 19 December 1901; *Chicago Tribune,* 18 December 1901; *Washington Post,* 18 December 1901.

[23] 18, 19 December 1901; Robert M. LaFollette, *Autobiography: A Personal Narrative of Political Experiences,* 734.

[24] Roosevelt to Charles Ransom Miller, 23 December 1901, Morison, *Letters,* 3:211.

[25] Roosevelt to Joseph B. Bishop, 2 January 1902, ibid., 215.

alty to the party leadership and at the same time his lack of patience with the Wisconsin Insurgency. A few months later, when word reached him that the LaFollette element was determined to defeat Spooner for reelection to the Senate, Roosevelt explosively asserted to some White House callers from Wisconsin, "That man Spooner is my right hand man and if you people of Wisconsin do not return him to the senate . . . it will be infamous."[26] Roosevelt also let it be known that he very much liked Charles Pfister, the Milwaukee millionaire who had joined forces with Payne and Spooner to destroy LaFollette.[27] Much that Roosevelt later learned about Spooner and LaFollette, especially in 1904 and 1906, he could have discovered easily long before. But Roosevelt was a party regular. He was very suspicious of anything that smacked of radicalism and he circulated in an environment unfamiliar and unsympathetic with insistent protest movements. It was, therefore, certainly understandable that he should ally himself with those who scorned the LaFollette Insurgents and other nuisance movements that were cropping up here and there. Roosevelt's appointment of Payne emphasized the wide gap between the national party leadership and the insurgency in Wisconsin, but more importantly it underscored Spooner's high standing with the president.

Roosevelt also appointed two influential Iowa politicians, Leslie M. Shaw and James S. Clarkson, to federal posts. This strengthened Allison and his Regency in their opposition to Governor Cummins and his Iowa Idea, and it helped disarm Hanna's political power. Clarkson was especially well prepared to combat Hanna's influence with Southern Negro Republicans.

In 1901 the situation in Iowa, more than that in any other state, worried Roosevelt and the party leaders. Albert B. Cummins, was more than willing to enter the United States Senate and had fashioned for that goal a formidable organization. As one of Allison's Iowa editor friends observed in November 1901, after Cummins's election to the governorship, "The Cummins political juggernaut is as relentless as the juggernaut of ancient

---

[26] Belle Case LaFollette and Fola LaFollette, *Robert M. LaFollette*, 1:149. See also *Wisconsin State Journal* (Madison), 24 April 1902.

[27] E. W. Keyes to Spooner, 4 January 1902, Spooner Papers.

times."[28] It was conceivable that political pressure would force Allison to forsake his eastern high-tariff allies, Aldrich and Platt, or force them to accept a compromise position on the tariff. Already the Iowa Idea had gathered some momentum outside Iowa. In December 1901, disgruntled Wisconsin Republican Joseph W. Babcock introduced a tariff bill in the House that seemed to embody the Iowa Idea, and it caused concern in high places. Moreover, there was a rumor afloat, albeit false, that Babcock and LaFollette might join forces.[29]

In December 1901, shortly after Payne's appointment to the cabinet, Roosevelt appointed Iowa's ex-governor, Leslie M. Shaw, as secretary of the treasury to replace Lyman J. Gage. The new treasury head was a small town Iowa banker-lawyer who had entered politics in 1896 to fight the Bryan scourge. He was elected governor in 1897 and again in 1899. He was on the best of terms with the Allison group and was an ultra-high tariff advocate. While he recognized the need for moderate currency reform, he was almost fanatical in his hatred of the Iowa Idea or tariff reform under any guise. In his new post, he soon proved to be an embarrassment to Roosevelt on the tariff issue, for he persisted in talking about the glories of high protectionism at the very time the president wanted his cohorts to give the matter the silent treatment.[30]

Shaw's record as governor disturbed even moderate reformers. An editor of the *Outlook* was shocked to discover that Shaw advocated no reforms whatsoever.[31] But Roosevelt in his desire to assure the friendship of Allison and to protect the hierarchy in general against the threat of the Iowa Idea did not concern himself with Shaw's negative record on reform.

Four months later Roosevelt selected Iowa's James S. Clarkson to fill the lucrative post of surveyor of the Port of New York.

[28] Robert P. Clarkson to James S. Clarkson, 17 November 1901, James S. Clarkson Papers.

[29] Dorothy Ganfield Fowler, *John Coit Spooner: Defender of Presidents,* 265; Stephenson, *Aldrich,* 180–81; James M. Swank to Allison, 20 February 1902, Allison Papers.

[30] Shaw to Aldrich, 3 August 1905, box 49, Biographer's Notes, Aldrich Papers; Roosevelt to Shaw, 31 July 1905, and Shaw to Roosevelt, 3, 10 August, 27 September 1905, Roosevelt Papers; Roosevelt to Shaw, 4 August 1905, Morison, *Letters,* 4:1299–1301.

[31] Elbert F. Baldwin to Allison, 7 January 1902, Allison Papers.

That appointment carried with it implications akin to the selection of Payne as postmaster general. Both men were skillful machine politicians, and, more important, both had on occasion battled against Mark Hanna and certainly welcomed any opportunity to renew the fray.

Clarkson could be helpful to Roosevelt in securing 1904 delegates from New York, neighboring Pennsylvania, and the South, all strategically important places. In New York he would have the advantage of being outside and above the factions that were jealously and bitterly jockeying for power. In Pennsylvania he could make common cause with Senator Matthew Quay because of their mutual enmity toward Hanna.[32] In the South, Clarkson had valuable connections among Negroes and white defenders of Negroes. He had long been an ardent champion of the Negroes, embracing an abolitionist attitude.

During the Benjamin Harrison administration, when Roosevelt was a civil service commissioner, Clarkson was first assistant postmaster general. Roosevelt and the politically conscious public had observed the zeal, singleness of purpose, and dispatch which Clarkson then displayed as chief distributor of postmasterships.[33] He operated as a professional politician of the old school.

Allison and his loyal friend Senator Jonathan P. Dolliver initiated the Clarkson appointment. Allison had been as anxious to find for Clarkson a place in the federal service as Spooner had been to do the same for Payne. Over many years Clarkson had rendered yeoman service to Allison and in the 1890s he had travelled into the South to round up delegates for Allison's presidential nomination bid.[34] Upon learning of the death of the incumbent surveyor of the Port of New York, Allison and Dolliver quickly contacted New York's Boss Platt, whom Roosevelt distrusted but in whose state the appointee would be working.

[32] Roosevelt to Henry C. Payne, 8 July 1902, Morison, *Letters*, 3:285–86; James S. Clarkson to William Loeb, 13 September 1902, quoted in ibid., 328 n–29; Clarkson to Matthew S. Quay, 17 September 1902, Clarkson Papers; Roosevelt to Clarkson, 29 September 1902, and Roosevelt to John Proctor, 28 March 1903, Morison, *Letters*, 3:332–33, 459.

[33] *New York Times*, 15 April 1902.

[34] Cripps, "Lily White Republicans," 21, 25, 28, 43, 101–02; Leland L. Sage, *William Boyd Allison: A Study in Practical Politics*, 277–78.

They obtained Platt's endorsement of Clarkson as a fellow anti-Hanna man. The eager pair then hurried to the White House, where, carefully avoiding reference to their visit with Platt, they obtained Roosevelt's endorsement. Much to their amusement, which they managed to suppress, Roosevelt expressed fear that Boss Platt would object. When the deed was done, Dolliver informed Clarkson that "I never felt so good over a thing since my wife agreed to marry me." He also thought it was a "funny situation." If Roosevelt, he explained, had known that Platt was inclined to support Clarkson, that fact "would probably have queered" their efforts for him. If Platt, on the other hand, had known that Roosevelt was "bent on giving" the position to the Iowan, "he would have had his doubts about it."[35]

There was an additional reason why Roosevelt might well have hesitated to appoint Clarkson. Not only had Clarkson been a spoilsman during the Harrison administration, but Roosevelt had been one of those who had caustically criticized him for his conduct. Civil service reformers referred to Clarkson as "the 'Headsman' of the Harrison Administration" for his wholesale removal of Democratic postmasters.[36] In addition, Clarkson had written an article, published in the *North American Review*, in which he assailed the merit system in general and the Civil Service Commission in particular. Civil Service Commissioner Roosevelt, in an address before the Civil Service Reform Club at St. Louis, had replied that Clarkson "and his friends believe that they ought to be paid for supporting the party. . . . There is a certain difference between being paid with an office and being paid with money, exactly as there is a certain difference between the savagery of an Ashantee and that of a Hottentot, but it is small in amount."[37] Little wonder the *Times* reported that many people were slow to credit the report of the appointment of "spoilsmonger" Clarkson, "before the funeral services" of his predecessor were held.[38]

[35] 12 April 1902, Clarkson Papers; Roosevelt to Charles R. Miller, 10 July 1902, Morison, *Letters*, 3:290–91.

[36] *New York Times*, 18 April 1902; see also: *New York Times*, 13, 16, 20 April 1902; *New York World*, 15 April 1902.

[37] Quoted in *New York Times*, 18 April 1902.

[38] Ibid., 15 April 1902.

As with the Payne appointment, good-government reformers raised eyebrows and antimachine men in the appointee's home state were more than disappointed. Roosevelt explained to one lady that in the Harrison days Clarkson had indeed made appointments and removals for political reasons, but for that "he is in no way to be criticized," for "Until some law can be devised affecting postmasters no other course is possible."[39] It was well for Roosevelt that the lady had not read his 1893 letter to Carl Schurz in which he stated, "Under Clarkson as under his predecessor all of the fourth class postmasters, practically, were changed, but Clarkson worked with the utmost brutality, exulting in his efforts to do the thing faster than his predecessor."[40] But now Roosevelt was sufficiently worried to warn Clarkson "to be particularly careful not to get into any conflict with the Civil Service Commission." He added, "As you know, I am rather a crank on the Civil Service Law."[41] Whitelaw Reid's Republican *New York Tribune*, cautious while it waited to determine what element or faction was destined to control the party at the time of the 1904 presidential election, took the safe course. It completely ignored the Clarkson appointment.

Booker T. Washington was another key figure in rounding up 1904 convention delegates in the South for Roosevelt.[42] The Tuskegee Institute principal had become acquainted with Roosevelt in 1900, five years after he emerged as an important Negro spokesman. In 1901 he became President Roosevelt's chief adviser on southern patronage. Roosevelt's awareness of the plight of Negroes and his approval of the vocational training at Tuskegee Institute certainly contributed to his interest in Washington. On the day McKinley died, Roosevelt wrote Washington expressing his regret over being unable to fulfill his promise to visit Tuskegee. He also said he wished to see Washington soon, "to talk over the question of possible future

[39] Roosevelt to Harriot Sumner Curtis, 12 May 1902, Morison, *Letters*, 3:262.
[40] 23 August 1893, ibid., 1:335.
[41] 5 May 1902, ibid., 3:256.
[42] Much of the interpretation of Booker T. Washington's role in the Roosevelt administration is based on the authors' interviews with Louis R. Harlan, History Department, University of Maryland, and Thomas R. Cripps, History Department, Morgan State College, Baltimore, Maryland.

appointments in the South exactly on the lines of our last conversation together."[43]

The coming 1904 election was on Roosevelt's mind when he brought Washington into his political circle. In order to attract southern Negroes and whites into his camp, Roosevelt needed to broaden the base of the Republican party in the South. Otherwise, the small clique of Republicans who constituted the core of the party there and selected from among themselves the delegates to conventions, would deliver their votes as Hanna directed. They felt obligated to Hanna, who had labored effectively to reward them with federal jobs and other acts of kindness. They would be suspicious of Roosevelt because the friendly Hanna would remind them that the new president was a Civil Service reformer and that his postmaster general, Henry C. Payne, had been a prime leader in the 1900 attempt to whittle down the size of the southern delegations to national Republican conventions. Roosevelt therefore recruited Washington to help form a party that would include both Negroes and whites and would represent responsible business and professional leaders. With offers of such attractive positions as judgeships, Roosevelt and Washington hoped to attract to the party paternalistic southern whites of high social stature. They considered the Gold Democrats an especially promising group to cultivate. These well established citizens had already broken once with the Democratic organization because of its surrender in 1896 to the free silver panacea, and thus they seemed subject to persuasion.

There soon followed a series of conversations between these two ambitious, vigorous, and shrewd leaders. A dinner meeting of the two at the White House in mid-October 1901 caused a public furor in the South and created some political difficulties. It identified Roosevelt with the Negro cause and thereby made it harder for him to break down racial barriers in southern Republican organizations. But that was the only political mishap the new president experienced as he moved to change the party to better suit his purposes and better respond to the require-

[43] 14 September 1901, quoted in Thomas Robert Cripps, "The Lily White Republicans: The Negro, the Party, and the South in the Progressive Era" (Ph.D. dissertation, University of Maryland, 1967), 100–101.

ments of the times. He made no apologies for the dinner, but in 1908 he privately stated, "There is plenty of room for question as to the wisdom of my having had Booker Washington to dinner, and however firmly convinced I may be that I was morally right, I will cheerfully admit that the matter is one for entirely legitimate difference of opinion."[44]

Roosevelt and Washington, meanwhile, maintained a mutually respectful and friendly relationship. Both men were positive, astute, and compassionate. They understood each other and the problems each faced, and even managed to retain a sense of humor about their relationship. On one occasion in mid-1903, Washington sent a newspaper clipping to Roosevelt that, he said, contained a true story about his encounter with an elderly Florida colonel. "Suh, I am glad to meet you," the colonel said. "Always wanted to shake your hand, suh. I think, suh, you're the greatest man in America." Washington modestly responded, "Oh, no," to which the colonel pugnaciously asked, "Who's greater?" "Well," said the Tuskegee educator, "there's President Roosevelt." "No suh," roared the colonel, "Not by a jugful: I used to think so, but since he invited you to dinner I think he's a blank scoundrel." To this story Roosevelt replied: "I think that is one of the most delightful things I have ever read. It is almost too good to believe."[45]

At the time Roosevelt became president, the Republican party had long since abdicated its once assumed championship of the Negro. Moreover, it soon failed dismally to respond even mildly to his gestures toward a more enlightened role. The fact that his efforts were manifestly very limited served to emphasize the hollowness that had replaced a once conspicuous Republican moral fervor.

Roosevelt's actions on the Negro question were in part a by-product of his efforts to acquire friendly delegates to the 1904 Republican presidential nominating convention and in part a direct reflection of his civilized attitude toward institutionalized

[44] Roosevelt to Richard Watson Gilder, 16 November 1908, Morison, *Letters*, 6: 1359.
[45] Washington to Roosevelt, 9 July 1903, Roosevelt to Washington, 13 July 1903, and clipping from *Baltimore Herald*, 3 July 1903, Roosevelt Papers.

cruelty. He believed that the current mistreatment of Negroes, with its attendant poverty, lynchings, and burnings, was not only morally wrong but totally unnecessary. Roosevelt accepted the then generally held belief that Negroes were inherently inferior to whites. Nevertheless, his particular interpretation of biological evolution led him to conclude that better environment for Negroes could very greatly improve them. All the while, however, his devotion to Anglo-Saxon superiority took precedence over his optimism for the improvement of any other group, white or colored. But unlike most whites, Roosevelt refused to dismiss the Negro problem. Moreover, in dealing with such successful and accomplished non-Anglo-Saxons as Booker T. Washington, Roosevelt treated them as equals. Any inherent inferiority he may have believed they possessed was to him inconsequential.

Most of the other members of the Republican leadership and those who served as principal advisers were generally silent on the Negro issue. Like McKinley before them, they clearly preferred to make no comment, and Roosevelt made no effort to recruit their services on behalf of this dispirited mass of humanity.[46] Thus, what the president did was with him a personal, rather than an organized party, policy. True, Spooner made some remarks in the Senate in answer to the racist outbursts of Senator Benjamin Tillman, but his actions were likewise personal.[47] "The truth is," Spooner said in reply to a letter from an admirer, "the southern statesmen are putting the negro question up to us in a new form, revolutionary, impudent and impossible."[48] In early 1906 Spooner said of the southern problem, "God only knows if it can ever be solved. I fear it can not be."[49]

Elihu Root seemed obsessed with the fear that the government might coddle individuals to such an extent as to deprive them of initiative and pride. He likewise feared the government would

[46] Apparent through the paucity of correspondence on the subject between Roosevelt and the other top party leaders.

[47] See Charles W. Cansler to Spooner, 26 January 1903, Spooner Papers.

[48] Spooner to Edward C. Porter, 29 March 1903, and similarly in Spooner to Thomas P. Ivy, 29 March 1903, Spooner Papers.

[49] Spooner to Neal Brown, 14 March 1904, Spooner Papers.

regulate private enterprise into collapse. That attitude, coupled with his very self-conscious Nordic bias, made it unthinkable for him to extend a helping hand to Negroes. Root was a devotee of sociologist Madison Grant, the widely proclaimed exponent of Nordic superiority. Even three decades later, Root still held these views when he praised Grant's racist book *The Conquest of a Continent.*[50]

Early in the Roosevelt administration, Root told a Union League audience that the effort made during the Reconstruction Era to elevate the Negro race through the ballot had failed.[51] A few days later, upon discovering that newsmen and editors gained the impression that he was currently against restoring the ballot to Negroes, Root hastened to explain that his sole aim had been to encourage discussion of the problem, not "to fix the responsibility for the failure or to discuss the remedy."[52] Thereafter, he left speech-making on the Negro question to Roosevelt and Spooner.

The attitude of Lodge, likewise, showed an absence of enthusiasm for a return to the pre-1877 Republican championship of the Negro. In 1890 Lodge had steered the pro-Negro Federal Elections bill, or "force bill," through the House, but thereafter he joined the Republicans who adopted a "let well enough alone" position. Following the southern excitement over the Booker T. Washington-Roosevelt dinner, Lodge wrote to the president that the southern uproar was "melancholy and disappointing." He said that he was "always hoping that they will learn and broaden, and then comes a thing like this showing the narrow solidity and imperiousness which are so disheartening. But they surely will learn and we must go on hoping."[53]

Lodge's growing doubts concerning the capacities of Negroes probably inhibited his actions on the subject. He finally came to believe that "the negro advances only when there is an admix-

[50] Elihu Root to Madison Grant, 11 June 1934; see also Grant to Root, 15 June 1934, and Richard E. Gutstadt, director, Anti-Defamation League, Chicago, to "The Publishers of Anglo-Jewish Periodicals," 13 December 1933, Root Papers.

[51] *New York Times*, 3 February 1903; *Churchman*, 14 February 1903, clipping, and Charles M. Harvey to John A Sleicher, n.d., box 53, Roosevelt Papers.

[52] Root to Albert Shaw, 16 February 1903, Root Papers.

[53] 19 October 1901, Roosevelt Papers.

ture of white blood and when there is the pressure of a surrounding white population to sustain him." For evidence, he cited the situation in Haiti and the Aruwhimi dwarfs whom Stanley had found in precisely the "same condition as that in which they were described to be by Herodotus."[54]

Had Roosevelt and his associates been prepared to face up to their party's failure to aid Negroes and deal with the southern attitude, they would have followed up the Booker T. Washington dinner episode with other appropriate actions. Instead, Roosevelt did nothing, clearly choosing to avoid raising the matter into a political issue. He made no explanation, no apology for having invited Washington to dine with him; neither did he follow that action with subsequent invitations. In this the politically realistic Washington himself concurred. The failure of the two to dine together again showed that they placed political expediency above their belief that society at all times should afford equal opportunity to all people and that, under all circumstances, people should treat each other on the basis of their individual worth.

Nevertheless, the fact that party leader Roosevelt issued the invitation in the first place constituted a tangible indication that a new type of person with a new outlook on the race question was in the White House. The episode was a dramatic reminder to the Republicans that historically they were committed to decent treatment of the Negro.

Roosevelt had on another occasion demonstrated disregard for an individual's color. When he assumed his duties as vice-president, he appointed as a messenger a Negro named Pinckney who had served him in that capacity when he was governor of New York. Roosevelt learned, however, "that there was considerable opposition to the appointment," that it was "against precedent to have a colored man as messenger in the Senate," and that he had better "reconsider the appointment." Roosevelt's immediate reaction was the exclamation, "Pinckney is appointed." The *New York Tribune* slyly remarked, "the smile that followed

---

[54] Lodge to Charles Francis Adams, 1 May 1906, copy in box 105, Roosevelt Papers.

showed that at last he had obtained his long wish for an opportunity of being strenuous."[55]

Later in the Roosevelt administration, when some southerners expressed anger because John Wanamaker, a member of the board of trustees of Tuskegee, dined with Washington in New York, Roosevelt commended Seth Low for publicly protesting the outburst. Roosevelt wrote to Low, "The South must be made to understand that it can not in the same breath demand that northerners allow it the complete liberty it desires and yet decline to allow that same liberty to northerners."[56]

An aspect of Negro-white relations which revealed the bankruptcy of the Republican party's and the nation's leadership on racial matters was the party's failure to act vigorously to stop the great wave of Negro lynchings and burnings that blighted the years Roosevelt was president. Only Roosevelt himself did anything conspicuous to discourage the practice. His efforts, however, were limited to an attempt to arouse the public. He spoke forth personally and called upon editors and writers, such as Lyman Abbott, to do likewise. But he did not ask the party leadership to consider the problem, despite the fact that decent citizens both North and South were horrified at one of the most disgraceful situations in the history of the country.

Graphic accounts of lynchings appeared in newspapers, telling the public about the problem, which was not entirely confined to the South. The *New York Tribune,* in a front-page story entitled "Burned Negro to Death," described a mob watching the father of an allegedly murdered girl ignite the fire around the victim, who was tied to a stake, in Limon, Colorado.[57] In 1902 the *New York World* and the *Washington Post* published identical accounts about the fate of a Negro in Corinth, Mississippi. Five thousand spectators were there. According to the papers, "The affair was conducted almost as if it had the sanction of the law." "There were special places reserved for women and a roped-off space for the newspaper correspondents." The cry was

---

[55] 15 June 1901.
[56] Seth Low to Roosevelt, 6 September 1905, Roosevelt to Low, 8 September 1905, Roosevelt Papers.
[57] 17 November 1900.

"Burn him," and "hundreds of women . . . screamed out 'Burn him.' . . . Meanwhile special trains were arriving . . . each with a crowd anxious to see the burning." The account ended: "Suddenly the flames reached the man. His eyes rolled. He grappled at the chains with his hands. Then he was all ablaze, and in ten minutes he was dead. But for three hours the crowd watched the bones char themselves away to white ashes."[58]

Negro lynchings increasingly incensed Roosevelt. The inhumanity shocked him and the unrestrained lawlessness of it alarmed him. He shared the apprehensions of substantial citizens in their concern for life and property when mob rule took over. He discussed the subject with other angry people. He was in doubt as to what to do about it, stating to one friend, "I wish to Heaven our course were clearer in the lynching business."[59] He finally decided to speak out on the matter, but he told *New York Evening Post* editor Rollo Ogden that he would "prefer to have it come . . . in a way that makes it my duty to act," though he added, "I may have to *make* an opportunity."[60] He did, however, wait for an event that afforded an excuse to speak forth. Such an opportunity came in connection with a three-day race riot in Evansville, Indiana. In the course of a letter, released for publication, to Indiana's Governor Winfield Taylor Durbin, commending him for his courageous action in ending the riot, Roosevelt wrote at length, and with skill and eloquence, about the nature and consequences of mob rule in general and lynching of Negroes in particular. Appealing to the better sense of citizens, he stated that "even where the real criminal is reached, the wrong done by the mob to the community itself is well-nigh as great. Especially is this true where the lynching is accompanied with torture." He reminded his readers that "There are certain hideous sights which once seen can never be wholly erased from the mental retina. The mere fact of having seen them implies degradation." The president called upon other leaders to play a role, saying that "Surely all public men, all

[58] *New York World*, 29 September 1902; *Washington Post*, 29 September 1902.
[59] Roosevelt to Lucius N. Littauer, 22 July 1903, Morison, *Letters*, 3: 526.
[60] Roosevelt to Ogden, 29 July 1903; see also Ogden to Roosevelt, 28 July, 3 August 1903, Roosevelt Papers.

writers for the daily press, all clergymen, all teachers, all who in any way have a right to address the public, should with every energy unite to denounce such crimes and to support those engaged in putting them down."[61] Roosevelt thus performed his duty, as he saw it, by reminding the public of the horrible implications of lawlessness, but he called for no legislative action on the matter. He clearly took for granted the prevailing view that control of such matters resided with state and local authorities.

The party leadership, including Roosevelt, not only failed to take positive action against lynching, it also sidestepped the southern disfranchisement movement, which each year deprived more Negroes, in more areas, of the vote. There was a growing movement afoot to attack the latter problem through enforcement of the clause in the Fourteenth Amendment which prescribed that any state depriving citizens of the franchise would lose a corresponding number of representatives in the House. At the turn of the century, Congressman Edgar D. Crumpacker introduced into Congress a measure to implement that approach. In 1900 at least a third of the Republicans in the House supported it, but the top leaders and even Booker T. Washington himself thought it inadvisable to stir up political conflict between the North and the South.[62]

These Republican opponents of direct political action felt it was better to spend money and effort educating Negroes in such institutions as Tuskegee and to work with southern moderates to eliminate lynchings. President Roosevelt, very much in accord with moderate northern reformers and with Booker T. Washington, accepted the long-term educational and law enforcement approach. At the same time, he continued his efforts toward his main goals—to reverse the drift toward lily-whitism in southern Republican organizations and to insure delegate support for himself in the 1904 convention.[63]

[61] Roosevelt to Winfield Taylor Durbin, 6 August 1903, Morison, *Letters*, 3: 540.
[62] Cripps, "Lily White Republicans," 75, 93–94, 99–100.
[63] Authors' interviews with Louis R. Harlan, 1967–1968.

VI

ROOSEVELT, ALLISON, AND SPOONER CONFRONT THE INSURGENTS 1902-1903

REPUBLICAN INSURGENCY in the Middle West was a major concern of the party hierarchy in 1902–1903. Roosevelt, Spooner, and Allison were the most concerned. The problem confronting Spooner was so completely confined to state politics that it was inadvisable for an outsider, even the president, to interfere. However, Roosevelt was able to come to the rescue of the beleaguered Allison. Allison welcomed his help and serving the senator's interest increased Roosevelt's influence and power. Some of the aid he gave came indirectly from his actions on the trust problem and the coal strike, but Roosevelt's speech-making in the Middle West was of most significance.

Roosevelt launched his popular "trustbusting" in February 1902 when he ordered Attorney General Philander C. Knox to initiate a suit against the Northern Securities Company. This application of the hitherto moribund Sherman Act against the J. P. Morgan-James J. Hill-Edward H. Harriman railroad holding company served as a fillip to the already great popularity of Roosevelt in the traditionally antimonopoly Middle West. The similar suits that followed kept alive Roosevelt's reputation as a trustbuster.

In mid-September 1902, before Roosevelt went on his speaking tour, Republican leaders held a "secret" political strategy meeting at Roosevelt's Oyster Bay, New York, home. From the standpoint of public relations, this was the most meaningful leadership conclave during his administration. Most of the top political strategists—Aldrich, Allison, Spooner, Hanna, Lodge, and Payne—were there, although Platt remained in Connecticut to open the State Republican Convention with a speech praising Roosevelt.[1] Hanna, suffering from rheumatism, came reluctantly. He grumbled at Aldrich before the meeting, "Our strenuous President does not appreciate that we 'old fellows' are hardly able to keep up with his procession."[2]

The event was a model of political professionalism. The "secret" meeting was known to newsmen in advance, and at its close the participants disclosed some information and hinted at more. The widespread speculation thus produced was a reminder to the public of the unity in the top echelon of the Republican party structure. The meeting was, moreover, well timed, for it came shortly before Roosevelt visited the Middle West to convince voters and leaders that wise men in Washington could best handle the trust and tariff problems.

Tariff and trust issues, of course, dominated the discussion at Oyster Bay. Of these, the tariff took precedence. Easterners clearly wanted no action whatsoever on the tariff, but Spooner and Allison were still looking for some means to assuage the unrest in their Middle West.[3] The conferees had no solution on which they could agree, so they left it for Roosevelt to bury the issue as best he could in his speeches. They clearly hoped that no one would force the issue to the forefront.[4]

---

[1] George B. Cortelyou to Allison, 25 August 1902, and Aldrich to Allison (telegram), 26 August 1902, Allison Papers; *Washington Post*, 13, 17 September 1902; *Chicago Tribune*, 15, 17 September 1902; *New York Sun*, 17 September 1902; *New York World*, 17 September 1902. The *New York Tribune* ignored the "secret" conference.

[2] 2 September 1902, Aldrich Papers.

[3] *Milwaukee Journal*, 2 October 1902; Spooner to Allison, 2 October 1902, Allison Papers; Platt to Aldrich, 18 November 1902, Aldrich Papers.

[4] For individual concern over the prevalence of public talk of possible tariff reform legislation, see: Whitelaw Reid to M. C. Sechendorff, 1 February 1902, Reid Papers; Albert Clarke to Aldrich, 11 February 1902, Aldrich Papers; James M. Swank to Allison, 20 February 1902, Allison Papers; *New York Times*, 3 April 1902; John Carter Rose to Roosevelt, 28 May 1902, and James R. Sheffield to Roosevelt, 11 September 1902, Roosevelt Papers. Minnesota's Congressman James A. Tawney, a high protectionist, wrote to Allison, 2 September 1902, "Don't you think, for the good of the party in the west, some of the eastern Republicans prominent in

However, their hopes were dashed when, without forewarning and even while the Oyster Bay conference was in progress, the respected House Speaker David B. Henderson made it known widely and convincingly that tariff reform agitation was rife in his Iowa congressional district. In a surprise announcement, he declined the proffered Republican nomination for reelection to Congress because he would not comply with the insistent public demand in Iowa to use tariff revision to destroy trusts. The Iowa Idea not only forced this old-timer to the sidelines[5] but kept the tariff issue very much alive.

Henderson's action immediately became a national cause célèbre of great concern to the party hierarchy.[6] Newspaper reporters, fuming over the secrecy surrounding the Oyster Bay discussions, found consolation in Henderson's employment of the tariff issue at a time when the hierarchy wanted it buried, and his dramatic resignation, which disrupted the House of Representatives.

The significance of Henderson's resignation was related to his unique position in the House. He was the Senate Four's main instrument for control of the House. Since 1901, following the resignation of the more independent "Czar" Thomas R. Reed, Henderson had been Speaker. He was also a long-time, loyal member of Allison's closely knit Iowa party machine. Henderson had solicited and obtained the support of the Four when he sought the Speakership.[7] His retirement posed a danger to the top Republican leadership. The increasingly disgruntled House Republicans might select as Speaker some less tractable colleague. Growing House resentment over the Senate Four's control of their proceedings could lead to the selection of proud, testy, independent "Uncle Joe" Cannon of Illinois or even tariff revisionist Joseph W. Babcock of Wisconsin.

---

the councils of the party should say less against a limited revision of the tariff?" (Allison Papers).

[5] See George E. Mowry, *The Era of Theodore Roosevelt, 1900–1912*, 117–18.

[6] Spooner to Allison, 9 October 1902, Allison Papers; see also Spooner to Robert G. Cousins, 27 September 1902, Spooner Papers.

[7] Henderson to Allison, 27 January 1898, 20 April 1899, and John C. Spooner to Allison, 27 May 1899, Allison Papers; Grenville M. Dodge to Mark Hanna, 12 May 1899, Dodge to Henderson, 25 May 1899, Root to Dodge, 22 January 1903, Dodge Papers; Willard Hoing, "David B. Henderson: Speaker of the House," *Iowa Journal of History* 55 (January 1957): 5, 6.

The aspect of gravest immediate concern, however, was Henderson's outburst on the tariff, making it impossible to submerge the issue. Upon learning of Henderson's announcement, the leaders at Oyster Bay were at first incredulous, but soon recovered enough to issue a plea that Henderson change his mind. Senators Hanna, Lodge, Spooner, and Aldrich joined with the National Republican Congressional Committee in a telegram to Henderson which in effect urged him to reconsider.[8] Henderson refused, stating again his "growing repugnance and conviction against the doctrine that free trade medicine will cure the trusts." He added a list of other grievances, such as "the dirty mud slinging of Waterloo Republicans, . . . and all because I made a faithful and good soldier postmaster, and turned down a young fellow who owned a petty newspaper."[9]

Henderson was clearly not his usual self, either professionally or personally. Although quick tempered, he normally was a genial, popular, story-telling party man.[10] In fact, party devotee Arthur Goldsborough had reported a few weeks earlier in a gossipy letter that he had recently met Henderson at a gay luncheon in Washington. "Forty two bottles of champagne were drunk and twenty one speeches made." Speaker Henderson, the "greatest in the country" at the art, was the toastmaster and was "almost the whole show."[11]

Many of Henderson's acquaintances therefore believed that he had not given the real reason for his announcement.[12] Leslie M. Shaw pointed out, according to the *Dubuque Daily Times,* that a year earlier Henderson had not objected when the party took the same tariff stand as in 1902.[13] Roosevelt, according to the *New York Sun,* was also skeptical and indignant.[14] Iowa's Clarkson thought that perhaps Henderson, aged sixty-two, had failed to keep his political fences in good repair and younger men were forcing him aside. Clarkson, himself aged sixty and

[8] Leland L. Sage, *William Boyd Allison: A Study in Practical Politics,* 285.
[9] Henderson to Allison (telegram), 17 September 1902, Allison Papers.
[10] Hoing, "Henderson," 9; Champ Clark, *My Quarter Century of American Politics,* 1: 372–73.
[11] Arthur Goldsborough to Mrs. [no initials] Pryn, 23 August 1902, Charles S. Hamlin Papers.
[12] Sage, *Allison,* 284–88.
[13] 17 September 1902, clipping, box 48, Biographer's Notes, Aldrich Papers.
[14] 18 September 1902.

very active as a Roosevelt lieutenant, was not very convincing when he stated that "It was ever thus," that "old generations go and new generations come, and we who are old must realize it and not get bitter over it." Clarkson was then showing no signs of retiring because of age.[15] Several decades later, a Washington newsman stated that Henderson had acted so precipitously less because of the tariff than because a certain United States senator had accused the one-legged Henderson of betraying his daughter and threatened to take Henderson's life unless he immediately left Washington.[16] Despite conflicting rumors regarding his intention,[17] Henderson remained at his post until March 3, 1903, when his term expired.

Henderson's resignation certainly hurt his party and ended his political career. In October, Spooner wrote to Allison that Henderson's action "has intensified the tariff and trust question, and tended to make both more of an issue than they otherwise have been."[18] Grenville M. Dodge wrote to Henderson from New York that people "here in the East give you credit for having laid down a great future in support of a principle, as they make a vast difference here between your position and the Iowa [Idea] platform."[19] But certainly Henderson had no "great future," for very soon Cummins reported to a cohort that the Speaker's withdrawal and his antitariff reform statement, "instead of hurting us," had destroyed him. "Everything is going well, and the 'Iowa Idea' is gathering adherents every day."[20]

Soon after the Oyster Bay conference, Roosevelt went to the Middle West. He delivered his major addresses in Cincinnati, Ohio, on September 20, and in Logansport, Indiana, on September 23. He hoped to diminish the mounting popularity of the Iowa Idea. This difficult undertaking called for a professional touch. Roosevelt needed to be a subtle educator rather than a bombastic purveyor of scorn and abuse. As a national Republican he could not risk alienating business interests, nor

[15] James S. Clarkson to Andrew B. Humphrey, 20 September 1902, Clarkson Papers.
[16] Neil MacNeil, *Forge of Democracy: The House of Representatives,* 119.
[17] Leslie M. Shaw to Allison, 8 November 1902, Allison Papers.
[18] 9 October 1902, Spooner Papers.
[19] 16 October 1902, Dodge Papers.
[20] Albert B. Cummins to John Kemble, 2 October 1902, Cummins Papers.

could he antagonize that vast body of Republican farm and small-town voters of the Middle West. If he were simply attacking Democrats, he could lambast them as ridiculous, irresponsible, and vicious, but he confronted fellow Republicans. He had somehow to build up voter resistance to the clearly attractive Iowa Idea. He was required to approach a national issue, as LaFollette was confronting state issues, with logic, reason, and facts, not just emotion.

Roosevelt's strategy included the use of a cutlass on the Iowa Idea (though he never actually mentioned that term in his speeches), severing it into two parts. In short, he isolated the tariff problem from the trust problem and then dealt with them separately. He also cleverly discredited the Iowa Idea through his use of the word trust as a synonym for large corporation rather than monopoly. He then proceeded to show the unfairness and futility of applying the Iowa Idea to all goods made by large corporations. Roosevelt was unfair in this interpretation because the Iowa Idea never embraced any such broad definition of trusts. In essence he was using against Insurgent Republicans essentially the approach his party had traditionally applied to the Democrats. The Republicans had labeled Democratic tariff proposals as "free trade" schemes and then had proceeded to decry the dangers inherent in free trade. Having defeated Grover Cleveland with that tactic, they felt they could do likewise to Governor Cummins.

Roosevelt correctly argued that the application of free trade to goods made by large corporations would be unfair to some producers and ineffectual in other cases. He used his "good" and "bad" trust argument, stating that "some . . . corporations do well and others do ill." He effectively pointed out, too, that in many cases free trade would bring competition from foreign producers that would harm small domestic producers more than it would hurt large corporations. To illustrate the limitations of the Iowa Idea, he shrewdly referred to the unpopular Standard Oil Company and the unpopular coal mine owners. He reminded the audience at Cincinnati that while the Standard Oil Company and other trusts controlled the production of hard coal, tariff revision would have no effect on the price of coal and coal oil because there was no tariff on coal.

Roosevelt insisted that the nation could deal intelligently with tariff and trust problems only when it considered them separately. Giving publicity to business transactions involving interstate commerce had been Roosevelt's usual remedy since he became governor of New York. Now he felt publicity was not enough, that eventually trust regulation must come. "We need additional power and we need knowledge," he said, but he placed the emphasis on caution and slowness. He admitted regretfully that "ultimately the nation will have to assume the responsibility of regulating these very large corporations which do an interstate business." While something could be done with existing laws, "it is difficult to say how much can be accomplished." He felt that a constitutional amendment was needed. It would be difficult to frame and obtain passage of a suitable amendment, but the "very fact that there must be delay in securing the adoption of such an amendment insures full discussion and calm consideration on the whole subject, and will prevent any ill considered action."[21]

On the tariff question, Roosevelt emphasized the danger that might result from a "violent surgical operation" on the rates. No nation, he insisted, could "stand the ruinous policy of readjusting its business to radical changes in the tariff at short intervals." He emphasized, as he had done when vice-president, under the tutelage of Spooner, that "What we really need . . . is to treat the tariff as a business proposition." Then in essence he endorsed the tariff commission approach, stating, "we need to devise some machinery by which, while preserving the policy of a protective tariff, . . . we would be able to correct the irregularities and remove the incongruities produced by the changing conditions without destroying the whole structure."[22]

Spooner was pleased with Roosevelt's speeches, especially his

[21] *Chicago Tribune,* 21 September 1902; *New York World,* 21, 22 September 1902; *New York Times,* 22, 23 September 1902; *New York Tribune,* 22 September 1902.
[22] *Chicago Tribune,* 21, 24 September 1902; *New York Tribune,* 23, 24, 26 September 1902. At Noblesville, Indiana, 23 September, Roosevelt declared regarding "the great industrial combinations" that "We do not war on them. We war on any evil in them, and you can reach that evil, I am certain, only through exercising national control over them." (*New York Times,* 24 September 1902.) See also Lodge to William H. Moody, 24 September 1902, Lodge Papers.

remarks on the tariff, and he wired him that they would "bear rich fruitage."[23] Not only had Roosevelt been considerate enough to come westward to help with the situation there, but he had dealt with the tariff question with the same commission approach Spooner had been advocating for the past seven years. In fact, a *Minneapolis Tribune* editorial, entitled "Spooner to the Rescue," credited the Wisconsin senator with having contributed the tariff commission idea to Roosevelt.[24] Spooner, himself, in a letter to Allison praising Roosevelt's Logansport speech, remarked, "Some of it you recognized undoubtedly as familiar."[25]

While Spooner was resigned to the do-nothing policy of the eastern contingency in the party leadership, even though he felt they were not fully aware of the intensity of feeling in the Middle West, Allison was not. In October, he confided to Spooner, "Our friends Lodge, Aldrich, et al, will realize by the time we assemble next winter that politically something must be done and it would have been wiser for all if that something had been done at the last session instead of waiting now, as we will be obliged to, until the beginning of the new Congress."[26]

Hanna was the least happy, but for a very different reason. The idea of a tariff commission was completely foreign to his political thinking. It was inconceivable that Hanna, who had used the fear of a "free trade" Congress as a means to obtain big business largesse for the party, could accept the removal of tariff-making from political control. But Roosevelt wrote to Spooner in regard to his own tariff remarks at Logansport, "I only hope Uncle Mark does not mind it. I am really very fond of him."[27] In this hope, Roosevelt may have been overly optimistic, for a few days previously Hanna had addressed a Republican rally in Akron, where he declared, "A year ago I gave you a piece of advice, 'Let well enough alone.' . . . Today I say 'stand pat.'" He believed the tariff "good enough as it is." With an eye to the Democrats, he scornfully added that "If the

[23] 26 September 1902, Roosevelt Papers; see also Roosevelt to Spooner, 1 October 1902, Morison, *Letters,* 3: 335.

[24] Quoted in *Milwaukee Journal,* 2 October 1902.

[25] 9 October 1902, Allison Papers.

[26] 11 October 1902, Spooner Papers.

[27] 1 October 1902 Morison, *Letters.* 3: 335.

time shall come when the tariff needs revision, it will be done by the men who made the tariff."[28]

Roosevelt returned to Washington for a knee operation and to confront the worrisome labor-operator crisis in the anthracite coal industry. Public anger was growing at the inconvenience, cost, and impending shortage of coal during the approaching winter.[29] Lodge, more concerned with the political situation in the East than with Republican insurgency in Iowa and Wisconsin, wrote to the president toward the end of September that "Despite Henderson and the tariff and the trusts" the party would do satisfactorily in the 1902 election if it were not "for the rising price per ton of coal." Frightened and angry at the operators, he pressed Roosevelt to do something or other about it, but *"not in public,* of course."[30]

Roosevelt did act on the coal crisis and in so doing demonstrated to a high degree his complete mastery of his position as head of his party and as president. He showed in an impressive manner that he had the will and the skill to capitalize politically on events and at the same time to be of genuine public service. The coal strike crisis was outside the mainstream of recent Republican experience and hence there was no tested formula for the president. He did not employ the crude and cruel bludgeoning tactics used by President Cleveland in the 1894 Pullman strike, even though at that time Roosevelt had praised the Democratic president's performance.[31] Instead he brought the leaders of the contending groups together and compelled them to make an agreement that ended the strike. It was a difficult task and he received considerable public acclaim for this accomplishment, which further enhanced the popularity of his party in the 1902 election and subsequent elections. He increased the power and prestige of the presidency, some of it

[28] Quoted in *New York World*, 28 September 1902.

[29] Roosevelt to Lodge, 27 September 1902, Morison, *Letters*, 3: 331–32. For accounts of this well-known episode, see Robert H. Wiebe, "The Anthracite Strike of 1902: A Record of Confusion," *Mississippi Valley Historical Review* 48 (September 1961): 229–51; William Henry Harbaugh, *Power and Responsibility: The Life and Times of Theodore Roosevelt*, 166–81.

[30] 22 September 1902, Henry Cabot Lodge, ed., *Selections from the Correspondence of Theodore Roosevelt and Henry Cabot Lodge, 1884–1918*, 1: 528–29.

[31] Roosevelt to Anna Roosevelt, 22 July 1894, Morison, *Letters*, 1: 391. In the letter Roosevelt wrote, "Cleveland did excellent, so did [Richard] Olney."

at the expense of the arrogant fringe in the business world. And he advanced the labor union movement a little by conspicuously working with union president John Mitchell and forcing recalcitrant coal operators to accept a portion of the union demands.

In the coal crisis, Roosevelt called upon a few selected colleagues, principally Hanna, Lodge, and Root, for assistance. The others in the hierarchy were as much outside the circle as all the top leaders had been on the occasion of the Booker T. Washington invitation and the Northern Securities Company indictment. How much on the outside some of them were was apparent in the private exchange that took place between Allison and Spooner. In early October, when Roosevelt was sending additional troops into the coal fields and preparing for federal seizure of the mines, the cautious constitutional lawyer Spooner expressed to Allison his belief that it was a dangerous experiment, "beyond the Federal jurisdiction" and "in the end it encouraged the strikers and stiffened up the operators."[32]

Allison disagreed, believing that the president had to act because of the pressure on him. Moreover, because his action was "one of friendly interference without any real Executive power, it was constitutional."[33] Allison doubtless agreed with the view of his old friend and political associate General Grenville M. Dodge, who wrote from New York to entreprenuer Horace Porter that "our people are growing so that they think if we could go to war to keep somebody in Cuba from starving, the President of the United States has a right to take on the question of our freezing to death for want of fuel, and on the stump anyone with . . . eloquence could make that plain." Dodge predicted victory in the 1902 election, partly because even though there was some unrest in the East due to the coal episode, "poor people here are getting coal cheaper than they had it before."[34] They did not actually face freezing to death,[35] but many appeared to be haunted by the possibility.

Roosevelt certainly did his part to maintain unity and strength

[32] 9 October 1902, Allison Papers.
[33] Allison to Spooner, 11 October 1902, Spooner Papers.
[34] 15 October 1902, Dodge Papers.
[35] Wiebe, "Anthracite Strike," 243–44.

in the party during the summer and fall of 1902, though he did irritate some members of the financial community, mainly those in Wall Street. He performed with superb political acumen as a law enforcer on the trusts, as a conciliator on the tariff issue, and as a mediator on the coal strike.

The overall outcome of the 1902 election was gratifying for the Republicans. The party experienced no serious losses at the hands of either insurgent Republicans or Democrats. In the main areas of insurgency, most notably Wisconsin and Iowa, the LaFollette and Cummins forces further entrenched their organizations, but neither made any direct moves of defiance against Allison or Spooner. True, the Iowa election was not held until 1903, but when it did come, it was largely a repetition of the 1901 performance, with the 1901 statement on the Iowa Idea simply reaffirmed, without fanfare or emphasis.[36]

It was soon apparent that the chief sponsors of the Iowa Idea found it a mixed blessing and were seeking a way out of this dilemma. It was fine as a means for winning elections within Iowa and in some other areas where agricultural and railroad interests dominated politics. But nationally Roosevelt's attack on it, together with the scorn many other Republicans heaped upon it, made the Iowa Idea a distinct liability. Politicians identified with it could not hope to obtain any favors whatsoever at the hands of the national leadership.

Facing this predicament, proponents attempted to redefine the Iowa Idea. Shortly after Roosevelt's attack, Governor Cummins explained to a *Washington Post* reporter that the plan did not encompass any change in basic, traditional Republican policy on the tariff. He said, "It is not necessary to the business of the country that monopolies exist, and ambitious men should be informed that they cannot have both monopolies and the tariff. You can be sure they will choose the course most profitable to them." The *Washington Post* correspondent contrasted that very mild view with the declarations of Republican tariff revisionist Babcock of Wisconsin when he wrote, "The governor's

[36] Dorothy Ganfield Fowler, *John Coit Spooner: Defender of Presidents*, 298; Robert M. LaFollette, *Autobiography: A Personal Narrative of Political Experiences*, 280; Sage, *Allison*, 288–99; John Luchsinger to Spooner, 13 December 1902, Spooner Papers.

statement compares with some of the Babcock interviews as blue skim milk with hot scotch."[37] But in actuality Congressman Babcock was also retreating from his tariff reform views. Doubtless an important factor in his more moderate position on the tariff was the possibility that the House might elect him Speaker.[38] Clearly, Cummins and his friends hoped they had heard the last of the Iowa Idea. Eventually Director of the Mint George E. Roberts, a tariff reform crusader and the person fellow Iowans generally credited with authorship of the Iowa Idea, insisted that Cummins had distorted its meaning to take advantage of "the anticapitalistic feeling" in Iowa.[39]

Roosevelt continued to keep a close watch on the Iowa situation. The tariff persisted as the central issue in the power struggle within that state's Republican organization. Allison continued to walk on eggs. Shaw, Iowa's former governor and now secretary of the treasury, was constantly tempted to make high protectionist pronouncements as uncompromising as those of Cannon or Hanna, while Roberts and Cummins defensively let everybody know they were still dedicated to tariff reform in general. They simply crusaded for reciprocity instead of the Iowa Idea. They also worked jointly to obtain the House Speakership for Babcock.[40]

Roberts used the *Des Moines Register* as a vehicle for tariff reform. In 1902 he had bought a controlling interest in that important Republican organ. In the spring of 1903, Lafe (Lafayette) Young, editor and publisher of the *Des Moines Capital,* informed Aldrich that "Robert's paper" caused many people to believe that Roosevelt favored tariff reform, otherwise he "would call a halt on him." Young urged Aldrich to talk to the president about it.[41] Soon the *Register* ceased its crusade, and in May a *Register* editorial stated that it favored "the abandonment, for the present at least, of all idea of immediate tariff revision."[42]

[37] *Washington Post,* 30 September 1902.
[38] See George E. Roberts to Albert B. Cummins, 13 November, 10 December 1902, Cummins Papers.
[39] George E. Roberts memorandum, box 48, Biographer's Notes, Aldrich Papers.
[40] Roberts to Cummins, 13 November, 10 December 1902, Cummins Papers.
[41] 20 March 1903, box 48, Biographer's Notes, Aldrich Papers.
[42] Quoted in *New York Tribune,* 13 May 1903. On 12 April 1903, the *Tribune* printed a piece entitled "End of Iowa Idea."

For Roosevelt and others to persuade Cummins to abandon his tariff reform talk required patience and tact. The ambitious Cummins possessed considerable pride. Roosevelt talked with him personally and attempted to influence him through Allison and other Iowans. In January 1903, upon returning to Iowa after a visit with Roosevelt, editor A. B. Funk reported to Cummins that Roosevelt hoped Cummins would go slowly on his tariff reform. The president, he said, "spoke in kindly terms of you and your speeches. It is difficult for him to conceal in private conversation the interest he feels in the tariff and the extending of our trade relations, and his contempt for the 'stand pat' notion, but under the pressure of great party and national necessity he is trying to be diplomatic to the extent necessary to keep in working relations with Congress and the party leaders."[43] Cummins gradually quieted down and by the time the Iowa Republicans met in July for their state convention he was willing to accept an Allison-made compromise on the tariff and monopoly planks in the platform.[44]

In 1902 and 1903, Wisconsin, unlike Iowa, was on the periphery of the Roosevelt-dominated national scene. Spooner was the only link between the two, but a very important link. To have the Republican insurgency unseat Spooner would greatly injure the pride of the Republican hierarchy and would lessen its power.

After LaFollette assumed the governorship in January 1901, he and his Insurgents were so relentless with their reform drive and Spooner and his Stalwarts so adamant in their opposition to it that by the end of 1902 it should have been clear to old-time Republican leaders that the Wisconsin movement was more than a "flash-in-the-pan." But understandably the Spooner Stalwarts and like-minded fellow Republicans elsewhere were not prepared to take the requisite careful look. In the course of their battle against LaFollette and his Insurgents, some Stalwarts, though not Spooner himself, did occasionally admit they had

[43] Funk to Cummins, 29 January 1903; see also Funk to Cummins, 26 January 1903 and Cummins to Funk, 29 January 1903, quoted in Ralph Mills Sayre, "Albert Baird Cummins and the Progressive Movement in Iowa" (Ph.D. dissertation, Columbia University, 1958), 200–201.

[44] Sayre, "Cummins," 202–07; Sage, *Allison*, 290.

underestimated the power of the opposition. But even then they proceeded to repeat the same errors over and over again. They failed to recognize that to meet the LaFollette Insurgent challenge they needed to do more than engage the enemy in political skirmishes. They needed to give serious consideration to their opponent's tax reform and election reform programs.

The Stalwarts lacked not only an effective program but even effective leadership. Spooner through it all played an Olympian role,[45] pretending to remain above the state conflict as he attended to national matters. Now and then he exhorted his followers to battle relentlessly against the Insurgents, but his only significant contribution was use of his federal patronage power. Until the end of 1902, he adhered to his 1900 announcement that he would not seek reelection to the Senate when his term expired in 1903. He remained aloof, even in the face of the repeated pleas of his followers that he assert positive leadership against the Insurgent advance.

With Postmaster General Payne also in Washington, where he now concentrated on the furtherance of Roosevelt's political fortunes, Stalwart affairs in Wisconsin rested in the hands of such blundering amateurs as the wealthy Pfister and "has-been" Keyes.[46] With so many young men gravitating toward LaFollette, the Stalwarts were left in sore need of attractive, able, and aggressive recruits for party service. The best they could produce as a possible candidate for the governorship was a state senator named John M. Whitehead, who was unpopular, especially among the German-Americans, because he was an outspoken prohibitionist. He had other drawbacks as well. Keyes for a time "doubted very much if the railroads will submit to such a nomination."[47]

The series of tactical blunders by the Stalwarts during LaFollette's first term as governor began in early 1901, when they used their control of the state legislature to defeat the Insur-

---

[45] Spooner to John Hicks, 8 November 1902, Spooner Papers.
[46] E. W. Keyes to Spooner, 3, 4, 17 April 1902; Robert Eliot to Spooner, 19 April 1902; *Milwaukee Journal*, 15 April 1902, and *LaCrosse Chronicle* (Wisconsin), 17 April 1902, clippings—all in Spooner Papers.
[47] Letters to Spooner from E. W. Keyes, 8 January, 19, 23 June 1902, Henry Fink, 11 April 1902, and John Luchsinger, 12 May 1902, Spooner Papers.

gents' railroad tax and direct primary bills. Then the Stalwarts in the legislature organized a Republican League of Wisconsin to destroy the governor in the 1902 election. They operated on the assumption that the LaFollette movement was but a passing phase already on its way to oblivion. Edwin D. Coe, an old-time professional political manager and patronage recipient who was loyal to Spooner, believed that "no such stuff is going to win for long; it is just the foam and froth on the surface of the stream which can last but for a little while and has no power to turn a wheel."[48]

By the spring of 1902, however, many Stalwarts were far from certain that they had been wise in their cavalier treatment of LaFollette. He clearly possessed a substantial and well-organized army of followers. Strangely, though, of the numerous Stalwarts who wrote to Spooner, none was yet prepared to even hint that basic in their trouble was the close relationship between their leaders and big business interests. An Oshkosh editor and former minister to Peru, John Hicks, however, expressed concern in an early 1902 letter to another veteran of Wisconsin politics, Assistant U.S. Secretary of the Treasury Horace A. Taylor. Hicks castigated his fellow Stalwarts for bungling affairs so much as to insure LaFollette's renomination. He believed it was a bad mistake to have antagonized LaFollette on the primary election bill. "The convention had declared for it, the people wanted it, and the legislature in good faith should have passed the law. Fighting it as so many Republicans did made LaFollette a martyr and every man in the state who favors the law looks upon him as its exponent and representative." Hicks pointed out that the establishment of the Republican League further emphasized the high-handedness of the Stalwarts.[49]

Having thus touched on one of LaFollette's great sources of popularity, his appeals to the democratic process, Hicks then turned to the governor's other major asset—Stalwart alignment

[48] Coe to Spooner, 3 July 1902; see also letters to Spooner from Horace A. Taylor, assistant secretary of the treasury, 23 May 1901, and E. W. Keyes, 8, 19 January, 3, 25 April 1902—all in Spooner Papers.

[49] Hicks, editor of the *Daily Northwestern* (Oshkosh, Wisconsin), to Taylor, 2, 10 April 1902, enclosed in Taylor to Spooner, 14 April 1902, Spooner Papers.

with big business. "Our strength in the state," Hicks correctly said, "has always been with the farmers and working men. Once run a dividing line between this class and the railroad interests, and you make trouble. Whether a voter likes LaFollette or not, he is forced to choose between him and the monopolies and trusts." He concluded that if the trouble "is not fixed up at the next state convention it will become a permanent division and the supremacy of the party gone." Taylor forwarded the letter to Spooner and urged him to seek reelection to the Senate, but Spooner still refrained from announcing his candidacy.[50] Democrat Ellis B. Usher was "forced to the conclusion that the Stalwarts have committed suicide."[51]

At the state convention in mid-July, the Insurgents compounded Spooner's predicament. The delegates passed a resolution which commended "the official career of Hon. John C. Spooner" but then diabolically called upon him to endorse the Insurgent-constructed party platform, which included an emphatic call for taxation of railroad corporations and for a meaningful direct primary law. After praising Spooner, the resolution read, "We again express our regret for his announced determination not to serve the state another term in the senate and should he now find it possible to reconsider this decision and express his willingness to stand as a candidate in harmony with the sentiments, and in support of the platform principles here adopted by Wisconsin Republicans in state convention, and for the election of a legislature favorable to their enactment into law, his decision would meet the general approval of Republicans everywhere."[52]

In response, Spooner sulked for the next two months, while more and more party members became fearful that enough of his followers would desert to the Bourbon-controlled Democratic party to cause a Republican defeat in the November election.[53] To avoid such a catastrophe, concerned Republicans,

[50] Ibid.

[51] *Milwaukee Journal*, 15 April 1902.

[52] *Milwaukee Sentinel*, 17 July 1902, quoted in Fowler, *Spooner*, 296; see also Belle Case LaFollette and Fola LaFollette, *Robert M. LaFollette*, 1: 151.

[53] Willet M. Spooner to H. C. Reed (Spooner's secretary), 16 September 1902, Spooner Papers.

including Postmaster General Payne, attempted to induce Spooner to swallow his pride, support the state platform and ticket, and reconsider his refusal to run for reelection. An overwhelming majority of the Republican candidates for the legislature pledged to vote for his reelection and the LaFollette-controlled Republican State Central Committee endorsed him.[54] In September, the committee urged him "to make a speaking campaign in this state in support of the ticket."[55] Hopeful Republicans reported to Spooner that LaFollette was injecting into his speeches complimentary remarks about the Senator.[56]

Spooner's manner softened. In October he returned from the East to campaign. But he did so under the auspices of the Congressional Campaign Committee rather than the State Central Committee, and he showed something less than enthusiasm for the state platform and ticket. He refused to mention the platform, and his remarks regarding the ticket were subject to different interpretations. For example, in the course of an address in Milwaukee on October 13, someone in the audience called out, "What is the matter with LaFollette?" "If my friend had waited a few minutes," Spooner replied, "I would have told him to vote for the whole ticket from Governor LaFollette down."[57] Most people interpreted that to mean that he endorsed the ticket *below* the governorship, and the senator did nothing to alter that impression.[58]

On October 25, LaFollette abandoned, momentarily, his studied restraint toward Spooner and thereby undid much that the workers for party harmony had accomplished. The occasion was a political rally in Appleton, at which LaFollette replied with startling forthrightness to a question from the audience. The questioner wanted to know whether he favored the unconditional return of Spooner to the U.S. Senate. "I will raise my

[54] Willet M. Spooner to Spooner, 27 September 1902, ibid.; Fowler, *Spooner*, 296–97.

[55] James A. Stone, editor and a member of the State Central Committee, to Spooner, 16 September 1902, Spooner Papers.

[56] Willet M. Spooner to Spooner, 2 October 1902, and Isaac Wing to H. C. Reed, 25 October 1902, ibid.

[57] Quoted in LaFollette, *LaFollette*, 1: 154.

[58] Ibid.; Spooner to Frank J. Tucker, 27 September 1902, and *Chicago American*, 27 October 1902, clipping, Spooner Papers.

voice for the re-election of John C. Spooner to the United States Senate," LaFollette declared, "when Senator Spooner raises his voice for the principles of the platform adopted at the state convention at Madison."[59] A Spooner henchman, Henry Fink, wrote immediately to the senator, "That little whelp [LaFollette] was mad to let the cat out of the bag. . . . *He will fail in his purpose.* Let us keep cool and continue the even tenor of our way."[60] When a reporter questioned him, Spooner smiled and said only, "I am doing all I can for the Republican state ticket from the Governor down."[61]

In November, LaFollette won reelection by the second largest off-year majority any Wisconsin governor had ever received.[62] The unhappy Spooner doubtless wondered why it was that of all the national Republican leaders he alone had to suffer such humiliation. Elsewhere things were better. Root wrote to Mark Hanna on March 5, "Congratulations on the artistic style in which you have done up the circus" in Ohio.[63] At the same time, Root was able to write to Platt, "Believe in my sincere congratulations on the conduct of Connecticut under your leadership."[64] Aldrich, however, had his troubles in Rhode Island. A combination of independent Republicans and Democrats elected a reform-minded physician, Democrat Lucius F. C. Garvin, to the governorship.[65]

Spooner continued to sputter, but he did not retire from politics. He wrote to Platt that LaFollette "will pursue me to the extent of his capacity and malignancy. What the result will be I do not know and as to it I am quite indifferent."[66] But he was far from indifferent to the future and in mid-December informed his followers that he would accept reelection to the Senate.[67]

Wisconsin Republicans still wished to avoid the necessity of

[59] Quoted in LaFollette, *LaFollette*, 1: 154–55.
[60] 25 October 1902, Spooner Papers.
[61] *Chicago American*, 27 October 1902, clipping, ibid.
[62] LaFollette, *LaFollette*, 1: 156.
[63] 5 November 1902, Root Papers.
[64] 5 November 1902, ibid.
[65] For the Rhode Island situation see our discussion of the background to Aldrich's 1904 difficulties in chapter 8 below.
[66] 7 November 1902, Spooner Papers.
[67] Henry Fink to Spooner, 11 December 1902, and John M. Whitehead to Spooner, 11 December 1902, ibid.; LaFollette, *LaFollette*, 1: 156.

making a choice between Spooner and LaFollette. In January 1903, the legislature returned Spooner to the Senate by a unanimous vote of the large Republican majority.[68] It was clear to a rapidly growing number of people, however, that Spooner was clinging too closely and too exclusively to a Republican party blueprint that was fading. There was irony in Spooner's observation that same autumn concerning his long-time Bourbon Democrat friend, William F. Vilas of Wisconsin, a one-time powerful political leader in the Middle West. With good reason Spooner said that "Vilas somehow cannot get over the traditions of the Democratic party of his youth. The progress and growth of the country does not seem to make any impression upon some minds."[69] He might have added, however, that on conspicuous issues in Wisconsin—the direct primary, corporation taxes, and railroad regulation—Vilas was at least as much in step as Spooner himself with the growing public demand for more democracy and more positive governmental control.[70]

Back in Washington during the winter and spring of 1903, Spooner helped direct one final Stalwart stand against LaFollette's state reform program. The battle revolved mainly around the primary election, railroad taxation, and rate regulation. Although there were other notable items on LaFollette's agenda which the legislature passed in significant number, the basic power struggle continued to center on LaFollette's attempt to destroy the big business-political alignment in the state Republican organization. To achieve this goal, he needed more strength in the legislature.

Spooner persuaded the legislature to postpone final enactment of a primary election measure, using his brother, Philip Spooner, president of the Madison Traction Company, as his agent, and ostensibly remaining completely out of the fray himself. His brother worked among the state legislators to substitute for the LaFollette proposal a bill which could not go into effect for two years, inasmuch as it included a provision for a referendum. The intent of this delaying tactic was to prevent an in-

---

[68] Fowler, *Spooner*, 298.
[69] Spooner to W. P. Warner, 1 October 1902, Spooner Papers.
[70] Horace Samuel Merrill, *William Freeman Vilas, Doctrinaire Democrat*, 247.

flux of LaFollette supporters into the state legislature, who could, in turn, insure LaFollette a seat in the United States Senate.[71] Six weeks later, in late March, a Stalwart wired to Spooner, "The Primary bill passed . . . in exactly the form you suggested."[72]

A few days after this victory, the relieved and elated Spooner wrote hypocritically to a Chicago friend, declaring that he was "utterly opposed to such a primary law as Mr. LaFollette would wish, although I have taken no part in it out there, because of the peculiar circumstances which have surrounded me." He told his friend that the Insurgent measure would make LaFollette a boss, and noted that he did not believe in bosses, "and especially I do not believe in such bosses as Mr. LaFollette." Spooner thought that such a primary law "would destroy the [Republican] party machinery, which is necessary in order to fight the [Democratic] political enemy of the party." The senator, however, failed to explain what the Insurgent primary measure might also do to the Democratic party machinery. Spooner felt that the consequence would be the emergence of "a lot of personal machines." The system would thereby "make every man a self-seeker, would degrade politics by turning candidacies into bitter personal wrangles and quarrels." Overlooking the fact that he himself had first entered the Senate as the hand-picked choice of the powerful Senator Philetus Sawyer, Spooner stated that he did "not see how under such a scheme the office would be likely to seek the man." Also concealing his own fear of LaFollette's popularity with the voters, Spooner hypocritically told his friend that he was "a good deal in favor . . . of the fullest freedom to the electorate." As for LaFollette, "He is for LaFollette and, to my apprehension, cares little for the party."[73]

Throughout the winter and spring of 1903, Spooner's Stalwarts fought valiantly to defeat LaFollette's legislation on the railroads. While LaFollette's immediate goal was railroad taxation, he also sought to establish a commission with power over

[71] Philip L. Spooner to Spooner, 11 February 1903, and J. L. Sturtevant to Spooner, 21 May 1903, Spooner Papers.

[72] J. W. Babcock to Spooner, 26 March 1903, ibid.; see also H. C. Reed to Spooner, 26 March 1903, ibid.; Fowler, *Spooner*, 299–300.

[73] Spooner to S. M. Booth, 28 March 1903, Spooner Papers.

railroad rates. If enacted, these measures would be a severe blow to the big business-Stalwart alliance. In mid-February, Keyes reported from the state capital to Spooner, "The railroad magnates here yesterday produced a good impression."[74] A few weeks later he wrote him that "The manufacturers and business men of the state are swarming through the Capitol in opposition to the Assembly Commission and Rate Bill. It is thought that bill will be killed in the Assembly."[75] A small-town editor reported late in the spring, "The manufacturing interests of the state are almost solidly arrayed against" LaFollette because of the "rate commission bill, which the assembly turned down."[76] LaFollette was convinced that those manufacturing "interests" enjoyed such advantageous rebate privileges with the railroads that a rate-making commission would hurt them sorely. Spooner and the Stalwarts prevented the establishment of a railroad commission for the time being, but they were unable to defeat a railroad taxation measure and the creation of a commission to investigate railroad rate practices. Two years later, the legislature passed a railroad commission measure.[77]

Personally, Allison and Spooner had weathered the storm. Both easily won reelection to the Senate and the immediate crisis for the Republican leadership subsided. Allison and Spooner also continued, apparently secure, in their powerful positions as members of the Senate Four and as close allies of the president.

[74] 12 February 1903, ibid.
[75] 1 April 1903, ibid.
[76] J. L. Sturtevant to Spooner, 21 May 1903, ibid.
[77] LaFollette, *LaFollette*, 1: 158, 170, 189–92.

VII

CANNON, TRUSTS, AND CURRENCY TO THE FORE 1903

THE REPUBLICAN LEADERSHIP in 1903 concentrated on Congress. A new assertiveness was evident in the House of Representatives, which reflected, on the part of both House members and their constituents, a growing discontent with the status quo. In January, House Republicans selected "Uncle Joe" Cannon as Speaker. The Senate Four demonstrated that they understood the necessity of concessions to public demands for reform and to the insistence of both the House and the president on a greater and more positive role in party policies. Congress enacted some moderately important legislation, especially on the trust problem. The Republican inner circle admitted Cannon into its deliberations and wrestled unsuccessfully with the currency question. The period between Cannon's selection as Speaker in January and his official election to the office in March afforded him time and opportunity to employ his considerable talent for ingratiating himself with fellow members. For the party command especially it was a successful year.

Roosevelt pressed for trust legislation in his December 1902 message to Congress and in January issued a public statement on the subject, again asking for legislation. Meanwhile, Attorney General Knox worked for and with the president to promote measures to improve and increase the federal government's control over business. The administration program called for a law to help the government expedite cases under the antitrust and interstate commerce laws, an increase in the appropriation for this work, enactment of an antirebate law, and means and power to use publicity to induce businesses to perform in the public interest. By the end of the session, in early March, Congress had acceded to these requests. It provided law enforcement agencies with improved means to bring offenders to justice, enacted the Elkins Antirebate Act, created a Department of Commerce and Labor, and set up a Bureau of Corporations.

The act creating a Bureau of Corporations as a branch of the Department of Commerce and Labor pleased Roosevelt the most and proved the most important. The bureau's function was to provide the president with information on individual trusts, which he could at his own discretion publicize and present to the Justice Department as a basis for indictments. The publicity feature was the key item in Roosevelt's plan. By threatening monopolists with publicity of their exploitive practices, he hoped that the government could "persuade" them to mend their ways. Hence, through "gentlemen's agreements," litigation would be unnecessary.[1]

The maneuvers employed in creation of the Bureau of Corporations reflected the degree to which various segments of the political-business world were anxious to advance or prevent governmental supervision of big business. It became apparent that the House of Representatives and President Roosevelt were the most interested. The Senate lacked enthusiasm but recognized the political necessity for compromise. A few big business leaders, notably the Morgan group, showed interest in creating a means for close government-business relations but backed away from Roosevelt's bid for effective governmental supervision. Most businessmen remained watchfully on the sidelines, apparently counting on the Senate Four and other like-minded politicians to protect their interests.

In the initial stages, when the bill creating a Department of

[1] For detailed accounts of the 1903 trust legislation see: Arthur M. Johnson, "Theodore Roosevelt and the Bureau of Corporations," *Mississippi Valley Historical Review* 45 (March 1959): 571–77; Gabriel Kolko, *The Triumph of Conservatism: A Reinterpretation of American History, 1900–1916,* 69–72; Hans B. Thorelli, *The Federal Antitrust Policy: Origination of an American Tradition,* 530–56; Claude Barfield, Jr., "Theodore Roosevelt and Congressional Leadership: Trust Legislation in 1903," paper presented at annual convention of the Organization of American Historians, 23 April 1965, Kansas City, Missouri.

Commerce and Labor carried no authorization to interfere with business, some representatives of business encouraged the move.[2] They clearly wanted a Department of Commerce and were even willing to include the word Labor in its title in order to obtain the support of congressmen from labor constituencies. They reasoned that if agriculture had a department, it was only fair and logical that other economic endeavors should have the benefit of a tax-supported department.

Consequently, in January 1903 business lobbyists were in Washington working for the cause. George W. Perkins, who was close to J. P. Morgan and a friend of Roosevelt, sent an associate, William C. Beer, to Washington from New York to work for the bill and to keep in constant touch with him. Railroaders James J. Hill and Charles S. Mellen sent an experienced lobbyist, Timothy E. Byrnes, who had valuable connections with politicians, including Iowa's Congressman William P. Hepburn, a member of the important Interstate Commerce Committee. "Fortunately," Beer reported to Perkins, "last summer, Mr. Byrnes had contributed $2500 to Hepburn's campaign fund. So with the advent of Mr. Byrnes today Hepburn warmed up in great shape."[3] Later, when the House debated the measure, "Hepburn closed in a rousing speech for the bill."[4]

The lobbyists found the work congenial and were optimistic about the outcome. Almost everyone wanted the bill passed. They decided to concentrate first on the House, where they saw no serious obstacle to its passage, and then turn to the Senate, where they counted on Aldrich to help. In fact, Aldrich even scheduled a conversation with Speaker Henderson to help speed the measure to enactment before the March 3 adjournment of Congress. On January 6, Beer wrote to Perkins that in actuality, "Five minutes of talk between *you* and [Congressmen] Dalzell and Grosvenor will pass the bill."[5] Republicans John Dalzell of Pennsylvania and Charles H. Grosvenor of Ohio were important House leaders and always friendly to business interests. Dalzell, moreover, was chairman of the Rules Committee.

[2] Barfield, "Roosevelt and Congressional Leadership," 10.
[3] 16 January 1903, George W. Perkins Papers.
[4] Beer to Perkins, 15 January 1903, ibid.
[5] Beer to Perkins, 6 January 1903, ibid.

The lobbyists got along well with Roosevelt's able private secretary, George B. Cortelyou, who represented the president in the task and later became the first secretary of the new department. On January 15 in one of his reports to Perkins, Beer amusedly said, "While I was consulting with Cortelyou today the President came in and after a little taffy said: 'How is my friend—my *very good* friend—George Per-Kins?' I replied," Beer continued, "that you were in good health but working mighty hard." Roosevelt responded, "'After a few little things are out of our way, I am going to *com-mand* him to go a-way for s-i-x-ty days. And in that time to neither do nor think of doing a single thing.' (teeth)." Roosevelt "intimated that you and he were or are doing something, and that after work you are to rest. He was jovial—away up—and I am sure he feels that the Department of Commerce is his baby and his alone."[6]

Nevertheless, Roosevelt clearly was not happy with Congress. Certain members of Congress, especially Littlefield in the House and Quay in the Senate, were a severe strain on his patience. He wrote his son Kermit, "I am having a terrific time trying to get various things through Congress and I pass my days in a state of exasperation, first, with the fools who do not want to do any of the things that ought to be done, and, second, with the equally obnoxious fools who insist upon so much that they cannot get anything."[7]

The lobbyists and political managers of the bill experienced a little unanticipated trouble in the House, but they handled it without great delay. Henderson, whose tenure as Speaker would not expire until the new Congress assumed control in March, proved to be difficult. Roosevelt and Aldrich conferred with him, but the lobbyists later discovered that Henderson was interested in something other than the usual confab with political leaders. Clarkson, who served as Henderson's agent in

<hr />

[6] 15 January 1903, ibid. For Roosevelt-Perkins cooperation on the measure, see also: Roosevelt to Perkins, 26 December 1902, and 26 June 1903, Morison, *Letters*, 3: 399, 506; memorandum, 3 January 1903, on a telephone conversation between Cortelyou and Beer (in New York), who spoke for Perkins, box 7, George B. Cortelyou Papers; Cortelyou to Philander C. Knox, 5 February 1903, Knox Papers.

[7] 17 January 1903, Morison, *Letters*, 3: 406; on Littlefield, see Roosevelt to Taft, 19 March 1903, ibid., 450; on Quay, see Albert J. Beveridge to George W. Perkins, 8 January 1903, Albert J. Beveridge Papers.

the matter, sought to obtain from Perkins a definite promise of aid in establishing Henderson's anticipated new legal career in New York. Shortly thereafter, Henderson cleared the way for quick passage. Perkins did aid Henderson but in 1905 poor health forced him to retire, and in early 1906 he died.[8]

Thus, with the generous help of business lobbyists, the administration's political managers obtained early passage in both the House and the Senate of the Department of Commerce and Labor bill, with its toothless Bureau of Corporations. It then went to a House-Senate conference committee. Roosevelt, desirous of something more meaningful, was in no mood to accept defeat. He promptly set about persuading the conference committee to add an amendment that would provide the Bureau of Corporations with the important publicity feature.[9]

The canny Roosevelt attempted to obtain his goal by implying that unless moderates accepted his modest proposal, he would give his full support to the more drastic and popular Littlefield bill, then before Congress. That punitive measure, sponsored by Congressman Charles E. Littlefield of Maine, authorized the Interstate Commerce Commission to deny corporations the privilege of engaging in interstate commerce if they failed to obey the commission's orders. Roosevelt acted indirectly, using the services of Cortelyou, Knox, and a friendly correspondent. On January 30, 1903, Cortelyou wrote Knox, "The President has asked Mr. Henry S. Brown, correspondent of the New York Herald, to see you, and would be glad if you would explain to Mr. Brown as fully as you can the trust legislation it is thought can be secured at the present session, notably, the bill to expedite cases under the Sherman Act, the Nelson amendment [to authorize the publicity feature Roosevelt sought], the Elkins bill, and the entire Littlefield bill." Having thus placed the Littlefield bill on the agenda for Roosevelt, Cortelyou closed with, "Mr. Brown is a personal friend of the President, and is

[8] William C. Beer to George W. Perkins, 11 January 1903, and James S. Clarkson to Perkins, 17 January 1903, Perkins Papers; O. O. Stealey, *Twenty Years in the Press Gallery*, 309; see also *Washington Post*, 11 February 1903.

[9] Barfield, "Roosevelt and Congressional Leadership," 14–15; George B. Cortelyou to Philander C. Knox, 30 January 1903, Knox Papers; *New York Herald*, 2, 3 February 1903; *New York Times*, 2, 3 February 1903; Johnson, "Bureau of Corporations," 575.

I believe quite well known to you. The President desires me to express to you his great interest in having Mr. Brown understand the situation regarding this matter."[10]

Earlier in the month both Roosevelt and Knox had indicated that they favored the Littlefield bill. But about ten days before the end of January the rumor spread that the president had decided against sponsoring it.[11] Now he again gave it his approval, apparently making the Senate Four and the less adventuresome of their business constituents nervous.

Oddly, however, the story that appeared in the *Herald*, three days after Cortelyou's January 30 letter, made no mention of the Littlefield bill, but did suggest that the president doubtless would call an extra session of Congress if it failed to approve the other three measures.[12] Perhaps Roosevelt had changed his mind about the Littlefield bill, fearful that it was too popular for the safety and harmony of the Republican party. In any case, the direct encouragement he had previously given the Littlefield forces and the growing popularity of the measure aided Roosevelt immeasurably in bringing the Senate leaders into line in support of the bill the conference committee had amended to include the publicity feature Roosevelt so much desired. Moreover, Roosevelt saw to it that the actual exercise of power over business was centered in the president. The Bureau of Corporations would gather statistics on businesses, which the president could either publicize or keep confidential, as he saw fit. This afforded him personal power to evaluate and deal with trusts on the basis of their being either "good" or "bad."

In the evening of February 7, Roosevelt, with masterly timing, recruited additional public support. He announced to the press that John D. Rockefeller, Sr., had telegraphed influential senators urging them to vote against the bill. Actually, however, Rockefeller, who paid little attention to politics, was not among the Standard Oil people who employed that device to block passage of the bill. But there was no question that most Standard

---

[10] Cortelyou to Philander C. Knox, 30 January 1903, Knox Papers.

[11] Barfield, "Roosevelt and Congressional Leadership," 12.

[12] *New York Herald*, 2 February 1903. There is a typed copy of this and some later *Herald* news stories in the Knox Papers.

Oil executives were angry over the proposed legislation. John D. Rockefeller, Jr., and John Archbold were among the signers of telegrams to the senators. O. H. Platt's friend, John H. Flagg, was also one of them. Flagg wired Platt, "We are opposed to all the proposed trust legislation except the Elkins anti-discrimination bill. Mr. Archbold with our counsel go to Washington this afternoon. Please give them audience and assistance." Platt administered a severe rebuke to Flagg for his role in the affair.[13]

The measure now moved rapidly toward final enactment. On February 10, 1903, the House passed the bill, 250 to 10, with the disgruntled Littlefield and nine Democrats opposed. The Senate passed it immediately with a voice vote.[14] Everybody concerned with the relations between business and government obtained a measure of satisfaction from the outcome. Roosevelt gained the most and the earnest Littlefield House reformers, the least. Businessmen were relieved to discover that their worst fears were groundless. Some businessmen, such as Perkins, doubtless reacted in the same way as the *Wall Street Journal,* which declared on March 4, "the industrial corporations will in time discover that they gain more in their credit and in the market standing of their securities by a wise publicity than they can possibly lose by the partial exposure of their affairs." The *New York Sun* expressed satisfaction with the president's achievement, pointing out that businessmen could trust Roosevelt to employ his publicity power with discretion.[15] Anti-Roosevelt sentiment in business circles tended to dissipate whenever it appeared that the alternative to his acceptance of "good" trusts was the legalist, inflexible position that no trust was "good," all were bad. Hence, ironically, such probusiness organs as the *Sun* were sometimes grateful for the moderate Roosevelt.

Roosevelt took satisfaction from his experience in working

[13] Flagg to Platt, 6, 11 February 1903, Platt Papers; see also *New York Times,* 8, 9 February 1903; Johnson, "Bureau of Corporations," 577.

[14] Johnson, "Bureau of Corporations," 577; Thorelli, *Federal Antitrust Policy,* 553–54.

[15] 17 February 1903. For Wall Street reaction in the context of the impending 1904 presidential election, see chapter 8 below.

with Congressional leaders. In March he wrote a lengthy letter to Taft, explaining that it had made him "feel respect and regard" for that group of senators including Aldrich, Allison, Spooner, O. H. Platt, Hanna, Lodge, and "one or two others, who, together with men like the next Speaker of the House, Joe Cannon, are the most powerful factors in Congress." Roosevelt explained that although he differed with all of them on certain important issues, "they are the leaders, and their great intelligence and power and their desire in the last resort to do what is best for the government, make them not only essential to work with, but desirable to work with." On the issues affecting federal relations with business, "with both Hanna and Aldrich I had to have a regular stand-up fight before I could get them to accept any trust legislation; but when I once got them to say they would give in, they kept their promise in good faith, and it was far more satisfactory to work with them than to try to work with the radical 'reformers' like Littlefield."[16]

Shortly after creation of the Department of Commerce and Labor, a new session of Congress began, with Cannon as Speaker of the House. Cannon's accession to the Speakership brought about a definite shift in the distribution of power, although not at the expense of party regularity or of unity in the party command. There was already a widespread spirit of revolt in the House, which the wily Cannon capitalized upon. He emerged as a powerful spokesman for the House, at the expense of the Senate Four.[17]

Cannon, who was sixty-seven when he became Speaker, had been in the House most of the time since 1873, representing a rural Illinois district. He was a thoroughgoing traditional midwestern Republican. While Allison and Spooner, from neighboring Iowa and Wisconsin, long since had become oriented to the political partnership between the East and the Middle West

[16] Roosevelt to Taft, 19 March 1903, Morison, *Letters*, 3: 450.

[17] For Roosevelt-Cannon relations see letters from Roosevelt to Kermit Roosevelt, 8 January 1903, Morison, *Letters*, 3: 401; to Hugh H. Hanna, 29 January 1903, ibid., 413–14; to Cannon, 25 February 1903, ibid., 434; to Taft, 19 March 1903, ibid., 450; to Grenville M. Dodge, 22 April 1903, ibid., 466; William Rea Gwinn, *Uncle Joe Cannon, Archfoe of Insurgency: A History of the Rise and Fall of Cannonism*, 78–79; L. White Busbey, *Uncle Joe Cannon: The Story of a Pioneer American*, 216–19.

(and hence had come to take into consideration the views of Platt and Aldrich when forging Republican policy and tactics), Cannon was more parochial, more closely related to his rural, small-town Illinois constituency.

From the outset, as a loyal party man and by attending to the interests of his constituency, Cannon found it a relatively simple matter to remain in office and to move gradually up the House seniority ladder to the Speakership. As he moved upward, his reputation grew as an intelligent, reliable, shrewd, picturesque figure. He was often crude and, as Speaker, was frequently dogmatic and offensively dictatorial. But he was hard working and sincere and possessed a refreshing forthrightness. In the course of a House debate in 1890, a Democratic member twitted him for reversing himself on a position he had taken a year before on a constitutional interpretation. Cannon replied, "The gentleman knows that in this popular body members from time to time do and perhaps always will do, under a supposed partisan necessity, that which lies in their power to do, and then, having done it, the desire to be sustained makes them claim a construction of the Constitution to justify that which nothing in sound sense or morals can justify else."[18]

Cannon affected the dress and mannerisms of a country rube, perhaps in a spirit of defiance against eastern manners. He made himself conspicuous by his sometimes crude language, homespun suits, and unkempt appearance, and by spewing tobacco juice. His personal appearance, even if he had worn clothes more in keeping with his official position, would have inspired publicity. The president's daughter, "Princess Alice," later recalled that "Mr. Cannon was an aquiline-faced, chin-bearded, old fellow, so typically a politician or legislator that no cartoon ever seemed to exaggerate him." On one occasion when she was to play poker with Cannon, a "celebrated player," William Howard Taft warned her of what to expect. "President Taft . . . told me I had better be careful not only to play my cards close, but to avoid getting between Uncle Joe Cannon and a close spittoon."

[18] U. S., *Congressional Record*, 51 Cong., 1 sess., 1890, 94, part 1, 957, quoted in William A. Robinson, *Thomas B. Reed, Parliamentarian*, 212; see also Richard Bartholdt, *From Steerage to Congress*, 119.

Alice at first believed he was joking, but "Uncle Joe, when he sat down at the poker table demanded" a spittoon. He had to settle for an umbrella stand. Cannon "used it freely and frequently throughout the evening." At the poker game he proved to be "a serious and rather tedious" player. "He would pick up his hand slowly, tuck in his chin, lean back, squint at it, and ask for cards as if weighing his words," and he "had all the poker clichés."[19]

It had been a frustrating and at times embittering experience for Cannon to serve in the House while Henderson was Speaker and the Senate Four treated the House as a rubber stamp. The day before he took office as Speaker, Cannon gave vent to his feelings in a most dramatic way. Word reached the House that the Senate had just passed the Sundry Civil Appropriations bill. The measure included a manifestly indefensible grant of $47,000 to South Carolina, which Senator Benjamin R. Tillman of that state had maneuvered into the bill. At the time the measure arrived, the House members were sleepily slouched in their chairs, for it was almost dawn. But Cannon awakened them with suddenness. He jumped to his feet and, with his left arm waving like an uncertain swordsman, poured forth his anti-Senate resentment. Red of face, he angrily warned that the Senate "must change its method of procedure, or our body, backed up by the people, will compel that change; else, this body, close to the people, shall become a mere tender, a mere bender of the pregnant hinges of the knee, to submit to what any one member of another body may demand of this body as a price for legislation." His colleagues, clearly entertaining the same feelings toward the Senate, burst forth with great applause. They had found a leader, a spokesman.[20]

At the same time, powerful Republican Main Street had found a spokesman. The business and professional men of rural America were very influential in their communities. Local bankers, small factory owners, doctors, editors, merchants and clergy-

---

[19] Alice Roosevelt Longworth, *Crowded Hours: Reminiscences*, 46, 170.
[20] Blair Bolles, *Tyrant from Illinois: Uncle Joe Cannon's Experiment with Personal Power*, 8–9; Nathaniel W. Stephenson, *Nelson W. Aldrich: A Leader in American Politics*, 214–15.

men in one way or another wielded impressive influence over the farmers and wage earners of their communities. Joe Cannon, because of his business connections in Danville, Illinois, was closer to middle western town and country life than any of the top Republican leaders. Allison had his Dubuque connections, but he had become so oriented to the East and to Washington that his town relationship lacked the air of authority that surrounded Cannon. One small-city banker reminded his senator, when a certain pro-big-city bank measure was under discussion, of the power of Main Street. He said that it "gives the central banks much power over the smaller fish, but it's 'the little fish' that count most when it comes to a popular vote."[21] It surprised nobody that Roosevelt found Cannon a useful ally.

During 1903, the Republican leadership not only wrestled with the trust problem, but also confronted a currency crisis. Financiers, especially in Wall Street, became alarmed over money scarcity in the financial centers. A crisis threatened early in the year, subsided in the early summer, returned with greater force in August and finally ended in the fall. In October, lawyer Henry Taft looked back at the scene in Wall Street, where he had his office, and reported that seemingly "only two classes of persons have not lost money during the summer, viz: (1) those who had none and (2) the liars."[22] Throughout those dreary months in the business world, the currency stringency stimulated the already substantial interest in reform. Business demands for legislation, along with the threat of a protracted economic depression, caused Republican leaders to contemplate action. They discussed among themselves what reforms to endorse and whether or not to summon a special session of Congress to enact the reforms. They finally decided to do nothing.

Roosevelt was in a very uncomfortable position. In addition to his natural concern over the economic implications of the crisis, he faced a threat to his own political future. He could not afford to go into the 1904 election campaign in the midst of a continuing economic crisis. However, he could find no re-

[21] N. B. Van Slyke, Madison, Wisconsin, to Spooner, 18 February 1903, Spooner Papers.
[22] Henry Taft to Taft, 27 October 1903, Taft Papers.

lief proposal that his colleagues in the party hierarchy could agree upon. He placed the blame for his predicament on the bankers of the country because they had failed to unite on any plan, leaving their political representatives in an impasse.[23] In the midst of the crisis, Roosevelt wrote to his friend, New York Congressman Lucius N. Littauer, "One great trouble is the absolute inability to get anything like unity of judgment among the financiers." Roosevelt believed that if the financiers of the East could "formulate a plan in conjunction with the western bankers, both city and country . . . we would have a good chance of putting it through.[24] He explained to Grenville M. Dodge in April, before the crisis reached an acute stage, that while he could speak definitely on the tariff, because it was a composite of the views "of men as diverse in feeling as Hanna, Spooner, Aldrich and Allison," such was not the case with the currency problem. "In financial measures I do not want to find that I am asking for something which the leaders of the party in Congress violently oppose, unless, of course, it is necessary."[25]

The party hierarchy was well aware that the currency system needed reform. Despite that knowledge and still fresh memories of the Panic of 1893 with the ensuing years of economic suffering, they could not bring themselves to face up to the fact that another devastating panic might occur at any moment. Weak patchwork legislation remained the outer limits of their plans. Senator Aldrich proposed a bill which provided for additional currency to be issued on selected state, municipal, and railroad bonds. It was a pale gesture compared to the Fowler plan for assets currency.

The party leadership was well aware that each fall and early

[23] For examples of 1903 banker concern and divergence in views on possible solutions, see letters to Spooner from N. B. Van Slyke (banker), 18 February, William B. Banks (banker), 20 February, E. J. Perry (banker), 24 February, James Blair (broker), 25 February, 30 March, William Carson (banker), 2 March, and A. P. Frame (banker), 11 August—all in Spooner Papers; Leslie M. Shaw to Grenville M. Dodge, 25 June 1903, Dodge Papers; George E. Roberts to Allison, 1 September 1903, Allison Papers.

[24] 22 July 1903, Morison, *Letters*, 3: 524–25.

[25] 22 April 1903, Dodge Papers. The copy of the same letter in Morison, *Letters*, 3: 466, is slightly inaccurate, because two words, namely "it is," were indecipherable in the Roosevelt letterbook copy. See also Roosevelt to John Byrne, 29 December 1903, Morison, *Letters*, 3: 684.

"The Senate Four" confer at the home of Nelson W. Aldrich in 1903.
Left to right: Orville H. Platt, John C. Spooner, William B. Allison, Nelson W. Aldrich.

Senator Nelson W. Aldrich
of Rhode Island in 1902
Courtesy of the Library of Congress

Senator William B. Allison of Iowa
Courtesy of the Library of Congress

Senator John C. Spooner
of Wisconsin in 1902
Courtesy of the Library of Congress

Senator Orville H. Platt
of Connecticut in 1902
Courtesy of the Library of Congress

William Howard Taft in 1908
Courtesy of the Library of Congress

President William McKinley
Courtesy of the Library of Congress

President Theodore Roosevelt in 1904. *Courtesy of the Library of Congress*

Booker T. Washington,
Presidential Adviser,
in 1902
Courtesy of the
Library of Congress

A Democratic campaign button of 1904   A Republican campaign button of 1904
Courtesy of the Smithsonian Institution

Attorney General
George W. Wickersham in 1909
Courtesy of the Library of Congress

Attorney General Philander C. Knox
Courtesy of the Library of Congress

Senator Henry Cabot Lodge
of Massachusetts in 1901
*Courtesy of the
Library of Congress*

Secretary of State Elihu Root in 1907
Courtesy of the Library of Congress

Speaker of the House
Joseph G. Cannon
in 1909
*Courtesy of the
Library of Congress*

"Uncle Joe" Cannon as Speaker of the House.
Courtesy of the Library of Congress

" Sh ! Do not speak, or else you'll wake the tariff."

And just then Speaker Henderson came along.

Speaker Henderson and the tariff issue in 1902
John T. McCutcheon, in *Cartoons by McCutcheon*, Chicago, 1903

PRESIDENT ROOSEVELT: "I could ride that critter, but I haven't any intention of trying it."

President Roosevelt stands a safe distance from tariff revision
Minneapolis Tribune, November 11, 1901

A consequence of the Republican-business partnership
New York American, September 13, 1904

The Republican command in action. *Chicago Record Herald,* May 9, 1908

SOMEBODY'S DARLING

Senator Aldrich is unhappy over proposed changes in his currency bill
Philadelphia Inquirer, April 11, 1908

NICE BIG APPLE FOR THE ELEPHANT, BUT HE DOESN'T SEEM TO WANT IT.

A Roosevelt contribution to the 1908 Republican campaign
Brooklyn Eagle, February 8, 1908

LOST BALL!

Tariff revision eludes Taft
Brooklyn Daily Eagle, May 6, 1909

JUST BEGINNING TO REALIZE HIS STRENGTH

The Sherman Antitrust Law in the Taft administration
Register and Leader, Des Moines, Iowa, October 4, 1911

President Roosevelt's dream of a successful hunt
Courtesy of the Library of Congress

"THEY WILL MISS ME WHEN I'M GONE"

As defeat looms for the Republican Party in the 1912 election
Brooklyn Daily Eagle, October 2, 1912

winter there was a dire shortage of money in eastern banks because so much of it was sent into the rural areas to move the crops to market. In the spring of 1903, Platt reported to Root that he "found in New York quite a sentiment among the people who are called financiers" for an extra session of Congress in early October, "in order to give plenty of time for the passage of some measure of financial relief before the customary December money stringency comes on." Platt did not, however, think it as important "as they regard it."[26] For many years, Henry L. Higginson of Boston had been reminding political leaders of the need for new currency legislation. In June 1903, he urged Roosevelt to call an extra session of Congress and pointed out that "We have rather outgrown our means for the time, and we have decidedly poor financial laws. We rely simply on greenbacks as a basis, and we need a more elastic and a larger basis than the greenbacks supply." He added the political warning, "If a considerable disaster comes to the land through financial trouble which is not necessary, it will be visited on the heads of the Republican party and with justice."[27]

Grenville M. Dodge, writing from Wall Street to fellow Iowan Allison, urged legislative action. In early May he was "impressed more this year than ever before" by the length of time the financial strain persisted, which was "the best indication" to him "that it is going to be serious."[28] At the end of the month he reported that "money just now is easy on account of the lack of speculation, but if speculation should commence again when crops are assured, we will be in trouble." On the possibility of governmental action, he reported that there was some optimism in Wall Street. "Spooner has been here and has given a good deal of strength to the financial feeling that something is going to be done that will help us."[29] A month later, when excessive speculation on the stock market was draining money from normal business requirements, Dodge was as angry and perturbed as was Higginson up in Boston. "I want to say to

[26] 6 April 1903, Platt Papers.

[27] 11 June 1903, Roosevelt Papers; see also John George to Spooner, 8 August 1903, Spooner Papers.

[28] 4 May 1903, Allison Papers.

[29] Dodge to Allison, 29 May 1903, ibid.

you just as positively as I can," he wrote Allison, "that unless you [leaders in Washington] provide some method of furnishing money for the business of this country you will have the greatest tumult about your ears, and about the ears of Congress, and the Republican party will get the worst rapping it ever received for not being able to provide money for taking care of the business brought about by the prosperity they claim to have made." He warned Allison to "look out when the crops move."[30] But Allison, along with Roosevelt and the other leaders in Washington, remained calm as they worked to produce a measure that they could agree upon. In August, Dodge was somewhat less perturbed, for "Everything seems to be prosperous except for the people who have to borrow money." But he still hoped for legislative action on the basic problem.[31] Spooner was among those caught in the sharp market decline. Throughout the summer his broker sent pleas for more and more margin money.[32] Spooner mortgaged property to meet the demands. He borrowed $30,000 from his wealthy friend Russell A. Alger, a former political leader and cabinet member from Michigan.[33]

Arguments over possible remedies for the currency crisis were essentially the same in 1903 as they had been before passage of the Gold Standard Act of 1900. But Roosevelt, unlike his predecessor McKinley, was very directly involved in the discussions. Roosevelt in turn brought into the discussion Speaker Cannon, Secretary of the Treasury Leslie M. Shaw, and some members of the financial community. On both occasions, Aldrich, Platt, Allison, and Spooner were major participants.

Aldrich and Platt spoke for the financial interests of the East. Their basic views were widely known. They showed no inclination to foster any comprehensive currency reform and were especially opposed to assets currency. Aldrich feared it would open the way to dangerous inflation, or in his words would be "letting the camel's head into the tent."[34] Shaw said Aldrich's

[30] 29 June 1903, ibid.
[31] Dodge to Allison, 5 August 1903, ibid.
[32] See, for example, A. A. Housman and Company (brokers) to Spooner, 18 May, 1 June, 8 July, 4 August, 19 September 1903, Spooner Papers.
[33] Spooner to Alger, 20 June 1903, and H. C. Reed to Alger, 18 July 1903, ibid.
[34] Quoted in Shaw to Roosevelt, 10 August 1903, Roosevelt Papers.

opposition to assets currency flowed from his logical projection of the scheme. If it became permissible to issue currency on such assets as municipal and other bonds, then "the Granger States will immediately demand that real estate mortgages be made the basis, and then the populists will want Government warehouses and [then] currency based on warehouse receipts." That, Shaw added in explaining Aldrich's views to Roosevelt, "has already been asked [for] you remember."[35] Shaw also pointed out what everybody knew, that "no financial measure can pass the Senate without Senator Aldrich's consent." His "great power," moreover, was "based on merit."[36]

The evidence at hand bearing on Aldrich's merit as an expert on currency was far from impressive, as was evident in the Aldrich bill. The measure called for such severe restrictions and charges that it was highly unlikely that banks, other than the largest and most powerful, could obtain the additional currency the bill afforded. The requirement that only certain carefully selected types of securities, most notably municipal and railroad bonds, would be eligible paper for the funds, angered representatives of non-Wall Street regions. Western and southern politicians pointed out that only the large Wall Street banks possessed a significant number of railroad bonds. They also pointed out that the only eligible municipal bonds prescribed were those of cities and counties whose populations exceeded 50,000. This discriminated against banks in small communities, which held a proportionately large number of bonds of small municipal and county governments. The Aldrich bill, moreover, contained no provision that afforded any degree of currency elasticity. As early as March 1903, it was apparent even to Aldrich that Congress would refuse to enact his measure.[37]

To devise a measure acceptable to Congress, Aldrich invited top Senate Finance Committee members Platt, Spooner, and

---

[35] Ibid.; see also Shaw to Roosevelt, 24 July 1903, Roosevelt Papers; Shaw to Grenville M. Dodge, 25 June 1903, Dodge Papers.

[36] Shaw to Roosevelt, 28 July 1903, Roosevelt Papers.

[37] U. S., *Congressional Record*, 57 Cong., 2 sess., 1903, 36, part 3, 2550–54; *New York Times*, 19, 27 January, 10, 26 February, 2, 3 March 1903; *Nation*, 25 December 1902, 22 January, 12 February, 5 March 1903; Stanley Markowitz, "The Aldrich-Vreeland Bill: Its Significance in the Struggle for Currency Reform, 1893–1908" (Master's thesis, University of Maryland, 1965), 28–31.

Allison to a meeting at his Rhode Island home. None of them approached the conference with optimism. Shortly before going, Platt wrote musingly to his friend Flagg, "On the sixth of August I go down to Aldrich's as one of a sub-committee, to consider financial matters. Sometimes I think it is almost a farce that I should be taking part in proposed legislation affecting our financial system, and at other times I think perhaps I know fully as much about it as those who are better financiers." Then, after discussing the pros and cons of assets currency and adding that he was "all at sea about the matter," Platt went on to place the problem in historical and international perspective. "If we, in this country, could have a national bank, or a governmental connection with a strong bank, as in England, France, Germany, and other commercial countries, and thus do away with the sub-treasury, I think we would be better off." But, he added, "that is impossible, in view of public sentiment." Recalling the heated controversy of the Andrew Jackson era, Platt remarked, "The national bank idea was sound finance, but its experience made every one opposed to a national bank, and you have only to mention one now, to stir up the whole community to hostility." He thought it was "manifest that we cannot revive the idea of a national bank." He thought tax reduction would be "the real remedy for money stringency" but that too he believed to be "difficult of accomplishment."[38]

Roosevelt sent a word of encouragement to Aldrich, and asked, "Is there anything for me to do now?" In discussing the prospects for acceptable action in the House, the president added that Uncle Joe Cannon "is very obdurate as regards anything being done but I think if we take the old boy the right way he will stand with us."[39] Next day, Roosevelt again wrote to Aldrich, this time clearly uneasy over the pressure business interests were exerting upon him. "Do you want to see me about the financial situation? I suppose you have got your eye on it. I hope you are keeping in touch with Shaw. Mr. [Henry Clay] Frick was out here and thinks we ought to have an extra session in September, but as yet I don't see it that way."[40] New

[38] 29 July 1903, Platt Papers.
[39] 22 July 1903, box 48, Biographer's Notes, Aldrich Papers.

York banker Jefferson Seligman also called on Roosevelt, "wild with fear of a panic."[41]

After the Rhode Island meeting in mid-August, the Four went down to Oyster Bay to report to the president. They had little, however, to add to the Aldrich bill. They favored some minor, but as yet not formalized, changes in that measure and indicated that they approved of a special session of Congress in October to act on the problem.[42]

When the Senate Four and the president settled on the Aldrich bill, they were unduly optimistic about its chances in Congress. They were not fully aware of the difficulties in getting the House to follow their instructions, and that on certain issues they lacked sufficient persuasiveness to obtain the cooperation of the narrow-minded Cannon. Roosevelt was correct in his earlier observation that Uncle Joe was "very obdurate as regards anything being done" on the matter.[43] It soon became apparent that their sponsorship of even a modified Aldrich bill was not taking the "old boy the right way." The Aldrich approach was anathema to Cannon, who was also opposed to Fowler's assets currency proposal. Both approaches represented the interests of large banks. Cannon not only represented the small-town banks but was himself a small-town banker. Back in the early 1870s, he and his brother William had pooled their savings to open the Vermilion County Bank in Danville, Illinois. That bank, which later became the Second National Bank of Danville, prospered enough to permit the Cannon partners to acquire the majority stock of the gas, electric light, and street railway companies in Danville.[44]

During the 1903 summer crisis, Cannon argued that greedy Wall Street financiers had brought the problem upon themselves by tying up funds in their speculative ventures. New York Congressman Lucius M. Littauer reported to Roosevelt on July 27 that "After Mr. Cannon's return from his visit to you, he re-

---

[40] 23 July 1903, Morison, *Letters*, 3: 526–27.
[41] Roosevelt to Leslie M. Shaw, 22 July 1903, ibid., 526.
[42] Roosevelt to Cannon, 13 August 1903, ibid., 565.
[43] Roosevelt to Aldrich, 22 July 1903, box 48, Biographer's Notes, Aldrich Papers.
[44] Gwinn, *Uncle Joe Cannon*, 16–17. At his death in 1926, Cannon left an estate of a half-million dollars. (Ibid., 16.)

mained but one day" in New York City, "and despite every endeavor, I could not get him to visit a single banker, nor [would he] permit anyone to call on him."[45] Cannon clearly did not believe that the current situation was critical enough to warrant passage of legislation to rescue Wall Streeters.[46] He also kept one eye on the political situation, using it as a reason, or excuse, to oppose legislation. Secretary Shaw, who was at the time advancing a mild compromise plan in a vain effort to obtain agreement between Cannon and the Senate Four, reported to Roosevelt on one occasion that Cannon "expressed the opinion that if the proposition I submitted to him were on the statute books, it would be a good thing, but he was afraid of any legislation that would result in Bryanistic harangues against legislation in the interest of banks."[47]

In mid-August nobody could report progress. Roosevelt felt impelled to report to Hugh H. Hanna, then in Russia as a member of the Commission on International Exchange, that "As for the financial situation here, the trouble largely is the wide difference of opinion among those to whom we should look for expert knowledge."[48] At the same time, Platt expressed concern to Aldrich. He was especially worried over what the president might end up doing after talking about the financial situation and proposals with nearly everybody within his reach. Platt feared that Roosevelt might accept the views of the wrong person, so he urged Aldrich to keep in close touch with the president. "If you do this, he may accept your ideas as his own, and push them." Otherwise, "he will be filled up with others from various parties, and be working against what we think is the right thing." For the same reason, Platt thought it very important that Aldrich arrange a conference between J. P. Morgan and the

[45] 27 July 1903, Roosevelt Papers. Whitelaw Reid's, and hence his *New York Tribune's* attitude was similar to Cannon's. Reid attributed the current crisis to speculative activity. He said, "no legislative device can prevent people from suffering when they flood the market with enormous over issues of securities representing water." He also believed "that whether from a political or a business point of view it would be disastrous to attempt wholly remodelling the currency laws on the eve of a Presidential campaign." Reid to Donald Nicholson, 31 August 1903, Reid Papers.

[46] L. M. Littauer to Roosevelt, 27 July 1903, Roosevelt Papers.

[47] 24 July 1903, ibid.

[48] 19 August 1903, ibid.

president, to insure proper thinking on the part of the latter.[49]

The Senate Four, concerned over Roosevelt's possible action, over their own inability to produce an acceptable bill, and over Cannon's opposition to any legislation, exerted their influence to prevent an extra session of Congress. They operated through Allison, who conferred with Cannon and then wrote to the president. In his letter to the president, Allison said that he and Cannon believed there was no emergency and hence no immediate need for a special session to enact currency legislation. "In view of the early coming Presidential election," moreover, "is it not likely that much debate will be had for political ends, and will not this currency question be made the occasion for the exploitation of all the plans that ingenuity can invent, wise or otherwise," and "will it not be urged in certain quarters that we substantially admit that our currency legislation has been a failure?" Nor did he cease his lament there. "If we admit an emergency would not the country be placed in a condition of unrest? And suppose Congress should delay prompt action, or in the end take the wrong action, or pass experimental legislation, the effect of which would not be presently visible, or suppose views are found to be so widely divergent as that no action would be taken, thus placing us at a disadvantage in the next campaign on that question."[50]

By fall the anxiety of the party leaders dissipated and they convinced themselves that they need not, after all, formulate new currency legislation. Instead, they engaged in half-hearted discussion about minor repair measures, placed great emphasis on the superiority of the existing system, and saw no real need to pursue the difficult task to improve upon it. On September 3, Roosevelt reported to Lodge, "The Wall Street situation is greatly improved. The chance of a panic seems to be pretty well over." He believed, however, that "the check to the boom and the Wall Street disturbance generally will have some effect on the whole business world and times will not be so good for the next year or so as they have been during the past year or so." In assessing the blame, Roosevelt said, "The fault belongs

[49] 17 August 1903, Platt Papers.
[50] 19 August 1903, Allison Papers, and a copy in Aldrich Papers.

wholly of course to the speculators, the promoters who have overcapitalized the great trusts, and the reckless, greedy and over-sanguine men generally." While adding that "of course these people and a considerable number of their followers will not wish to shoulder the blame and will put it on me if they can," the president failed to suggest a possible remedy.[51]

In mid-September, Platt observed that it would be advantageous if Congress passed the main features of the Aldrich plan, but he doubted that such would occur. Moreover, he believed that the "Fowler plan and all others which involve asset currency, . . . look to the complete change of the currency system, and it . . . would be folly to attempt such a change . . . in this congress, on the eve of a presidential election. We have a safe currency now. It is also an abundant currency for the ordinary conditions of business." He was inclined, however, to favor some minor legislation in order to make the system a little more elastic.[52] Six weeks later, in late October, he concluded that current gold production made it unnecessary for Congress to make provisions for increasing the money supply, "and if the banking institutions were what they should be instead of being speculative concerns, they could always provide easily for the shipment of money necessary to move crops." To Platt, "It is not more money we want—it is more sense about money."[53]

By early October, the leadership had decided definitely against a special session. Allison stated publicly that Congress was not going to act immediately on the matter. The *New York Times* editorialized disgustedly, "We suppose that the dictum of the venerable Senator Allison of Iowa must be taken as conclusive of the intention of the majority in the Senate to take no steps toward the improvement of the currency."[54]

Some of the leaders, however, believed that it was no longer feasible to sweep the problem completely under the rug. In early November, Spooner wrote to his friend Frank G. Bigelow,

[51] 3 September 1903, Morison, *Letters*, 3: 587.
[52] Platt to John H. Flagg, 14 September 1903, Platt Papers; see also Platt to Albert J. Beveridge, 14 September 1903, Beveridge Papers.
[53] Platt to John H. Flagg, 28 October 1903, Platt Papers.
[54] 12 October 1903. For further expressions of disgust over the failure of Congress to act on the matter, see: *New York Times*, 27 August 1903; *Nation*, 27 August, 8 October 1903.

president of the First National Bank in Milwaukee, that the Senate Committee on Finance "will provide this winter for the appointment of a commission to consider and report a full financial scheme for the country, the report probably to come in after the Presidential election, so that it may be taken up at the succeeding session." He asked Bigelow if he would be willing to serve on the commission.[55] Spooner also took steps to improve his knowledge of finance, ordering from the publishers a copy of Davis R. Dewey's *Financial History of the United States.*[56]

Some businessmen showed more enthusiasm for reform than most political leaders. In November, after the immediate crisis had ended, John Byrne, a railroad president and founder in 1896 of the Democratic Honest Money League of America, advocated that Congress or the president create a commission to study and make recommendations on the matter.[57] Henry L. Higginson did likewise, explaining to the president that "The truth is, banking is well understood both here and abroad, and such a commission as you could appoint would give us a system that would last indefinitely. Such a system would be a great blessing and monument."[58]

Roosevelt questioned the feasibility of the commission approach. He pointed out that the Four and Speaker Cannon in effect represented such diverse interests that they could not unite the Republicans in Congress behind it. Roosevelt explained to Byrne, "Of course, the real difficulty comes from the fact that the different sections of the country seem to look at this question in different ways. If all the bankers and businessmen of New York City felt alike, that of itself would be a stimulus to action by Congress; and if in addition the country bankers in districts like those in which Speaker Cannon lives felt the same way, we should be almost sure of legislation; but at present even the New York business world has but an indistinct idea of what it wants, and the country bankers of the Mississippi valley do not eye favorably what they have seen of the New York proposi-

---

[55] 3 November 1903, Bigelow Papers.
[56] Spooner to Longmans, Green and Co., 14 November 1903, Spooner Papers.
[57] Mentioned in Roosevelt to John Byrne, 29 December 1903, Morison, *Letters,* 3: 684.
[58] 6 November 1903, Roosevelt Papers.

tion."[59] In Roosevelt's annual message, delivered December 7, 1903, his remarks on the subject were brief and general. "The integrity of our currency," he said, "is beyond question, and under present conditions it would be unwise and unnecessary to attempt a reconstruction of our entire monetary system."[60]

Republican leaders gradually retreated from the remaining pressures to produce currency reform. Public fickleness helped them and the Panamanian revolution diverted public attention. When Roosevelt and his political strategists prepared for the 1904 election, they discreetly passed over currency reform as a subject for campaign discussion. The Senate Committee on Finance decided against establishing the commission to formulate the "full financial scheme" Spooner had mentioned. In fact, although in his early November letter to banker Bigelow he had been emphatic about the commission, three weeks later Spooner wrote to him in very vague terms about the intentions of the leaders regarding currency reform.[61]

Banker-politician George E. Roberts, the director of the mint in Washington, understood the situation. This alleged "father of the Iowa Idea"[62] wrote Allison, "Public opinion is evidently largely against anything in the way of 'asset' currency," the only acceptable approach to the problem. He believed "The difficult thing to overcome is the popular prejudice that is based upon the experience of the country with the wild-cat banks" which had issued insecure asset currency. However, Roberts was convinced that the nation could "not go on indefinitely with government bonds as a basis for bank note currency. The country is growing, its business is increasing, while the supply of government bonds is likely to become smaller."[63]

As 1903 drew to a close, the Republican leadership remained intact and voters seemed to be relatively complacent. The national financial crisis had ended before party leaders had been forced to become embroiled in controversy over currency reform

[59] 29 December 1903, Morison, *Letters*, 3: 684; see also Roosevelt to Higginson, 7 November 1903, Roosevelt Papers.

[60] James D. Richardson, *A Compilation of the Messages and Papers of the Presidents*, 14: 6787.

[61] 3, 28 November 1903, Spooner Papers; Stephenson, *Aldrich*, 229.

[62] Leland L. Sage, *William Boyd Allison: A Study in Practical Politics*, 282.

[63] George E. Roberts to Allison, 1 September 1903, Allison Papers.

legislation. The party command, with Roosevelt taking the lead, had brought the trust problem under control for the time being by continuing trustbusting and by inducing Congress to enact legislation that somewhat satisfied public and business demands. One of these measures, the law establishing the Bureau of Corporations, had the additional advantage of affording the restless Roosevelt an opportunity to experiment with his plan to control monopolies rather than destroy them. The promotion of seasoned Cannon to the Speakership of the House and also into the inner circle of the party leadership reminded the public that men of caution still led the party. Only the presence of Roosevelt offered any likelihood of a modernization of party policy.

VIII

THE ELECTION OF 1904

THE ELECTION OF 1904 was a stunning victory for the ebullient, gifted Roosevelt and a disappointment for some key old-time members of the Republican leadership. In state contests, men of lesser stature gained votes at the expense of established leaders. Identification with the popular Roosevelt forestalled an even greater decline than this in the power of the Senate Four. The condition of southern Negroes was a matter of more than usual national consideration in the election, largely because "friend-of-the-Negro" Roosevelt was a presidential candidate and because the Republican platform contained a proposed plan to reverse the Negro disfranchisement movement. Southern whites were convinced that the northern Republicans were launching a movement to nullify the Compromise of 1877, which had reassigned southern Negroes to southern control.

Opposition to Roosevelt in the presidential contest was abysmally weak. The continued low state of the Democratic party made it unnecessary for the Republican party to go beyond a routine, formal presentation of its traditional platform and a mere parade of the names of the candidates. The national Democratic party was still hopelessly divided between Bryanism and Bourbonism. Presidential candidate Alton B. Parker was a dedicated champion of political inertia. William Howard Taft remarked in the summer of 1904, "The great difficulty about the Democratic party is that it is not a party at all, in the proper sense of that term. It is a conglomeration of irreconcilable elements that have no solidarity so far as carrying through any policy affirmatively is concerned."[1]

Until it was all over, nevertheless, Roosevelt's managers kept a careful watch on every possible quarter from whence a threat to his election might arise. This included danger spots in the Republican network itself. They found a few possible threats worthy of attention. The rumored bid of Mark Hanna for the presidency, or at least for control of the convention so that he could select the candidate, annoyed the Roosevelt forces, although the basic weakness of Hanna's position was apparent to them. Only anti-Roosevelt wishful thinkers, mostly angry business leaders and loyal party workers, looked upon Hanna as a serious contender. Newsmen, anxious for dramatic stories, found in Hanna material for front-page accounts. His prominence and colorful personality captured readers' attention much more easily than such dull men as Alton B. Parker. Newsmen overlooked the cold fact that Hanna's candidacy in reality was a house of sand.

Hanna's well-known identification with machine politics and big business made it impossible for the Republican party to present him as a presidential candidate. Ironically, moreover, Hanna could not even count on the machine element in his party, for such men as Thomas C. Platt, Henry C. Payne, and Matthew Quay were among his political enemies. Hanna was also particularly vulnerable on the conspicuous tariff issue. He was identified with an uncompromising defense of the Dingley Tariff at a time when there was widespread recognition that it was a disgraceful, unjust measure, and a growing feeling that the Republican party should reexamine its rigid ultraprotectionist policy. Hanna was, in short, a "standpatter." Although he bowed in the direction of governmental encouragement of foreign trade, he needed to demonstrate that interest more strongly. He urged subsidization of the nation's shipbuilders and the construction of the Isthmian canal, but he failed to follow McKinley's example on tariff revision.

Roosevelt's position in the White House and as head of his party gave him a distinct advantage over Hanna or any other possible candidate. Roosevelt's triumph in the 1902 anthracite coal crisis had endeared him to wage earners much more conspicuously than did the earnest efforts of the less highly placed

¹ Taft to Horace D. Taft, 4 August 1904, Taft Papers.

Hanna. Too, Roosevelt early used his power to obtain friendly delegates from the southern Republican rotten boroughs where Hanna had previously maintained notable popularity. Above all else, only the most obtuse of politicians could have blinded themselves to the fact that to deny the nomination to a first-term occupant of the White House was at best a herculean task and that to attempt such a thing when Roosevelt was that occupant bordered on the ridiculous. Some who knew this to be true, however, were well aware of the unpredictability of politics. An accident *could* happen. In May 1903, O. H. Platt wrote Albert J. Beveridge, "It is a year before the nominating convention, and in the interval many things may happen."[2] Platt had heard that Hanna wanted the Ohio State Republican convention of May 1903 to postpone until the next year any endorsement of Roosevelt's candidacy. Among the rumored reasons for the action was that Hanna wanted the nomination himself. The president, upon learning of Hanna's plan, promptly telegrammed Hanna to choose between him and an open political fight. Hanna meekly surrendered.[3]

Another and final flurry of pro-Hanna sentiment came in late 1903 in the wake of the substantial Republican election victory in Ohio. The victory not only assured Hanna's reelection to the Senate but appeared to some people to increase greatly his chances for the presidency. The political realists, however, were not impressed. It was one thing for Ohio Republicans to defeat Democrat Tom L. Johnson, mayor of Cleveland, for governor; it was quite another to defeat Theodore Roosevelt.[4]

While loyal Hanna followers engaged in wishful thinking over the prospects of his nomination, he never more than fleetingly considered himself a serious contender. On January 19, 1904,

[2] 30 May 1903, Platt Papers; see also Beveridge to Platt, 26 May 1903, ibid.
[3] Charles P. Taft to Taft, 25, 26 May 1903, Taft Papers; Roosevelt to Henry Cabot Lodge, 27 May 1903, Morison, *Letters*, 3: 481–82; Joseph B. Foraker, *Notes of a Busy Life*, 2: 109–11; Nathaniel W. Stephenson, *Nelson W. Aldrich: A Leader in American Politics*, 221–22.
[4] Whitelaw Reid to Donald Nicholson (of *New York Tribune* staff), 6 November 1903, Reid Papers; J. H. Woodward to Roosevelt, 14 December 1903, enclosing Scott C. Bone to Woodward, 11 December 1903, and Woodward to Bone, 14 December 1903, Roosevelt Papers; E. W. Keyes to Spooner, 17, 19 December 1903, Spooner Papers.

Charles G. Dawes recorded in his journal the substance of a visit he had had that day with Hanna. Dawes concluded that Hanna did not intend to become a candidate. Hanna "said that he had refused to become a candidate for the nomination notwithstanding the solicitation of J. P. Morgan, George F. Baker, J. J. Hill and other magnates whom he named, but had promised them that he would not advocate the nomination of Roosevelt before the convention, thus giving them the opportunity to get another candidate." Hanna was convinced, moreover, that nobody could defeat Roosevelt for the nomination. The Ohioan expressed bitterness toward the president, charging him with untruthfulness. Hanna stated, moreover, that he would not manage the campaign, "that if he did and won, Roosevelt would claim all credit and if he lost, Roosevelt would accord him all blame."[5]

The shallowness of Hanna's popular appeal became apparent in January 1904. In state after state Republican conventions endorsed Roosevelt.[6] Some delegates, nostalgic for an earlier day, announced that they personally favored Hanna, but they endorsed Roosevelt because the voters wanted it that way.[7] A few diehard businessmen, however, were not prepared to surrender. A group of ten railroad presidents publicly urged Hanna to run. Roosevelt expressed amused satisfaction upon learning that Hanna had to carry the burden of their endorsement.[8] This was a reminder to the public of the many caricatures of Hanna which Homer C. Davenport, cartoonist for the *New York Journal*, had produced, depicting Hanna as a "bloated money bag." In mid-January, W. Murray Crane of Massachusetts, soon to become a United States senator, wrote Lodge, "Senator Hanna is rapidly losing ground, and the impression is going out that he is

[5] Charles G. Dawes, *A Journal of the McKinley Years*, 361–63. Early in the previous year, John M. Maxwell, secretary to David M. Parry, president of the National Association of Manufacturers, stated, "Mr. Hanna is not as strong as he was with the business people, because of his flirting with Organized Labor." Maxwell to Albert J. Beveridge, 16 January 1903, Beveridge Papers.

[6] Harvey Polster, "Mark Hanna and the Republican Hierarchy, 1897–1904" (Master's thesis, University of Maryland, 1964), 108–09.

[7] *Washington Post*, 19 January 1904.

[8] Paul Morton to Roosevelt, 18 January 1904, and Roosevelt to Morton, 19 January 1904, Roosevelt Papers.

doing the party a real harm by his actions." Moreover, "I feel sure from what I can hear, that he also realizes it, and that he will make a definite statement soon which will clear the air." Crane believed that "The great thing for the President to do now, is to be as silent as possible."[9]

On February 15, 1904, Hanna died of typhoid fever, causing genuine and widespread sorrow. He had been a likeable, hard-working, decent political servant as he managed campaigns and collected party funds from industrialists. Professional politicians who had worked with him on the organizational level, from members of the National Committee down to small-fry local workers, felt the greatest sorrow, and some of them showed bitterness. They resented, among other things, Roosevelt's "domineering tactics" in making the 1904 platform.[10] Lodge reported to the president that when he arrived at the national convention hall in Chicago in June, "The old National Committee crowd were making their last struggle with the inevitable. . . . They had in the centre of the hall over the platform a perfectly colossal oil painting of Hanna, nothing of McKinley and little bits of lithographs of you stuck about in the flag clusters on the top gallery."[11]

A core of wealthy businessmen constituted the other potentially serious obstacle to the Roosevelt candidacy. This cabal was centered in Wall Street, but its power and influence fanned out into various bank-railroad-industrial centers. It was essentially a power struggle between Roosevelt on the one hand and on the other, J. P. Morgan, James J. Hill, Edward P. Harriman, their business empires, and the John D. Rockefeller-controlled Standard Oil Company.[12] To a lesser degree, it was a struggle between Roosevelt and those angry and fearful men who objected to his role in the 1902 anthracite coal strike.[13] Many other

[9] 15 January 1904, Lodge Papers.
[10] Joseph W. Blythe to Allison, 12 May 1904, Allison Papers.
[11] 25 June 1904, Roosevelt Papers.
[12] *New York Evening Post,* 12 June 1903; Franklin Murphy to Roosevelt, 9 October 1903, Roosevelt Papers; Platt to C. S. Mellen, 25 January 1904, Platt Papers.
[13] *New York Evening Post,* 12 June 1903; Lodge to Roosevelt, 2 June 1903, Roosevelt Papers; Whitelaw Reid to Roosevelt, 9 February, 14 July 1904, Reid Papers; Taft to Horace D. Taft, 4 August 1904, Taft Papers.

people just did not like Roosevelt personally, regarding him as bumptious, arrogant, overbearing, conceited, and a renegade from his own social class. A few newspapers, most notably the *New York Sun,* reflected a virulent anti-Roosevelt attitude.[14]

Roosevelt expressed bafflement as to why businessmen were angry over his role in the coal strike. They criticized him, he told his friend Joseph Bucklin Bishop of the *New York Commercial Advertiser,* for employing in his instructions to the anthracite coal commission, phraseology in one sentence which Elihu Root had provided him, and in another, phraseology "which both the operators and the miners had themselves used, substantially" in their requests to him. Bishop, in reply to Roosevelt's initial letter to him on the matter, declared, "It is insane, . . . I think it is inspired by Morgan and reflects his bitter personal feeling toward you. There is in his circle in Wall Street an undercurrent of hatred toward you of which this is a surface indication."[15]

The Wall Street-centered Roosevelt haters never really became an organized opposition. They had nowhere to go, no leadership, no program, no way to command a significant following, and no ready-made outside leader or party to which to turn. All they could do was threaten to withhold financial contributions to the election campaign, thereby increasing the power of William Jennings Bryan. These disgruntled Wall Streeters and their associates elsewhere, in considering various ideas aimed at preventing Roosevelt's election, demonstrated conspicuous political naiveté. They talked of an alignment with Bourbon Democrats through whom they would "buy" the Democratic party nomination, as Bryan described the move, and then deliver it to some trustworthy member of that party. Possible

[14] See, for example, an editorial, "Might Makes Right," in *New York Sun,* 22 April 1903; Paul Dana to Roosevelt, 15 November 1901, Roosevelt to Harrison Gray Otis, 5 August 1903, James R. Sheffield to Roosevelt, 30 January 1904, Roosevelt Papers.

[15] Roosevelt to Bishop, 13, 27 October 1902, Morison, *Letters,* 3: 349, 369; Bishop to Roosevelt, 25 October 1902, Roosevelt Papers. According to Bishop, at some time or other Morgan in person asked Roosevelt to "send your man to my man" to settle their differences. The only apparent indication that this meeting took place is the account in Joseph Bucklin Bishop, *Theodore Roosevelt and His Times, Shown in His Own Letters,* 1: 184–85.

recipients of their largesse were Grover Cleveland, Richard Olney, Arthur P. Gorman, and Alton B. Parker.[16] They even hoped
to persuade the Republican party to deny Roosevelt the nomination. They reasoned that through Mark Hanna, they could
"influence" the choice of convention delegates, especially those
from the South. And they pondered the possibility of rewarding
Hanna with the nomination.[17] A few talked about Spooner as a
nominee, but as Whitelaw Reid wrote in April 1903, "Spooner
seems to keep up very close relations at the White House for a
man really in training to oust the present incumbent."[18] Irate
anti-Roosevelt men also threatened to withhold campaign funds
if Roosevelt was nominated. C. S. Mellen, president of the
Northern Pacific Railroad, quoted J. P. Morgan as having stated
that the party could not raise as much as $10,000 in Wall Street
for the reelection of Roosevelt if he should be nominated.[19]

Roosevelt forces handled the unhappy Wall Street opposition
with consummate skill, and even the Democrats unwittingly
contributed mightily. The phalanx Roosevelt had at his command was truly impressive. In particular, he had the mighty
Senate Four, corporation lawyer Elihu Root, highly placed
Henry Cabot Lodge, and Whitelaw Reid's *New York Tribune*.
The role of the Roosevelt champions varied widely. The aging
and ailing O. H. Platt wrote long letters to sulking businessmen
and to his friend Flagg. Through Flagg, the senator had an especially good entrée into high places, for Flagg was a Standard
Oil Company attorney.[20] Elihu Root, highly respected in Wall
Street, was a great asset. In early February 1904, Root gave a
pro-Roosevelt address to the blue-ribbon New York Union
League Club. As Root himself later reported to a London friend,
"The Union League Club speech was designed to meet the very

[16] Bishop to Roosevelt, 29 January 1904, Roosevelt Papers; Charles E. Perkins to
Charles S. Hamlin, 2 April 1904, Hamlin Papers; *Wall Street Journal*, 18 February
1903.
[17] James S. Clarkson to Leigh S. J. Hunt, 9 October 1903, Clarkson Papers;
H. T. Dobbins to Roosevelt, 30 December 1903, and Roosevelt to Dobbins, 2
January 1904, Roosevelt Papers; Dawes, *Journal*, 361–62.
[18] Reid to I. N. Ford, 20 April 1903, Reid Papers.
[19] *New York Evening Post*, 12 June 1903.
[20] See in particular Platt to Simon J. Fox, 18 December 1903, and Platt to John
H. Flagg, 30 December 1903, Platt Papers.

insidious and dangerous attempt to undermine President Roosevelt's influence" led by the Northern Securities Company group and anti-labor union people.[21] Roosevelt also chose Root to deliver the keynote address at the national convention.

Aldrich was a little slow in giving unequivocal support to Roosevelt's candidacy, apparently not wishing to become involved in a political hassel with his Wall Street friends. He remained silent until it became apparent even to his anti-Roosevelt friends in the financial world that there was no realistic way to stop Roosevelt. In December 1903, the president asked George G. Hill, a *New York Tribune* correspondent, to obtain and publish statements from prominent members of Congress endorsing him. Hill told Roosevelt that he expected no definitely positive response from Aldrich but would make the attempt. Sure enough, Aldrich, unlike Spooner, Allison, and Platt, said that although he was in favor of the Roosevelt candidacy and would endorse it in practical, quiet ways, he felt it would be no advantage to Roosevelt for him to give out an interview endorsing him.[22] By the spring of 1904, however, Aldrich began to work for his political chief. He reminded Wall Streeters that Roosevelt was safer than any Democrat because of the tariff question. In a rare newspaper interview he said, "the fundamental difference between the two parties on the tariff question will be the principal, if not the only, issue of the campaign."[23]

In general, all members of the leadership gave every appearance of having the same view Lodge expressed in a letter to Roosevelt in the spring of 1903. Lodge had just spent three or four days in New York, where he had observed "some soreness in the group interested in the [Northern Securities Company] merger, but I think it is by no means general, even in Wall Street, . . . and is already subsiding." Lodge was certain that in the nation as a whole, by moving against the Northern Securities Company merger, the Roosevelt administration had been

[21] Root to J. St. Loe Stratchey, 23 March 1904, Root Papers; see also Whitelaw Reid to M. C. Seckendorf, 6 February 1904, Reid Papers; Philip C. Jessup, *Elihu Root*, 1: 415–16.

[22] George G. Hill memorandum, box 48, Biographer's Notes, Aldrich Papers.

[23] *New York Herald*, 5 May 1904; see also A. B. Shelton memorandum, box 48, Biographer's Notes, Aldrich Papers.

"immensely strengthened." The politically wise Lodge concluded with the reminder, "All that is necessary, I think, is to be careful that no idea should be given that we are entering on a general plan of harrying the corporations. There are some of our opponents who are only too anxious to give that impression, and we want to disabuse the public mind of it."[24]

Roosevelt took numerous steps of his own to assuage the feelings of distraught businessmen. Over and over again he emphasized his opposition to indiscriminate trustbusting, saying that in actuality he was friendly toward "good" trusts. The fact that the government until 1905 initiated no major trust suit following the indictment of the Northern Securities Company in 1902, except the one against the unpopular meat-packers, underscored Roosevelt's moderation.

The modest nature of the 1903 legislation on business, most notably the Elkins Antirebate Act and the Bureau of Corporations measure, afforded business interests no ground for angry complaint. The administrators of laws and regulations, moreover, were manifestly fair and friendly toward business. Likewise, Roosevelt took a conspicuously cautious, moderate position on the tariff, currency, and labor-employer questions. For the benefit of all those who feared violence and loss of property, Roosevelt pointed out on numerous occasions that his reform activity was a protection against anarchy and socialism. When, for example, the *New York Sun,* the coal operators, and other anti-labor union interests condemned his role in the anthracite coal strike, he asked, "Do they not realize that they are putting a very heavy burden on us who stand against socialism; against anarchic disorder?" Too, he wondered if these detractors found much comfort in the speeches of Bryan, Tom Johnson, and Richard Olney.[25]

Gradually, beginning early in 1903, Wall Streeters became more accustomed to Roosevelt's presence in the White House and had an opportunity to observe his basically moderate approach. Grenville M. Dodge, writing to Allison from New York about the tight money situation there, stated, "Roosevelt grows stronger

[24] 2 May 1903, Roosevelt Papers.
[25] Roosevelt to Joseph B. Bishop, 13 October 1902, Morison, *Letters,* 3: 349.

in New York all the time." He also remarked that Cleveland was "not as strong in the East as one would think from what the papers say," and if nominated "he would pretty nearly divide his party in two."[26]

Some newspaper editors demonstrated realism. The Republican newspapers of New York praised Roosevelt for his successful effort to create a Bureau of Corporations. The *Wall Street Journal* predicted that business interests eventually would be pleased with the publicity feature of the bureau's procedures.[27] Even the *New York Sun* had praise for Roosevelt. In discussing the publicity feature, that paper remarked that business interests were fortunate to have Roosevelt as president because they could trust him and the men he selected as administrators not to take undue advantage of the power to publicize corporate affairs.[28]

Even the Democratic papers of New York were gentle in their criticism of the Republican record. The *New York Herald* mildly suggested that the trust measures Congress had passed in the current session were of little use, but it had friendly words for the administration. "In the case of the Beef Trust and in the injunctions whereby he stopped discrimination in railway rates," the *Herald* editorialized, "Attorney General Knox demonstrated that many abuses can be remedied by the enforcement of the existing laws." In its discussion of a new law to improve the administration of the Sherman Act, the *Herald* quoted Knox as saying, "The law to expedite the hearing of cases and giving an appeal directly to the Supreme Court from the court of first instance assures within a reasonable time authoritative decisions, in the knowledge of which future legislation, if necessary, can be confidently framed."[29]

New York newspapers defended the Roosevelt-Knox indict-

[26] 4 May 1903, Allison Papers.

[27] 4 March 1903.

[28] 17 February 1903; see also *New York Evening Post,* 16, 17 February 1903; *New York Tribune,* 16 February 1903; *Wall Street Journal,* 18, 19, 24 February, 4 March, 4, 8, 10, 14 April 1903.

[29] 16 February 1903. There appears to be no available evidence to corroborate the statement made years later that at that time Roosevelt assured business interests, through Aldrich, that he would not seek further trust legislation. The supposed evidence for this in the Knox papers seems to be nonexistent.

ment of the Northern Securities Company. In June 1903, the *Wall Street Journal* discussed the matter in an article entitled "Sober Second Thoughts." "Quite apart from the fact that the Northern Securities scheme was illegal, it is certain," the *Journal* declared, "that the check given to this form of enterprise was salutary from every point of view." It asked, in the light of recent evidence of "reckless finance," where the nation might "be today if the law had not been set in motion against the Northern Securities Company? . . . Suppose, for instance that we had had a flood of Securities Companies doing business in all parts of the country as was threatened for a while after the organization of the Northern Securities Company." The result, the *Journal* felt, would have been a "carnival of speculation and a manufacture of securities on an unheard of scale," and the ultimate result, "a panic of extraordinary severity." Because that did not occur, "A great many people who cried out against what they affected to regard as an attack upon property interests have today cause for heartfelt gratitude that halt was made when it was made."[30] On the same day, the *New York Evening Post* quoted a "very prominent foreign banker" as saying that while the president "may have enemies" in Wall Street, "he has just as strong friends." Many cautious Wall Street men who found "the Northern Securities litigation . . . a bitter pill to swallow at the time, . . . see it in a new light now, since the over issue of securities has been plainly demonstrated."[31] Three days later, banking editor William J. Boies of the *Post* assured Roosevelt that the "merger litigation has been a veritable boomerang in your favor, even in the section where the bitterest opposition arose."[32]

Ever since the 1902 indictment of the company, Roosevelt himself had remained almost silent on the subject. His defenders, however, sobered unhappy Wall Streeters by pointedly asking them if they preferred that he deliberately avoid his responsibility as a law enforcer and wink aside the laws they happened not to like. The *Wall Street Journal* reminded the financial world of its stake in law enforcement and of Roosevelt's record in that

[30] 12 June 1903.
[31] 12 June 1903. For the same view on overissues of securities see Platt to Simon J. Fox, 18 December 1903, Platt Papers.
[32] 15 June 1903, Roosevelt Papers.

regard. "Wall Street should remember" the *Journal* emphasized, "that of all sections of the body politic none is more dependent upon the law than itself." Roosevelt, it added, "has ever stood for rigid execution of the law without fear or favor."[33] In March 1904, the United States Supreme Court declared that the formation of the Northern Securities Company was in violation of the Sherman Act. The Roosevelt administration's "attack on Wall Street" was thereby vindicated.[34]

Whitelaw Reid, who cherished his position as ambassador to Great Britain and wanted very much to be reappointed to that position, did what he could through letters and through his *New York Tribune* to help the Roosevelt cause. In a letter written in September 1903 to his friend and neighbor Mrs. W. S. Cowles, who was Roosevelt's sister, Reid reported on Edward H. Harriman's recent remarks when a guest at the Reid home. According to Reid, Harriman had not only come to Roosevelt's defense but claimed he was also trying to persuade Morgan to support the president. "Mr. Harriman casually mentioned to me that he had seen Mr. Pierpont Morgan the previous day" and that Morgan was unhappy about the policy of the administration. Moreover, Morgan had predicted that the moneyed classes would refuse to give Roosevelt the necessary financial support and that a Cleveland Democrat would win the presidency. "Mr. Harriman went on to say that he had suggested to Mr. Morgan the overwhelming probability that the President would be nominated, and the certainty that it was to the interest of the moneyed classes to have the Republican nominee elected rather than take their chances with the Democracy." Harriman "then intimated that at present the labor unions seemed to be putting the President under more obligations to them than to the capitalists, and that it seemed to him to the interests of the capitalists to relieve that situation, and have at least as much claim upon him as the labor unions would have."[35] In October 1903, James S. Clarkson reported that "Generally speaking, aside from the Rockefellers and Goulds, the feeling toward the President has

---

[33] 18 February 1903; see also Platt to Simon J. Fox, 18 December 1903, Platt Papers.
[34] *New York Tribune*, 15 March 1904.
[35] 14 September 1903, Reid Papers.

been growing better in New York among the high financiers."[36]

By January 1904, even before Hanna died, the anti-Roosevelt movement among the financiers completely collapsed. In fact, no Republican and very few Democrats showed any indication of taking on the unenviable chore of engaging Roosevelt in political combat. Moreover, as William Howard Taft said, even if someone managed to obtain the nomination in place of Roosevelt, that person would go to defeat at the polls "because it would inevitably follow that the person so nominated would be nominated because he had yielded to the undue influence of speculating capitalists in Wall Street."[37] Mrs. Whitelaw Reid did her bit by remarking at a dinner party of influential New Yorkers that she "thought the thing for the business men to do was to stop talking about their injured feelings and go to work to keep the Republican party in." She warned them that though "they themselves would no doubt vote the Republican ticket . . . their violent talk would keep others from doing so."[38]

By the end of January, there was a near stampede to the Roosevelt banner. Joseph B. Bishop reported to Roosevelt that "Everybody, including some of the bitterest of your enemies whom I have known, are now saying that your nomination is certain and they are afraid your election is equally certain." He felt that the anti-Roosevelt *New York Sun* and certain Wall Streeters had overplayed their cards. "Bryan rubbed it in finally when . . . he charged that the moneyed interests had been trying to buy the Democratic nomination. This had effect only because of its absolute truth." Bishop ended, "With all my heart I congratulate you."[39] O. H. Platt's friend Flagg reported on Bryan's devastating jibes at Wall Street. "The Republicans here," he said, "are exultant, while the Democrats are correspondingly crestfallen." Flagg could not see how it was possible in the Democratic party "to reconcile the radical differences of the

[36] Clarkson to Leigh S. J. Hunt, 9 October 1903, Clarkson Papers.

[37] Taft to William M. Butler, 5 February 1904, Taft Papers.

[38] Elizabeth Mills Reid to Anna Cowles, 26 January 1904, enclosed in Cowles to Roosevelt, 29 January 1904, Roosevelt Papers.

[39] Joseph B. Bishop to Roosevelt, 29 January 1904, Roosevelt Papers; see also Bishop to Roosevelt, 19 January 1904, ibid.; E. W. Keyes to Spooner, 31 January 1904, Spooner Papers.

two wings" unless Bryan "should turn tail, and he does not appear to know enough to do that."[40]

There was no sensible move left for Wall Streeters if they wished to influence the 1904 election outcome, other than to help Roosevelt defeat the Democrats. They contributed huge sums to that end. The Roosevelt forces, in turn, made several gestures of friendliness toward Wall Streeters. Besides having Root as keynote speaker at the National Convention, they chose the trustworthy Cortelyou to manage the campaign. The convention choice of wealthy, colorless Senator Charles W. Fairbanks of Indiana for second place on the ticket was also a concession to them. Lodge, reporting to Roosevelt on the nomination, said, "Harriman . . . insisted on Fairbanks."[41] An inexperienced delegate, in seconding the Fairbanks nomination, amused his audience with the pronouncement that his constituency "realizes that sound money makes sound banks, and sound banks make Senator Fairbanks."[42]

On the broader front, Roosevelt and his cohorts performed with the same skill they had employed with the petulant Hanna and with uneasy business leaders. Roosevelt presented an adroitly constructed formula to attract voters, summed up in the phrase "A square deal for every man."[43] The term "Square Deal" caught the fancy of the public. It graphically described the feelings of hosts of people who looked to government to insure and advance the well-being of the deserving. In this era of relative prosperity, voters welcomed the generalized, inspirational aspects of Roosevelt's Square Deal and his dedication to moderate reform and to law and order. They agreed with him that these ingredients of the Square Deal were the best possible defense for their security and prosperity against such extremists as un-

---

[40] John H. Flagg to Platt, 30 January 1904, Platt Papers; see also letters to Platt from Flagg, 5 February 1904, Charles F. Brooker, 18 January 1904, C. S. Mellen, 25 January 1904, ibid.; to Roosevelt from Henry Clews, 19 January 1904, James R. Sheffield, 30 January 1904, Jacob H. Schiff, 31 January 1904, Roosevelt Papers; Thomas Dolan to Root, 5 February 1904, and Root to Henry White, 26 February 1904, Root Papers; Whitelaw Reid to Moreton Frewen, 14 January 1904, to R. L. Fearn, 28 January 1904, to M. C. Seckendorf, 6 February 1904, to Roosevelt, 9 February 1904, Reid Papers.

[41] Lodge to Roosevelt, 25 June 1904, Roosevelt Papers.

[42] Quoted in Claude G. Bowers, *Beveridge and the Progressive Era*, 209–10.

[43] Roosevelt to Ray Stannard Baker, 27 August 1904, Morison, *Letters*, 4: 908.

restrained monopolists, irresponsible labor leaders, corrupt political bosses, anarchists, and socialists. Roosevelt's vigor and record of accomplishment elevated the Square Deal above mere demagoguery and platitudes.

Roosevelt decided it was unnecessary and unwise for him to "take to the road" during the 1904 campaign. He already had made many public appearances and statements. He did not reveal a specific program until after the votes were counted, lest he create controversy and thereby lose more supporters than he gained. He and his friends worked hard to produce a platform couched in terms as innocuous as possible. The president dominated the preconvention platform construction, relying heavily on the counsel of the Senate Four. He also employed the political skill of Lodge, who assembled the various proposed planks for the platform. Roosevelt virtually ignored the Hanna men on the National Committee, much to their annoyance.[44]

Root, meanwhile, worked on his convention address. As an administrator in both the McKinley and the Roosevelt administrations and as a corporation lawyer and close friend of "trustbuster" Roosevelt, Root symbolized the traditional Republican consensus. He wrote his speech to reflect the continuity in the McKinley-Roosevelt regimes.[45] At the convention itself, Root and Lodge were particularly active and conspicuous in their promotion of Roosevelt. Following the convention, the elated Lodge wrote to Roosevelt, "Root says that after the way in which he and I strained and racked our consciences in what we said of you in speech and platform it will be necessary for us to join some church which is able to give full absolution."[46]

In general, the platform as adopted reflected the party hierarchy's views.[47] The only people who could be offended by the statements on such supposedly controversial issues as the tariff, currency, and the trusts were Democrats and the reformers whose

[44] *New York World*, 3 May 1904; Lodge to Platt, 11 May 1904, and Platt to Lodge, 16 May 1904, Platt Papers; J. W. Blythe to Allison, 20 May 1904, Allison Papers.

[45] Roosevelt to Root, 2 June 1904, and telegram and letter, 14 June 1904, Morison, *Letters*, 4: 812, 833; Philip C. Jessup, *Elihu Root*, 1: 421–22.

[46] Lodge to Roosevelt, 25 June 1904, Roosevelt Papers.

[47] Kirk H. Porter and Donald J. Johnson, *National Party Platforms, 1840–1956*, 137–43.

proposals were ignored. The platform included no call for new legislation on the touchy railroad rate question. It did, however, give cursory attention to the Negro disfranchisement question, despite a desire on the part of the leadership to ignore this pressing matter.

Party leaders gave particular attention to the tariff issue. They began on that problem early. Clearly, they all wished to keep the issue out of Congress as long as possible. They scrutinized carefully the various proposals before them, including the late McKinley's reciprocity approach and most particularly the Iowa Idea. Although the popularity of the latter was in decline, the leaders wished to make certain that the convention did not give it any attention.[48] They were very solicitous of Joseph W. Blythe, Allison's chief state political aide. An unfounded rumor circulated that Roosevelt intended to place railroad attorney Blythe in charge of the campaign in all the western states. Such a move would constitute a warning to the Iowa tariff-reform crowd and would also please the railroad interests.[49]

Roosevelt showed great caution on the tariff question when he advised Root on his keynote speech. Upon receipt of a rough draft of the speech and Root's request for suggested alterations, the president wired, "Speech admirable in every way. Have no suggestion to make except that instead of saying 'The tariff will presently need revision' it might be better to say, 'The tariff *may* presently need revision and if so should receive it at the hands of the friends and not the enemies of the protective system.'" On the same day, he also wrote a letter to Root, mostly on appointment matters but with a brief tariff statement included. "I do not believe that the platform will *declare* for tariff revision," he said, "but I think it will leave the door *open* for tariff revision, and I wanted your speech to be along the same

[48] On preparation of the tariff plank, see: Lodge to Roosevelt, 2 May 1903, 6 June 1904, Roosevelt Papers; Roosevelt to Allison, 5 May 1904, and Lodge to Allison, 5, 11, 18 May 1904, Allison Papers; Ebenezer J. Hill to Platt, 10 May 1904, and Platt to Hill, 12 May 1904, Platt Papers; Roosevelt to Lodge, 8 June 1904, and Roosevelt to Henry C. Hansbrough, 15 June 1904, Morison, *Letters*, 4: 824–25, 834.

[49] Lloyd Bowers to Taft, 15 April 1904, enclosed in Taft to Roosevelt, 18 April 1904, and J. E. Forbes to Roosevelt, 5 March 1904, enclosing clipping from *St. Louis Globe Democrat*, 2 March 1904, Roosevelt Papers.

lines." Both Root's speech and the platform reflected Roosevelt's views.[50]

The party leaders gave only routine attention to the other major economic questions, the trusts and the currency. On those matters, no insurgency within the Republican party threatened, and the McKinley-Roosevelt administration was in a somewhat better position to "point with pride" to a record of achievement than was the case with the tariff. They proudly reminded the public of the Gold Standard Act, the Bureau of Corporations, and the Northern Securities Company case. They could also heap scorn upon the Democratic party for its poor record and point out Democratic flirtation with the free-silver panacea.

Republican leaders had no remedy for the Negro disfranchisement movement in southern and border states, no proposals to end lynchings and burnings or alleviate the economic plight of the great mass of Negroes. Lower echelon Republicans were, however, able to insert a moderate plan for action in the 1904 platform. It called upon Congress to implement the clause in the Fourteenth Amendment which provided that states which unconstitutionally deprived Negroes of the franchise were subject to a corresponding reduction in their numerical representation in the House of Representatives.[51] Since 1900, Indiana's Congressman Edgar D. Crumpacker had been the chief sponsor of this plan, appropriately called "Crumpackerism."[52]

Roosevelt and his close advisers on the race question believed the proposal was morally right but that it could spell nothing but trouble for both the Republican party and race relations. The president appeared to feel that if he asked Congress to act on it, his party colleagues there would engage in a disruptive, fruitless wrangle that would end in a humiliating defeat for him and a setback for the Negroes. Sectional antagonism and racial feeling would grow in intensity, diminishing progress for Negroes through the mutual efforts of North and South, whites and Negroes. Lodge, who had suffered a bitter defeat in Congress

[50] Roosevelt to Root, 14 June 1904 (telegram and letter), Morison, *Letters,* 4: 833; see also Roosevelt to Root, 2 June 1904, ibid., 812; Porter and Johnson, *Platforms,* 138.

[51] Porter and Johnson, *Platforms,* 137–43.

[52] John B. Wiseman, "Dilemmas of a Party out of Power: The Democracy, 1904–1912" (Ph.D. dissertation, University of Maryland, 1967), 25.

back in 1890 when he sponsored the Force bill, a Negro franchise measure, shared Roosevelt's apprehension over Crumpackerism. He wrote to the president, "The proposition is an absolutely righteous one, but your objection and mine still holds that
it is demanding something in all probability we shall not have
the nerve to do."[53] Roosevelt replied in similar vein. "I am sorry
they put in the suffrage plank," he said, "just as I should depre-
cate a plank endorsing your old so-called 'force bill,' which I believed in thoroughly as a matter of abstract right, but which there
is no use in backing when we are perfectly certain to be unable
to carry it through."[54]

Booker T. Washington argued that congressional enactment of
Crumpackerism would actually reduce Negro suffrage because
it would lead to increased Negro disfranchisement in the border
areas. States there would be willing to take a slight reduction in
congressional representation in order to rid themselves legally of
their strong pockets of Negro political power.[55] "The minute Congress recognizes the right to the reduction of representation, on
the account of color," Washington declared, "that minute our
case will grow worse."[56] Washington felt that rather than legalize disfranchisement, as the Crumpacker approach would do, it
would be preferable to have Congress investigate and act upon
individual cases where it appeared that fraudulent voting practices prevailed.[57]

Washington opposed anything that might lead to racial strife.
He had close ties with northern educators, publicists, and philanthropists, whom he was trying to interest in the Negro. Racial
unrest, he also believed, would discourage northern investors in
the South. He reminded Roosevelt, "There is a large amount of
Northern capital invested in Southern enterprises, and this makes
a large element in the North sensitive about anything that stirs
up the South." He further pointed out that if Roosevelt appeared
to be closely allied with Negroes, he would weaken his position
with labor unions, for employers tended to hire Negro laborers

[53] 25 June 1904, Roosevelt Papers.
[54] 28 June 1904, Morison, *Letters*, 4: 849.
[55] Washington to T. Thomas Fortune, care of Phil Waters, 22 November 1904,
Booker T. Washington Papers.
[56] Washington to John C. Dancy, 28 November 1904, Washington Papers.
[57] Washington to Roosevelt, 10 August 1904, Roosevelt Papers.

to replace white laborers who were on strike.[58] He advised Roosevelt to make no reference whatsoever to the "Southern question" in his "formal letter of acceptance."[59]

Roosevelt revealed the complexity of his feelings on the racial problem in an exchange of letters with his friend Lyman Abbott, editor of *Outlook* magazine. Abbott was on close terms with Booker T. Washington and was emphatic in his opposition to the suffrage plank on the grounds that it would foolishly arouse southern enmity.[60] On August 8, 1904, Roosevelt wrote Abbott that "though I have permitted myself the luxury of uttering my indignation privately to you and some other good friends, you will notice that during all the time I have been President and in the years before, I have never said a harsh thing of the South, and I have done my level best so to handle myself as to divide the [Benjamin R.] Tillman and [J. K.] Vardaman types from their antitypes."[61] Privately the president expressed more anger at white southerners than did Abbott, although he was careful to exempt certain individuals from his attacks. Roosevelt emphasized that to accept the current Negro disfranchisement as permanent was out of the question. He held as intolerable a system that denied the vote to illiterate Negroes but not to illiterate whites. After stating that "the thing that astounds me is the queer dough-faced indifference with which the North submits on this matter," Roosevelt proceeded to illustrate his feeling by citing the example of Congressman John Sharp Williams of Mississippi. Williams represented a district of 48,000 whites and 143,000 Negroes, but the whites there, Roosevelt pointed out, "suppressed this colored vote so absolutely by force, by fraud, by every species of iniquity" that it is pointless, "after the Democrats have nominated their candidate," for either a Negro or a white man to vote. "At the last election Williams did not have a single vote against him and but 1400 for him." What is more, "this man

[58] Ibid.

[59] Washington to Roosevelt, 29 July 1904, ibid.

[60] Abbott to Roosevelt, 4 August 1904, enclosing *Outlook* editorial dated 12 March 1904, and Abbott to Roosevelt, 17 December 1904, enclosing *Outlook* editorial dated 13 December 1904, Roosevelt Papers. Among other notable opponents of the Negro suffrage plank were Henry S. Pritchett and Whitelaw Reid. See: Pritchett to Roosevelt, 6 December 1904, Roosevelt Papers; Reid to Henry E. Tremaine, 15 December 1904, Reid Papers.

[61] Roosevelt Papers.

comes to Congress and declaims against our policy in the Philippines on the ground that it is a contravention of the Declaration
of Independence and of 'the consent of the governed' theory"
but "represents those who would deny to the negro, not only the
right to vote, but the right to hold any office or do any work
which a white man wants to hold or to do."[62]

But in 1904 Roosevelt, in his public statements and performance, was being very much the politician, and nothing transpired to convince him that it would be good politics to stir up
the Negro question. When moderates such as Booker T. Washington and Lyman Abbott exuded great caution on the matter
and such old political hands as Lodge and the Senate Four did
likewise, it was not surprising that Roosevelt failed to launch a
crusade of righteousness and justice for the Negro.

Although the president's decision to deliver no campaign
speeches made it easy for him to escape public discussion of
the race question, he felt it imperative to say something about
the overall problem in his public letter of acceptance of the
nomination, but even then he avoided a direct reference to the
suffrage plank.[63] Employing the counsel of Booker T. Washington, Spooner, Root, and others in the preparation of his letter,
Roosevelt discussed important public questions in detail, giving
special attention to the tariff.[64] Incidental to his lengthy remarks
about the Philippines, where he said we have "been true to the
spirit of the fourteenth amendment," he reminded the public that
"at home the principles of the fourteenth and fifteenth amendments have been in effect nullified."[65]

In a personal letter to railroad president John Byrne, Roosevelt disclosed some of his thinking on the race question prior to
writing his letter of acceptance. "What I have decided to do [in
the letter of acceptance] is this: Not to commit myself to any
policy at all, and to touch the issue as lightly as I can without
seeming to dodge it, and then simply to say that we can solve

[62] Roosevelt to Abbott, 26 July 1904, Morison, *Letters,* 4: 866–68.
[63] Spooner to Roosevelt, 15, 22 August 1904, enclosing memorandum; Roosevelt
to Spooner, 26 August 1904; Roosevelt to Booker T. Washington, 29 August, 10
September 1904—all in Roosevelt Papers.
[64] "Letter of Acceptance," Roosevelt to Cannon, 12 September 1904, Morison,
Letters, 4: 921–43.
[65] Ibid., 941–42.

the complex color problem here at home[66] only if we approach it in the spirit with which Governor Taft and Luke Wright, ex-Confederate, have done their work in the Philippines." Thus, he pointed out, "by this I do not promise any legislation or executive action by the federal Government, and I hold up a Democrat and an ex-Confederate as a man upon whose actions we should model ours." Roosevelt added, "I feel far too deeply on this subject to be willing to make it an issue for partisan advantage." He concluded, "Not to get the election would I say one word that would add difficulty to the work of those, like Judge [Thomas G.] Jones, a life-long Democrat in Alabama, who are honestly working for the solution of the color problem in the South."[67]

Roosevelt succeeded in his goal to "touch the issue lightly" without actually "seeming to dodge it." His acceptance letter helped dampen Crumpackerism as a popular issue in the North, and, at the same time, the friendly, respectful recognition he gave to Negro citizens brought an enthusiastic response from Booker T. Washington. In his effort not to dodge the issue altogether, Roosevelt wrote in general terms of the American dream. "This government," he said, "is based upon the fundamental idea that each man, no matter what his occupation, his race, or his religious belief, is entitled to be treated on his worth as a man and neither favored nor discriminated against because of any accident of his position."[68] Washington immediately indicated to the president that these words were "so strong, fundamental and comprehensive" that he thought they should be "re-written on White House paper for lithographing" and "appear with the President's signature, in all the best Negro newspapers in . . .

[66] He originally wrote "in our southern states," but crossed it out and inserted the words "at home."

[67] 31 August 1904; see also Roosevelt to Byrne, 13 August 1904, to Booker T. Washington, 18, 29 August, 10 September 1904, 9 March 1905, including clipping from *New York Evening Post*, 14 February 1905—all in Roosevelt Papers; "Address at the Lincoln Dinner of the Republican Club of the City of New York, February 13, 1905," in Hermann Hagedorn, ed., *The Works of Theodore Roosevelt*, 16: 343; Thomas Robert Cripps, "The Lily White Republicans: The Negro, the Party, and the South in the Progressive Era" (Ph.D. dissertation, University of Maryland, 1967), 106–08.

[68] "Letter of Acceptance," Roosevelt to Cannon, 12 September 1904, Morison, *Letters*, 4: 929.

the country." Furthermore, he felt they should be "put in an attractive form for hanging upon walls" and put in "sections of the country where it would accomplish much good."[69] Washington did not, however, request for his lithograph the sentence that followed in Roosevelt's letter. This sentence included the remark that even in America "there is painful difficulty in the effort to realize this ideal" that every man "is entitled to be treated on his worth as a man."[70]

Despite his restraint on the Negro question, white southern Democrats in the campaign were indignant at Roosevelt for the recognition he gave Negroes and at the party in general for the suffrage plank in the platform. Many newspapers carried on an effective campaign on both these issues.[71] In Maryland, beginning in 1903, Democrat Arthur P. Gorman used the famous Booker T. Washington-Roosevelt dinner to advance his disfranchisement effort and to discredit Roosevelt. At a meeting in Baltimore, he showed pictures on a screen of the president and Washington dining together and charged the president with trying to force social equality with Negroes. Gorman told his audience that he "wanted to know what the President and Booker T. Washington talked about when they lunched together."[72] In Maryland and in several other states, Democratic workers passed out large campaign buttons depicting a Negro dining with President Roosevelt, with the word "Equality" inscribed on it.[73]

Some Negro Republicans also attempted to build political strength by circulating "Equality" buttons and pictures.[74] One of these buttons, which pictured Washington and Roosevelt dining together, was almost identical to the one Democrats circu-

[69] Washington to William Loeb (secretary to Roosevelt), 15 September 1904, Roosevelt Papers.

[70] "Letter of Acceptance," Roosevelt to Cannon, 12 September 1904, Morison, *Letters*, 4: 929.

[71] Wiseman, "Party out of Power," 24–25.

[72] *Cleveland Gazette*, 14 November 1903.

[73] Roosevelt to Lyman Abbott, 29 October 1903, Morison, *Letters*, 3: 639; Roosevelt to Silas McBee, 15 December 1904, Roosevelt Papers; *Chicago Post*, 14 January 1904, in clipping books, Washington Papers.

[74] *Chicago Examiner*, 18 September 1903; *Cincinnati Enquirer*, 24 September 1903; *Norfolk Virginia Pilot*, 26 August 1904—all in clipping books, Washington Papers.

lated among white voters.[75] When white peddlers from the North sold pictures of the dinner to southern Negroes, Mississippi Congressman Thomas Spight declared in the House of Representatives that these vendors should be lynched. The dinner, Spight said, "had done more to inflame the passions of the Negro and give him a perverted idea of his importance and his near approach to social equality than anything that had been done in the last ten years." In his opinion Washington should have had sense and self-respect enough to refuse the invitation.[76] An Indianola, Mississippi, sheriff arrested agents selling the pictures "for violating the obscene literature law."[77] In their respective campaigns, both Negro Republicans and white Democrats used pictures and buttons depicting Roosevelt leading an assault of Negro troops up San Juan Hill.[78]

Roosevelt was bitterly disappointed with this display of southern bigotry and the obvious failure of his attempt to revive the Republican party in the South through moderation. In the election, Roosevelt received less popular support in the former Confederacy than had McKinley four years previously, in contrast to his stunning victory in the North. Negro disfranchisement had made inroads into the Republican strength in the South and it was spreading further.

In an exasperated letter to Robert U. Johnson, a *Century Magazine* editor, the frustrated Roosevelt blamed on others some of his failure to create harmony in the South. Referring to Roosevelt's election victory, Johnson had hopefully suggested to the president, "The solemnity of the exceptional tribute to you from the people [in the North] will I am sure move you to a magnanimity toward the South which will break up what is left of a dangerous sectionalism."[79] The president curtly replied, "For three years I have been more than magnanimous towards the South; and the dangerous sectionalism has gone on . . . and I

[75] See campaign button and picture collection, Smithsonian Institution, Washington, D. C.

[76] *Baltimore Evening Herald,* 17 March 1904.

[77] *Washington Times,* 11 March 1904, and *Baltimore Sun,* 12 March 1904, in Theodore Roosevelt Scrap-Book, 4 January–1 April [1904], Roosevelt Papers.

[78] *Hartford* (Connecticut) *Courant,* 3 September 1904, and *Chicago Post,* 14 January 1904, in clipping books, Washington Papers.

[79] Robert Underwood Johnson to Roosevelt, 11 November 1904, Roosevelt Papers.

think partly because men like you in the North have hesitated to speak as you ought to have done about this attitude in the South."[80] To those with whom he had worked during the past three years on the Negro question, Roosevelt wrote with sadness and with obvious bafflement over what course to pursue next.[81]

Roosevelt held the prevailing view that his own party as well as the Democratic party had pursued the wrong course after Lincoln's death. He felt that his own trouble with the southern question emphasized the "infinite damage done in reconstruction days by the unregenerate arrogance and shortsightedness of the southerners, and the doctrinaire folly of radicals like [Charles] Sumner and [Thaddeus] Stevens."[82] Crumpackerism was a modern expression of the spirit of the Radicals. The older Republicans who still remained active in the party felt more kinship to the Reconstruction Radicals than did Roosevelt and his cohorts. The older group put Crumpackerism in the 1904 platform. Professional politician Roosevelt knew how to round up Negro convention delegates and how to flatter Booker T. Washington, but he did not know how to attain the more difficult goal of equality for the Negroes or harmony between the North and the South. On the other hand, he was not quite prepared to abandon hope. In early 1905, in the course of an exchange of letters with Root about the plight of the Armenians in Turkey, Roosevelt informed Root, "I have plenty of evils to fight here at home, evils connected with race prejudice, especially against the negro, evils connected with the tyranny of corporations and the tyranny of the labor unions."[83] He devoted much thought to those very matters, but on the Negro question he took no militant stand, had no comprehensive program to offer. He did, however, continue to appeal to the decency of moderate southern whites, decry lynching, support the educational efforts of Booker T.

[80] Roosevelt to Johnson, 12 November 1904, Morison, *Letters,* 4: 1030.
[81] Roosevelt to Henry S. Pritchett, 14 December 1904, ibid., 1066–72; Roosevelt to Pritchett, 26 December 1904, Roosevelt Papers; Roosevelt to James Ford Rhodes, 15 December 1904, Morison, *Letters,* 4: 1072–73; Roosevelt to Nicholas Murray Butler, 20 December 1904, Roosevelt Papers.
[82] Roosevelt to James Ford Rhodes, 29 November 1904, Morison, *Letters,* 4: 1050.
[83] Roosevelt to Root, 13 May 1905, ibid., 1175.

Washington, and appoint a few more Negroes to minor federal positions.

At the state level in 1904, two key Republican leaders faced crucial problems. Republican insurgency and the Democratic bid for power forced Spooner's career into a sharp and fatal decline in Wisconsin and administered a severe blow to Aldrich's political machine in Rhode Island. Spooner's predicament was the more critical.

For a few months in 1903 and until May 1904, Republican Stalwarts believed the Insurgency had run its course. In February 1904, Philip L. Spooner wrote his brother, "In every county there is an unquestionable defection from LaFollette."[84] The Stalwarts took heart from the fact that LaFollette had been unable to secure a rate-making railroad commission and the type of primary election law he had sought. In a test of strength, the Stalwarts mistakenly believed they could administer a *coup de grace* to LaFollette, whose house of cards, they thought, was resting on a mound of sand. They grossly underestimated LaFollette's power and attempted to demonstrate their strength at the May 1904 regular state convention. Much to their consternation and anger, however, LaFollette dominated the convention. The Stalwarts claimed that the Insurgents, operating through the Insurgent-dominated State Central Committee, had deprived them of their rightful representation. Thereupon, they walked out and held a rump convention of their own, claiming it was the legal one. Thus two separate conventions selected two separate slates of candidates for state offices, adopted two separate state platforms, and selected two separate delegations to the national convention.[85]

The battle over delegates to the national convention brought the Spooner-LaFollette battle to national attention. It also brought President Roosevelt, other prominent national party

[84] 8 February 1904; see also letters to Spooner from: Philip L. Spooner, 23 April 1904, Joseph W. Babcock, 20 September 1903, John Luchsinger, 13 December 1903, Edwin D. Coe, 21 December 1903, 19 March 1904, E. W. Keyes, 17, 21 February 1904, R. S. Cowie, 22 March 1904, Spooner Papers.

[85] Russel B. Nye, *Midwestern Progressive Politics: A Historical Study of Its Origins and Development, 1870–1958*, 175; Harold U. Faulkner, *Politics, Reform and Expansion, 1890–1900*, 46; Dorothy Ganfield Fowler, *John Coit Spooner: Defender of Presidents*, 303–06.

leaders, and the national party organization into the controversy. The credentials committee had to decide between the LaFollette delegates and the Spooner delegates, both pro-Roosevelt. The president viewed the Wisconsin situation as "very, very ugly" and declared, "I am at my wit's end how to keep out of it."[86] From neighboring Iowa, Blythe wrote to Allison, "In Wisconsin I do not see what is left for the conservative element except the right of revolution."[87]

Roosevelt and the party leaders feared a Republican split in Wisconsin would enable the Democrats to carry the state. They felt a personal friendship for Spooner, though they did not like the way he handled LaFollette. They believed that compromise was in order and Spooner stubbornly refused to compromise.[88] On the other hand, Roosevelt and the Republican leadership took a dim view of LaFollette, who was a political nuisance to them. Nicholas Murray Butler wrote Roosevelt in May 1904 that "LaFollette is made out of the same sort of stuff as [Hazon S.] Pingree was and as Bryan is. He is more or less of a fanatic and cannot be conciliated by any ordinary methods,"[89] to which Roosevelt replied, "In my judgment you read LaFollette exactly right when you compare him to Pingree."[90] The late Pingree, as Republican mayor of Detroit and governor of Michigan, had ignored the leaders of his own party in fighting what seemed to him to be the corrupt alliance between business and politics in his party.[91]

Roosevelt turned the Wisconsin problem over to a group of seasoned eastern politicians—Aldrich, Reid, Lodge, and William E. Chandler—hoping they could work out a compromise. When a delegation of LaFollette supporters called on the president to present their side of the story, he sent them to Aldrich. The spokesman for the Insurgent group, Irvine Lenroot, recalled that "After I had talked about twenty minutes Aldrich

[86] Roosevelt to Nicholas Murray Butler, 21 May 1904, Morison, *Letters*, 4: 802.
[87] 20 May 1904, Allison Papers.
[88] Roosevelt to Platt, 9 December 1903, and Platt to J. Kean, 23 May 1904, Platt Papers; Roosevelt to Spooner, 14, 25 January, 10 April 1904, Spooner Papers.
[89] 19 May 1904, Roosevelt Papers.
[90] Roosevelt to Butler, 21 May 1904, Morison, *Letters*, 4: 802.
[91] Nye, *Midwestern Progressive Politics*, 175; see also Roosevelt to Lodge, 21 October 1896, Morison, *Letters*, 1: 563.

interrupted me and said, 'I don't think that I care to hear any more. To be frank with you I don't care a damn about the merits of your case but I want Roosevelt to carry Wisconsin and as a matter of practical politics I would like to see the matter of delegates compromised.'" Aldrich ended with a promise to "'see Spooner and see if I can get him to call off the fight inasmuch as you say your slate of delegates will also support Roosevelt.'"[92]

The Aldrich-Reid-Lodge-Chandler group, with the concurrence of Roosevelt, hoped that the Wisconsin contestants would accept a compromise, each agreeing to have half its delegation seated at the convention. But much to the annoyance of the negotiators, Spooner flatly refused to accept the arrangement. The canny LaFollette agreed to it and doubtless thereby acquired some goodwill with the national leaders and among the voters.[93] The contest then went to the convention's credentials committee, where Spooner's high position in the national party insured him victory. None of the Insurgent delegates obtained official recognition, but LaFollette had gained a moral victory and in the long run a political victory. It was far more important to him that he win reelection to the governorship than that his pro-Roosevelt delegates be seated at the national convention.

Flushed with victory, the Spooner Stalwarts injudiciously requested an injunction from the Wisconsin Supreme Court to bar the LaFollette ticket from the official ballot as a legal Republican party slate. "It is not a struggle for leadership, power or patronage among Republicans with whom I am acting," Spooner insisted, but "a struggle to prevent the disintegration and Bryanization of the Republican party in Wisconsin."[94] He and the other Stalwart lawyers discovered, however, that it was

[92] In "Memoirs of Irvine Lenroot," Irvine L. Lenroot Papers; see also William Loeb to Aldrich, 27 May 1904, Aldrich Papers; Belle Case LaFollette and Fola LaFollette, *Robert LaFollette*, 1: 178–79.

[93] William E. Chandler to Aldrich, 4 June 1904, Aldrich Papers; Chandler to Robert M. LaFollette, 15 March 1905, copy in Aldrich Papers; Whitelaw Reid to R. L. Fearn, 13, 15, 20 June 1904, and Reid to Chandler, 15 July, 2 November 1904, Reid Papers; Roosevelt to Henry C. Payne, 15 July 1904, and Roosevelt to Lodge, 22 July 1904, Morison, *Letters*, 4: 859, 863–64; George G. Hill to Spooner, 3 August 1904, Spooner Papers.

[94] Spooner to George A. Benham, 1 July 1904, Spooner Papers.

far from easy to find a sound legal base for their request, and on October 5, 1904, the state supreme court ruled against them.[95]

Late in September, a few days before the court decision, a *McClure's Magazine* article on Wisconsin politics by Lincoln Steffens appeared on the newsstands. It contained a devastating attack on the Stalwarts and extolled LaFollette and his reform program.[96] Two weeks later, Spooner wrote Albert J. Beveridge of Indiana, "The situation in this State is hell."[97]

Uncle Joe Cannon, always on the alert to serve fellow members of the House, attempted to rescue Wisconsin congressmen allied with Spooner. But after talking with some LaFollette aides he concluded that the Insurgents were in no mood to moderate their anti-Stalwart antagonism. On October 14, Cannon reported to House colleague J. W. Babcock of Wisconsin, "the LaFollette people are for hell all along the line."[98] The angry Insurgents felt no need to make concessions. William E. Chandler reported to Reid, "LaFollette is having it all his own way" and Spooner is in a "most humiliating position" and is "losing his temper and his influence." Reid replied a few days before the election that he wished Spooner "had been less unbending."[99] LaFollette won reelection by a comfortable 50,000 plurality, and Roosevelt carried the state with an even larger count.

In the East, meanwhile, Aldrich experienced election difficulties in Rhode Island, but his machine managed to win the election because the popular Roosevelt drew voters to the Republican ticket. It was, nevertheless, a very close contest. Angry citizens and ambitious politicians had become sickened at the nature and operation of the state Republican machine. Boss Charles R. Brayton operated the machine by controlling the state senate. Through money he collected from the Providence

[95] George G. Greene to John M. Olin, 23 August 1904, enclosed in Olin to Spooner, 24 August 1904, ibid.; LaFollette, *LaFollette*, 1: 185.

[96] Lincoln Steffens, "Enemies of the Republic: Wisconsin," *McClure's Magazine* 23 (October 1904): 564–79.

[97] 14 October 1904, Spooner Papers.

[98] 14 October 1904, copy in box 25, Cortelyou Papers.

[99] Chandler to Whitelaw Reid, 30 October 1904, and Reid to Chandler, 2 November 1904, Reid Papers; see also Roosevelt to George B. Cortelyou, 6 October 1904, Morison, *Letters*, 4: 973–74.

"trolley gang" and other special privileged interests, he bribed voters and officeholders in both rural and urban Rhode Island. In 1901 he augmented his already considerable power when he ordered the enactment of a measure, the Brayton Law, that gave the senate complete power over state patronage. The governor, henceforth, could not appoint even minor officials without senate approval. Already the governor's power was hedged in by lack of authority to demand reports from department heads without the approval of the legislature. Brayton also saw to it that a property qualification for voting kept city councils out of the reach of poor citizens who might be unhappy about the high costs of trolley rides, electricity, gas, and telephone service.[100]

In 1902 a Brown University professor, Sidney A. Sherman, had written a forthright article in the *Annals of the American Academy of Political and Social Science* describing the power of the Brayton-Aldrich machine. Without using the actual names of persons, he said that boss Brayton "has for years been building up political control of these rotten boroughs, until today he is master of the legislature." Sherman went on to state that Brayton nevertheless did not exercise his great power "to further his own political fortunes, but as the agent of a small group of men, who, besides completely controlling the state politically, have during the last ten years obtained by his assistance a practical monopoly of electric traction lines, electric lighting, and bay and harbor transportation in the state."[101] Soon journalists spread the story far and wide. Edward G. Lowry wrote devastating articles on the Rhode Island situation which appeared in the *New York Evening Post* and Waldo L. Cook wrote similar articles in the *Springfield Republican*. After the election, Lincoln Steffens published an attack in *McClure's Magazine.*[102]

The reform agitation alerted some businessmen to the dangers inherent in business unpopularity with the public and caused

[100] Erwin L. Levine, *Theodore Francis Green: The Rhode Island Years, 1906–1936,* 4–6.

[101] Sidney A. Sherman, "Relations of State to Municipalities in Rhode Island." *Annals of the American Academy of Political and Social Science* 17 (May 1901): 472–73.

[102] *New York Evening Post,* 7 May 1903; *Nation,* 12 November 1903; Lincoln Steffens, "Rhode Island: A State for Sale," *McClure's Magazine* 24 (February 1905): 337–53.

some franchise seekers to postpone requests. A key figure in the Providence Telephone Company, R. G. Hazard, wrote to Aldrich in early 1902 that while some of his associates thought they could get a franchise from the legislature "of value to the Telephone Company," he questioned whether it was desirable "to agitate this matter at the present time." He felt it unwise to obtain "rights which will afterwards be said by the sore-headed people who have not got them, to have been secured through favoritism or even less permissible agencies."[103]

The general discontent attracted many people to the Democratic party and caused independent political groups to emerge. Wage earners, ever increasing in numbers, were incensed by the failure of the Brayton-dominated state government to enforce the state ten-hour work law. They organized a Central Labor Union and joined forces with the Democrats. Moreover, many young, politically ambitious men were putting life into the Democratic party. A Providence acquaintance of Aldrich wrote to him that "while the Democratic party is raising up a large number of bright young men who scent the battle and are eager to fill positions" in the party, in the Republican party "every position" in Providence and the state "is filled by fossils who are no earthly good to the party."[104]

The revolt in Rhode Island first evidenced real strength in 1902 and 1903 when Democrats and Independent Republicans united forces to elect, and next year to reelect, Democrat Lucius F. C. Garvin to the governorship. A physician by profession and a longtime member of the legislature, Garvin sought to clean up his state, employing the popular reform formula of restoring the government to the people and bringing corporations under governmental control. He favored proportional representation, the Initiative, and the single tax.[105] Machine members became alarmed, but the *Providence Journal*, mouthpiece for the machine and the "trolley gang," bravely asserted that "These banded hosts of evil, led by the clergymen, college professors,

[103] Hazard to Aldrich, 13 February 1902, box 48, Biographer's Notes, Aldrich Papers.
[104] Joseph P. Manton, Providence, R. I., to Aldrich, 16 December 1902, Aldrich Papers.
[105] *Providence Evening Telegram*, 1–14 October 1902.

philanthropists, and other well-known rascals of the State, have won a temporary victory," but the voters would soon recover their senses.[106] Machine members were especially angry at the Episcopal bishop of Rhode Island, William N. McVickar, who headed a committee that circulated antimachine material. In his reform efforts, the bishop made especial use of the articles of journalist Lowry.[107]

Aldrich showed definite signs of concern, for he spread the word that he planned to abandon politics in 1904 when his current term in the Senate ended. That news caused consternation in business circles and brought forth offers of substantial financial support for the 1904 election in the state.[108] Aldrich then had a change of heart. Not only did he show a new interest in politics, but he even took command of the Rhode Island campaign. Brayton allegedly was ill that year.[109]

What Aldrich lacked in experience as a campaign manager and campaigner, he made up for in expenditure of effort and money. He spent $40,000 or $50,000 of his own money, along with the sums others generously contributed to the cause. It was reported that the National Association of Manufacturers and the American Protective Tariff League sent $300,000, which the party returned because the money was not needed.[110]

Many Catholics were on very good terms with Aldrich, although he was not a churchman. The student body of a Catholic school contributed clerical services to the Aldrich cause. The children wished to express their gratitude to Aldrich for the support he had given in Congress to an Indian mission. They addressed envelopes containing pamphlets describing Aldrich's kindness to the Indians.[111] There were other evidences of Aldrich's good relations with Catholics. Miss Josephine Patten later remarked that Aldrich and Cardinal Gibbons were close friends. "His love for the Cardinal," she said, was the reason

---

[106] Quoted in *Nation,* 12 November 1903.

[107] *Nation,* 12 November 1903; *New York Evening Post,* 7 May 1903; Platt to Lynde Harrison, 25 November 1904, Platt Papers.

[108] Ex-Congressman John W. Wright memorandum, box 48, Biographer's Notes, Aldrich Papers.

[109] Josephine Patten memorandum, ibid.

[110] Major James W. Abbott memorandum, ibid.

[111] Ibid.

Aldrich contributed generously to the Catholic University of America. Aldrich regularly attended Gibbons's annual dinners in Washington.[112]

In 1904 Aldrich and his associates invested in the newspaper publishing business in an obvious attempt to influence the election outcome. They purchased the *Pawtucket Times* and made plans, which failed to materialize, to buy the *Providence Evening Telegram* and the *Providence Journal.*[113] Associated with Aldrich were two of the most powerful businessmen of Rhode Island, Samuel Pomeroy Colt, president of the Industrial Trust Company and the United States Rubber Company, and Marsden J. Perry, president of the Union Trust Company. They planned to engage journalist David S. Barry to edit the *Providence Journal.*[114] In the proposed five-year contract with Barry was the statement, "Your editorial policy is to be independent in politics and news, but you are to oppose by all proper means the socialistic and anarchistical tendencies of the labor unions and similar organizations."[115]

Aldrich met directly with voters and urged such colleagues as Spooner and Platt to campaign for him in Rhode Island. Although Spooner was too busy with his own election troubles, the thoroughly entrenched veteran Platt complied. He recognized the gravity of the situation and was convinced that Aldrich "must give some personal attention to the matter, which, heretofore, he has not done."[116] Aldrich attended "old home day" in his native hamlet of Foster. There he delivered a felicitous talk in defense of the morality of rural Rhode Island. In response to the widespread charge of vote buying in Foster, he talked about "Christian values." "I have been brought in constant contact," he declared, "with every phase of public, private and business life with the natives and residents of these towns, and I know by

---

[112] Josephine Patten memorandum, ibid.

[113] Barry, "Aldrich's Career," box 50, and Samuel P. Colt to Aldrich, 11 July 1904, copy in box 48, Biographer's Notes, Aldrich Papers.

[114] Barry, "Aldrich's Career," ibid.

[115] Aldrich and R. S. Howland to David S. Barry, 26 February 1904, box 48, Biographer's Notes, Aldrich Papers.

[116] Platt to Henry R. Reed, 2 September 1904, Platt Papers; see also Platt to Reed, 5 November 1904, and Platt to Aldrich, 12 November 1904, ibid.; Aldrich to Spooner, 28 September, 9 October (telegram), 1904, Spooner Papers; Nathaniel W. Stephenson, *Nelson W. Aldrich: A Leader in American Politics,* 250–51.

personal experience that they will not suffer by comparison with the people of any other section or state."[117]

In the end, however, it was very probably Roosevelt's popularity that prevented disaster at the polls for the Rhode Island Republican party and that sustained it in the years ahead. The president defeated Parker in the state by almost 17,000 votes, while the Republican candidate for governor won by less than 1,000 votes.[118] Such a victory afforded Aldrich slight confidence that he had surmounted the clamor against him.

Nationally, the election outcome was above all else a personal triumph for Roosevelt. James S. Clarkson, veteran of many campaigns, stated in his letter of congratulation to the manager of the national campaign, "Roosevelt's popularity and your management have lifted the party up again into an actual majority in the nation, as against an uncertain plurality for many years past."[119] Old-timers, moreover, including the supposedly entrenched Spooner, Aldrich, and Allison, could not fail to observe that without Roosevelt their home-state constituencies would have been frail support. His great success worried them.[120]

[117] *Providence Telegram,* 16 September 1904.

[118] *Review of Reviews,* 15 November 1904; Stephenson, *Aldrich,* 250.

[119] James S. Clarkson to George B. Cortelyou, 11 November 1904, Cortelyou Papers.

[120] Stephenson, *Aldrich,* 250–51.

IX

THE PARTY LEADERSHIP
CONFRONTS BIG BUSINESS
1905-1906

THE SWEEPING ELECTION VICTORY of 1904 provided the Republicans with more power than they were
willing to use, for they were clearly afraid to apply their great
power to effect modernization of the party policies. Their promises to the voters had been very vague, and they had not even
agreed among themselves on an agenda, let alone on what positions to take on important issues. They simply had not dared to
face the political turmoil that could erupt in their own party if
they made an effort to enact constructive legislation on the
tariff, trusts, and currency, recognizing that such turmoil might
endanger the alliances between the East and the Middle West
and between the party command and big business. On the Negro
problem, the party leaders lacked sufficient interest to launch a
crusade to educate and arouse the public. Hence, not surprisingly, the overall legislative record in the next four-year term
was unimpressive. The leaders adeptly avoided action on the
tariff, dealt with but one segment of the trust problem, took a
small, hesitant step in the direction of currency reform, and
skirted the Negro problem. They deserved praise, however, for
the measures they did enact. Congress passed the Hepburn bill
in 1906, which provided for railroad rate regulation, and the
pure food, drug, and meat inspection acts, measures which
underscored Republican recognition of a need for some federal
controls.

At the outset of the maneuvering on the tariff and railroad

rate issues, there was widespread uncertainty regarding Roosevelt's probable course. The president had been elected in his own right and had won so decisively that the question arose in everyone's mind, including his own, how much concession he would make to Aldrich, Platt, Allison, Spooner, and Cannon. Uncle Joe Cannon, worried and always on the alert to recruit allies, wrote in his congratulatory note to Cortelyou, "The sweep was so clean that we will have to both pull the load and apply the brakes."[1]

Three days after the election, Platt asked Aldrich, "What are we going to do with our victory! It worries me." He added, "I am beginning now to ask the opposition's question, 'What will he [Roosevelt] do next?'"[2] Before the votes were counted, and hence before the enormous popular endorsement of Roosevelt was known, Platt had been less worried. In a preelection letter to his friend John H. Flagg, he confessed that he was "interested to know" how Roosevelt would "behave himself when he has a term of his own." Platt concluded that "he will be on his good behavior, for he has not . . . made any announcement to the effect that he will not be a candidate for a second term," and "I think he believes enough in himself, so that he thinks he will be so necessary to the country at the end of his first term, that the people would not want anyone else." But, Platt added, "That is not said in a spirit of criticism, for I like him, and believe that he will be conservative, and that if he has any disposition to be otherwise, he will take advice."[3] Roosevelt jarred Platt's equilibrium immediately after the election when he stated that he would not seek another term. Platt thereafter showed obsessive concern that Roosevelt, anxious to make a quick record, would ignore his advice to put off tariff reform.[4]

The tariff question, which Roosevelt privately showed every indication of hoping to keep from reaching Congress, sorely tested his political acumen. Both opponents and advocates of tariff revision brought intense pressure on the president as he

---

[1] Cannon to George B. Cortelyou, 13 November 1904, box 25, Cortelyou Papers.
[2] 12 November 1904, Platt Papers.
[3] 25 October 1904, ibid.
[4] Louis A. Coolidge, *An Old-Fashioned Senator: Orville H. Platt of Connecticut*, 384–94.

led his party, step by step, away from that question to the less controversial railroad rate issue. His first definite step in that strategy came in mid-November when he indicated to newsmen that he would not deal with the tariff issue in his December 1904 annual message to Congress, but that later he would submit a special message on the subject (which he never did).

Tariff reformers, with the aid of such newspapers as the *New York Times,* sustained a steady flow of demands for new legislation, making it necessary for the Republican leadership to operate gingerly if they wished to keep the question out of Congress. It was perfectly clear, and had been since the 1897 tariff debates, that one of the last things the Republican leadership wanted was a new round of tariff discussions in Congress. They had at hand well-rehearsed, tiresome reasons for postponing action, believing that if they unleashed the question in Congress the ensuing battle could tear asunder their party. The Republican-business alliance and the Republican East-Middle West alliance might well break at the seams. Roosevelt and the other top leaders hoped that economic prosperity was great enough to keep tariff agitation within bounds.

The accumulated evidence of the inadequacies of the Dingley Tariff, the increased interest in foreign trade, and the general political discontent in the country combined to create an atmosphere of expectancy on tariff reform. Large numbers of people assumed that Congress would act soon. An active participant in the 1904 campaign, William Howard Taft, wrote in August to his brother Horace, a low-tariff advocate, "I have a feeling that there will be a very real and strong movement for a revision of the tariff among the Republicans in the next Congress."[5] The *New York Evening Post* interviewed one thousand people listed in *Who's Who in America* on the subject of tariff revision. Ten to one, the survey showed, they favored revision.[6]

Roosevelt harkened the most to his colleagues in the party leadership, but at the same time he kept in touch with others, including congressmen, senators, and governors. To Benjamin Wheeler, president of the University of California, who had told

[5] 4 August 1904, Taft Papers.
[6] *New York Evening Post,* 22 December 1904.

him "You have got to revise the tariff," Roosevelt said shortly after the election, "I feel exactly as you do."[7]

New Yorkers Elihu Root and Nicholas Murray Butler, who counseled Roosevelt, reflected the foreign-trade-oriented views of New York businessmen, even though they professed greater interest in the welfare of consumers and manufacturers. As active Republicans, they were also very conscious of the reviving strength in New York of the tariff-reform Democrats. The day after the election, Butler suggested to Roosevelt, "We cannot longer go before the country with the statement that the *tariff*, if revised at all, must be revised by its friends, unless in the next Congress we begin to revise it voluntarily, not as a matter of political necessity, but in response to economic needs."[8] The harassed Roosevelt responded next day with, "I have already begun the effort to secure a bill to revise and reduce the tariff."[9]

Root wasted no time. On November 16, he wrote a lengthy letter to Roosevelt reporting that he had found "in talking with representative Republicans from all parts of the Country, evidence of a widespread conviction that in many respects the present tariff is too high." Placing the emphasis upon the attitude of manufacturers, and oddly ignoring the New York commercial and financial interests, he said, "This conviction is being constantly strengthened by the manufacturers themselves, who do not hesitate to say in private conversation that the present rates of duty are wholly unnecessary to protect their respective industries." By way of illustration, he noted that "many men in the steel industry, in the glass industry, in the shoe industry, and in many others have made these statements in my hearing."[10] He might well have added that the shoe manufacturers and tanners were pressuring politicians such as Lodge in their home states to get hides placed on the free list. Too, he could have been more specific in the case of the steel industry, where rates could be lowered substantially without placing the industry in

[7] Wheeler to Roosevelt, 13 November 1904, and Roosevelt to Wheeler, 21 November 1904, Roosevelt Papers.

[8] 9 November 1904, ibid.

[9] 10 November 1904, Morison, *Letters*, 4: 1027.

[10] 16 November 1904, Root Papers. Root then held no official position, having resigned as secretary of war to return to his law practice. In July 1905, he became secretary of state following the death of Secretary John Hay.

competition with foreign producers and where steelmen preferred to have Roosevelt engage in a tariff revision crusade rather than break up the steel trust. Root did go so far as to say, "There is also an impression, which is undeniably gaining ground, that in many directions the excessive duties enable combinations of great manufacturers to exact higher prices than are reasonable in view of cost and risk of production." In short, the spirit of the Iowa Idea, if not the plan itself, was in the ascendancy.

Root then pleaded for revision. He urged that it be taken up "promptly upon the opening of the next session of Congress, that all possible preparation in the way of material and threshing out of the specific questions involved should be made before the fourth of March, next, and that an extra session of Congress should be convened immediately after your inauguration to revise the tariff, unhampered and undelayed by the performance of any other duty whatever."[11]

Platt, Aldrich, and Cannon were opposed to any tariff revision whatsoever. The ailing, seventy-year-old Platt was fanatical on the subject. He wrote frantically to political colleagues and business friends about his fears and lamented to his industrialist friend Charles F. Brooker, "I wish it were possible for us to get along without any legislation whatever for the next twelve months."[12]

In mid-November, Platt wrote to Aldrich that he would like to talk with him and with the president about the dangers ahead. "I see the newspaper correspondents are fixing things all up for" the president, "even to an extra session after the short one, to revise the tariff, and further prosecutions and legislation regarding trusts." But it "is a time to go slow; it is time for the president to drop the strenuous life, and take up the simple life for a while. He ought not, in my judgment, to make one single positive recommendation in his next message—there is no occasion for it."[13] Platt talked with Roosevelt and reacted explosively when he learned that the president favored a special session of

---

[11] 16 November 1904, Root Papers. For a strikingly similar letter see Nicholas Murray Butler to Roosevelt, 5 December 1904, Roosevelt Papers.

[12] 21 November 1904, Platt Papers. See also Coolidge, *Platt*, 521–23.

[13] 12 November 1904, Platt Papers.

Congress to deal with the tariff. He was also horrified at Roosevelt's suggestion, borrowed from Root's letter, that a joint congressional "commission" study the question and make recommendations.[14] Platt feared that the old tariff hands, especially Aldrich and himself, would lose control of the situation if the matter escaped their own committee and fell to a commission in which House members might have a strong voice. He reminded Aldrich, who had failed to indicate sufficient concern, "You know as well as I do, that a joint commission composed as suggested, would be entirely valueless, so far as getting our ideas accepted, is concerned." Platt pleaded with Aldrich to exert pressure on Roosevelt, for "I cannot think he knows as much about the difficulties of amending the tariff as you and I do."[15]

Aldrich reported to Platt that he had talked briefly with the president on November 15, at which time "He told me that he was thinking about an extra session, but that nothing would be done about matters of importance until we were all together." Aldrich agreed about the dangers inherent in the "commission" and believed that if the president adhered to his promise "he would not commit himself or the party to any line of action. . . . all will be well and we can arrange to carry out any plan we can agree upon." Also, he doubted if there was pressure enough for revision to make necessary an extra session. In fact, he was "at a great loss to know" where the alleged pressure came from. As far as he was aware, "there was absolutely *no demand* for tariff revision."[16] Aldrich clearly was trying to reassure the excited elder statesman.

Like Aldrich, middle westerners Allison, Spooner, and Cannon seemed content to let the tariff matter rest until the situation became clearer. Trusting Roosevelt's promise to be cautious, they were more than happy to remain in the background. The experienced Allison could take satisfaction in the predicament of his erstwhile antagonist Cummins, who now confronted the tariff problem. Cummins, moving into national politics with a

[14] Platt to Roosevelt, 21 November 1904, and Platt to Aldrich, 21 November 1904, ibid.
[15] 25 November 1904, ibid.
[16] 19, 23 November 1904, ibid.

Senate seat his goal, desired the goodwill not only of the national leaders but of his Iowa tariff reform friends as well. On November 21, Cummins called on Roosevelt to urge tariff reform, but he carefully avoided pressing his demands. In fact, Cummins soon increased his efforts to disassociate himself from the Iowa Idea.[17] In December, in a reference to his relationship to the Iowa Idea, he declared, "I never claimed that I was in the least departing from established Republican principles or accepted economic thought."[18] He continued to be very much interested in tariff revision, along with other reforms, but he talked now more about reciprocity than about the tariff as an aid to trusts.[19] Like Roosevelt and LaFollette, Cummins had come to believe that railroad regulation was a safer issue than the tariff. Early in 1905 he wrote to LaFollette, "We are in just the same sort of fight here, with some different phases, that you are having in Wisconsin, and I have to bear the brunt of it."[20]

Spooner remained on the sidelines. His past experiences with tariff legislation had been unfortunate and by 1904 most of his Wisconsin constituents were so interested in LaFollette's crusade that they paid little attention to the tariff question. Spooner explained to one citizen who did show some interest, "I think after a little we have got to revise two or three schedules of the tariff, but I do not look for any general shake up. . . . The demand for revision is not so pronounced as it was a year or so ago."[21]

Speaker Cannon emphatically opposed downward revision. He had always been as wedded to high protectionism as Platt. In addition to seeing its economic implications, the shrewd Cannon understood the politics of the tariff issue, some of which he had learned the hard way. His 1890 election defeat was in part attributable to the emotionalism the McKinley Tariff had engendered. His long service in the House, moreover, had underscored for him the political dangers inherent in the issue. During

[17] See Cummins to M. Converse, 6 February 1905, and Cummins to Alvin H. Sanders, 12 August 1905, Cummins Papers.
[18] Cummins to D. A. Valentine, 22 December 1904, ibid.
[19] Cummins to Alvin H. Sanders, 12 August 1905, ibid.
[20] 3 April 1905, ibid.
[21] Spooner to Henry D. Smith, 25 December 1904, Spooner Papers.

the 1904 campaign, traveling in a private car, Cannon made protectionist speeches in fifteen states. In Iowa he remarked about the Iowa Idea, "We don't pay much attention to that over in Illinois where I live, and really, you don't seem to be paying much attention to it here in Iowa."[22] In December, Roosevelt wrote Nicholas Murray Butler that "Uncle Joe Cannon represents the feeling of the rural Middle West in his strong opposition" to any action on the tariff.[23] Later Cannon even boasted of his flat refusal to approve Roosevelt's plan for a special session of Congress to take up the question.[24]

Platt and Cannon remained adamantly opposed to any concessions whatsoever, and Aldrich appeared to be in substantial agreement with them. Aldrich's position as chairman of the Senate Finance Committee and his connection with businessmen, who entertained conflicting views on the tariff, caused him to be somewhat circumspect on the matter and to refrain from definite support for either side. Because the party had made no promise to the voters in the 1904 campaign, no commitment forced Roosevelt to defy Republican leaders in Congress.

Roosevelt explained to Nicholas Murray Butler on December 2, "I am having great difficulty on the tariff business." He added, "I am going to make every effort to get something of what I desire in the way of an amendment to the present law; but shall not split with my party on the matter, for it would be absurd to do so."[25] A week later he indicated to Butler that he "must get some kind of substantial agreement among the leaders" before he called a special session of Congress on the matter.[26]

On January 7, 1905, at Roosevelt's request, the party leaders held a conference on the tariff question. The conference consisted of the president, Senators Aldrich, Spooner, O. H. Platt, and Allison, House Speaker Cannon, and House members Sereno

[22] William Rea Gwinn, *Uncle Joe Cannon, Archfoe of Insurgency: A History of the Rise and Fall of Cannonism*, 90–92.

[23] 2 December 1904, Morison, *Letters*, 4: 1055–56.

[24] L. White Busbey (Cannon's secretary) memorandum, box 48, Biographer's Notes, Aldrich Papers; see also Busbey, *Uncle Joe Cannon: The Story of a Pioneer American*, 207–08; Roosevelt to Cannon, 30 November 1904, Morison, *Letters*, 4: 1052–53.

[25] Morison, *Letters*, 4: 1055.

[26] 9 December 1904, ibid., 1062.

E. Payne, John Dalzell, Charles H. Grosvenor, and James A. Tawney.[27] The conferees issued no statement. Thereafter, in public, standpatters Platt and Cannon appeared to be complacent. Aldrich continued to be circumspect but indicated in the summer that he favored some rate reduction.[28] Allison and Spooner remained noncommittal and Roosevelt created the impression that he believed Congress would want a special session very soon in order to revise the tariff. But none of the conferees said anything definite and all remained as quiet as possible.[29]

The Republican leaders, Roosevelt in particular, watched carefully for signs of mounting tariff revisionist sentiment. They experienced no significant pressure for legislation, nor did they encourage any. In fact, Roosevelt made it a point to quiet any insurgency in the party on the question. Moreover, the general increase of interest in the railroad rate issue and in "trustbusting" kept interest in tariff revision at a minimum.

The president paid particular attention to the areas where the tariff issue was supposedly most alive. In November 1905 he corresponded with Allison, who reported that he thought revisionist sentiment was "not so pressing as it was three years ago when you made a most admirable statement on the subject in your speech at Minneapolis." Nevertheless, Allison added, there existed "considerable agitation for immediate revision in certain localities and particularly is this true in some of the Western States." In Iowa, however, those Republicans who "would be glad to see revision believe that under the circumstances it is unwise to attempt it now, because of the marked divisions in our own party on the subject."

Allison expressed complete agreement with Roosevelt's statement, written to him November 9, 1905, that in his judgment, very reluctantly arrived at, Congress would not enact a reform

[27] See Roosevelt's schedule of appointments, in Morison, *Letters*, 4: 1373–74; *New York Tribune*, 6, 7 January 1905, included J. W. Babcock on the list; *New York Times*, 7 January 1905, included Eugene Hall, Theodore E. Burton, and G. E. Foss, but not Babcock.

[28] Roosevelt to Leslie M. Shaw, 4 August 1905, Morison, *Letters*, 4: 1300.

[29] *New York Tribune*, 6, 7, 9, 11 January 1905; *New York Times*, 7 January 1905; L. White Busbey memorandum, box 48, Biographer's Notes, Aldrich Papers; Busbey, *Cannon*, 211–14.

tariff measure "because the enormous majority of your colleagues either decline to take up the subject at all, or wish to approach it only as the Massachusetts reciprocity people wish to approach it—that is, from the standpoint of having the tariff revised purely with the interests of their own particular localities in view." Roosevelt wanted to avoid "such a position as Cleveland got into when he succeeded in forcing tariff revision, only to get a bill so bad that he would not sign it, and yet let it become a law, so that the whole proceeding worked great mischief to the people at large and helped split his party in two."[30]

Roosevelt carefully avoided personal involvement in public discussion of the issue, ignored rumors that could place him on the defensive, and made a positive effort to prevent his close associates from action that might cause public speculation about his views and plans. He showed special concern over the activities of his cabinet members. One of them in particular, Secretary of the Treasury Shaw, an old-time Iowa ultraprotectionist, was very difficult. An opponent of the Iowa Idea who had failed to stop the ambitious Cummins, Shaw seemed determined to spread the impression that the Roosevelt administration regarded the Dingley Tariff as sacred. He had persistently tried to get Roosevelt's permission to let him announce in a speech that the administration would never employ tariff revision as a means to increase public revenue. In the course of an exchange of long letters with Shaw, the president stated, "I entirely agree with all you say as to the dangers which accompany tariff revision or any attempt at it, but as yet I am not sure whether there are at least equal dangers in avoiding tariff revision." In the same letter Roosevelt insisted, and correctly, that he was not discriminating against Shaw or any antirevisionist. As evidence of his impartiality, he pointed out that he had blue-penciled a draft of a speech Taft planned to deliver at the Ohio convention, in which Taft "committed himself unreservedly to a big lowering of duties." Roosevelt also told Shaw that he had requested Root, who agreed with Taft, not to commit himself.[31]

[30] 11 November 1905, Roosevelt Papers; Roosevelt to Allison, 9 November 1905, Morison, *Letters*, 5: 72.

[31] Roosevelt to Shaw, 4 August 1905, Morison, *Letters*, 4: 1299–1301; see also:

The efforts of ardent tariff revisionists made it difficult for the Republican leaders to suppress the issue. The *New York Times* writers were especially on the alert for opportunities to advance the cause of tariff reform. In May 1905, a wishful-thinking *Times* correspondent in Washington thought he found evidence that the Republican leaders were laying the groundwork for a tariff revision drive when Congress convened in the fall. The zealous reporter took his cue from a Washington correspondent for the Republican *Ohio State Journal* of Columbus, whose story stated, "there is a strong possibility that at the next session of Congress the Republican leaders will face the situation squarely and set about the enactment of a new law that will meet the new requirements."[32] The *Journal* reporter offered no evidence for his supposed scoop, but the *Times* correspondent surmised it rested on the actions of a Panama Canal Commission meeting, then being held in Washington. The exhorbitant prices American tariff-protected steel companies charged the canal builders for certain materials then available from Europe for far less money disturbed the commission, which retaliated with a threat to give the business to foreigners. At this point, the *New York Times* correspondent and editorial staff concluded that the action of the Panama Canal Commission was actually a White House device to expose the need for a reduction in the tariff duties on steel. *Times* writers took advantage of this opportunity to write several "news stories" and lengthy editorials on what they believed to be the tariff reform intentions of the Republican leadership for the next session of Congress. To support their conclusions, they made much of the lone *Ohio State Journal* story.[33]

Some individual Republican politicians who favored tariff revision for reasons of their own welcomed events that kept alive the movement. Henry Cabot Lodge was then under great

---

Roosevelt to Shaw, 31 July 1905, Shaw to Roosevelt, 3, 10 August, 27 September 1905, H. C. Lodge to Roosevelt, 10 June 1905, W. Murray Crane to Roosevelt, 7 August 1905, Roosevelt to Aldrich, 8 August 1905—all in Roosevelt Papers; Shaw to Aldrich, 3 August 1905, box 49, Biographer's Notes, Aldrich Papers.

[32] *Ohio State Journal*, 14 May 1905, quoted in a *New York Times* editorial, 23 May 1905.

[33] *New York Times*, 16, 17, 18, 20, 23 May 1905. The *New York Tribune* ignored the matter.

pressure in Massachusetts from the intense activity of reciprocity crusaders. He felt that Congress could no longer avoid the issue[34] and he tried to persuade Roosevelt to that view. Operating on the assumption that lower rates would increase imports and thus revenues, Lodge argued that the federal treasury's need for additional revenue compelled rate changes, and he employed the Panama Canal affair as an argument. He wrote to Roosevelt, "The performance about materials for the canal ought to strengthen revision," and added, "That the manufacturers should show greed is human nature but the stupidity in their own interest which leads them to charge us more than they charge a foreign government is to me so huge as to be incomprehensible."[35] A week later he wrote the president, "The Panama materials business has forced on tariff revision."[36]

Despite scattered episodes that revealed the continued desire in certain areas for tariff revision, most notably in the West and in Massachusetts, the party leaders were able to keep the issue under control. They were thereby freed to concentrate their energies on railroad rate regulation. Politically, this was considerably safer.

Roosevelt just as carefully did his best to elevate the smaller, but less controversial, railroad rate question into an issue of great public interest. The subject was not even mentioned in the 1904 party platform, but nevertheless it had promising possibilities. It had been an important issue in several states, and clearly the time for federal action was past due.

Under mounting pressure from Iowa cattle raisers and other shippers, Iowa's Senator Jonathan P. Dolliver wrote a letter to Allison, a few days after the 1904 election, indicative of the need for and interest in railroad rate regulation. "I have thought a good deal of the matters we talked over when I was at your house just before the landslide, and it looks to me as if conservative men in Congress would be compelled to take notice of the fact that we have practically no machinery for adjudicating

[34] All the Massachusetts congressmen called for revision. See, for example, Lawrence B. Evans, *Samuel W. McCall, Governor of Massachusetts*, 130–31.

[35] 3 June 1905, Henry Cabot Lodge, ed., *Selections from the Correspondence of Theodore Roosevelt and Henry Cabot Lodge, 1884–1918*, 2: 129.

[36] 10 June 1905, ibid., 137.

the question of the reasonableness of railroad rates, and I believe that while the supervisory power of the Government is essentially non-judicial, still the question of whether a rate fixed by a commission is reasonable and if not what modification in it ought to be made in order to make it so, may be a judicial question." Dolliver raised questions about the quality of rate bills then pending before Congress. He said they "have not originated with members of either House, but are the product of the lobby's [*sic*], representing what private interests I do not know."[37] Within in a few months, both the dynamic Dolliver and the aging and ailing Allison were in the thick of the battle over rate regulation.

The program Roosevelt finally decided to present to Congress was in essence a reaffirmation of the Square Deal but with one very specific item added, a definite call for legislative action on railroad rate regulation. He asserted in his December 1904 annual message to Congress that control of railroad rates was "the most important legislative act now needed as regards the regulation of corporations."[38] He asked for nothing else.

Roosevelt's inclusion of the railroad question in his address startled, even angered, some conventional Republicans. The Washington correspondent for the *Springfield Republican,* Richard Hooker, later recalled, "In spite of any protestations to the contrary, the message of 1904 was a genuine shock to the old line conservatives." They felt, Hooker said, "that Roosevelt, in injecting the transportation issue into his message, when it had not been a part of the platforms and an issue in the campaigns, was guilty of a great offense. They were filled with dismay; and execrations of his action were general, abounding in charges of political bad faith."[39]

As a political goal, railroad rate regulation nevertheless provided Roosevelt and the Republican party with an opportunity

---

[37] 12 November 1904, Allison Papers.

[38] Hermann Hagedorn, ed., *The Works of Theodore Roosevelt*, 15: 226.

[39] Richard Hooker memorandum, box 48, Biographer's Notes, Aldrich Papers. In this memorandum, he also stated: "There were no rumors current at the time that he had turned to transportation stressing because he had agreed to stress that since he was not to be allowed to stress the tariff. In fact, assertions to that effect are not believed to have much foundation; for there was not the slightest indication of the existence of such an arrangement, and it would have been almost impossible for its existence not to have become known to that small group of correspondents who were the confidants alike of Roosevelt and the Aldrich group."

to add substance to the rhetoric of the Square Deal and at the same time retain the traditional party structure of alliances. The geographical alliance between the East and the Middle West, as well as the closely related one between the party leaders and big business, needed just such an infusion of reform activity if the leaders hoped to keep party insurgency from assuming dangerous proportions and promoting a Democratic revival. With the greatest danger to the party centered in the crucially important Middle West and the increasingly important expanding states farther west, Republican leaders could now demonstrate with effective legislation that they were on the way toward an effective control over the power of big business or trusts. It seemed relatively safe to crusade for regulation of one business giant, especially if that one was the railroad network.

During the ensuing months, Roosevelt helped focus public attention on rate regulation. He made speeches, wrote letters, and conferred with key men. William Howard Taft also crusaded for regulation. At the same time, consideration of the question in the House of Representatives, together with the clamor of irate shippers and railroad interests, heightened public interest in the subject.[40] Not until early 1906, however, did the movement reach a climax.

Meanwhile, the top Republican leaders experienced sharp clashes within their own elite circle. They failed to maintain a solid front in the face of powerful conflicting demands from the railroads, the shippers, and the aroused public. Roosevelt and Aldrich were the main contenders but none escaped. Ultimately, in May 1906, the Hepburn bill became law.

Journalists of protest, whom Roosevelt labeled muckrakers in early 1906, stimulated public interest in railroad rates and related issues. Ray Stannard Baker wrote articles for *Colliers* and for *McClure's Magazine* on the railroads. At the same time, journalist attacks on the Senate, or "Millionaire's Club," and on the state machines of certain senators reached great intensity. In late 1904 and early 1905, Lincoln Steffens presented in *McClure's Magazine* his scathing attacks on the state machines that sustained the power of Spooner and Aldrich. In the fall of

[40] Gabriel Kolko, *Railroads and Regulation, 1877–1916*, 102–07.

1905, Thomas W. Lawson's series on "Frenzied Finance," which included searing anti-Senate material, began to appear in *Everybody's*. In January 1906, the *Arena* suggested that the Senate was "becoming more and more a machine for registering the will of Wall-street campaign contributors and the puppet of privileged wealth."[41]

Also in January 1906, the respectable *Cosmopolitan Magazine* began a series of devastating articles entitled "The Treason of the Senate," by David Graham Phillips. These articles made the most of the close alliance between powerful senators and powerful business interests. Phillips used facts, but through a clever use of words, he implied that more corruption existed than he could actually demonstrate. He even managed to create the nonsensical illusion of shady dealing on the part of Henry Cabot Lodge.[42]

It was unusual and even startling for the venerable Platt to receive a scolding letter from as influential a fellow Connecticut citizen as Charles Hopkins Clark, editor of the *Hartford Courant*. In answer to a typical Platt letter calling for more action on a rate bill, Clark wrote the senator in February 1905, "It doesn't seem as if the gentlemen who make up what is so frequently called through the country the rich man's club of America realize the delicacy of the position of the United States Senate." No extremist himself, Clark accepted the reputation of Platt himself as "poor and honest," but went on to emphasize that "The corporate interests of the country have such a tremendous hold upon the Senate, and money goes so far in securing position there, that the country at large is in a state of feeling toward that body which I am confident its better members do not realize. The country is dead tired of being in the hands of dictatorial monopolists."[43]

The journalists' impact was twofold. The articles of Ray Stannard Baker urged railroad rate regulation, and Upton Sinclair's *Jungle* portrayed even more dramatically the need for regulation of the meat-packing industry. The attacks on the

[41] George E. Mowry and Judson A. Grenier, Introduction to David Graham Phillips, *The Treason of the Senate*, 26.
[42] Ibid., 1–46.
[43] 10 February 1905, Platt Papers; see also Coolidge, *Platt*, 462–65.

.

august Senate had a sobering effect on all thoughtful politicians, in and out of that body. Feeling themselves under close scrutiny, Republican leaders closed ranks and attempted to counteract the stigma of the "Millionaire's Club" label. Aldrich even seriously considered suing David Graham Phillips for libel for his article entitled "Aldrich, the Head of It All," one of the "Treason of the Senate" series in *Cosmopolitan Magazine.*[44]

The senators for the most part conducted their debate on the railroad rate bill in a dignified manner and couched their disagreements in legalistic rather than economic terminology whenever possible. They also avoided conspicuous association with railroad people. Roosevelt, who at times indulged in self-righteous attacks on corruption as vitriolic as those of Phillips, chose now to join forces with his beleaguered fellow politicians, thereby gaining their gratitude and greater cooperation.

Shippers dependent on the railroads, angry to the point of desperation, augmented their already militant and powerful pressure groups to obtain governmental protection from the railroads. They carried on an intense campaign for redress of rate discrimination between communities, regions, and businesses; such discrimination seemed to them an even greater grievance than whether or not overall rates were excessive. The *New York Times* in March declared that "the crying evil of railroad administration is not high rates, but unfairly discriminating rates, secret rebates, and tricks and devices which favor one shipper at the expense of others."[45]

The shippers placed Spooner high on the list of recipients of their pressure. His mail contained many detailed letters, especially from Milwaukee, giving specific information on rate discrimination. In February 1905, the secretary of the Merchants and Manufacturers Association of Milwaukee reminded Spooner that his city was "being discriminated against by common carriers in the transportation of grain between territory in the west . . . and the Atlantic seaboard cities." He said Milwaukee was destined to "lose its position as a grain market unless these inequalities in transportation charges can be remedied."[46]

---

[44] Barry, "Aldrich's Career," box 50, Biographer's Notes, Aldrich Papers.
[45] 5 March 1905.

A Milwaukee manufacturer of hardware specialties complained to Spooner that his firm was unable to develop a market in Minneapolis "because rates on these finished goods are almost as low from Pittsburg [*sic*] to Minneapolis as they are from Milwaukee to Minneapolis, giving a manufacturer of our line at Pittsburg a very considerable advantage as he saves all the freight on [steel] raw material which we are obliged to pay." He added that for the past five years his appeals to the Western Traffic Association, charged with the rate adjustment function, had netted no results. "You understand that this Association consists of about eight or ten Roads and to make a change requires the concurrence of all of them. As we do business with only two or three, the rest are not particularly interested in our welfare and are not inclined to vote in our favor, especially as it is easier for them to leave rates alone than to begin correcting them." He added that freight officials of the Chicago, Milwaukee and St. Paul Railroad acknowledged that the "rates were entirely wrong."[47]

Railroad leaders were worried. Most of them found it easy to appear receptive to rate reform suggestions, but certainly all of them, in actuality, were opposed to any thoroughly effective rate regulation legislation. They hoped for laws that would remove the danger of cutthroat competition between roads and protect them from shippers with power enough to obtain special costly favors from railroads, but they wanted to retain actual control of rate-making. They also wanted Congress to legalize pooling arrangements, which the Supreme Court had declared unconstitutional. They believed that if they could again organize associations, or pools, to establish rates for all the member companies, competition between them would disappear. Former Senator William E. Chandler wrote to LaFollette, "The railroads are going to accept ostentatiously governmental regulation; but they are not going to agree to effective governmental control of rates." He believed, "They mean to get more than they yield

---

[46] L. C. Whitney to Spooner, 15 February 1905, Spooner Papers; see also letters to Spooner from: Whitney, 6 February 1905, S. G. Courtion, 18 January, 10 February 1905, Robert Eliot, 21 March 1903, Edward P. Bacon, 10 January, 5 March, 9 May 1906—all in Spooner Papers.
[47] E. R. Wagner to Spooner, 30 March 1905, ibid.

—to get pooling and to grant only feeble power over rate-making."[48] Richard Olney and some other railroad attorneys made another suggestion. They proposed a bill authorizing Congress to create a special commerce court to settle disputes over rates. Experience showed that judges were very conscious of the "rights of property."[49]

Railroad men in the Middle West and West were the most worried. They hoped that Spooner could help them and attempted to persuade him that their companies were popular in Wisconsin. Between February 6 and February 25, 1905, Spooner received 160 letters and telegrams from Wisconsin businessmen (clearly railroad-company inspired) urging him to use his influence in Congress to postpone railroad rate regulation. The messages, most of them telegrams, emphasized the role of railroads in current prosperity, the good behavior of railroads, and the unreliability of government commissions. They cautioned against any but the mildest new legislation. A Wisconsin banker said, "My attention has been called by valuable railroad clients of ours to some drastic" proposed legislation. He argued that "the shipper is not everything" and that Congress should consider such matters as the continued value of railroad securities.[50]

An Allison informant on many questions for many years, Grenville M. Dodge, was one of those who threw some light on the state of confusion and worry among railroad men. His connections with the Union Pacific in particular and railroad men in general placed him in close touch with rumors. In early 1905 he reported to Allison from New York a rumor that the Senate Commerce Committee had decided against taking any action on rate regulation. News of that, he said, caused "almost all" of "the railroad people" to change over "from the view of accepting action by the commission on a reasonable rate to a determination to fight it." After noting that of course Allison knew the temper of the Senate better than he, Dodge offered the opinion that the

[48] 24 December 1904, quoted in a note, box 48, Biographer's Notes, Aldrich Papers.

[49] Olney to Daniel S. Lamont, 17 December 1904, and Olney to Samuel W. McCall, 22 December 1904, Richard Olney Papers.

[50] William B. Banks, president, First National Bank, Superior, Wisconsin, to Spooner, 21 February 1905, Spooner Papers.

majority in the Senate, because of the "feeling there is in the country" and "the influence of the President," would not allow that committee decision to prevail. He feared, however, that the senators would as a result "get in such an antagonistic position that we will get some radical legislation." But, "with the present temper of matters" still not out of hand, if the senators got together they doubtless could agree "to give the commission certain powers, and then have the court decide within sixty days whether it is a reasonable or unreasonable rate." He added, in closing, that such a law would keep the railroads from cutting rates "as they have been doing lately," but he confessed that very few railroad men agreed with him.[51]

In December 1905 a railroad "peace committee," representing most of the railroads west of Chicago, went from Chicago to Washington to seek a peace treaty with the Interstate Commerce Commission.[52] Conscious that their defiance of the Elkins Act had stimulated the movement for new legislation, this committee carried with it a promise from the railroads to obey the law henceforth. Albert S. White of Chicago, who had friends on the committee, wrote Spooner, "I am sure this offer will be made in good faith," and urged Spooner to give them a hearing. He asserted, "The Railroads would have taken this step long ago but there is a certain '*Amour Propre*' that prevented them from becoming informers against each other." But now it is for them "a matter of self preservation to see that its provisions are enforced against those roads which seek to evade it."[53]

Taft reported to his brother Charles toward the end of 1905 that he thought the railroads were "beginning to realize that the situation is becoming more and more interesting for them." Robert Mather, president of the Rock Island Company, "told me," Taft added, "that their Senators, meaning thereby those Senators upon whom they could count for allegiance, had come to him with a statement that, while they were conscientiously opposed to the President's proposition the President had so roused the people that it was impossible for them to stand

---

[51] 12 May 1905, Allison Papers.
[52] Kolko, *Railroads and Regulation,* 125.
[53] 27 December 1905, Spooner Papers.

against the popular demand, and, therefore, he was one of those who favored a compromise with the President."

Southern railway leaders were worried lest they lose their unique advantage. Samuel Spencer, president of the J. P. Morgan-controlled Southern Railway, was particularly active in persuading Congress to be gentle with the railroads. Taft explained to his brother Spencer's opposition to Roosevelt's call for an effective rate regulation law. If passed, such a law "would have a greater effect on the southern railways than on any other system in the whole country, because the inequalities and discriminations between localities are more marked there. I don't know why it should be so, but I knew it while on the Bench." Taft added, "there are many complaints on that account, and the reason why [Senator Joseph] Foraker and Spencer are squealing so thus becomes apparent." Foraker, a conspicuous friend of the railroads, advocated that all shipper complaints about railroad rates go directly to the courts. Taft explained to his brother that Foraker had been "General Counsel for the Southern Railway under Spencer," and his "relation to Spencer has always been close."[54]

The railroad interests found it very difficult to recruit supporters among politicians. Resentment and suspicion of railroads made it impossible for them to check the movement for reform. In Wisconsin, LaFollette obtained a railway-commission law and an effective railroad taxation law. Roosevelt, in his December 1904 message to Congress, had pointedly asked for federal rate regulation. During 1905, the president and William Howard Taft helped keep the public aware of the need for effective control.[55] In May 1905, in a widely quoted banquet address to the Democratic Iroquois Club in Chicago, the president declared, "Personally I believe that the Federal Government must take an

[54] 3 December 1905, Taft Papers; see also Lucien Tuttle, president, Boston and Maine Railroad, to Lodge, 11 November 1905, Lodge Papers; see also Roosevelt to Ray Stannard Baker, 22 November 1905, Morison, *Letters*, 5: 88; David M. Potter, "The Historical Development of Eastern-Southern Freight Rate Relationships," in Richard M. Abrams and Lawrence W. Levine, eds., *The Shaping of Twentieth-Century America* (Boston, 1965), 24–61 passim; Kolko, *Railroads and Regulation*, 128 n–29.

[55] Belle Case LaFollette and Fola LaFollette, *Robert M. LaFollette*, 187–92; *New York Tribune*, 10 May 1905; *New York Times*, 12 May 1905; Roosevelt to Lodge, 20 April 1905, Morison, *Letters*, 4: 1167.

increasing control over corporations. I trust there will be no halt in the process of assuming such national control, and the first step toward it should be the adoption of a law conferring upon some executive body the power of increased supervision and regulation of the great corporations engaged primarily in Interstate Commerce." He also said that the statements of Taft and Knox on the subject were the same as his own.[56] A few days later he told a Denver audience that the national government must "assume a supervisory and regulatory function" over transportation.[57]

Taft spoke out forthrightly in public and even more so in private in favor of legislative action to harness the roads. In his May 1905 address to the International Railway Congress, meeting in Washington, Taft declared, "What I am strongly in favor of . . . is that we shall have a body that shall decide things and that these things shall be decided within a reasonable time, finally by the courts."[58] Later in the year, in a letter to his brother Horace, he said he was "sorry to say so" but the "railroad men of the country have been . . . violating the law so long that they are very anxious not to be put in a position where they can be subjected easily and quickly to control." Indignantly, Taft asserted that his "experience with most railroad men" convinced him that "they are exceedingly lawless in their spirit, and that they don't wish to be measured by anything but the standard of success."[59] To Henry Cabot Lodge, Taft pointed out "that the evil lies" not in excessive rates but "in the discrimination in favor of and against individuals and places."[60]

Throughout 1905, Roosevelt looked with confidence on the prospects for effective rate regulation. He reported to Lodge in the spring that although the "railroads have been making a most active campaign against my rate-making proposition" and "think they have it beaten," personally he did not believe they

[56] *New York Times*, 11 May 1905; *New York Tribune*, 11 May 1905.
[57] *Nation*, 18 May 1905.
[58] *New York Times*, 12 May 1905; see also *New York Tribune*, 10 May 1905.
[59] 16 December 1905, Taft Papers.
[60] 13 February 1906, ibid. Nebraska citizens were greatly distressed because railroad service had become increasingly undependable and inadequate under the policies of James J. Hill. Richard Lowitt, "George W. Norris, James J. Hill, and the Railroad Rate Bill," *Nebraska History* 40 (June 1959): 137–45.

had succeeded. Roosevelt thought them "very shortsighted not to understand that to beat it means to increase the danger of the movement for the Government ownership of railroads."[61]

In his December 1905 annual message to Congress, the president indicated that he saw an inherent political danger in any threat to railroad property rights. To quiet such fears, he recommended that Interstate Commerce Commission decisions on rates should be "subject to review by the courts."[62] The president's view in general was, as Taft put it, one of willingness to compromise, "so long as the hose carriage is painted red, that is, so long as the principles enunciated by him are incorporated in the bill."[63]

Roosevelt also, as never before, selected the best possible aides and pointedly avoided contacts with individuals who might embarrass him. Through written correspondence and White House visits, he conferred with many knowledgeable and influential persons of the nonpolitical world. He carried on a correspondence with muckraker Ray Stannard Baker,[64] Benjamin Wheeler, president of the University of California, and Charles W. Eliot, president of Harvard University. He wrote Eliot, "To my mind, the questions that we group together under the head of industrialism far outweigh all questions connected with the tariff, and I am inclined to say all questions connected with the currency." Roosevelt added that "Sooner or later the nation must undertake the regulation of all the great corporations engaged in interstate commerce."[65] Reform-minded Wheeler reported to him in June 1905 the complaint of Edward H. Harriman that he and other railroad men felt they could not talk to Roosevelt on the subject without being suspected of special pleading. Harriman, according to Wheeler, viewed the

[61] Roosevelt to Lodge, 24 May 1905, Morison, *Letters*, 4: 1193.

[62] Hagedorn, *Works of Roosevelt*, 15: 275–76.

[63] Taft to Charles P. Taft, 3 December 1905, Taft Papers; see also Henry Cabot Lodge to Henry L. Higginson, 1 December 1905, Lodge Papers; Kolko, *Railroads and Regulation*, 275–76; Nathaniel W. Stephenson, *Nelson W. Aldrich: A Leader in American Politics*, 277.

[64] Baker to Roosevelt, 7, 8, 11, 13, 18 September, 17, 25 November 1905, Roosevelt Papers; Roosevelt to Baker, 3 September, 13, 20, 22, 28 November 1905, Morison, *Letters*, 5: 25, 76, 83, 88, 100.

[65] 8 December 1904, Roosevelt Papers.

"impending legislation with an unjustified horror."[66] Roosevelt replied that he liked Harriman and would be glad to talk with him, as he had previously. "But," he concluded, "I am awfully afraid there is not much to talk over in this railroad matter at present. Our difference is on a simple proposition, and all I can say is that I think they are all wrong in opposing our proposition, while they think we are all wrong in pressing it." Harriman was at that time engaged in what he called a railroad "campaign federation" to block passage of rate-making legislation.[67]

Most railroad men, however, were less blatant than the irascible Harriman in their antiregulation activity. President Charles E. Perkins of the Chicago, Burlington and Quincy Railroad, and his friend Henry L. Higginson agreed that Harriman's methods in general were "most injudicious." Bostonian Higginson thought that "perhaps they are the natural outcome of a greedy nature."[68] Higginson believed, moreover, that even though railroad leaders and the railroads had served the nation well, they as "public servants have very great and grave responsibilities to fulfil,—have done in many cases wrong things," and perhaps they "had better be controlled."[69]

Just as the president's December 1904 message to Congress had given impetus to extended public debate over rate regulation, his 1905 message set the tone of an important four-month Senate debate on the subject.[70] By this time, the Republican leadership agreed that some legislation was necessary but could not agree on the nature and extent of governmental control. In early February 1906 the House passed the Hepburn bill, which

[66] 19 June 1905, ibid.
[67] 20 June 1905, Morison, *Letters*, 4: 1243.
[68] Higginson to Charles E. Perkins, 27 August 1906, Higginson Papers.
[69] Higginson to Henry Cabot Lodge, 29 March 1906, Lodge Papers.
[70] For the debate see: John M. Blum, *The Republican Roosevelt*, 87–105; Leland L. Sage, *William Boyd Allison: A Study in Practical Politics*, 296–305; Stephenson, *Aldrich*, 283–313; Kolko, *Railroads and Regulation*, 110–47; Robert H. Wiebe, *Businessmen and Reform: A Study of the Progressive Movement*, 51–56; Robert M. LaFollette, *Autobiography: A Personal Narrative of Political Experiences*, 403–18; Leon Burr Richardson, *William E. Chandler, Republican*, 657–74; Dorothy Ganfield Fowler, *John Coit Spooner: Defender of Presidents*, 343–51; Mark Sullivan, *Our Times: The United States, 1900–1925*, 3: 226–74; Francis Butler Simkins, *Pitchfork Ben Tillman, South Carolinian*, 419–40; Joseph Benson Foraker, *Notes of a Busy Life*, 2: 211–27.

represented the national consensus on rate regulation but was too vague to fully satisfy either Roosevelt or the railroads. The bill then went to Aldrich's Senate Committee on Interstate Commerce, where a real battle began. The contest was primarily between Roosevelt and Aldrich over the role of judicial review. Roosevelt hoped the final measure would specifically restrict the power of the courts to a narrow review, while Aldrich, representing railroad opinion, wanted a guaranteed broad court review. Narrow review would confine the role of the courts to procedural review, that is, whether or not both sides were given a fair hearing. Broad review would permit the courts to review the evidence itself upon which the commission had made its decision.

Aldrich lacked sufficient power in the Senate Committee on Interstate Commerce to force the inclusion of a broad review provision in the bill. So he persuaded a majority coalition of Republican and Democratic committeemen to send the Hepburn bill to the floor of the Senate for debate and amendment, without committee endorsement. Aldrich selected committee member Benjamin R. Tillman of South Carolina as the floor leader. Under ordinary circumstances, that assignment would have been in the hands of Jonathan P. Dolliver of Iowa, also a committee member. Both Tillman and Dolliver enthusiastically favored an effective law. Aldrich, however, disliked the unruly Iowa Republican. The clever Aldrich apparently also hoped that the selection of Tillman, a Democrat and Roosevelt's bitter enemy, would disrupt the proponents of a strong bill. Although unhappy over the Aldrich maneuver, the politically professional Roosevelt did not let it deter him. In reporting on the episode to Whitelaw Reid, ambassador to Great Britain, the president said on March 1, 1906, "Aldrich did what I have rarely seen him do: he completely lost both his head and his temper. But it won't have any effect in the long run and I shall get just about the bill I have been fighting for."[71]

By late April both the Roosevelt and the Aldrich forces

[71] Morison, *Letters*, 5: 170; see also *Theodore Roosevelt: An Autobiography*, 435–36; Thomas Richard Ross, *Jonathan Prentiss Dolliver: A Study in Political Integrity and Independence*, 205–06.

recognized each other's strengths and weaknesses. Both had failed to form a winning coalition among Republican and Democratic factions. Roosevelt faced the possibility of complete failure, but even if the Aldrich forces should pass a broad review bill, the Supreme Court might declare it unconstitutional. William Howard Taft believed the court could not constitutionally employ broad review over decisions of an administrative agency, but he did believe that some sort of statement on the court's role should appear in the bill. Roosevelt, however, came to recognize that he could not obtain sufficient support from lawyers, in and out of the Senate, on his narrow review position. Regardless of how they felt privately, they were not prepared to commit themselves openly to any but the vaguest statements on the role of the courts. Overly cautious, they wanted the measure to indicate that the courts had the power to participate in rate decisions but also to leave it to the discretion of the judges whether or not the courts should engage in narrow or broad review.[72] Aldrich, on the other hand, saw the potential danger in failure to get some legislation to meet the popular demand for regulation, and recognized that he had underestimated Roosevelt's ability to function as a tactician when under fire. Aldrich ceased to inquire, as he once had of a White House caller, "Well, how is the rudderless leader this morning?"[73]

On April 14, Roosevelt delivered his famous muckraker speech against excesses in general. He spoke about the dangers to society inherent in the writings of "the wild preachers of unrest and discontent," but at the same time he made clear his desire to correct the injustices to society resulting from the unrestricted amassing of great fortunes and corporate power. He called for a federal inheritance tax and increased governmental control over business. In the latter connection, he specifically referred to railroad rate regulation as "a beginning in the direction of

[72] Taft to Horace Taft, 3 March 1906, and Taft to Philander C. Knox, 28 March 1906, Taft Papers; Allison to Jonathan P. Dolliver, 23 August 1907, Allison Papers. Moreover, Richard Olney observed in mid-March that "While the Interstate Commerce Act reaffirms the common law in the requirement of reasonableness, neither the statute nor the common law furnishes any definite standard for the determination of what is reasonable." Olney to Joseph B. Foraker, 16 March 1906, Olney Papers.

[73] George G. Hill memorandum, box 49, Biographer's Notes. Aldrich Papers.

[a] serious effort to settle some of these economic problems." This railroad rate regulation, he insisted, should not "be exercised in a spirit of malevolence toward the men who have created the wealth, but with the firm purpose both to do justice to them and to see that they . . . do justice to the public at large." There was much in the speech that showed the lawmakers Roosevelt's reasonableness. He said, "the reform that counts is that which comes through steady, continuous growth; violent emotionalism leads to exhaustion." He declared that "if the present unrest is to result in permanent good," it must be "translated into action . . . marked by honesty, sanity and self-restraint."[74]

Both Aldrich and Roosevelt now found it possible to resolve their differences. Roosevelt was prepared to retreat and, because he had been cautious in his public statements, could do so without seeming to give in to Aldrich and the railroads. Aldrich, who no longer held his former paternalistic attitude toward the youthful president, showed more willingness to come to terms. It was a matter of choosing the best time. They made particular use of two members of the old Senate Four.

Normally the president and the Senate Four would have resolved their differences before the measure reached the Senate floor. This time, however, the situation was too complex. Outside pressures on them differed in degree and kind. Platt died in the spring of 1905. The ailing Allison and Spooner were in such weak positions in their home states that they hoped to escape taking a positive stand on the controversial court review aspect of the bill. They clearly hoped that Aldrich and Roosevelt would settle the matter before they had to cast their votes. After the measure reached the Senate floor with the court review issue still unresolved, Spooner and Allison became conspicuous. Both sponsored amendments to end the deadlock through compromise.

Spooner, a friend of the railroads, applied his superior legal talents to retain for them the broad review power of the courts and at the same time to satisfy the demands of the well-organized, insistent shippers of Milwaukee and the antirailroad

[74] *New York Tribune,* 15 April 1906.

rural voters of Wisconsin.[75] He offered several amendments to the Hepburn bill that were compromises. In preparing his amendments, Spooner consulted in particular railroad expert John W. Midgley, whom he had known in earlier days in Wisconsin. Midgley was currently manager of the Railway Clearing House Bureau in Chicago.[76] To a lesser degree, he sought the advice of Lloyd W. Bowers, general counsel for the Chicago and Northwestern Railroad Company.

With Bowers's help, Spooner formulated one of these amendments to protect both the shippers and the railroads in situations where litigation was in process. Shippers contended that under a system of elaborate court review, they might have to pay excessive rates for an indefinite period before they could obtain redress. The railroads, on the other hand, wished to insure protracted court review of interstate commerce decisions that reduced rates. The Spooner amendment, which Roosevelt and Allison temporarily favored, would allow railroads to obtain a suspension of rate changes in dispute until the courts decided the matter but would require the roads to place in escrow the amount of money in dispute. The escrow feature would protect shippers against delaying tactics on the part of the railroads. Unfortunately, the amendment did not include a plan to distribute the escrow money equitably in the event the railroads lost the case. Numerous parties might conceivably have legal claim to the money, namely, the producers, the middlemen, the shippers, and the consumers.[77] In early March, in a politic letter to influential Milwaukee shipper Edward P. Bacon, the president reduced the shipper pressure for the Spooner amendment. Roosevelt stated that he favored keeping the amendment in reserve for Congress to pass a few months later if it then appeared necessary. Meanwhile, he did "not regard it as a vital matter one

[75] See E. W. Keyes to Spooner, 4 February 1906, Spooner Papers.

[76] For this correspondence on the railroad industry, see: Spooner to Midgley, 15 January, 3 March 1906, and Midgley to Spooner, 25 January, 3, 8, 12, 23, 28 March, 27 April, 11, 26 May, 1, 4, 26 June 1906, Spooner Papers; Midgley to Roosevelt, 28 May 1906, copy in ibid.; see also Midgley to Roosevelt, 12, 15 October 1904, and Charles A. Prouty to Roosevelt, 24 October 1904, Roosevelt Papers.

[77] Bowers to Spooner, 8 January 1906, and Burton Hanson, general solicitor, Legal Department, Chicago, Milwaukee and St. Paul Railway Company, to Spooner, 30 April 1906, Spooner Papers; Sage, *Allison,* 301.

way or another."[78] At the time, Roosevelt still hoped the Hepburn bill would limit the courts to a narrow review and also that it would prevent undue delay of cases in the courts. Those features would reduce the need for Spooner's escrow proposal.

Roosevelt finally recruited Allison to present an administration-formulated compromise proposal on the court review question. Allison, weary, in ill health, and caught in the conflicting currents of loyalties to old-time associates, had remained largely in the background.[79] But it was fortuitous that he was still in the Senate when the time arrived for compromise. Roosevelt induced him to sponsor what all parties to the arrangement conspicuously called the "Allison Amendment." This ended the long contest over the Hepburn bill.

On May 3, because Allison was ill, Aldrich presented the Allison amendment to the Senate. It stated that the courts would have the power to review Interstate Commerce Commission changes in rates but left to the courts themselves the decision on how narrow or broad to be in their performance. The Senate readily accepted this amendment, thereby restoring the Hepburn bill to virtually the same measure the House had passed earlier, which had said nothing about review.[80]

On May 18, 1906, the Senate passed the Hepburn bill, 71 to 3. The vote in its favor was as overwhelming as that in the House four months before. Only one Republican, Ohio's Joseph B. Foraker, voted against it. Many railroad lawyers and officials expressed gratitude to him for his singular performance.[81]

Enactment of the Hepburn Act was a distinct achievement for the Republican party. Despite the strain the debate had placed on the long-standing political-business and East-Middle West partnerships, the party emerged intact. Both Roosevelt and Aldrich felt they had triumphed. Roosevelt achieved an advance in governmental regulation of business. Aldrich thought he had obtained broad court review. Soon, however, when the

[78] 9 March 1906, Morison, *Letters*, 5: 173–74.
[79] On Allison's feelings of uncertainty and worry, see Allison to Aldrich, 19 October 1905, Aldrich Papers.
[80] See Sage, *Allison*, 302–04; Blum, *Republican Roosevelt*, 102–05.
[81] Borne out in letters to Foraker, March–June 1906, Foraker Papers, as reported in Jeanette Nichols memorandum, box 49, Biographer's Notes, Aldrich Papers.

courts determined their proper role, they chose narrow review.[82]

Before adjournment, Congress also enacted pure food, drug, and meat inspection measures. In these notable achievements, however, the Republican top leaders played a less important role than in railroad rate regulation. Lesser politicians, writers, and a concerned public persuaded Roosevelt to endorse these reforms. The president, in turn, pressured Speaker Cannon and other key House members to advance the legislation. Aldrich, who had opposed regulation of these industries, now allowed the measures to slip through the Senate without his vote, either for or against. Allison and Spooner paired, with Allison later remarking that he favored the reforms.[83]

That summer, Roosevelt took satisfaction from the 1906 legislative record. He said of the food, drug, and meat regulation measures that they were "along the same general line" as the interstate commerce law and "second only to it importance."[84] In a letter to Root on August 18, he declared he had "never known Congress to do quite as well as this Congress has done." He mused, "it is not often that an administration can say with greater truth than we can that we have carried out with signal success the policies we have undertaken."[85] Despite these achievements, however, the party command had a relatively slight legislative record and most of Roosevelt's years in the White House were behind him.

[82] Blum, *Republican Roosevelt*, 104–05.
[83] George E. Mowry, *The Era of Theodore Roosevelt, 1900–1912*, 207–08; Gwinn, *Cannon*, 106–13; Fowler, *Spooner*, 331, 333–34; for a comprehensive account of the meat inspection measure, see John Braeman, "The Square Deal in Action: A Case Study in the Growth of the 'National Police Power,'" in John Braeman, Robert H. Bremner, and Everett Walters, *Change and Continuity in Twentieth-Century America*, 42–80.
[84] Roosevelt to James E. Watson, 18 August 1906, Morison, *Letters*, 5: 375.
[85] Ibid., 367.

X

AN EPIDEMIC OF
POLITICAL CAUTION
1906

AFTER ENACTMENT of the Hepburn Act and the pure
food, drug, and meat inspection measures, the Republican
party approached the 1906 election with caution and felt the
need to strengthen its public image with voters. Times were still
good and there were no tangible evidences of panic, yet many
people feared that further governmental reforms might lessen
prosperity and expressed increased concern for law and order as
a protection for individual and property rights. The Republican
leadership shared the general uneasiness over extremists. They
were concerned over socialism, labor union agitators, and Negro
lynchings. Hence they concentrated more on law enforcement
than on new legislation. During the 1906 election campaign,
Roosevelt made only one notable speech calling for increased
governmental control of business and as he directed the campaign he urged his followers to be circumspect on economic
reform issues.

Roosevelt's restraint in his drive to extend governmental supervision over business came from his uneasiness over the growth
of the Socialist party, the increase of reform zeal in segments of
the Democratic party, and the increase in labor union activity.
But he was even more disquieted by the worsening relations
within the Republican-business partnership. Many businessmen
resented the Hepburn Act and the continued relentless enforcement of the Sherman Act against trusts, and some took unkindly
to Roosevelt's attempt to restrain trusts through the Bureau of

Corporations. Many hesitated to enter into "gentlemen's agreements" with the government whereby they would promise to be good and report their operations to the bureau and president as evidence of their good faith. They clearly preferred running the risk of adverse publicity and even prosecution to exposing all their activities to unpredictable government officials. It was the restlessness within the party itself, rather than the efforts of outside reformers, which most worried the top leadership, and in particular party chieftain Roosevelt.

In late June, George W. Perkins, whose function was partially to keep J. P. Morgan informed, wrote a long letter to Morgan, then in London, on the mood of Americans with money to invest. Perkins reported that although prosperity was at a high level and appeared to be mounting ever higher, investors, especially those with moderate sums, showed definite concern for what the future held for business. "I do not believe," he said, "that in my experience I have ever known a time when so many people of moderate holdings have expressed their inability to decide what to do."[1]

As a devotee of orderly business practices, Perkins placed the cause of the current uneasiness in a broader context than rash political interference with business, although he did not rule out the government's actions as a factor. Perkins felt that of late "we have had so much to disturb confidence in American business methods and management of corporations that it is not any wonder that the average investor has not, in a general way, known where he was at; but within the last two or three weeks especially, it seems as though things had [sic] crystalized somewhat and people are beginning to wonder whether or not any security is exempt from ultimate attack, in some form or another."[2]

Perkins indicated he believed the performance of the Roosevelt administration was a contributing factor to the current uneasiness in the business world. The tone of his remarks, however, suggested approval rather than censorship of the government's activity. He was friendly toward the government in his

[1] 25 June 1906, Perkins Papers.
[2] Ibid.

account of its actions on trusts. The Justice Department, acting upon information which Roosevelt's Bureau of Corporations had obtained, was prosecuting the Standard Oil Company for violating the Elkins Act. On that matter Perkins reported, "I have been rather surprised that the final decision of the President and his Cabinet and the Attorney General to begin criminal proceedings against the Standard Oil Company should have had such a depressing effect as it has had during the last few days." He had thought that investors had already discounted that event, because the president had over a month earlier "plainly stated" that he was referring the Bureau of Corporations report on the matter to the attorney general, "who would decide what action or actions should be brought against the corporation or its officials."[3] Perkins had in mind the president's special message to Congress on May 4, 1906, in which he summarized the bureau's findings and pointedly stated, "The report shows that the Standard Oil Company has benefited enormously up almost to the present moment by secret rates, many of these secret rates being clearly unlawful."[4]

Perkins expressed optimism about the eventual effect of the increased governmental supervision of business. He predicted that more indictments against railroads were on the way. "I really believe," he added, "that while the treatment is mighty heroic, it is going to work out for the ultimate and great good for the railroads." He held the same view toward the long-term effect of the pending measure to regulate the meat-packers. It was destined to add to their profits because government certification of meat would add greatly to their foreign market.[5]

Clearly Perkins understood the prevailing Republican leadership's attitude of restraint and the pressures upon them. He told Morgan, "As to the Government's further action, in the way of turning up new work to be done, I very much doubt if it will amount to anything." He believed "the powers that be feel that they have made splendid political capital out of what

[3] Ibid.
[4] Quoted in Arthur M. Johnson, "Theodore Roosevelt and the Bureau of Corporations," *Mississippi Valley Historical Review* 48 (December 1961), 584–85.
[5] Perkins to Morgan, 25 June 1906, Perkins Papers.

has been done in connection with the packers, the Standard Oil Company and minor matters, and are ready to rest on their laurels for some time." Politically, he said, "with the masses, the record is probably a very good one with which to go before the country, but, as I have said above, the treatment was pretty heroic and no one can tell what effect it will have in other directions meanwhile." As for the 1906 election, Perkins made no prediction but reported that many people anticipated a great increase in the Socialist vote. He also noted that many people believed that "when Congress convenes in November a determined effort will be made to crowd through some sort of a tariff revision bill."[6]

Roosevelt was the central figure in the Republican 1906 campaign effort. He concentrated on electing as many Republicans as possible, regardless of their views on public questions. He apparently felt that any Republican in office was better than any Democrat, doubtless reasoning that party discipline could keep recalcitrants in line. He went to the rescue of beleaguered candidates who had demonstrated no affinity for reform. He himself offered no definite reform program for Congress to enact, although in early September he did on one occasion, in Harrisburg, Pennsylvania, renew his call for governmental control of business.

Until the end of August, Roosevelt remained pessimistic over the election outcome. He thought the public was unhappy with the Republican party. In a letter to Elihu Root, then on tour in Latin America, he expressed his doubts concerning future reform. His "experience of the past," he said, led him to conclude that "the time has about come for the swinging of the pendulum" away from the party in power. The voters feel "it is time for a new deal." He concluded, "it is possible we may win," but "I should not be at all surprised at a heavy defeat."[7] He nevertheless accepted the possibility of defeat philosophically. "Isn't it a great comfort to feel that in such circumstances it really does not alter the fact that during the time we have been in office we have accomplished great substantive work for good, and

---

[6] Ibid.
[7] 18 August 1906, Morison, *Letters,* 5: 367–69.

that while some of what we have done will be swept away, a very large part will remain?" Calling upon history for confirmation, he referred to Alexander Hamilton, about whom he had been recently reading. In Hamilton's "few years of public life, which ended by his seeing the actual triumph of the men and the seeming triumph of the principles to which he was most opposed, he nevertheless accomplished an amount of work which has remained vital and effective until the present day."[8]

Roosevelt worked closely with the cochairmen of the congressional campaign committee, Speaker Cannon and party whip James E. Watson of Indiana, assuring his friend Lodge in advance that he would "convulse the goo-goos and mugwumps with horror" by "making as strong a plea as I know how for the election of a Republican Congress."[9] He did exactly this in a letter to Watson, by prearrangement designed for public consumption and issued on August 18. He began his letter with a plea for the continuation of the current organization of Congress. "With Cannon as Speaker," he said, "the House has accomplished a literally phenomenal amount of good work." By example, he encouraged the campaign managers to guard against involvement in campaign debates on any important reform proposals. He concentrated his remarks mostly on the achievements of the past session of Congress, praising them because they were so very moderate.[10]

The campaign managers were on the alert to stamp out brush fires that threatened Republican candidates. They were particularly on the defensive from needling tariff revisionists and labor union leaders. Roosevelt handled the southern Negro problem separately and at a later date, inasmuch as it did not threaten any of the candidates during the campaign.

Demands by organized labor as well as the sporadic outbursts by unorganized labor became an increasing cause of political concern. As urban-industrial America grew in political power and rural America declined, and as tension mounted between

[8] Ibid.
[9] 9 August 1906, ibid., 349.
[10] Roosevelt to Watson, 25 July, 18 August 1906, ibid., 336, 372–78; to Cannon, 15 August 1906, ibid., 359–60; to Lodge, 15 August 1906, ibid., 361.

Republican-oriented employers and Republican-oriented wage earners, it appeared that the Republican party would eventually experience a schism over the conflict. In December 1903 Roosevelt had realized the party would ultimately have to deal with the labor question. In a lengthy letter to Carl Schurz at that time, the president stated, "Of course the two great fundamental internal problems with which we have to deal (aside from the problem of mere honesty, social and governmental, which after all enters into both the others) are the negro problem in the South, and the relations of capital and labor, especially organized capital and organized labor, to one another and to the community at large."[11]

Thus far, the party leaders had avoided the increasingly complex and explosive problem of worker-employer antagonism and had kept it on the periphery of the party agenda. The national party had in general enjoyed the support of wage earners because of the McKinley-Hanna record of friendliness and Roosevelt's handling of the anthracite coal strike. Roosevelt's Square Deal appealed to wage earners. Only his cavalier attitude toward striking western miners marred his good relations, when he showed no sympathy for them and condoned the use of armed force.[12] He was, however, on friendly terms with Samuel Gompers, president of the American Federation of Labor, and he endorsed some measures Gompers wanted Congress to enact, including one providing for a literacy test for immigrants.[13]

As the 1906 election approached, Roosevelt showed constant concern over the labor vote. He knew that a substantial number of Republicans were unalterably opposed to labor unions. As Whitelaw Reid tactfully said to him, "Some of your warmest supporters would not like to admit the necessity of trades unions."[14] Roosevelt had been worried about the labor situation

[11] 24 December 1903, ibid., 3: 679.
[12] See, for example, Roosevelt to George W. Alger, 20 March 1906, ibid., 5: 188–89.
[13] William Rea Gwinn, *Uncle Joe Cannon, Archfoe of Insurgency: A History of the Rise and Fall of Conservatism*, 113; Samuel Gompers, *Seventy Years of Life and Labor: An Autobiography*, 1: 243–44.
[14] 14 July 1904, Reid Papers.

in 1904 until the Democrats failed to become effective labor champions, and now he was even more concerned.[15]

In 1906 Speaker Cannon and the Labor Committee in the House were in a quarrel with Gompers and the AFL. The House had failed to pass the labor bills Gompers's organization desired. Gompers in person then presented a document to key House leaders called "Labor's Bill of Grievances," which included the charge that unsympathetic committees in Congress had suppressed labor legislation. Cannon and Charles E. Littlefield of Maine retaliated. Cannon delivered a tirade against Gompers which must have pleased the National Association of Manufacturers, then engaged in a successful antilabor crusade, and which aroused the ire of organized labor members. In August, the American Federation of Labor announced its determination to defeat Cannon, Littlefield, and other antilabor House members in the 1906 election.[16]

Although Roosevelt regretted the House performance because it was "bad business to solidify labor against" the party, he came to the defense of the House members under attack.[17] In his "public letter" to Watson, the president reminded voters that "In addition to dealing with the proper control of capitalistic wealth, Congress has also taken important steps in securing to the wageworkers certain great rights." The only specific item he cited, however, was the LaFollette-sponsored employers' liability law.[18]

[15] See Roosevelt to Jacob G. Schurman, 31 August 1903, Morison, *Letters*, 3: 581; to Lyman Abbott, 5 September 1903, ibid., 592–93; to Theodore Roosevelt, Jr., 24 October 1903, Roosevelt Papers; to Root, 2 June 1904, Morison, *Letters*, 4: 811; Root to Roosevelt, 13 June 1904, Root Papers; Whitelaw Reid to Roosevelt, 14 July 1904, Reid Papers; Roosevelt to Cannon, 12 September 1904, Morison, *Letters*, 4: 925–26, 928–29; Paul Morton to E. P. Ripley, 31 December 1903, copy in Roosevelt Papers; Hermann Hagedorn, ed., *The Works of Theodore Roosevelt*, 16: 368.

[16] Gwinn, *Cannon*, 113–14; L. White Busbey, *Uncle Joe Cannon: The Story of a Pioneer American*, 333–38; Blair Bolles, *Tyrant from Illinois: Uncle Joe Cannon's Experiment with Personal Power*, 46–48, 49; Harold U. Faulkner, *The Decline of Laissez Faire, 1897–1917*, 295–96; Gompers, *Autobiography*, 2: 171–72, 239; Roosevelt to Henry Cabot Lodge, 13 October 1906, Henry Cabot Lodge, ed., *Selections from the Correspondence of Theodore Roosevelt and Henry Cabot Lodge, 1884–1918*, 2: 244.

[17] Roosevelt to James Wilson, 11 September 1906, Morison, *Letters*, 5: 403–04.

[18] Roosevelt to James E. Watson, 18 August 1906, ibid., 376–77.

Roosevelt also dispatched Secretary of War Taft to campaign for candidates whom the AFL and other labor groups had singled out for special attack. Taft spoke in Littlefield's Maine bailiwick and went to Idaho to help Governor Frank R. Gooding.[19] The Western Federation of Miners was bent upon defeating Gooding for reelection because he had tried to bring to trial the union laborers allegedly involved in the 1905 murder of former Idaho Governor Frank Steunberg. Roosevelt said that "next to beating William Randolph Hearst" in his bid for the governorship of New York, he was "most anxious to see Gooding elected in Idaho."[20]

In August Roosevelt reported to Root that "The tariff is of course what will cause us the most trouble."[21] But also in August he wrote Lodge that the issue was largely confined to "certain regions in the West." Roosevelt suggested to Lodge that what he characterized as "that idiot revision feeling" might possibly have continued in the West because it had "arisen somewhat later in that section" and hence had not yet run its course. In any case, Lodge, who a year before had been convinced that the party must no longer postpone tariff revision, was relieved to discover that the sentiment for it had subsided in Massachusetts, having "touched high water mark a year ago." Lodge thought it very apparent "that the great prosperity of the country has cooled off those who would change the tariff."[22] Meanwhile, Roosevelt, always uneasy about the tariff despite hopeful signs, insisted that the party campaigners follow a very cautious, carefully

[19] Roosevelt to Cannon, 15 August 1906, to Lodge, 15 August 1906, to Root, 18 August 1906—all in ibid., 360, 361, 367; to James Wilson, 11 September 1906, Roosevelt Papers; Taft to Albert Douglas, 29 July 1906, to Henry M. Hoyt, 10 September 1906, to Albert Chatfield, 11 September 1906, to E. J. Hill, 20 October 1906—all in Taft Papers; Gwinn, *Cannon*, 113; Gompers, *Autobiography*, 1: 244–46.

[20] Roosevelt to Alice Roosevelt Longworth, Morison, *Letters*, 5: 488–89. For more on the labor issue in the campaign, see *Commercial-News*, Danville, Illinois, 16 August 1906, clipping; Cannon to William Loeb, 16, 22 September 1906; Boies Penrose to Roosevelt, 19 September 1906; Cannon to Roosevelt, 14, 22 September 1906; Roosevelt to F. P. Sargent, 5 September 1906; Sargent to Roosevelt, 7 September 1906—all in Roosevelt Papers; Roosevelt to Gifford Pinchot, 15 September 1906, to Cannon, 17 September 1906, Morison, *Letters*, 5: 413–14.

[21] 18 August 1906, Morison, *Letters*, 5: 367.

[22] Roosevelt to Lodge, 9 August 1906, ibid., 5: 349; see also Lodge to Roosevelt, 8, 11, 28 August, 27 October 1906, Roosevelt Papers.

hedged approach. He persuaded ardent high-protectionist Cannon to abandon his plan to announce publicly that the Dingley Tariff needed no revision.[23]

While Roosevelt found it easy enough to keep the top leaders in line, some of the more ardent tariff revisionists chose to argue the matter. Beveridge, flushed with his success as a leading advocate of the meat inspection measure, tried to persuade Roosevelt to press for tariff revision in the next Congress. The president asked him to consider whether there was any chance that the Republicans in Congress would even entertain the idea, let alone enact the type of measure that would avoid bringing disaster in the presidential election. Beveridge treated those "considerations as irrelevant."[24]

Taft, a tariff revisionist, whom Roosevelt assigned to deliver a September speech in Maine to aid congressional candidate Littlefield, could not resist the temptation to inject the tariff question into the address. But he first cleared the matter with Roosevelt, who raised no objection, inasmuch as Taft did not call for immediate revision.[25] Taft stated that since passage of the Dingley bill, changes in business conditions made it wise and just to "revise the schedules." But, he added, just how soon "the feeling in favor of revision shall crystallize into action cannot be foretold."[26]

Mrs. Taft, with the presidency in mind and on one of those rare instances of being in agreement with Roosevelt, whom she jealously mistrusted, thought her husband had made a mistake. "I shouldn't wonder if your dragging the tariff into that Maine speech would cost you the nomination," she wrote him. Two days later, still worried, she was sorry he kept "bringing in the tariff, as it seems to be unnecessary and not a special issue at

[23] Roosevelt to Cannon, 15 August 1906, Morison, *Letters*, 5: 359–60; Cannon to Roosevelt, 17 August 1906, Roosevelt Papers.

[24] As reported in Roosevelt to Lodge, 27 September 1906, Lodge, *Roosevelt and Lodge Correspondence*, 2: 233; see also Albert J. Beveridge to Roosevelt, 21 August 1906, Roosevelt Papers; Roosevelt to Edgar D. Crumpacker, 30 July 1906, Morison, *Letters*, 5: 339.

[25] Taft to Roosevelt, 27, 28 August 1906, Roosevelt Papers; Roosevelt to Taft, 1 September 1906, Morison, *Letters*, 5: 392.

[26] Quoted in Henry F. Pringle, *The Life and Times of William Howard Taft: A Biography*, 1: 289.

this time, and calls down comments." The Washington papers "give so much prominence to it, that you would suppose it was the principal point of the speech."[27] Taft replied that he probably did talk too much about the tariff and "you are quite right in supposing that this will be another ground for opposing me on the part of powerful interests, but it is relevant, it comes in natural." Also, "It is important to meet the discussion of the Democrats."[28]

It became increasingly clear, meanwhile, that Roosevelt hoped he would not need to press for immediate revision. In a letter to Taft on September 1 he said the vital factor in the situation was the crystallization of sentiment, which he believed would not occur in time to achieve revision before the 1908 presidential election. By the time that election approached, he believed, it would be wise "to announce that there shall be tariff revision by the Republican party immediately after the election."[29]

On August 31, a speech by William Jennings Bryan in Madison Square Garden suddenly altered the nature of the election campaign. Bryan startled the nation with the declaration that he had "reached the conclusion that railroads partake so much of the nature of a monopoly that they must ultimately become public property and be managed by public officials."[30] Soon afterwards he backed away from his "socialistic" outburst, but too late to repair the damage he had inflicted on the Democratic party, which lost considerable potential support among moderates. Although weary or afraid of Roosevelt's extension of federal power, they now shuddered at the suggestion of socialism and looked to the Republican party for protection. On September 4, Roosevelt wrote Root that Bryan "has helped us, as he came a bad cropper in his much heralded great speech."[31] On the same day, the president also wrote Lodge, "I drew a sigh of relief after reading Bryan's speech."[32] Bryan's remarks afforded

[27] Mrs. Taft to Taft, 27, 29 October 1906, Taft Papers.
[28] Taft to Mrs. Taft, 1 November 1906, ibid.
[29] Morison, *Letters*, 5: 392; see also Spooner to Reuben M. Kessler, 29 December 1906, Spooner Papers.
[30] Paolo E. Coletta, *William Jennings Bryan: Political Evangelist, 1860–1908*, 377.
[31] Morison, *Letters*, 5: 395.
[32] Ibid., 397.

Roosevelt increased maneuverability in reviving his crusade for more federal control over business.

The recent performance of certain businessmen, most notably Edward H. Harriman and the managers of Standard Oil, reinforced Roosevelt's decision to press forward with his antitrust drive. The president's current irritation with the Standard Oil "people," as he habitually referred to the management of that giant concern, revolved around their failure to abide by the Elkins antirebate law. Roosevelt had hoped that his power to publicize any Bureau of Corporations evidence of violations of the law would achieve compliance without litigation. But the Standard Oil "people" had responded with defiance, and by the summer of 1906 the angry and disappointed president ordered the Justice Department to take legal action.[33] The Standard Oil experience made it clear to Roosevelt that Congress would have to increase governmental controls or continue to channel many trust cases into the courts.

The arrogance of Standard Oil irritated the president all the more because it contrasted sharply with the more cooperative policy of the United States Steel Corporation with the Bureau of Corporations. Elbert H. Gary, head of the huge, Morgan-dominated concern, exuded affability in his conversations with the president. This "reasonableness" reflected the Morgan empire's awareness of the importance of good relations with the government and the voters. On June 25, 1906, George W. Perkins wrote Morgan, "There has been a good deal of a favorable nature in the papers during the last two or three weeks, comparing us with the Standard Oil and its companies." In an understatement, Perkins added, "Judge Gary has been most wise and vigilant in all that he has done in this connection."[34]

In early October, Roosevelt reported to Lodge, "I have been

[33] Charles Saul to James R. Garfield, 25 May 1905; Virgil Kline to Garfield, 13 June 1905; Garfield to Kline, 1 December 1905; Herbert Knox Smith to Garfield, 14 August 1906; Smith to Garfield, 31 August 1906; William H. Moody to Garfield, 9 November 1906—all in Bureau of Corporation Records, Record Group 40, National Archives, cited in William Buchanan, "Theodore Roosevelt and the Business Community" (Master's thesis, University of Maryland, 1968), 48–49; Gabriel Kolko, *The Triumph of Conservatism: A Reinterpretation of American History, 1900–1916*, 122–23.

[34] Perkins Papers; see also Ida M. Tarbell, *The Life of Elbert H. Gary*, 178–86.

more shocked than I can say by the attitude of some of the corporation men within the last two or three weeks." He cited in particular the Standard Oil Company and Harriman. The indignant Roosevelt explained to Lodge that "the Standard Oil people informed [Boise] Penrose that they intend to support the Democratic party unless I call a halt in the suits begun against" them. Moreover, although "they did not use the naked brutality of language which Harriman used . . . they did state in substance that they could buy what favors they needed" if the Democrats won the election.[35]

Roosevelt's anger at Harriman was largely personal. Frequently since the president had ordered the indictment of the Northern Securities Company in 1902, the proud, independent railroad tycoon had shown his dislike of him. In early October 1906, Roosevelt's irritation turned into fury when he learned the details of a conversation between Harriman and New York Republican leader James Sherman. Roosevelt reported the episode to Lodge in early October: "Last week Jim Sherman called upon E. H. Harriman for a contribution. Harriman declined flatly to give anything" and said "he had no interest in the Republican party and that in view of my action toward the corporations he preferred the other side to win." According to Roosevelt, when Sherman reminded Harriman of the much greater hostility toward corporations in the Democratic party, Harriman replied "that he was not in the least afraid, that whenever it was necessary he could buy a sufficient number of Senators and Congressmen or State legislators to protect his interests, and when necessary he could buy the Judiciary. These," Roosevelt added, "were his exact words."[36] Roosevelt also was incensed over Harriman's alleged charges that Roosevelt had reneged on a promise to appoint Chauncey Depew as ambassador to France and that in 1904 Roosevelt had asked Harriman to raise $250,000 for the Republican presidential campaign.[37] Roosevelt declared, probably correctly, that "Any such statement is a deliberate and wilful untruth—by rights it should be characterized by an even shorter

---

[35] 8 October 1906, Morison, *Letters,* 5: 452–53.
[36] Ibid.
[37] Roosevelt to James S. Sherman, 8 October 1906, and enclosing 1904 correspondence between Roosevelt and E. H. Harriman, Morison, *Letters,* 5: 447–52.

and more ugly word. I never requested Mr. Harriman to raise a dollar for the Presidential campaign of 1904."[38]

On October 4, Roosevelt carried his anger to the public. Bryan's "socialistic" speech made it politically safe for the president to lash out against irresponsible men of great wealth, as well as against "demagogs and agitators." In a speech at Harrisburg, Pennsylvania, Roosevelt castigated these extremist enemies of society. He placed greatest emphasis on the "need to check the forces of greed." He made clear his belief that the Constitution afforded the federal government sufficient power to increase "Supervision over and control of the great fortunes used in business" in the interest of "the general public." The Constitution granted to the federal government, he declared, power beyond "the enumerated powers," an "inherent power" to operate "in all cases where the object involved was beyond the power of the several states." Pennsylvania's Philander C. Knox, who had left the cabinet in 1904 to enter the Senate, told the president it was the strongest speech he had ever made. Lodge thought likewise.[39]

Election day brought victory for the traditional professionals in both parties. There were no upsets. Cannon of Illinois, Foraker of Ohio, and George W. Norris of Nebraska won with substantial majorities. The Cummins forces gained strength in Iowa and Gooding won in Idaho. In some state contests, however, the victories were something less than impressive. In Rhode Island, the Republicans retained most of their usual positions, but Democrat James H. Higgins captured the governorship and his party made notable gains in Providence. The closeness of Charles Evans Hughes's victory over William Randolph Hearst in New York caused some consternation. The large minority vote for John B. Moran in Massachusetts disheartened Lodge, but he found the result in New York "even more depressing." Though gratified over the election of Hughes, Lodge was upset "to think of the thousands of Republican workingmen and the great mass of the Democratic party who voted for Hearst and Moran," and he thought this "melancholy to the last degree."

[38] Ibid., 447.

[39] Roosevelt to Lodge, 8, 16 October 1906, ibid., 452–53; Lodge to Roosevelt, 18 October 1906, Lodge, *Roosevelt and Lodge Correspondence,* 2: 249–50; George E. Mowry, *The Era of Theodore Roosevelt, 1900–1912,* 209.

He believed "we have got a terrible struggle before us to save the country from a movement which strikes at the very foundation of society and civilization."[40] Spooner also felt that "the escape by so narrow a vote in the great State of New York from Hearst shows an unhealthy condition of the popular mind."[41]

The narrowness of the victory in New York did not worry Roosevelt. He was too pleased with the Hughes victory and too angry at the men who refused to support the party to be pessimistic. He was "especially glad that we have won . . . without being indebted to the ultra-reactionaries, the Bourbons, the great financiers, who declined to support either the Republican Congressional candidates or Hughes." The president was also "astounded but greatly pleased, by the friendly leading editorial" in the *New York Times,* a paper he considered to be a "staunch and well-nigh subservient" ally of "these financiers."[42]

From a purely partisan view, Roosevelt had very good reason to be pleased. The defeats and near defeats for the party occurred primarily in local and state contests and, as Lodge wrote Roosevelt, "On the National side we did splendidly."[43] In a letter to his daughter Alice, Roosevelt expressed his relief and gratification at the election outcome. "I had no idea we were going to do so well in the Congressional campaign." Aside from the congressional victories, "Next to beating Hearst in New York, I was most anxious to see Gooding elected in Idaho. . . . Yes . . . it is a big victory for civilization, to have beaten those Western Federation of Miners scoundrels." He regarded it as "very gratifying to have ridden iron-shod over Gompers and the labor agitators, and at the same time to have won the striking victory while the big financiers either stood sullenly aloof or gave furtive aid to the enemy."[44]

The Negro question remained outside the 1906 campaign, but it continued as usual to haunt the Republican party. Roosevelt, in particular, found it troublesome and unrewarding. The top

[40] Lodge to Roosevelt, 7 November 1906, Lodge, *Roosevelt and Lodge Correspondence,* 2: 259.
[41] Spooner to W. T. Lewis, 9 November 1906, Spooner Papers.
[42] Roosevelt to Charles Sprague-Smith, 7 November 1906, Roosevelt Papers.
[43] 7 November 1906, Lodge, *Roosevelt and Lodge Correspondence,* 2: 259.
[44] Roosevelt to Alice Roosevelt Longworth, 7 November 1906, Morison, *Letters,* 5: 488–89.

party leadership in 1904 had ignored the Crumpacker plan that lesser party men had managed to insert in the national platform, and in 1906 the national leaders ignored the entire subject in their campaign documents for the congressional elections. Roosevelt left the Negro question out of his 1906 campaign effort because he had no Negro program to take to the people for endorsement.

In 1905 Roosevelt had delivered a number of speeches in the South and North that included discussion of the Negro problem but he was careful to emphasize the advantages of sectional harmony instead of militancy. He increasingly took occasion to praise the good people of the South, white and black, whenever he mentioned the problem.[45] But the emphasis in his utterance was invariably on the good white people of the South. To underscore his desire to obtain their aid in the Negro cause, Roosevelt reduced the number of Negro appointees in the South and also ceased to use the services of militant Negro champion James S. Clarkson.[46]

In the fall of 1906, Roosevelt wrote Charles W. Eliot, president of Harvard, "I have been at my wits' end in knowing how to deal with this negro problem." He believed the situation was bad wherever there were "large bodies of negroes," including the North. "Things are hideous in the South." He added, "I am certain that what I have done has been all right, yet often the results have been most unsatisfactory; and while I have in different States tried different experiments, none of them have come out so I am really pleased."[47]

In mid-August 1906, an incident focused national interest on the issue. A small band of Negro soldiers from three Negro companies stationed near Brownsville, Texas, furious at their treatment in the town, allegedly "shot up the town" in a ten-minute nighttime foray. One inhabitant was reported killed. In

---

[45] See, for example, editorial by Oswald Garrison Villard, *New York Evening Post*, 14 February 1905, enclosed in Booker T. Washington to Roosevelt, 9 March 1905, Roosevelt Papers; C. Vann Woodward, *Origins of the New South*, 465–66.

[46] Roosevelt to William H. Fleming, 20 August 1906, Roosevelt Papers; Thomas Robert Cripps, "The Lily White Republicans: The Negro, the Party, and the South in the Progressive Era" (Ph.D. dissertation, University of Maryland, 1967), 219–20.

[47] 28 September 1906, Roosevelt Papers.

early November, Roosevelt, always horrified over violent defiance of the law, ordered the dismissal of 160 veteran Negro infantrymen, virtually the strength of the entire three companies. All of the Negroes had refused to inform on the handful involved, so the president dismissed them all without honor, including six who had received the Medal of Honor. They automatically lost their claims for pensions and their right to reenlist. No one produced, then or later, any actual proof that any of the soldiers were involved in the episode. Roosevelt justified his intemperate performance as necessary to carry out his commitment to uphold the Constitution. However, he timed the release of his punitive order so that voters did not learn about it in time to be influenced in their voting. But the majority of the voters doubtless agreed with his action.[48] Many certainly agreed with historian Albert Bushnell Hart of Harvard University, who wrote Roosevelt, "You have seized the opportunity to read to the Negroes a very necessary lesson as to their responsibility for the maintenance of justice." Hart added that Roosevelt's performance also earned him the right to apply the same approach to "acts of violence by members of the white race upon the Negro."[49]

Negroes, however, were incensed. Many had looked to Roosevelt for at least a measure of help and were disappointed when they learned of his action. Booker T. Washington tried unsuccessfully to get the president to change his mind.[50] Mary Church Terrell, the wife of a judge, and a Negro member of the District of Columbia Board of Education, persistently tried to see Secretary of War Taft in an effort to persuade him to put off the discharge until the president returned from a Caribbean trip. Mrs. Terrell finally saw Taft, who wired the president, but to no avail. Taft believed it was reasonable to wait for a rehear-

---

[48] Emma Lou Thornbrough, "The Brownsville Episode and the Negro Vote," *Mississippi Valley Historical Review* 44 (December 1957): 469–70; William Henry Harbaugh, *Power and Responsibility: The Life and Times of Theodore Roosevelt*, 303–06; Mowry, *Era of Theodore Roosevelt*, 212–13; Joseph Benson Foraker, *Notes of a Busy Life*, 2: 231–37.

[49] 26 November 1906, Roosevelt Papers.

[50] Roosevelt to Washington, 5 November 1906; John Allison to Roosevelt, 21 November 1906; Charles W. Anderson to William Loeb, 30 November 1906—all in Roosevelt Papers.

ing to explain the president's full reason for his action.[51] He felt, however that Roosevelt's mass discharge of the soldiers was "entirely justified." In a January 1 letter to his brother, Taft explained that he felt sure the president did not pay "as much attention to my suggestion" for a rehearing "as he otherwise would have" because "I could not get at him, and because I had not been cognizant of the facts on which the order was issued." Taft felt he otherwise might have persuaded Roosevelt and "this makes it uncomfortable for me."[52]

Roosevelt remained unpersuaded and baffled by Negro reaction. He later wrote to Ray Stannard Baker about his great surprise upon discovering "the attitude taken by the enormous majority of the colored people in regard to the matter." He had failed to foresee, he explained, that so many Negroes would condone the refusal of the 160 soldiers to provide information on the riot. He believed white people would have complied with the request.[53] Doubtless some white people felt Roosevelt was injudicious in his sweeping discharge, but no significant protest emerged among responsible white people. Senator Foraker, who entertained hope for the presidency, saw in the incident an opportunity for political advantage and tried to crystallize Negro voter support behind him and thereby undermine Taft's presidential chances.

Foraker's action and that of other less conspicuous protesters led to an intemperate display of animosity at a Gridiron Club dinner, where Roosevelt and Foraker openly quarreled. Roosevelt continued to defend his Brownsville order.[54] In a letter to Lyman Abbott, he later explained that in his opinion "The only hope of the Negro in the South is to be treated each man individually . . . and not as a member of a race." The Brownsville episode, he emphasized, gave the "greatest possible impetus" to the southern white argument that Negroes could not be treated as individuals because they "always stand by their own criminals." Roosevelt added that Foraker and other defenders of the

[51] Cripps, "Lily White Republicans," 268–69.
[52] Taft to Charles P. Taft, 1 January 1907, Taft Papers.
[53] 30 March 1907, Morison, Letters, 5: 634.
[54] Thornbrough, "Brownsville," 477–78; Mowry, Era of Theodore Roosevelt, 213.

Brownsville troops were "engaged in a most dangerous effort to put a premium on murder and perjury among the enlisted men of the army . . . because the race to which they belong declines to consider the question of their guilt or innocence and says they should be restored to duty."[55] He looked upon agitators of the Brownsville matter as "creatures who have no place in the Republican party" and should be voted down. He recommended to Herbert Parsons, chairman of the New York County Republican Committee, that the way to meet such a "sinister movement" was to "tell the negro or white agitator who declaims about Brownsville that he is standing up for murder" and is like a defender of "bomb-throwers."[56]

Booker T. Washington quietly helped moderate Negro opposition. Though he had originally tried to persuade Roosevelt to reconsider the Brownsville order, Washington later considered the denunciation of the president too extreme. In a December letter to Negro newspaperman Ralph W. Tyler of Columbus, Ohio, he explained, "Of course it was natural that some protest should be made, but I fear there is too much of it," and concluded, "the American people will not stand for any length of time . . . abuse by any group of people of the President of the United States." He cautioned that "if our people in the North" go "too far there will be a reaction among the people, and the newspapers who have stood by us." Washington added, "I am doing all I can to check that folly."[57]

In the fall of 1906 a four-day race riot in Atlanta, Georgia, again forced the Negro problem to the forefront. Mobs of frenzied white people killed at least ten Negro youths; one white person was also killed. Newspapers had provoked the riot during an irresponsible election campaign by printing lurid accounts of supposed Negro assaults on white women. A crowd of whites, which grew in size to 10,000 or 15,000, dragged Negroes from streetcars to beat and kill them. Many Negroes raced into the slums and into the post office for protection.[58]

President Roosevelt failed to act on the Atlanta riot, consider-

---

[55] 10 May 1908, Morison, *Letters*, 6: 1026.
[56] 10 April 1908, ibid., 999.
[57] 5 December 1906, quoted in Thornbrough, "Brownsville," 476.
[58] Cripps, "Lily White Republicans," 265.

ing it a civil matter, unlike the Brownsville affair where he had constitutional authority to intervene as commander-in-chief of the armed forces. The Compromise of 1877 had reserved for the separate states jurisdiction over racial strife. The governor of Georgia finally called out the militia, and moderates, including Booker T. Washington who came down from New York, did what they could to restore order. Eventually the trouble subsided.[59]

Shortly after the riot, a group of concerned newspaper editors in Atlanta and former Governor Andrew J. Montague of Virginia asked Roosevelt to appoint a commission to investigate and make recommendations on the entire southern Negro problem. The proposal was initiated by Clark Howell of the *Atlanta Constitution*, who perhaps was ashamed of his paper's role in printing irresponsible articles before the riots. These concerned southerners urged Roosevelt to announce in his December 1906 annual message his intention to appoint such a commission. In response, Roosevelt tentatively included a mild and vague paragraph implying his endorsement of the commission idea and submitted a rough draft of the speech to several interested citizens. Howell and Montague approved of the draft, but Silas McBee, editor of the *Churchman*, gave only qualified approval.[60] McBee advised the president to "either leave it out altogether or erect it into a more important paragraph, expressing your positive judgment with regard to it."[61] Two days later Roosevelt decided to drop the reference. To Montague he explained, "probably it would be best to have some first-class Southern member—some Senator or Congressman of your stamp, my dear Governor—introduce the measure and then I could send in a special message backing it up." This, the president believed,

[59] Ibid., 267.

[60] Letters to Roosevelt from Clark Howell, 24, 31 October, 7 November 1906, A. J. Montague, 30 October 1906, William H. Fleming, 2, 9 November 1906, Silas McBee, 3 November 1906; Roosevelt to A. J. Montague, 5 November 1906— all in Roosevelt Papers; Roosevelt to Clark Howell, 26 October, 5 November 1906, Morison, *Letters*, 5: 472, 487–88. See tentative copy of address to Congress, sent to various people for their suggestions, dated 30 October 1906, box 113, Roosevelt Papers; see also Dr. Paul Paquin to Roosevelt, 5 December 1906, and Senator A. S. Clay to Roosevelt, 6 December 1906, Roosevelt Papers.

[61] Silas McBee to Roosevelt, 3 November 1906, Roosevelt Papers.

"would prevent there being any suspicion that I had some sinister, hidden purpose; and I am afraid that that suspicion would surely be called forth in the minds of some people if the suggestion came first from me."[62] To Clark Howell, he wrote that he was very doubtful about the recommendation for a commission because he was "very much afraid that a certain extreme element here in the North would misunderstand . . . and hail it as having . . . a sinister party purpose." He was afraid that "an exactly opposite element in the South, but an element no less radical and no less prejudiced, would make the same mistake."[63]

In his 1906 message, Roosevelt did refer at length to the Negro lynching problem. The shocking increase in lynchings in those years troubled many decent people, North and South. Roosevelt emphasized that "The greatest existing cause of lynching is the perpetration, especially by black men, of the hideous crime of rape—the most abominable," in his opinion, "in all the category of crimes, even worse than murder." In attributing a greater "perpetration" of rape to Negroes than to white men, Roosevelt presumably did not consider it rape for a white man to force his intentions on a helpless Negro woman, nor did he take into consideration how easy it was for a Negro who accidently touched a white woman to be accused of rape. He did recognize that "when mobs begin to lynch for rape they speedily . . . lynch for many other kinds of crimes" and a large number of the victims are "innocent of all crime." In Roosevelt's judgment, "the crime of rape should always be punished with death, as is the case with murder," and "assault with intent to rape should be made a capital crime . . . in the discretion of the court," but he emphasized in his message the necessity of "justice under law." He stated, "There is no question of 'social equality' or 'negro domination' involved; only the question of relentlessly punishing bad men." He exhorted the white people to help ferret out criminals, without indicating "the whole colored race," and, apparently with the Brownsville episode in

---

[62] 5 November 1906, ibid.
[63] 5 November 1906, Morison, *Letters*, 5: 487–88.

mind, pointed out that "respectable colored people must learn not to harbor criminals."[64]

Roosevelt linked the problem of crime with the need for more education for Negroes. He felt education would lessen the possibility of crime and believed "the best type of education for the colored man, as a whole" was that given at such schools as "Hampton and Tuskegee," where "young men and young women are trained industrially as well as in the ordinary public school branches." He added that "hardly any of them become criminals," especially of "the form of that brutal violence which invites lynch-law."[65]

Roosevelt remained discouraged over the prospects for better race relations. Finally, he even ceased pleading in speeches and letters. In 1911, he wrote confidentially to a young southern-born writer who had served as his secretary in Africa, "I do not believe that for a good many years I have said anything about the negro question." It seemed to him by that time that "it was just one of those questions" about which it was "best to say as little as possible, because notice of it inflames it." He went on to say that he believed that fundamentally "the North and the South act in just the same way toward the negro."[66] Roosevelt's own conventional approach to the Negro's plight doomed him to a very limited success with the problem.

[64] Hagedorn, *Works of Roosevelt*, 15: 351–54; on the extent of lynching see Booker T. Washington to Roosevelt, 17 October 1904, 4 January 1906, and Robert M. Stevens to Roosevelt, 13 November 1911, Roosevelt Papers.

[65] Hagedorn, *Works of Roosevelt*, 15: 354–55.

[66] Roosevelt to Warrington Dawson, 20 October 1911, Roosevelt Papers. Dawson was the son of New South leader Francis W. Dawson, editor of the *Charleston News and Courier*. See Woodward, *New South*, 145–46.

XI

THE ROOSEVELT-ALDRICH-
CANNON TRIUMVIRATE
1907-1908

THROUGHOUT THE FINAL TWO YEARS of the Roosevelt administration, the president, Senate leader Aldrich, and Speaker Cannon guided the Republican party. Aldrich and Cannon replaced the Four as the dominant figures in Congress. The concentration of party power in the Roosevelt-Aldrich-Cannon triumvirate, however, brought no appreciable change in Republican party policy. They clung to their habitual attitudes on the tariff, trusts, currency, and Negro questions. They exhibited no desire to initiate any significant legislation on any important matters, although the Panic of 1907 and the impending election campaign of 1908 finally forced them to enact emergency currency legislation. This drift boded ill for the party's future.

In day-to-day operations, the party commanders performed with professional skill. Roosevelt and Aldrich emerged from their contest over the Hepburn bill with enhanced mutual respect. They did not pretend to be friends, but they did maintain courteous relations. On one occasion, shortly after the 1906 election, Roosevelt good-humoredly asked Lodge to inform Aldrich that he had found it "touching to see the relief in his face on Saturday night—at the Gridiron when I said I wouldn't run again!" As a postscript to the letter, Roosevelt added, "Don't give Aldrich my message unless it is one of the days when he has a sense of humor." Lodge complied and reported back that Aldrich "was much amused."[1]

Cannon's ability and power to round up a majority vote in the House of Representatives made him useful in the top leadership, but he was otherwise a nuisance and an embarrassment to the party. His uncouthness and his conspicuous defense of the least defensible attitudes in rural and ultrareactionary Republicanism made him a liability. Nobody, however, was prepared to lead a movement to rid the party of this primitive politician who had cannily ridden the House seniority vehicle to the Speakership, where he just as cannily exercised dictatorial power. He had some powerfully placed followers. Many industrialists appreciated Cannon's standpat tariff position, his anti-labor-union views and his "nongovernmental-interference" philosophy. Small-town bankers felt secure with small-town banker Cannon in the Speaker's chair. Cannon's success in restoring the House to its once great political power pleased many House members, who had been unhappy with the recent rubber-stamp status of that body. Many individual congressmen were grateful for the numerous attentions the Speaker bestowed upon them. They found him honest, ingratiating, and helpful in their election campaigns and he remembered to hand out choice committee assignments to his loyal followers.[2]

The party's high command chose to leave serious legislative reform to local and state governments and paid little attention to the scattered reformers who moved from those levels into Congress. They tended to dismiss them as less dangerous to the nation and the Republican party than Hearst, Bryan, socialists, and labor agitators. They regarded freshman Senator LaFollette, elected in 1906, as able but something of a nuisance. Roosevelt occasionally, but grudgingly, acknowledged that the newcomer advocated some meritorious reform measures. At the time LaFollette entered the Senate Roosevelt was scornful of his advocacy of physical valuation of railroads as a basis for rate schedules, though soon he himself asked Congress to empower

[1] Roosevelt to Lodge, apparently 27 November 1906, Morison, *Letters*, 5: 503; Lodge to Roosevelt, 10 December 1906, Henry Cabot Lodge, ed., *Selections from the Correspondence of Theodore Roosevelt and Henry Cabot Lodge, 1884–1918*, 2: 262.

[2] See in particular Blair Bolles, *Tyrant from Illinois: Uncle Joe Cannon's Experiment with Personal Power*, passim.

the Interstate Commerce Commission to make such valuations.[3] In January 1907, Roosevelt admitted in a letter to William Allen White that "LaFollette often does real good in the Senate, and I like him a great deal better this year than last. . . . he often serves a very useful purpose in making the Senators go on record, and his fearlessness is the prime cause of his being able to render this service." In fact, said Roosevelt, "this winter I have grown to have a real liking for him."[4] But when Lincoln Steffens published an article in *Everybody's Magazine* in which he praised LaFollette for fighting against the fundamental evil of corporate power and accused Roosevelt and Taft of simply attacking individual evils, the president was furious. He informed Steffens in June 1908 that LaFollette's so-called "plan" consisted of a "string of platitudes." He added that LaFollette had been no help but rather a hindrance in the Senate's work on the railroad problem.[5]

The triumvirate failed to understand clearly the causes for the decline in power of the old-time Republican leaders in the Middle West and West and hence saw no impelling reason for immediate modernization of the Republican program. The decline of Allison's power in Iowa, for example, could be explained easily—he was ill and aged and his enemy there was the normal one, tariff revision. It appeared, moreover, that Roosevelt had the tariff question under his control. They found it even easier to explain Spooner's declining power—he had handled the LaFollette Insurgency ineptly. They showed no surprise when the disgruntled, hurt Spooner submitted his resignation from the Senate in March 1907, two years before his term expired. They understood why he abandoned politics for a lucrative career as a corporation lawyer in New York. But they chose not to examine carefully the underlying forces that had destroyed Spooner—his intimate connections with corporate interests, especially the railroads.

Ever since the devastating repudiation of Spooner and his Stalwarts in the 1904 Wisconsin election, the situation had

[3] Roosevelt to William Allen White, 31 July 1906, Morison, *Letters,* 5: 341.
[4] 5 January 1907, ibid., 541.
[5] 5 June 1908, ibid., 6: 1050–53.

grown rapidly worse for the old-timers. Even oldster Elisha W. Keyes, long-time great friend of the railroads and a Spooner henchman, had accepted the change and decided that LaFollette was not the ogre he had always thought him to be.[6] Keyes went so far as to express anger at the railroads when they eliminated free passes for politicians. He wrote Spooner, "For a generation or more" the railroads "have had their own way. They have paid in taxes what they wanted to. They had friends in the Legislature to help them out; and until the advent of the Great Reformer [LaFollette], there was no let or hindrance to their interests or wishes."[7] Times had indeed changed. Keyes even urged Spooner to vote for the pure food, drug, and meat insection measures, stating that their passage "will add so much of strength among the people. Of this there is no earthly doubt."[8] But Spooner could not bring himself to endorse such unprecedented federal encroachment upon private enterprise. Thus in the voting he paired with Allison, who favored the legislation.[9]

In his December 1906 annual message to Congress, Roosevelt indicated what he hoped the party would accomplish in terms of economic reform. His message was mild in tone, reflecting his interpretation of the temper of the times. He had surprisingly little to say on the need for business regulation, merely asserting that "In some method, whether by a national license law or in other fashion, we must exercise, and that at an early date, a far more complete control than at present" over great corporations which "do not operate exclusively within the limits of any one state." He expressed particular concern over the evils of "excessive overcapitalization" of corporations.[10]

The president demonstrated greater concern for the currency question in his message than he had done since the stock market crisis of 1903. The tight money situation worried him. He pointed out that since spring "there has been a fluctuation in the

[6] E. W. Keyes to Spooner, 9 February, 11 April 1906, Spooner Papers.
[7] Keyes to Spooner, 30 July 1905, ibid.
[8] Keyes to Spooner, 21 June 1906, ibid.; see also Keyes to Spooner, 4 February 1906, ibid.
[9] Dorothy Ganfield Fowler, *John Coit Spooner: Defender of Presidents*, 334–35, 335 n; Nathaniel W. Stephenson, *Nelson W. Aldrich: A Leader in American Politics*, 464–65.
[10] Hermann Hagedorn, ed., *The Works of Theodore Roosevelt*, 15: 363–65.

interest on call money from two per cent to thirty per cent; and the fluctuation was even greater during the preceding six months." Still worse, he said, was the scarcity of available money even at high interest rates. Roosevelt made it clear, however, that he was not urging the adoption of any particular plan for a more flexible currency system. Instead, he pointed out that "various plans have recently been proposed by expert committees of bankers" and that among those which "are possibly feasible and which certainly should receive your consideration is that [plan] repeatedly brought to your attention by the present secretary of the treasury [Shaw], the essential features of which have been approved by many prominent bankers and business men." Shaw's plan permitted national banks to use a specified proportion of their capital as currency when needed. A high tax on the notes would drive them from circulation when they were "not wanted in legitimate trade."[11]

In January 1907, through letters to Cannon, Aldrich, and Fowler, Roosevelt asked Congress for legislative action on the currency problem. He was careful to explain, however, that he recognized it was useless to expect any far-reaching reform legislation from the short session of Congress. He hoped that Congress, nevertheless, would enact certain minor currency reforms he had in mind and give serious study to more comprehensive reform. He wrote, "it seems to me clear that a sufficiently heavily taxed emergency currency should be provided, the tax being such as to secure the automatic contraction of the currency when the emergency does not demand it." In a footnote he added, "I realize that the emergency currency proposition may cause opposition."[12]

Roosevelt obliquely drew the attention of Cannon, Aldrich, and Fowler to the political danger that lay in inaction. "I am

[11] Ibid., 378–80; see also: Paul Morton to Roosevelt, 13 September 1906, and Leslie M. Shaw to Roosevelt, 30 November 1906, 27 October 1907, Roosevelt Papers; Shaw's address to meeting of Kentucky Bankers' Association, 10 October 1906, in Leslie M. Shaw, *Current Issues*, 368–73. For an earlier, less restrained expression of opinions, see T. P. Shouts to Roosevelt, 28 June 1906, and Roosevelt to Shouts, 29 June 1906, Roosevelt Papers.

[12] Roosevelt to Charles N. Fowler, 20 January 1907, Morison, *Letters*, 5: 558–59, 559 n; see also Roosevelt to Aldrich, 29 January 1907, box 49, Biographer's Notes, Aldrich Papers.

well aware," he wrote, "that the average constituency does not take much interest in the matter, because it does not know much about it, and therefore but a limited number of Senators and Representatives come in contact with any pressure about it." But, the president emphasized, "all the constituencies will take a most lively interest after the event if things go wrong." He reported, moreover, "there has [already] been a demand for radical action" on the problem.[13]

The currency issue frightened congressional leaders. Certainly Uncle Joe Cannon opposed "heavily taxed emergency currency" and shared small-banker disdain of assets currency in any form. Certainly Aldrich desired no alteration in the existing currency system, which afforded such great power and profit to the eastern banking community. Fowler, chairman of the House Committee on Banking and Currency and an ardent champion of assets currency, could not possibly accept any weak proposal Cannon and Aldrich might finally support. Congress did, however, go so far as to pass a minor currency measure; and the Senate instructed Aldrich's Finance Committee to investigate and report on the currency and credit situation. But the committee proceeded in a desultory manner.[14]

In early March 1907, a sudden drop in the stock market caused many worried businessmen to focus increased attention on Washington. Some of them demanded currency reform legislation, but others concentrated primarily on name-calling and blame-placing. Roosevelt haters stepped up their attacks. Railroad men, and most especially Edward H. Harriman, already angry at the enactment and enforcement of the Hepburn Act, now blamed Roosevelt for their inability to find a satisfactory market for new issues of railroad bonds and for the stock market decline.[15]

[13] Roosevelt to Charles N. Fowler, 20 January 1907, Morison, *Letters*, 5: 558–59.
[14] See Stanley Markowitz, "The Aldrich-Vreeland Bill: Its Significance in the Struggle for Currency Reform, 1893–1908" (Master's thesis, University of Maryland, 1965), 41–42; Robert H. Wiebe, *Businessmen and Reform: A Study of the Progressive Movement*, 63–64.
[15] For businessmen's attitudes, January–September 1907, see letters to Roosevelt from Nicholas Murray Butler, 21 January, T. P. Shouts, 1 February, 23 March, Jacob H. Schiff, 24, 28 March, Emlen Roosevelt, 28 March, 23 April, James S.

The Roosevelt-Harriman feud reached a new intensity. In March, stock of the Harriman-controlled Union Pacific Railroad Company dropped several points. This price decline came shortly after an unfounded rumor circulated around Wall Street that Roosevelt intended to take drastic action against Union Pacific for its supposed violation of railroad laws. When a newsman asked Harriman about the rumor, he replied, "I would hate to tell you to whom you ought to go for an explanation for all of this."[16]

Harriman might well have blamed his own blatant performance, not the government's, for causing investors to shy away from his company. A few days before the March stock market dive, a board of inquiry of the Interstate Commerce Commission questioned Harriman about his railroad practices. During and in reply to the questioning, Harriman expressed anger because the law would not permit him to add the Santa Fe, Northern Pacific, and Great Northern lines to his already large empire. To the specific question of a member of the board, "And your power would gradually increase so that your power might spread not only over the Pacific coast but over the Atlantic coast?" Harriman flatly answered, "Yes."[17] Nevertheless, these investigations, together with the bond and stock price decline, caused Harriman to retreat somewhat. In the middle of March he called for "the development of new friendly relationships and a spirit of cooperation between the railroads and the public . . . and the departments of government." The *Wall Street Journal* called Harriman's new attitude "a death bed repentance."[18]

Some businessmen expressed such vehement anger at Roosevelt that Harvard economist Frank W. Taussig felt moved to

---

Harlan, 28 March, Franklin K. Lane, 28 March, John J. Jenkins, 7 April, T. R. Tuckerman, 22 April—all in Roosevelt Papers; Roosevelt to Nicholas Murray Butler, 23 January, 1907, and to Paul Tuckerman, 16, 24 April, ibid.; to Jacob H. Schiff, 25 March, Morison, *Letters,* 5: 631; Taft to Mrs. Taft, 13 August, to Charles Taft, 18 August, to Henry Taft, 18 August, Taft Papers; Charles E. Perkins to Henry L. Higginson, 11 February, 25 March, 18 June, in Bliss Perry, *Life and Letters of Henry Lee Higginson,* 435–38.

[16] *New York Times,* 15 March, 1907. See also Roosevelt to William Z. Ripley, 19 January 1916, Roosevelt Papers.

[17] *Wall Street Journal,* 28 February 1907.

[18] 12 March 1907.

offer him moral support. Taussig informed the president that through conversations with businessmen he had discovered that the "bulk of the business community" did not believe the "existing financial depression is due to the policy of the government in regard to the railways." Taussig felt that the "check to railway extension is due chiefly to high rates charged on loans, and this is a familiar phenomenon in the later stages of all periods of rising prices." Roosevelt thanked the economist for his "kind and considerate letter" and sent it on to Boston's Henry L. Higginson for comment.[19]

Financier Higginson, writing to Roosevelt in early May, disagreed to some extent with Taussig's analysis. "This checked railway extension," he insisted "is not chiefly due to the high rate of charges on loans. High rates make people think before spending money, but they do not stop business." People were refusing to buy railroad securities, Higginson emphasized, because they "are frightened about the present and future legislation." The Boston financial sage was nevertheless philosophical about the situation. "The speculations of late years have arisen from the very great and steady prosperity of the country, and if such are not to come, we mortals must all be made over again." He did not believe that speculation did much harm and felt it was "all in the day's work."[20] But on some economic issues, Higginson was in agreement with many other businessmen. For example, he shared with them the feeling that the steel industry was exploitative. In late May he wrote Lodge, "The Steelmen have more than they can do, and I wish the tariff was lower and that they were making less money."[21]

Even though Andrew Carnegie could state in April, "the markets have recovered,"[22] the economy during the summer remained sluggish and businessmen continued to argue over whether or not Roosevelt and government interference had caused the trouble. The debate increased in August, when Judge

---

[19] 26 April 1907; Roosevelt to Taussig, 29 April 1907, Roosevelt Papers.
[20] 4 May 1907, ibid.; see also Higginson to Roosevelt, 26 March, 24 April 1907, ibid.; Roosevelt to Higginson, 11 February, 28 March, 12 August 1907, Morison, *Letters*, 5: 584–85, 633–34, 745–49.
[21] 28 May 1907, Lodge Papers.
[22] Carnegie to Roosevelt, 7 April 1907, Roosevelt Papers.

Kenesaw Mountain Landis of the federal district court in Chicago made an important decision against Standard Oil. Landis upheld the government's contention that Standard Oil accepted rebates in 1,462 cases from the Harriman-controlled Chicago and Alton railroad and hence violated the Elkins Act. He fixed the fine at $29 million. More disturbing to the Standard Oil people was the government suit in September 1907 to dissolve the company and prosecute its leaders as criminals.[23]

In September, a government attorney reported to Attorney General Charles Bonaparte that the Standard Oil officials were "very much dispirited and alarmed," were now prepared to accede to the earlier Bureau of Corporations' request to examine the company records, and were ready to comply with the laws. But the matter drifted on. Except for a Circuit Court reversal of the Landis-imposed fine, the Roosevelt administration and Standard Oil never arrived at an agreement. Meanwhile a suit to dissolve the American Tobacco Company dragged on.[24]

The trust problem remained far from solved; neither the administration nor business interests were happy with the situation and Roosevelt was clearly at a loss for a solution. Businessmen willing to negotiate "gentlemen's agreements" wanted more assurances of continued government acceptance of their practices, and government officials disagreed among themselves as to whether such concessions would foster exploitative monopoly practices. Law enforcement had worked somewhat against the "bad trusts," but the performances of the Standard Oil Company, the American Tobacco Company, and Harriman attested to the need for a more precise policy. Roosevelt proved incapable of offering such a policy and so awaited proposals from others. He nevertheless retained his popularity with the public. His detractors in the business world were fewer in number and less influential than they pretended. Nor did he hesitate to strike out publicly at his critics in the business world. On August 20,

[23] William Henry Harbaugh, *Power and Responsibility: The Life and Times of Theodore Roosevelt*, 311; Gabriel Kolko, *The Triumph of Conservatism: A Reinterpretation of American History, 1900–1916*, 123.

[24] Walker Rumble, "Rectitude and Reform: Charles J. Bonaparte and the Politics of Gentility, 1851–1921" (Ph.D. dissertation, University of Maryland, 1971), 238–57.

1907, in the course of an address at Provincetown, Massachusetts, he stated that "it may well be that the determination of the government to punish certain malefactors of great wealth, has been responsible" for some of the current financial difficulty in the land. These men, he suggested, perhaps were attempting to discredit the government's business policy.[25]

Experienced observer Whitelaw Reid, after numerous conversations with businessmen, congressmen, and editors, reported in letters to his elderly in-laws that, in looking toward the next presidential election, "there seems to be no doubt that in the judgment of the best politicians he [Roosevelt] is enormously popular throughout the country, and may prove to be the only man whom the Republicans could elect." Reid recognized, however, that "intense bitterness" existed "in the East and especially among capitalists and railway men against the President." Reid reported on a luncheon meeting at which Paul Morton and Iowa's Congressman William P. Hepburn had suggested that "the capitalists would probably be better off" with Roosevelt in the White House another term "than with any other they might get in his place." Morton and Hepburn were not "sanguine about Taft's success" and believed the "country would have been in a better position if the railroads and Standard Oil could have been persuaded to devote their energies to obeying the law instead of trying to avoid it." Reid added that "Mr. Harriman's transactions, for example, were bound to bring trouble sometime" and that "probably the sooner it comes the less there will be of it." Reid simply refused to believe that Roosevelt "has done as much harm as the capitalists attribute to him."[26]

The economy drifted dully along through the summer and

[25] Hagedorn, *Works of Roosevelt*, 16: 84. When a justice department lawyer, James C. McReynolds, suggested that the government create a governmental receivership to run American Tobacco Company affairs until it conformed to federal regulation, Roosevelt wrote Bonaparte, "It looks as if we had at last struck a really efficient way of dealing with corporations that insolently defy the law." He included in a draft of his Provincetown speech a call to put "the trusts that are guilty of wrongdoing in the hands of receivers." Bonaparte persuaded him to omit it, stating that the technique was appropriate only "in certain contingencies and for certain purposes." Roosevelt to Bonaparte, 11 July, 2 August 1907, and Bonaparte to Roosevelt, 5 August 1907, Charles J. Bonaparte Papers, cited in ibid., 243–45.

[26] Reid to D. O. Mills, 31 August 1907, and to Mrs. D. O. Mills, 9 September 1907, Reid Papers.

into the fall of 1907 and then suddenly, in October, the most severe panic since 1893 hit Wall Street. Some observers had anticipated trouble but none had predicted anything so severe. The panic began with a false rumor about the soundness of a chain of New York City banks. People flocked to withdraw their funds from those banks, and the general fear brought into question the soundness of other banks. Real trouble ensued when depositors made a run on the Knickerbocker Trust Company. That institution was weak and on October 22 collapsed. The panic mounted and continued into the first week of November, when it ended, leaving in its wake the collapse of not only Knickerbocker but about a dozen smaller New York bank and trust companies, as well. Economic depression followed. During most of the first half of 1908, economic activity continued downward. Iron production declined 50 percent, railroad traffic receipts declined 11 percent, foreign trade lessened, and prices in general fell, while unemployment and bankruptcies mounted. By the middle of the year, however, liquidation had run its course and the economy turned upward. It kept on that general course until the 1910–1911 recession.[27]

The crisis, meanwhile, constituted both a political embarrassment and a political opportunity for the Republican leadership. Despite the long-standing need for currency reform legislation, the Republican party had failed to enact a single important measure to meet the obvious need for a more elastic currency. The party now had the opportunity to capitalize on the experience of bankers and public officials in the financial panic. Supposedly, men of influence would henceforth be more receptive to reform legislation. As it turned out, however, the lessons learned were too limited to jar the party leadership into significant modernization of the currency system. Likewise, the financial panic and the hard times that followed were too short-lived to unite bankers behind extensive reform.

While the Republican leadership failed to move the nation's currency system toward a more orderly financial structure, they did contribute indispensable service during the panic itself. President Roosevelt and his newly appointed secretary of the

[27] Harold U. Faulkner, *The Decline of Laissez Faire, 1897–1917*, 29–31.

treasury, George B. Cortelyou, unhesitatingly supported J. P. Morgan and his banker allies who took command in Wall Street, making government funds available to them for distribution to needy banks and trust companies. Roosevelt also acceded to a Wall Street request that he refrain from antitrust action against the U. S. Steel Company, which planned to purchase the Tennessee Coal and Iron Company. Morgan and his associates had engineered the deal, ostensibly as a means to save a large brokerage firm that was overcommitted with stock in the Tennessee concern. Possibly the bankers took undue advantage of the president, but financial catastrophe might have occurred if they had acted otherwise.[28]

Roosevelt's December 1907 annual message to Congress, presented a few weeks after the Wall Street panic, served as a prologue to the legislative drama. Roosevelt by implication told the anxious banking community and Congress that it was now their turn to perform. With some minor additions, he merely inserted into the document the same paragraphs on the currency situation that had appeared in his 1906 message.[29] When preparing the message, Roosevelt revealed to his friend Lodge that his desires on the currency question went beyond what he planned to recommend. "He would like," Lodge wrote in confidence to Higginson, "to recommend a Central Bank, but he thinks it best not to undertake too much and that it would be better to leave the Central Bank to Congress."[30] Roosevelt pointedly showed much more interest in other matters involving economic-finance policy.

In the message, the president prefaced his limited treatment of the currency problem with a more extensive discussion of the need to increase regulation of corporations. On corporation control he included direct quotations from his 1905 and 1906 annual messages, but with additions. After stating that "The most vital need is in connection with the railroads," he showed that he had moved closer to LaFollette's position by asserting

[28] See Harbaugh, *Roosevelt*, 311–15; Ida M. Tarbell, *The Life of Elbert H. Gary*, 196–206.
[29] James D. Richardson, *A Compilation of the Messages and Papers of the Presidents*, 15: 7080.
[30] 18 November 1907, Higginson Papers.

that there should be a new law to give the "Interstate Commerce Commission power to pass upon the future issue of securities" and "to make a physical valuation of any railroad."

The president, moreover, showed an increased interest in both the taxation and the tariff questions. He reiterated his earlier interest in inheritance and income taxes and urged enactment of laws to provide these reforms, pointing out that such nations as Great Britain and France were more advanced than the United States in their tax systems. Although acknowledging satisfactory results of the "present tariff law," he reminded the voters of the "constantly growing feeling among our people that the time is rapidly approaching when our system of revenue legislation must be revised."[31]

In 1908, in response to the panic, the president and Congress took up the matter of currency legislation. The contest pictured in bold relief the nature and strength of the Republican top leadership. Roosevelt conducted himself with impressive restraint and acumen as he moved in and out of the fray. He had no particular currency plan in mind, but he was determined that some measure emerge that would protect the party from defeat in the 1908 presidential election. As the debate developed, Republican insurgency in Congress played a conspicuous role. Aldrich proceeded with his usual imperious manner and his usual willingness to compromise when the pressures reached a certain point. This time, in contrast to 1906, when Roosevelt had opposed Aldrich in the Hepburn bill battle, the president worked with him. They had to contend with Insurgent Republican LaFollette, erratic Republican Beveridge, and Fowler-led revolt in the House. Speaker Cannon discovered he could not keep his fellow Republicans in line without the help of Roosevelt and Aldrich.

At the outset, public attention focused on the currency debate in the Senate. Aldrich, as Finance Committee chairman, reluctantly placed currency reform on the Senate agenda. Roosevelt's message in December 1907 had called for currency reform and at the same time J. P. Morgan had urged Aldrich to get a law to provide for emergency currency. The New York magnate argued

---

[31] Richardson, *Messages and Papers of the Presidents*, 15: 7071–80, 7082–84.

that such a measure would go far to restore public confidence and thus hasten recovery.[32]

Morgan and his associates, however, left it to Aldrich to translate their demands into a legislative measure and then to obtain its enactment. Lodge later reported, in a letter to Higginson marked "Personal," that Aldrich, "when he was consulting the people in New York . . . asked the two leading bankers there, when they met him at Morgan's office, to draft a bill." Aldrich had found this unrewarding. "Hearing nothing from them at the end of a week he went to see one of them and asked him where the bill was. The reply was, 'We haven't been able to draw one. We could not even agree among ourselves, and we do not know how.'" Lodge added, "I have not yet succeeded in getting any bill from our Boston Bankers."[33]

On January 7, 1908, Aldrich introduced into the Senate a measure that was essentially the Aldrich bill of 1903. It authorized the use of railroad and certain other bonds but not commercial paper as a base for emergency currency. The political conflict that followed reflected the bitter antagonism among bankers. Noneasterners argued, with reason, that the eastern bankers held a disproportionately large share of bonds, especially railroad bonds, and hence the scheme would add primarily to their power, profit, and currency supply. Moreover, antagonism toward railroads, with their overextended issuance of bonds, caused rural people from the South and West to regard the Aldrich bill as a scheme to allow railroads and eastern banks to make undue profits from railroad bonds. The recent difficulty experienced by railroads and investment bankers in marketing new railroad bonds was further basis for suspicion in antirailroad circles. But Aldrich held, also with reason, that carefully selected railroad bonds provided a particularly stable base for currency, whereas paper from small banks might not. In January, it appeared that he would have his way in the Senate.[34]

On February 10, when Senate debate on the Aldrich bill

[32] Markowitz, "Aldrich-Vreeland Bill," 55; Wiebe, *Businessmen and Reform*, 72–73; *Wall Street Journal*, 6 January 1908.
[33] 11 January 1908, Higginson Papers.
[34] Markowitz, "Aldrich-Vreeland Bill," 57; *Wall Street Journal*, 8 January 1908.

began, even the severest critics of the measure believed it would soon pass. But within a few weeks, Aldrich and his associates were making numerous concessions. Aldrich had expected the loud Democratic opposition that was forthcoming, but he was unprepared for the insistent, powerful opposition of Republican senators from the Middle West. Moreover, pressure outside the Senate mounted. By mid-March, while the debate was still in progress, numerous business and banker groups expressed great dissatisfaction. Even some eastern institutions, notably the New York Clearing House, the Merchants' Association of New York, and the Boston Chamber of Commerce, declared the measure would not end panics and called for more comprehensive reform.[35]

Aldrich had particular difficulty with two senators from the Middle West, Albert J. Beveridge and Robert M. LaFollette. These Insurgents wanted more comprehensive reform and believed the Aldrich measure afforded too much added power and profit for Wall Street bankers. Moreover, each of them took advantage of the political situation in Congress to advance a pet reform of his own. Beveridge wanted tariff reform; LaFollette wanted physical valuation of the railroads. Both men had considerable senatorial support. Even Allison said he could not possibly support the measure if it retained the railroad bond clause.[36]

In March, Aldrich, using J. P. Morgan's man George W. Perkins as an intermediary, sought to win over Beveridge. Beveridge indicated to his friend Perkins that much opposition to the bill would disappear if Aldrich would allow the Senate to take up tariff revision. Beveridge did not expect immediate passage of the tariff measure, but hoped Aldrich would allow it to get on the list of unfinished business for consideration in the next session. "You see," Beveridge said, "a do-nothing policy is a double-edged sword and cuts both ways."[37] Aldrich took Beveridge's demand under consideration.

[35] *New York Times,* 12 March 1908; Boston Chamber of Commerce, *Annual Report* (Boston, 1908), cited in Markowitz, "Aldrich-Vreeland Bill," 93; S. C. Mead, secretary, Merchants' Association of New York, to Taft, 23 March 1908, Taft Papers.

[36] *New York Times,* 18 March 1908; Markowitz, "Aldrich-Vreeland Bill," 98.

[37] Beveridge to Perkins, 12 March 1908, Perkins Papers.

More was required than a concession on the tariff to win the support of "Fighting Bob" LaFollette. Though his measure to use physical valuation of the railroads as a basis for establishing rates had been accumulating more and more adherents, the proposal remained untouched in the Senate Committee on Interstate Commerce. Now LaFollette saw an opportunity to get the matter before the Senate. He offered an amendment to the Aldrich bill, requiring in effect that the Treasury accept railroad bonds as security for emergency currency *"only after the Interstate Commerce Commission had ascertained the value of the physical properties of the railroads."* He also announced that, on March 17, he would address the Senate on the bill.[38]

On the evening of March 16, Roosevelt conferred at the White House with Aldrich, Beveridge, and Perkins. It was apparent that unless the leadership made concessions to Beveridge and LaFollette, the Senate would kill the Aldrich bill. Roosevelt served the cause principally as a political broker who was interested in the 1908 election and supported the Aldrich bill simply because it appeared to him to be the only way to forestall political danger. Nobody had offered a politically feasible alternative.[39]

The conferees decided to remove the controversial railroad bond clause from the Senate bill. They regarded this concession as a temporary expedient only, believing that they could reinstate the feature, as Perkins reported to Morgan, "when the fight comes in the House and it goes to Committee." They planned to camouflage the bond clause, however, employing words and phrases which New York banker George F. Baker and Aldrich would provide. The conferees found it relatively easy to make a concession to Beveridge on the tariff question, inasmuch as by then it was a foregone conclusion that after the presidential election Congress would have to take up the tariff question anyway. They agreed that the president would arrange for a commission to investigate tariff schedules and make recommendations to the next Congress. Beveridge, in turn, agreed to

[38] Robert M. LaFollette, *Autobiography: A Personal Narrative of Political Experiences,* 458–62.
[39] Roosevelt to Henry L. Higginson, 19 February 1908, Morison, *Letters,* 6: 949.

soften his earlier demands for more comprehensive tariff reform.[40]

Aldrich remained uneasy about LaFollette, who was scheduled next day to begin his speech on the bill. While he believed removal of the railroad bond feature would materially reduce LaFollette's influence, he nevertheless recognized that the Wisconsin leader had accumulated considerable support. Roosevelt, however, told Aldrich that he would give him "all the help he could."[41]

The next day, LaFollette began his three-day, carefully prepared speech, in which he declared that "in some ways no bill ever introduced in Congress was more significant of the control of the legislature by big business." He said this despite having learned just thirty minutes before his appearance on the floor that Aldrich had removed the railroad bond provision. He remarked in his speech that without doubt the friends of the New York bankers would later reinstate that provision. LaFollette was convinced that New York bankers had dictated the measure. When Aldrich interrupted him to state that he knew of no New York banker who favored the bill, LaFollette asked him if he knew anything of J. P. Morgan's attitude. Not everyone believed Aldrich's denial.[42] LaFollette's performance annoyed the proud Aldrich but did no serious damage to the measure.

Beveridge kept his promise to support Aldrich. He defended him against LaFollette's well-founded charge that Aldrich had pressed unduly for quick passage. He then asked Aldrich, possibly by prearrangement, whether he anticipated more comprehensive currency legislation in the near future. Aldrich replied that he favored adding a provision to the bill calling for a monetary commission to make a detailed study of the financial question.[43] By such concessions, Aldrich greatly strengthened

[40] George W. Perkins to J. P. Morgan, 16 March 1908, Perkins Papers; Markowitz, "Aldrich-Vreeland Bill," 95–97.

[41] George W. Perkins to J. P. Morgan, 16 March 1908, Perkins Papers. For unfounded speculation on the reasons for removal of the bond clause and its implications, see: *New York Times*, 17, 18, 19 March 1908; *New York Tribune*, 17 March 1908.

[42] Markowitz, "Aldrich-Vreeland Bill," 97–101; Belle Case LaFollette and Fola LaFollette, *Robert M. LaFollette*, 240–44.

[43] *Wall Street Journal*, 26 March 1908; Stephenson, *Aldrich*, 328–39; Markowitz, "Aldrich-Vreeland Bill," 101–02.

his position. At the same time, he relieved the minds of Allison and other uneasy fellow Republicans.[44]

In a special message on March 25, two days before the bill passed the Senate, Roosevelt gave incidental endorsement to the Aldrich bill. He stated, "The question of financial legislation is now receiving such attention in both Houses that we have a right to expect action before the close of the session. It is urgently necessary that there should be such action." Then he devoted two sentences to favoring postal savings banks.[45] Most of the message dealt with the need for new labor legislation.[46] On March 27, by a vote of 42 to 16, the Senate passed the bill. Only four Republicans voted against it.[47] But there was still trouble ahead.

Meanwhile, in the House, Cannon appeared to lack sufficient strength to prevent House consideration of a Fowler-sponsored measure to provide for assets currency and a guarantee of bank deposits. Cannon personally wanted no bank bill whatsoever, and especially not one that embraced Fowler's heretical schemes. The New Jersey congressman, however, was both popular and powerful. Amid this atmosphere of defiance of Cannon, the Aldrich bill arrived in the House.[48]

From March 30 to April 18, the Aldrich bill remained under the direct scrutiny of Fowler's Banking and Currency Committee. Fowler took full advantage of every opportunity to capitalize on the growing feeling in the country that the Aldrich bill was an unsatisfactory answer to the currency problem. Henry L. Higginson was among the important financiers whom he successfully cultivated. For many years Higginson had shown a lively interest in currency laws. He was dedicated to the gold standard but he also saw the need for more elasticity in the currency system and for a central bank. During the contest over

[44] In an exchange of letters, Allison and George E. Roberts agreed it would be foolhardy, pending study aimed to provide for a new permanent system, to violate the traditional relations between small and large banks. See Roberts to Allison, 29 February, 2 March, 14 April 1908, and Allison to Roberts, 6 March, 16 April 1908, Allison Papers.

[45] Richardson, *Messages and Papers of the Presidents*, 15: 7347.

[46] Ibid., 7343–44; *New York Commercial and Financial Chronicle*, 28 March 1908.

[47] Markowitz, "Aldrich-Vreeland Bill," 101–02.

[48] Ibid., 58.

currency legislation, Higginson corresponded frequently with Fowler and Lodge. He gave encouragement to Fowler and his assets currency crusade, and unmercifully needled his friend Lodge, who loyally supported Aldrich.[49] Higginson wrote Lodge as early as mid-January, "Fowler's bill is in the main, good, and inasmuch as we have come to a very serious place in our history, which has been neglected terribly, I think we must ask you gentlemen to take the matter up and try hard to do something better than the Aldrich bill." For emphasis he added, "Do not forget that whereas in former years we could draw on Europe for what money was needed in an emergency, we now can do no such thing. Our wants are altogether too large, and Europe cannot meet them."[50]

Fowler and his colleagues encouraged interested people to use the committee hearings to vent their fury and reach the public.[51] Most of those who testified at the hearings opposed the bill; only two of the forty who appeared advocated outright passage of the measure.[52] One prominent Iowa banker, Arthur Reynolds, angrily stated that over in the Senate, "watch dog of Wall Street" Aldrich had granted but a two-minute hearing to the pro-assets currency commission of the American Bankers Association.[53] Elmer Youngman, editor of *Bankers Magazine*, testified that his chief criticism of the bill was the "tremendous power" it afforded the secretary of the treasury. The "entire business interests of the country," he warned, "would be dependent on one man" if the bill became law.[54] Clearly, bankers and other businessmen, including many in New York, resented the alliance between the J. P. Morgan interests and the Repub-

[49] Higginson to Lodge, 3 December 1907, 21, 27, 29 January, 19 February, 3, 9 March 1908, Lodge Papers; Lodge to Higginson, 22, 29 November 1907, 11, 24, 28 January, 5 March 1908, Fowler to Higginson, 13, 19, 21 January, 7 February, 9 October 1908, Samuel W. McCall to Higginson, 4 March 1908—all in Higginson Papers.

[50] 13 January 1908, Lodge Papers.

[51] Markowitz, "Aldrich-Vreeland Bill," 104–05.

[52] Ibid., 109–10.

[53] Arthur Reynolds, testimony before the U. S. House, Committee on Banking and Currency, *Hearings, Aldrich Bill, S. 3023* (60 Cong., 1 sess., 1908), p. 10, cited in ibid., 108.

[54] Elmer Youngman, testimony, *Hearings, Aldrich Bill*, 9–15, cited in Markowitz, "Aldrich-Vreeland Bill," 107; see also George M. Reynolds memorandum, box 50, Biographer's Notes, Aldrich Papers.

lican leadership, especially the alliance between Aldrich and Morgan.

Even the two who favored passage of the bill were not enthusiastic about it. They were Charles G. Dawes, Chicago banker and one-time comptroller of the currency, and Charles C. Glover, president of the Riggs National Bank of Washington, D.C. Their answers to questions made it clear that they preferred commercial paper to bonds as the basis for emergency currency. They argued, however, that a bill based on that approach would not pass the Senate.[55]

The overwhelming majority of bankers and businessmen who testified at the House hearings expressed interest in having a new currency law, but they wanted one that was more comprehensive than the Aldrich bill. They advocated a currency commission to study the problem and left the distinct impression that they considered the Aldrich bill worse than no bill.

In mid-April, the situation in the House became critical, necessitating Roosevelt's intervention. On April 18, the committee announced that it had tabled the Aldrich bill, and three days later it summarily did the same to a substitute measure, the Vreeland bill.[56] Its author, Republican Congressman Edward B. Vreeland, a banker and businessman from Salamanca, New York, had already discussed his bill with Roosevelt on at least two occasions before introducing it as a replacement for the Fowler and Aldrich bills. Roosevelt hoped the banking and currency committee would accept this compromise bill, which included provision for emergency currency based on "any securities, including commercial paper." It thus included Aldrich's favored securities as authorized collateral for currency without employing the blasphemous term "railroad bonds."[57]

Despite the sharp set-back for Roosevelt and Cannon when the Fowler-dominated committee rejected the Vreeland bill, Roosevelt spread word that he was confident of the ultimate

[55] Charles C. Glover and Charles G. Dawes, testimony, *Hearings, Aldrich Bill*, 3–47, cited in Markowitz, "Aldrich-Vreeland Bill," 109–11; Charles G. Dawes, *A Journal of the McKinley Years*, 431–34.

[56] Markowitz, "Aldrich-Vreeland Bill," 112, 116.

[57] Ibid., 113–17; banker Charles C. Glover later related that he and Cannon had persuaded Vreeland to draft the bill. Glover memorandum, box 50, Biographer's Notes, Aldrich Papers.

outcome.[58] On April 27, the president sent another of his special messages to Congress. In it he remarked that he felt there was "good ground to hope" for further legislation "providing for temporary measures for meeting any trouble that may arise in the next year or two, and for a commission of experts who shall thoroughly investigate the whole matter, both here and abroad, so as to be able to recommend legislation which will put our financial system on an efficient and permanent basis."[59]

George W. Perkins remained on hand, although deliberately staying out of the limelight because of his connection with J. P. Morgan. He reported to Morgan that the president was making headway with his resolve to obtain a currency law, and that because it was politically the major item on his agenda, he intended to keep the restless Congress in session well into May, if necessary, in order to achieve his goal.[60] The *Nation* reported that all of the Republican leaders were placing great pressure on Congress to pass some sort of currency bill.[61]

On May 5, the first in a series of events occurred that culminated in passage of the compromise Aldrich-Vreeland bill. On that day, the House Banking and Currency Committee, still bent upon enactment of an assets currency measure, again refused, by a vote of 15 to 3, to send the Vreeland bill to the House floor, and on the same day Cannon and Roosevelt met privately to discuss the problem.[62] The immediate outcome was Cannon's call for a Republican caucus. The caucus voted 128 to 16 to bring the bill to the House floor. On May 13, Vreeland presented a resolution in the House to suspend the rules, discharge the Banking and Currency Committee from consideration of his bill, and then have a House vote on the measure. Trouble threatened momentarily, however, when the dictatorial Cannon refused to allow House discussion of the Vreeland bill and also of a Democratic-sponsored bill. House Democrats and a few Republicans denounced him for his tactics, but to no avail. With only fourteen angry Republicans defying the leadership and joining

[58] George W. Perkins to J. P. Morgan, 7 May 1908, Perkins Papers.
[59] Richardson, *Messages and Papers of the Presidents,* 14: 7189–90.
[60] 7 May 1908, Perkins Papers.
[61] 30 April 1908.
[62] Chronology, Morison, *Letters,* 6: 1619; Markowitz, "Aldrich-Vreeland Bill," 119.

the Democrats, who were solidly against the measure, the House quickly passed the Vreeland bill and sent it on to the Senate. The House vote was 185 to 145.[63]

In the Senate, the bill went to Aldrich's Finance Committee. Before the day ended, the committee drastically amended the bill and sent it to the Senate floor. The enacting clause of the original Vreeland bill remained, plus an amendment which replaced the substance of the Vreeland measure with the familiar Aldrich bill, which the House had earlier rejected. In less than an hour, the Senate, by a vote of 47–20, passed, or rather repassed, this version of the Aldrich bill. In the Senate, Aldrich was clearly in command.[64]

The amended bill then went back to the House, where Speaker Cannon took over. The House by-passed Fowler's committee, rejected Aldrich's amended portion of the bill, repassed the original Vreeland bill by a vote of 152 to 104, and sent it to the House-Senate conference committee. Many members chose not to vote, but Cannon had enough loyal cohorts to carry out his "responsibility" to the party.[65]

Then came the most meaningful, the most crucial, episode in the drama, a ten-day deadlock in the House-Senate conference committee. That committee had to resolve the conflicting currency views of bankers and at the same time prevent a collapse of the long-standing alliance between Republican leadership and business leadership. The committee was deadlocked between the Aldrich-dominated Senate forces and the Cannon-dominated House forces. Each side could boast the support of powerful top-level financial interests. It was a new experience for both Aldrich and Cannon.[66]

During the currency contest, the Aldrich-Morgan alliance had become increasingly unpopular in both political and business circles. Back in mid-February, Morgan had appeared in the Senate gallery to listen to Aldrich's speech on his bill. Newspapers and such critics as LaFollette made much of the visit.

[63] Markowitz, "Aldrich-Vreeland Bill," 119–23; L. White Busbey memorandum, box 50, Biographer's Notes, Aldrich Papers; *Wall Street Journal,* 5 May 1908.
[64] Markowitz, "Aldrich-Vreeland Bill," 123.
[65] Ibid., 124.
[66] Ibid., 124–26.

Morgan reportedly was "beaming throughout" Aldrich's speech. They also circulated the rumor that Morgan was the real author of the Aldrich bill.[67] Later the Morgan men operated in the shadows. Perkins and George F. Baker, president of the First National Bank in New York and a close ally of Morgan, represented Morgan in Washington. These men, however, soon found it expedient to work through the less well known Henry P. Davison, vice-president of Baker's bank. On May 27, Perkins wrote Morgan that Davison had done most of the work. "Baker and I felt," he added, "that in view of [the] constant criticism that has been made that [the] legislation was all for Wall Street neither he nor I had better be much in evidence."[68]

More and more people, meanwhile, blamed Aldrich for the continued conference committee deadlock and believed he would permit Congress to adjourn without enacting any bill. Even Perkins became irritated with him. Convinced that the most one could now expect was a measure to provide for a currency commission to make recommendations later, Perkins informed Morgan that "had Aldrich taken your advice last December and crowded through a very simple bill in the closing days of the first session the matter would have been out of the way."[69]

Roosevelt played the most active role in turning the tide toward compromise. He was, however, greatly handicapped in this endeavor by his unpopularity with many members of both houses of Congress. His aggressiveness, his increasing "radicalism" on economic matters, and his often uncalled-for impatience and scolding manner with Congress irritated many members who were already resentful of his power. At the time the currency problem was bottled up in the conference committee, Roosevelt wrote to editor Albert Shaw about his political difficulties, using his increasingly extravagant language of invective. "The ruling clique in the Senate, the House, and the National Committee," he said, "seem to regard every concession to decency as merely a matter of bargain and sale with *me*, which *I*

---

[67] Ibid., 80.
[68] Perkins Papers.
[69] 21, 22 May 1908, Perkins Papers; Markowitz, "Aldrich-Vreeland Bill," 126–27.

must pay for in some way or fashion." But he thought he would be able to "avoid a break" with that element.[70]

Perkins reported to Morgan on the intensity of the anti-Roosevelt sentiment in Congress. When the president asked for four battleships, "Congress voted two and then gloried in [the] fact they had refused to give [the] President what he asked for." According to Perkins, the fact that the country "ought to have [the] extra battleships did not seem to have anything to do with the question."[71] Roosevelt, however, did not let his quarrel with Congress divert him from his effort on the currency question. He cajoled members of Congress and allowed the rumor to spread that he would do all in his power to keep Congress in session until it passed a currency measure. Perkins felt that regardless of his past performance, Roosevelt's actions over the last four or five months were all to his credit, while Congress had a "do nothing policy to its credit."[72]

On May 27, five days before the scheduled adjournment of Congress, Aldrich, Cannon, and Vreeland agreed upon a compromise currency measure, the Aldrich-Vreeland bill, and steered it through the conference committee. It had the endorsement of Roosevelt. It allowed the use of any securities as a basis for emergency currency, including commercial paper which banking associations held. Thus the Aldrich-Morgan forces, in effect, kept the railroad bond clause, and the Cannon-Vreeland group retained the commercial paper provision. To placate Aldrich's fear that banks would be unwise in their use of commercial paper for currency purposes, the conferees included specific limitations on its use. To reduce Cannon's fear of the increased power of large banks and of federal authority, the bill restricted the issuance of currency to a "national currency association." In tacit recognition of the very limited nature of the bill, the conferees included a provision for a monetary commission to make a thorough study of the problem, after which it would submit to Congress recommendations for more comprehensive legislation.[73]

[70] 22 May 1908, Morison, *Letters,* 6: 1033.
[71] 21 April 1908, Perkins Papers.
[72] 22 May 1908, ibid.; Markowitz, "Aldrich-Vreeland Bill," 126–28.

Cannon rushed the Aldrich-Vreeland bill through the House. He held up the Public Building bill, laden with appropriations dear to the hearts of many congressmen, and also drastically limited floor debate, until the currency bill had passed. On May 27, it passed the House by a vote of 166 to 140, with 76 abstentions. Next day it went to the Senate.[74]

The final stage in the five-month series of maneuvers began when the bill reached the Senate amid rumors that LaFollette planned to stage a filibuster against it. Unhappy over the provision permitting railroad bonds for collateral, LaFollette began his filibuster at noon on May 29 to a packed audience. Democrats William J. Stone of Missouri and Thomas P. Gore of Oklahoma promised to participate. It was a hot, stifling day, but LaFollette talked on and on. He held the Senate floor for almost nineteen hours, and then, at 7:00 A.M. on May 30, Stone took over. He spoke until 1:30 P.M., and then Gore relieved him. Stone planned to return in two hours, but something went awry. The blind Gore, under the mistaken impression that Stone was on hand to relieve him, yielded the floor on schedule. Stone was out in the corridor and the presiding officer, Vice-President Fairbanks, quickly recognized Aldrich, a move that afforded an opportunity for a vote on the bill. It passed, with several votes to spare, 43 to 22, but 27 abstained.[75]

The Republican leadership had passed a crucial test, that of demonstrating at a politically important time that its alliances were still intact. There were signs of weakness, but the success was great enough to obscure them for the time being. The irrepressible Roosevelt, though furious at LaFollette, was exuberant. He declared he would go down to the Senate to "sign that bill." Thus the Aldrich-Vreeland law became the first significant cur-

---

[73] Markowitz, "Aldrich-Vreeland Bill," 129; *New York Times,* 28 May 1908; William Rea Gwinn, *Uncle Joe Cannon, Archfoe of Insurgency: A History of the Rise and Fall of Cannonism,* 132–33; Stephenson, *Aldrich,* 330, 476–77; Forrest Crissey, *Theodore E. Burton, American Statesman,* 195–96.

[74] Markowitz, "Aldrich-Vreeland Bill," 130–31; *New York Times,* 27 May 1908; *Wall Street Journal,* 28 May 1908.

[75] Markowitz, "Aldrich-Vreeland Bill," 131–38; LaFollette, *LaFollette,* 1: 245–56; LaFollette, *Autobiography,* 471–73; *New York Times,* 30, 31 May 1908. The Republicans voting in the negative were LaFollette, William E. Borah of Idaho, Norris Brown of Nebraska, and Jonathan Bourne, Jr., of Oregon.

rency measure to pass Congress since the Gold Standard Act of 1900. Congress adjourned on the same day.[76]

Though helping with the currency legislation, Roosevelt showed more interest in correcting the evils of the excessive concentration of wealth and power in the business world and in correcting evils in the judiciary. His experience with the arrogant Harriman and the Standard Oil Company strengthened his growing conviction that there was need for increased federal control of business. Roosevelt was not, however, prepared to push ardently for congressional enactment of any specific measure to increase federal control of business.

Although he had called for greater federal business control in his December 1907 message to Congress, Roosevelt cautiously restricted his specific recommendations to suggestions on how to increase railroad regulation. For that industry, he stated, "there should now be either a national incorporation act or a law licensing railway companies to engage in interstate commerce upon certain conditions," and the Interstate Commerce Commission should have the power "to make a physical valuation of any railroad." By limiting his statement to railroads, he did not face up to the broader constitutional question of the power of the federal government to regulate other industries.[77]

The hesitant and uncertain Roosevelt demonstrated his skill at political evasiveness when, in the spring of 1908, friends of big business confronted him with a specific proposal, the Hepburn bill, designed to reduce the strength of the Sherman Act. A product of the efforts of the National Civic Federation and the J. P. Morgan group, the Hepburn bill empowered the Bureau of Corporations, after making an investigation, to provide a corporation with a stamp of approval, thereby markedly reducing the danger of prosecution under the Sherman Act. The bill was in keeping with Roosevelt's personal views on control of business and he discussed its features with Seth Low, George Perkins, and other individuals urging its enactment. Roosevelt urged Congress to enact legislation embodying this approach,

[76] New York Times, 31 May 1908; see also Roosevelt to Kermit Roosevelt, 30 May 1908, Morison, Letters, 6: 1044.
[77] Hagedorn, Works of Roosevelt, 15: 415.

but he never flatly endorsed the specific bill that went there for consideration. Cannon sent the bill to the House Committee on the Judiciary, where it remained.[78]

Knowledge that he had so short a time left in the White House and had not accomplished more than a beginning in the direction of governmental control doubtless spurred Roosevelt to air his views in special messages to Congress. He sent these messages, however, at a time when members of Congress were deeply engrossed in the currency debate, impatient to return home for the 1908 election campaign, and in no mood to receive the president's embarrassing implication that they were derelict if they failed to take positive steps on such important matters as inheritance taxes, income taxes, trusts, railroads, and court reform. They were resigned to the necessity of tackling tariff legislation upon their return to Congress in the fall, but few of them had any taste for Roosevelt's "radical" schemes.

Despite the temper of Congress at the time, Roosevelt was determined to present his point of view. In the most notable of the special messages, that of January 31, 1908, he summarized his thoughts on the role of government in an industrial society.[79] The message included a forthright reminder to Congress and the public of the evils they must combat. In a letter to his son Kermit he justified his reasons for the message at this time, even though his advisers counseled against it. "As we approach

---

[78] George W. Perkins to J. P. Morgan, 16 March 1908, Perkins Papers; Roosevelt to Seth Low, 30 October 1907, Morison, *Letters*, 5: 824–25; 6 February 1908, ibid., 6: 925–26; 28 March 1908, ibid., 983; 1 April 1908, ibid., 986–87; 9 April 1908, ibid., 997; 21 November 1908, ibid., 1374–75; 24 November 1908, ibid., 1379; Roosevelt to Nicholas Murray Butler, 6 February 1908, ibid., 925; to Herbert Knox Smith, 14 April 1908, ibid., 1007–08; Richardson, *Messages and Papers of the Presidents*, 14: 7191–95; 15: 7343–46; *Des Moines Register and Leader*, 13, 26, 27 March, 7, 28 April 1908; Wiebe, *Businessmen and Reform*, 79–82; Kolko, *Triumph of Conservatism*, 132–37; James Weinstein, *The Corporate Ideal in the Liberal State: 1900–1918*, 80–81. Attorney General Charles J. Bonaparte advised the president against the proposed legislation. He clearly considered it too favorable to the business interests. See Bonaparte to Roosevelt, 2 December 1908, Bonaparte Papers. For discussions of Roosevelt's views and actions on business at that time, see Arthur M. Johnson, "Antitrust Policy in Transition, 1908: Ideal and Reality," *Mississippi Valley Historical Review* 48 (December 1961): 415–34; Robert H. Wiebe, "The House of Morgan and the Executive, 1905–1913," *American Historical Review* 65 (October 1959): 49–60; Rumble, "Charles J. Bonaparte," 267–72.

[79] The message is reprinted as Appendix III in Morison, *Letters*, 6: 1572–91.

nearer the convention more and more people will pay heed to what the candidates will say rather than to what the President may say, and this is well-nigh the last occasion I shall have to speak when all men, however unwilling, must listen." He felt sure, he added, that he was "on the right track" and that the message "says what ought to be said and that the ultimate effect will be good."[80]

On economic policy, the special message brought together into a consistent whole the product of his most advanced thinking on railroads, monopoly, labor, and the role of privately owned great fortunes. It indicated that his earlier interest in the labor-employer-government relationship had now become a major concern. He struck out, for example, at the misuse of injunctions in labor disputes. On the railroads, he declared, "The Interstate Commerce Commission should be empowered to pass upon any rate or practice on its own initiative." He also reiterated his view that the commission should have the "means to make a physical valuation of any road." He insisted that "In some form the Federal Government should exercise supervision over the financial operations" and also "a certain measure of control over the physical operation" of interstate railroads.[81]

On the control of big business in general, Roosevelt declared that Congress should provide for a "thoroughgoing supervision by the National Government of all operations of the big interstate business concerns." He lashed out against such abuses as "stock watering and over-capitalization." He emphasized the inadequacy of our laws and law enforcement to provide equal justice. "When the courts guarantee to the employer, as they should, the rights of the employer," he declared, "and to property the rights of property, they should no less emphatically make it evident that they will exact from property and from the employer the duties which should necessarily accompany these rights," but "hitherto our laws have failed in precisely this point."[82]

The dramatic aspect of the message epitomized Roosevelt's anger toward certain people and forces. He condemned wealthy

[80] 2 February 1908, ibid., 922.
[81] Appendix III, Morison, ibid., 1575–76.
[82] Ibid., 1576–78.

men who misused their power, and administered like treatment to nefarious members of the bench. He was careful, however, to remind his audience that he was not an enemy of all men of wealth and great economic power or of all judges. "For the honest man of great wealth," he insisted, "we have a hearty regard, just as we have a hearty regard for the honest politician and honest newspaper." As for the judges, Roosevelt emphasized that "Most certainly it behooves us all to treat with utmost respect the high office of judge; and our judges, as a whole, are brave and upright men." Late in the message he said, "No man should lightly criticise a judge; no man should, even in his own mind, condemn a judge unless he is sure of the facts."[83]

Some men of wealth and position were furious at Roosevelt for his attack on highly placed citizens, but more people were greatly pleased. His fellow Republican and friend Nicholas Murray Butler scolded him, and Democrat William Jennings Bryan praised him for his message.[84] "The feeling of sorrow and regret of which I speak," Butler declared, "is due chiefly to the form in which you couched the Message, but also in part to the fact that you as President have descended into the arena of ordinary newspaper and hustings debate, in order to attack those individuals and institutions that you do not like or that have attacked and criticised you."[85] Roosevelt, in a characteristically lengthy reply, in turn scolded Butler. Referring to what other people said in letters about the speech, Roosevelt declared that his "real supporters . . . have hailed it as they have no other speech or action of mine for a long time." He granted that he might be entirely mistaken about the overall popularity of the message, but said that the recent attacks on him made him regret "for the first time" that it was not early enough in his career as president to "have a showdown" with his enemies inside and outside the party. He believed "there would not be even a fight west of the Alleghenies; and if I were a betting man I should like to bet heavily on the fight in New York."[86]

Butler lamely replied. He attempted to assure Roosevelt that

[83] Ibid., 1578–83, 1586.
[84] See Roosevelt to Bryan, 4 February 1908, ibid., 923.
[85] 4 February 1908, Roosevelt Papers.
[86] 6 February 1908, Morison, *Letters*, 6: 924.

he supported his views and that his criticism of the message had "nothing whatever to do with corruption, or with Rockefeller, or with the *New York Sun,* or with anything else." He explained that it had "only to do with what" he believed was "the appropriate and dignified and effective attitude of the President of the United States towards his fellow-citizens and toward the Congress." Moreover, he wanted "to make plain" that "in the judgement of every real friend of yours whom I know, or have spoken to, or have heard from, you have made a most serious blunder in the form of your last message."[87] Henry L. Higginson, who sometimes spoke well of Roosevelt, believed that the president should now drop his insistent verbiage about the evils of the Standard Oil people. He wrote Lodge, "What the Standard Oil says about him is of no consequence. I do not think the Standard Oil has many friends among the population generally, and whether it abused the President or not I don't know nor care, but it does not seem to me dignified or worth while for the President to put out a proclamation defending his theories or himself." Roosevelt "has said all that is necessary—people have heeded it,—the corporations have heeded it, and anything more is injurious."[88] Despite his critics, Roosevelt continued his crusade until Congress adjourned and the 1908 election absorbed his attention.

As the Republican command prepared for the forthcoming presidential election, it still embraced an unflinching adherence to its oft tested formula for victory, its tie with big business and the alliance between the Republicans of the East and those of the Middle West. But the tie with big business was less conspicuous because of Roosevelt's presence and Platt's death. The alliance between the East and the Middle West was less secure without the unified power of the Senate Four. Most of the old guardians from the Civil War and Reconstruction era had either left or were in the process of withdrawing from the Washington scene. Among their replacements, only Theodore Roosevelt possessed great professional political skill and force. Now he too was preparing to withdraw. Few, if any, among the remaining

[87] 7 February 1908, Roosevelt Papers.
[88] 19 February 1908, Lodge Papers.

leaders, however, feared the outcome of the election because the Democratic party was still in a very weak state, but they did not enter the contest with enthusiasm. They regarded it as a chore and a bore.

By 1908, it appeared to be a foregone conclusion that the now less fearsome[89] William Jennings Bryan again would be the Democratic party standard-bearer and that again he would go down to defeat.[90] It also appeared that William Howard Taft would be the next president. Roosevelt indicated that he thought Taft was the best available man, and his fellow Republicans seemed to think likewise. Some few leaders were in a mood to quarrel with Roosevelt, but the best they could offer as an alternative was the aged vulgarian and political mossback, Uncle Joe Cannon. The campaign for him never developed.[91] In early March, Higginson reported that the Wall Streeters, as one of them said to him, would be "content if we could be sure of having Mr. Taft."[92] Higginson himself favored Taft, with Cannon as his second choice.[93] Lodge replied to his fellow Bostonian that he was "very glad to hear" what he had to say about Taft and that "I do not believe a better candidate, as Henry Adams said to you, was ever suggested."[94] George W. Perkins reported to J. P. Morgan from Washington that there was general agreement in political circles that Taft would be the next president but there was a notable lack of enthusiasm at the prospect and it would be easier to elect Roosevelt.[95] Nobody seemed to blame anybody for that sad state of affairs. Whitelaw Reid, in keeping with his habit of making certain that his underlings on the *New York Tribune* were in the proper political groove, wrote in May from London to a member of the staff, "The little I hear from the political world inclines me to think that Wall Street has made up its mind to Taft and expects his

[89] Root to Whitelaw Reid, 22 May 1908, Reid Papers.

[90] John B. Wiseman, "Dilemmas of a Party out of Power: The Democracy, 1904–1912" (Ph.D. dissertation, University of Maryland, 1967), 108–09.

[91] Gwinn, *Cannon*, 124–28.

[92] Higginson to Lodge, 3 March 1908, Lodge Papers.

[93] Higginson to Lodge, 19 February 1908, Lodge Papers. Earlier, on 14 June 1907, Higginson had written railroad president Charles E. Perkins, "tell me if Cannon would be a good President," Higginson Papers.

[94] Lodge to Higginson, 5 March 1908, Higginson Papers.

[95] 16 March 1908, Perkins Papers.

election." In fact, Reid explained, "Jacob Schiff told me this in so many words when he was here a few weeks ago, and I hear it from other financial quarters."[96]

Aldrich quietly supported Taft. In early June, following the routine nomination of Taft, crusty old William E. Chandler wrote Aldrich, "My dear friend I admire your ability and genius but abhor your conclusions. We should have beaten Taft if it had not been for you. I hope he will recognize the man who saved him." Chandler wondered, however, if the party could elect Taft, for "Every time he opens his mouth he puts his foot in it."[97]

There was something seriously wrong with a great political organization that stumbled apathetically into an election year in such a vulnerable condition. It was without either an adequate roster of leaders from which to select a politically attractive candidate or a list of proposals out of which to fashion a program. In fact the party lost its popular appeal when it lost Roosevelt as its leader.

The critical condition of the Republican party remained below the surface during the 1908 campaign, as various leaders and factions brushed aside nuisance Democrats. Nevertheless, the increased public interest in reform, combined with a lack of enthusiasm over the conspicuousness of the Taft-Aldrich-Cannon influences in the previously Roosevelt-dominated Republican party served to add some strength to the Bryan-controlled Democracy. The lack of an aggressive, crusading spirit in the Republican platform also aided the Bryan Democrats.[98] But at no time during the dull campaign did the Republicans become more than slightly nervous over the outcome.

In the early spring, before the convention, there appeared to be some danger of Negro defection[99] because of Roosevelt's action in the Brownsville affair, but Taft succeeded in escaping Negro condemnation on that matter because he was blameless

[96] Reid to Conde Hamlin, 21 May 1908, Reid Papers; see also William S. Cowles to Reid, 2 May 1908, and Roosevelt to Reid, 25 May 1908, Reid Papers.

[97] William E. Chandler to Aldrich, 4 June 1908, Aldrich Papers.

[98] Kirk H. Porter and Donald J. Johnson, *National Party Platforms, 1840–1956*, 157–63.

[99] Whitelaw Reid to Charles S. Francis, 16 March 1908, Reid Papers.

and had even left the door open for Negroes to conclude that he disapproved of Roosevelt's performance. But, on the other hand, Taft gave no indication that he would revive the one-time Republican championship of the southern Negroes' cause. In August, he wrote his friend Mabel Boardman, "The truth is that the negro question so far as the South is concerned in many of the States is a mere ghost of a past issue . . . and I don't propose to raise it again except in a discussion with the negroes themselves as to their course in the matter." He added, "My own judgement is that the best thing for the negroes is to allow the present status to continue until the Republicans can control some of the Southern States, and this will bring about an equal enforcement of the laws of eligibility for voting."[100] He offered no suggestions on how the Republicans might obtain that control of "some of the Southern States."

Taft's campaign consisted of reciting and endorsing the Roosevelt record. He seemed to be content to perform, as the Democratic *New York World* had predicted, as a Roosevelt proxy candidate.[101] He did, however, go further than Roosevelt on tariff reform. But the Roosevelt magnetism was lacking. Privately Taft made it clear to many people that he was in full sympathy with the growing movement to remove Cannon from the House Speakership. This greatly encouraged the angry anti-Cannon House members, who planned to dethrone Cannon with Taft's help if he was elected. "Confidentially," Taft wrote one supporter, "the great weight I have to carry in this campaign is Cannonism."[102]

On the other hand, Taft greatly appreciated Aldrich's help. He recognized that Aldrich had helped him obtain the nomination and shortly thereafter wrote him, "I am anxious to see you and talk with the coolest headed man in the country."[103] Their harmonious relationship continued. Aldrich came to the rescue

---

[100] 21 August 1908, Taft Papers.

[101] John L. Heaton, *The Story of a Page: Thirty Years of Public Service and Public Discussion in the Editorial Columns of the New York World,* 258–60.

[102] Taft to Fr. D. D. Thompson, 27 August 1908, Taft Papers; see also Taft to Charles F. Brooker, 12 September 1908, and to Roosevelt, 21 September, 9 October, 7 November 1908, ibid.; Henry F. Pringle, *The Life and Times of William Howard Taft: A Biography,* 1: 402–05; Gwinn, *Cannon,* 154–56.

[103] 27 June 1908, Aldrich Papers.

during the campaign when it appeared that Foraker, who was feuding with Taft, might withdraw from the Senate race to the detriment of the party in the election. Aldrich wrote to his fellow senator, at Taft's behest, that he should help the presidential candidate. He added, "The tendency in the West to elect a class of men to the Senate who mean nothing but mischief and destruction, if their ideas are adopted, should awaken in every patriotic mind a fear of the consequences. You must not leave the Senate."[104]

Taft won the presidency by a substantial majority. In the Middle West, however, in some of the contests for House seats and governorships, there were Democratic and reform-minded Republican gains large enough to serve as a warning that the spirit which had produced the Iowa Idea and the Wisconsin Idea was alive and thriving.[105] Without Roosevelt's help during the campaign, the regular Republicans might well have suffered a much greater defeat.

[104] 21 August 1908, ibid.; see also: Taft to Aldrich, 1 September 1908, ibid.; Taft to Arthur I. Vorys, 4 August 1908, Taft Papers.
[105] See George E. Mowry, *The Era of Theodore Roosevelt, 1900–1912*, 231.

XII

THE TAFT-ALDRICH-CANNON
TRIUMVIRATE
1909

THE TOP REPUBLICAN LEADERSHIP that emerged
following Roosevelt's withdrawal from the political scene
failed to meet its responsibilities and thereby contributed conspicuously to the rapid deterioration of the party. The new Republican command consisted of Taft, Aldrich, and Cannon.
These three appeared incapable of treating the Republican party
as a viable, national organization with a unified purpose and
showed no real interest in modernizing its traditional policies.
They did nothing to carry out the historic party commitment to
the Negroes or to champion any other humanitarian cause. They
allowed the currency question to remain buried in the slow-
moving Monetary Commission that Aldrich directed in leisurely
fashion. They honored the party platform promise to legislate
on the tariff, but the measure they sponsored was a political
nightmare for lesser party members, who saw it as a threat to
party unity. They showed no real comprehension of the trust
problem. They lacked Roosevelt's feeling for the need of increased governmental control over business and over businessmen who became greedy. President Taft preferred to fight and
punish business rather than develop a realistic program of governmental supervisory power. The new leadership allowed the
party increasingly to appear to be the servant of powerful
special interest groups. Even when the party contributed to
occasional reform projects, the leadership seemed unenthusiastic.
Nobody expected Aldrich or Cannon to sponsor reforms, but

many people took it for granted that Taft would carry on Roosevelt's modernization work. Instead, he seemed to go back toward McKinley in some things, toward Cleveland in some, and forward toward Roosevelt in others. He selected subordinates who added to this dual impression. Secretary of the Interior Ralph Ballinger showed a more conspicuous desire to serve selected business interests than had any member of McKinley's cabinet. Attorney-General George W. Wickersham engaged in trustbusting that went considerably further than the efforts of Roosevelt's trustbusting aides. He exhibited a combination of the moralistic zeal of the Roosevelt administration and the doctrinaire economic views of the Bourbon Democratic Cleveland administration.[1]

The personal political limitations of the top leaders, as individuals and collectively, was a major cause of the party's decline. Taft, as president and head of the Republican party, had the greatest power and the greatest responsibility, but he was woefully miscast for both those roles. He showed too little sensitivity to the feelings of other people, though his innate sense of decency and his dedication to the spirit of justice at times conveyed the impression that he was a "true friend of the people." His identity with Roosevelt made him at first seem a reformer. But he lacked sufficient knowledge and zeal to give real substance to that impression.

At the very outset of his administration, Taft's handling of the tariff issue revealed his inadequacies as a political leader. Occasionally during his years in Roosevelt's cabinet, he had shown an interest in tariff reform. His interest in lower rates on Philippine-produced goods, which his experience in those islands had taught him would greatly help the Filipinos, contributed to his tariff reform bent. His brother Horace, head of the Taft School, was a dedicated tariff reformer, and Taft took seriously the counsel of members of his family. For several years Roosevelt had expressed agreement with him that at least some tariff rates were excessive, and by 1907 he acknowledged to his friend Taft that after the 1908 election Congress should take up the matter.[2]

[1] See Wickersham to Richard Olney, 12 January 1912, Olney Papers.
[2] Taft to Roosevelt, 6 August 1906, and Roosevelt to Taft, 8 August 1907,

The 1908 platform only vaguely included tariff reform, calling for a special session of Congress after the inauguration to examine the matter, without specifying whether the tariff needed to be revised upward or downward.[3] Taft's 1908 campaign speeches, however, indicated his belief that some rates were too high and others were too low. Following the campaign he made clear his determination to push Congress into speedy action on the matter. He approached the project without the counsel of political champion Roosevelt or the aid of economic experts. He clearly intended to demonstrate at the outset of his regime that he could be an aggressive and successful political commander.

Taft's insistent, single-minded drive for early congressional action on tariff reform caused him to stumble immediately into an alliance with Aldrich and Cannon from which he never broke away. They were the two men best able to get quick action and without them he might get no action whatsoever. Nothing in Aldrich's political record precluded a working arrangement between the two men. As good Republicans, both Taft and Aldrich were protectionists, and both of them thought that some of the existing rates were too high.[4] This was true of Aldrich despite his flippant remark in April 1909 to the effect that the revisionist pledge in the Republican platform was not necessarily a downward revisionist pledge.[5] Even Taft felt some rates were too low when in August 1908 he wrote William Burgess of the United States Potter's Association, "All I can say is that in reading the report of the American Manufacturers Association, I became convinced that there were some industries that needed an increase in the tariff and the one which I felt was of chief importance was the pottery business." He added, "That is as far as I have gone in the matter of the tariff."[6]

Speaker Cannon presented the greatest initial obstacle to

Roosevelt Papers; see also Roosevelt to Taft, 3 August 1907, Morison, *Letters*, 5: 743.

[3] Kirk H. Porter and Donald J. Johnson, *National Party Platforms, 1840–1956*, 158.

[4] See, for example, Roosevelt to Leslie M. Shaw, 4 August 1905, Morison, *Letters*, 4: 1300.

[5] *New York Times*, 23 April 1909; Taft to W. H. Miller, 13 July 1909, Taft Papers. Lodge expressed the same view on the platform pledge.

[6] 24 August 1908, Taft Papers.

Taft's drive for quick action on the tariff. At first his record of "standpatism" on the issue and his vulgarity and dictatorial rule of the House troubled the president. But by the time the special session of Congress began, Taft had come to recognize Cannon's usefulness. In November following the election, however, Taft showed signs of panic. He became fearful that Cannon would employ his considerable power to prevent enactment of a defensible tariff revision measure. He wanted assurance that Cannon's cohorts, Sereno E. Payne, chairman of the Ways and Means Committee, and the Cannon-controlled Rules Committee would allow a genuine tariff revision bill to emerge from the House.[7]

A few days after the election, Cannon delivered a speech in Cleveland in which he acknowledged that lobbyists, pressure groups, and compromise would necessarily influence the forthcoming tariff legislation. He realistically stated, as a matter of course, that the Republican party would redeem its pledge for downward revision but that it would not be "a perfect revenue law . . . because all legislation is a compromise." He added, however, that "we will put on the statute books the best revenue law ever written," and "in the last analysis it will be the best that can be done by your representatives in Congress, with the approval of the President. . . . And under it we will march to further development of the great Republic."[8]

The naive Taft resented Cannon's speech. He privately wrote Root that it "was of a character that ought to disgust everybody who believes in honesty in politics and dealing with people squarely, and just because he has a nest of stand-patters in his House and so ensconced that we may not be able to move him is no reason why I should pursue the policy of harmony."[9] Finally, after Roosevelt and some concerned members of Congress interceded, Taft regained his composure and even exuded opti-

[7] Taft to Howard C. Hollister, 16 September 1908, to Harold T. Chase, 21 November 1908, to William Nelson Cromwell, 22 November 1908, to J. N. Dolley, 23 November 1908, to Frank L. Dingley, 23 November 1908, to Halvor Steenerson, 30 November 1908—all in Taft Papers.

[8] Quoted in Henry F. Pringle, The Life and Times of William Howard Taft: A Biography, 1: 403–04.

[9] Taft to Root, 25 November 1908; see also Taft to Roosevelt, 7 November 1908, and to Joseph H. Gaines, 1 December 1908; Horace Taft to Taft, 1 December 1908; Herbert Parsons to Calvin Cobb, 31 January 1923, enclosed in Cobb to Taft, 5 February 1923—all in Taft Papers.

mism. To William Nelson Cromwell, of Panama Canal fame, Taft wrote in early December, "Cannon and the other people in the House of Representatives seem disposed now to come down and 'play ball' and agree to do their duty as required by the platform of the Republican party."[10]

In December, Taft and Cannon met to talk over their differences. The meeting proved to be a success but its details were never revealed to the public. Several years later, however, Taft reminisced to a family friend that at the time of his conference with Cannon, the Ways and Means Committee was already working on a tariff bill. So after talking with Cannon, the president-elect "went down to see the Ways and Means Committee and reached an agreement with them about Philippine sugar."[11] He had not only obtained the reassurance he sought from Cannon, but had also performed successfully as a lobbyist for his pet project. Thereupon he withdrew temporarily from participation in tariff-making, trusting both Cannon and Aldrich to carry out the chore in their respective branches of Congress.

The Taft-Cannon truce had important consequences for the party. Above all else, it blunted Taft's great fury at Cannon and markedly reduced his earlier intention to join forces with angry House members to prevent Cannon's reelection to the Speakership. The most unfortunate aspect of the truce was the disappointment it brought to the anti-Cannon forces, who had counted on Taft's support. They considered tariff reform of much less importance than being rid of Cannon and therefore lost considerable faith in Taft's reliability as a dedicated reformer.

Taft, clearly afraid that the Insurgents lacked sufficient power to oust Cannon, justified his rapprochement in a letter to reformer William D. Foulke of Indiana, two days before the special session of Congress convened. "I ask you how a man of sense . . . can expect me to do otherwise than support the regular organization in the House. I should have been glad to

[10] 2 December 1908, Taft Papers; see also Taft to E. J. Hill, 2 December 1908, to J. L. Bristow, 5 December 1908, to William Worthington, 5 December 1908—all in Taft Papers; Roosevelt to Taft, 28 November 1908, Morison, *Letters*, 6: 1389.

[11] Taft to Mabel Boardman, 15 April 1912, Taft Papers; see also Taft to Horace Taft, 27 June 1909, ibid.

beat Cannon," Taft explained, "but I must rely upon the party and party discipline to pass the measures that I am recommending." Taft added, "one slight difficulty about reformers . . . is the indisposition to look ahead and take in the whole situation, and to magnify the importance of one particular thing . . . as compared with the whole plan of progress."[12]

Roosevelt had earlier counseled Taft to be cautious in dealing with the movement to demote Cannon. In November, in a letter to Taft that contained no reference to the tariff, Roosevelt in effect pointed out the sad fact that the House Republicans were in no position to produce any acceptable alternative for the Speakership and that Cannon was probably still very popular with them. Roosevelt said, "we cannot think of putting in some cater-cornered creature like [Theodore E.] Burton; and, moreover, if it is evident that four fifths of the Republicans want Cannon I do not believe it would be well to have him in the position of the sullen and hostile floor leader bound to bring your administration to grief, even tho you were able to put someone else in as Speaker."[13]

Cannon took full advantage of the tariff bill-making to forestall an attempt by Republican Insurgents and Democrats to unseat him. He enlisted the aid of key interests anxious to obtain high tariff duties on their products. Ex-House member Lucius N. Littauer, wealthy glove manufacturer of Gloversville, New York, proved useful. Popular in the House because he had been instrumental in obtaining a salary increase for the members, Littauer prevailed upon grateful former colleagues to remain loyal to Cannon. In return, Cannon used his power to obtain a substantial increase in the import duty on gloves. Cannon clearly made a similar arrangement with the Tammany Democrats in the House. The leadership of Tammany maintained friendly relations with the Standard Oil people. Cannon arranged for increased duties on petroleum products in return for Tammany support for his position as Speaker.[14]

[12] Taft to W. D. Foulke, 12 March 1909, ibid.

[13] Roosevelt to Taft, 10 November 1908, Morison, *Letters*, 6: 1340–41.

[14] Richard Lowitt, *George W. Norris: The Making of a Progressive, 1861–1912*, 147–49, 310 n, 311 n; Kenneth W. Hechler, *Insurgency: Personalities and Politics of the Taft Era*, 54–55; Taft to Horace Taft, 11 August 1909, Taft Papers; Stan-

The House Committee on Ways and Means, under the guidance of chairman Sereno E. Payne and with Cannon's help, quickly drew up a tariff bill and in March the House speedily approved it. The Payne bill, as it was called, provided for moderate tariff reduction. President Taft felt Cannon had kept his promise to carry out the tariff plank in the party platform. He later wrote his brother Horace that the bill "was a genuine effort in the right direction" and while the "step was not as great as I would have been glad to take, it contains much of what I approve." He added, "I shall be glad to sign a bill like the Payne bill, with the hosiery and glove schedules left out."[15]

After the bill went to the Senate, Taft continued to remain in the background. Partly he wanted to wait until the bill reached the House-Senate conference committee and partly he recognized his own limitations. By waiting until the bill reached the conference committee, he risked coming into the picture too late to obtain a good measure. He made it perfectly clear, however, that he would veto an unsatisfactory bill. In late March, before the Senate debate began, Taft explained to *New York Tribune* editor Hart Lyman why he had decided to refrain from earlier active participation in the matter. He stated, Lyman reported to Whitelaw Reid, that Roosevelt, "because of his personality and the state of public feeling at the time, was able to use a bludgeon with great effect. 'But I cannot do that,' he said; 'I must try to make Congress keep the party's promises by persuasion and conciliation.'" But to emphasize his determination to perform his duty, Taft added that "he could get along very well with only one term, and that he would not imitate Mr. Cleveland by letting a tariff bill of 'perfidy and dishonor' become law through an evasion of responsibility."[16]

The tariff debate in the Senate and the bill that resulted almost fatally damaged the alliances that had for so many years sustained the Republican party in its position of national dominance. To a large extent, Senator Aldrich's misguided judgment

ley D. Solvick, "William Howard Taft and the Payne-Aldrich Tariff," *Mississippi Valley Historical Review* 50 (December 1963): 428–29; Clarence R. Edwards memorandum, box 50, Biographer's Notes, Aldrich Papers.

[15] Taft to Horace Taft, 27 June 1909, Taft Papers.

[16] 27 March 1909, Reid Papers.

and arrogance caused the near disaster. In considering the Payne bill, the Aldrich-controlled Finance Committee precipitously raised duties on over 600 items. When a band of angry and ambitious Insurgent Republican senators sought to check Aldrich's efforts, he highhandedly applied his majority control in the Senate to rebuff them. Without Allison and Spooner in the Senate or Roosevelt in the White House, no one could hold Aldrich in check. The course he pursued was difficult even for him to control. His dominant position left him no opportunity to claim lack of power as an excuse for denying unreasonable requests for more rate increases, even when he wished to do so.

At the time, Senator Elihu Root wrote his friend Ambassador Whitelaw Reid, "We are having a dreadful time now about the tariff. Publication of the Payne bill woke up all the producers of the country and a bigger army than [free-trade crusader] Henry Watterson[17] ever dreamed of moved immediately on Washington to insist on full protection and an increase of duty for their own products and heroic reduction upon the products of everyone else, while all the importers and their foreign representatives here are on the verge of insanity over the increases that are included in the bill."[18] The same day, Taft wrote from the sidelines to James Ford Rhodes, "Aldrich is engaged in getting the bill through the Senate, and there is the place of special interests, and there is the most difficult place to deal with a recalcitrant minority."[19] The most obstreperous members of Taft's "recalcitrant minority" were Republican Insurgents from the Middle West: Wisconsin's Robert M. LaFollette, Iowa's Albert B. Cummins and Jonathan P. Dolliver, Indiana's Albert J. Beveridge, Minnesota's Moses E. Clapp and Knute Nelson, and Kansas's Joseph L. Bristow.[20]

The Insurgents used the debate to impress upon politically concerned people the unsatisfactory condition of the Republican top leadership, and most especially to expose Aldrich. They worked hard to acquaint themselves with statistical information on import goods. Though the available information was woefully

---

[17] Democrat Henry Watterson was editor of the *Louisville Courier-Journal*.
[18] 3 April 1909, Reid Papers.
[19] 3 April 1909, Taft Papers.
[20] James Holt, *Congressional Insurgents and the Party System, 1909–1916*, 30.

inadequate, they were able to display knowledge and oratory that greatly deflated the effect of the authoritarian and imperious Aldrich. His customary skill in tariff-making, using statistics business interests furnished him, seemed less impressive when the Insurgents appeared to be even better informed. Dolliver, always an eloquent performer, felt special cause to attack Aldrich. Dolliver had looked forward expectantly to the day when he would succeed his mentor Allison on the Finance Committee. Upon the death of Allison in the spring of 1908, however, Aldrich had passed over Dolliver in filling this and two other vacancies on the committee.[21] Mark Sullivan later recalled, "Slowly [Dolliver] would rise from his seat—and one felt that Aldrich cringed, for Aldrich, wholly a man of action and arrangements, was quite without arms or armor against such a foe as Dolliver." On another occasion, Sullivan noted that "Often Aldrich's only response was not to respond, to walk from the Senate floor, red-faced, for the first time in his life successfully defied."[22]

Some senators recognized that it was ridiculous and fraudulent to continue to rely so completely on a combination of oversimplified formulas, guesswork, and favoritism for determining tariff rates. The phenomenal growth of the nation's foreign trade and the complexities of its highly industrial society demanded a more sophisticated approach to economic questions. During the past several decades, starting in the 1880s, there had been a growing recognition of this need. Many economists and businessmen realized that politician-made tariff schedules were an absurdity. Spooner, Roosevelt, and lately Beveridge and LaFollette saw the wisdom of a tariff commission. LaFollette and Beveridge vainly attempted to include endorsement of the idea in the 1908 Republican party platform but did manage to include it in the minority report on the platform. Taft endorsed it during the campaign.[23]

---

[21] John C. Crockett memorandum, and Senator Reed Smoot memorandum, box 50, Biographer's Notes, Aldrich Papers; Mark Sullivan, *Our Times: The United States, 1900–1925*, 4: 358–60.

[22] Mark Sullivan, *The Education of an American*, 264; idem, *Our Times*, 4: 367.

[23] *Official Report of the Proceedings of the Fourteenth Republican National Convention . . . Chicago, Illinois, June 16, 17, 18 and 19, 1908*, 126–27; Belle Case LaFollette and Fola LaFollette, *Robert M. LaFollette*, 1: 258; Claude G. Bowers, *Beveridge and the Progressive Era*, 303, 304, 352–54.

In early 1909, while Congress was considering tariff revision, 700 people gathered in Indianapolis to attend a national tariff commission convention. They represented various business organizations, including the National Association of Manufacturers, the National Grange, and the National Live Stock Association. Several Indianapolis businessmen had initiated the idea, which had the endorsement of Taft and Roosevelt. Many speakers at the meeting criticized the current method of tariff-making.[24] But their efforts made only a slight impression on Congress.

During the tariff debate, Senator Beveridge led a movement to include in the bill a provision for a tariff commission. The opponents of the idea, with Aldrich as their spokesman, whittled away at the proposal until little remained of it, though enough was left to allow the president to create a fact-finding board, which many people referred to as a tariff commission.[25]

Clearly all the Republican senators, old-time ultraprotectionists and latter-day antitrust defenders of exploited consumers and farmers, were caught in a nonsensical Donnybrook when they debated the tariff issue among themselves. Those gifted with an ability to memorize and quote statistics held the stage. In the course of the debate, Senator Root reported privately to Whitelaw Reid that the "great obstacle to securing reductions arises from the fact that most of the men who are earnestly advocating them are as earnestly insisting upon retaining or increasing the Dingley duties on the products in which their own states are interested." By way of illustration, he pointed out that a few days before, the senators from the nonlumbering states in the Middle West had voted for free lumber, but subsequently most of them voted to increase the duty on barley.[26] In 1909, the party was still unprepared to render the subject proper treatment.

All of the Republicans, including the Insurgents, retained their traditional adherence to protectionism. Even the righteous

[24] Bowers, Beveridge, 304; Joseph F. Kenkel, "The Tariff Commission Movement: The Search for a Nonpartisan Solution of the Tariff Question" (Ph.D. dissertation, University of Maryland, 1962), 30; Taft to Henry Riesenber, 5 January 1909; to H. E. Miles, 18 January 1909; John C. Cobb to Taft, 13 February 1909—all in Taft Papers.
[25] Kenkel, "Tariff Commission Movement," 38, 41.
[26] Root to Whitelaw Reid, 29 May 1909, Reid Papers.

LaFollette, although too honest to deny the facts, never conducted a crusade to reeducate American farmers on the truth about the tariff. He acknowledged that high duties on farm products failed to net the economic benefits to farmers that Republican advocates habitually proclaimed as a matter of course, but he chose to emphasize in the debate only the excessive rates on non-Wisconsin-produced goods.[27] Neither did he show an inclination to educate the paper manufacturers of his home state on the manifest advantages to newspapers of lower duties on newsprint. Newspaper publishers were very unhappy with the four-dollar duty, but in answer to the complaint of one of them, President Taft was able to say, "Mr. LaFollette told me that in his judgement $4 was not an excessive rate."[28]

The Insurgents were obliged to let Aldrich carry the day. The most they could hope to accomplish from the tariff debate was to impress on their constituents back home that they dared to combat Aldrich. Aldrich remained top man in the Senate organization as chairman of the Finance Committee and as the new chairman of the Steering Committee. He was still an able debater on the Senate floor and commanded the loyalty of numerous senators to whom he had granted favors. His connections in the business world afforded him access to money and influence, which he could make available to his fellow senators. He could make or break a candidate whose strength was not deeply rooted in his state. True, he could not damage a LaFollette or a Cummins, but few senators had their popularity and gifts.

Aldrich conscientiously remembered to fulfill his promise of aid to colleagues who supported him. One such case was high protectionist Charles Curtis, a freshman senator from Kansas, who supported Aldrich in the tariff contest. It gratified Aldrich to have the help of a senator from a state with such Populist fame as Kansas. Curtis's support reminded solid citizens everywhere that the grand old Republican organization remained strong. Curtis, who had entered the Senate in January 1907, had long proved to be a cooperative Republican, not at all like the intractable Bristow from the same state. Roosevelt back in early

[27] See Aldrich to Taft, 11 February 1911, Taft Papers.
[28] Taft to H. V. Jones, 6 August 1909, ibid.; see also Taft to Melville E. Stone, 4 August 1909, ibid.

1907 had told Kansas editor William Allen White that "so far, my experience with Curtis has been rather more pleasant than with the average of his colleagues."[29] Roosevelt's remark was in response to a long letter from White, decrying the political situation in his home state. "Here in Kansas," White had declared, "I find every single general attorney of every railroad in the state, and every single newspaper that has ever been suspected of railroad alignment, solidly tied up with the Senatorial candidacy of Charles Curtis." The incensed White added that "Two railroad attorneys when I asked them why they were for Curtis, frankly told me in the confidence of friendship that orders came from higher up to be for Curtis and they are obeying orders."[30]

It was not surprising that in the Senate tariff contest Curtis and such other loyal middle western Republicans as Indiana's James A. Hemenway and North Dakota's Porter J. McCumber gave Aldrich their support. Soon Curtis wrote to Aldrich, "You will remember before leaving Washington, you told me to write you if we needed any assistance in the newspaper business in Kansas." With this in mind, he reported to Aldrich, "We [now] have an excellent chance to turn a good weekly newspaper at Emporia, Kansas, into a daily, and all the money has been raised by our friends except a thousand dollars." Curtis explained further that not only was Emporia "one of the most important points in the State," but was also "the home of William Allen White, who is publishing a paper against the present tariff laws." White was "in opposition to Mr. Miller the Congressman from that district, and all other members of the delegation who supported the bill." Furthermore, "The Kansas City Star, the Emporia Gazette and the Topeka Daily Capital are daily opposing the tariff measure and the republican [sic] congressmen who supported it and we need this paper very much."

In addition, Curtis had an opportunity, he said, "to arrange for two papers in the 6th district for five hundred dollars more. I think this fifteen hundred dollars would be well expended and hope you can see your way clear to have it sent me." Curtis added the incidental information that "In several of the districts

29 31 January 1907, Roosevelt Papers.
30 2 January 1907, ibid.

we have appointed newspaper men as Census Supervisors," and that "assisted greatly." Moreover, "As per your suggestion I have written Senator Hemenway."[31] About a week later, upon his return from one of his frequent trips to Europe, Aldrich wrote Curtis, "I enclose herewith check for $1500 as suggested, and I hope you may find it of use."[32] On the same day Aldrich indicated to Senator McCumber of North Dakota a willingness to aid him in a patronage case and an election matter. "I did speak to your late colleague before I left Washington" and told him what could be done for him. "I understood that he expected the place," Aldrich explained, "and was satisfied." Aldrich tactfully assured his fellow senator, "of course . . . your name was not mentioned in the conversation." Aldrich mysteriously added, "I have not forgotten to see as far as I could that no supplies were sent to your State antagonistic to your wishes. If you see any indication in that direction kindly let me know and I will attend to it at once."[33]

There were numerous other senators who for one reason or another followed Aldrich's lead in the tariff battle. Aldrich treated them well if he considered them worthy. Newspaper feature writer "Lincoln" wrote in the *Boston Transcript* at the time of the tariff debate, "Reed Smoot's recent rise to fame in the Senate is commonly ascribed to Aldrich," who seemingly "made and unmade the careers of the younger members."[34] Some Senators who had been close to President Roosevelt also supported Aldrich on the tariff bill. Two Massachusetts members, Henry Cabot Lodge and Murray Crane, and the new member from New York, Elihu Root, did so. In 1904, Root had privately advocated tariff revision.[35] Now that he was a senator, however, in the roll calls during the debate on the bill, he voted with Aldrich 104 times and against him 7 times, and failed to vote 18 times.[36] As a matter of course, Aldrich had the support of such standpat colleagues as Eugene Hale of Maine and Stephen B.

[31] 13 October 1909, Aldrich Papers.
[32] 22 October 1909, ibid.
[33] 22 October 1909, ibid.
[34] Quoted in *Providence Tribune*, 17 June 1909, clipping, ibid.
[35] Root to Roosevelt, 16 November 1904, Root Papers.
[36] Philip C. Jessup, *Elihu Root*, 2: 217.

Elkins of West Virginia. Shortly before the debate began, Elkins expressed his disgust with tariff revisionists. In a letter to White-law Reid, complimenting the ambassador on his recent widely heralded address on the greatness of Edmund Burke, Elkins incidentally mentioned his concern over the adverse effect the tariff revision movement was having on business. He blamed the president, at least in part, stating that "Taft is not yet over his Yale teachings. You know it takes about thirty years to cure the mischief [William Graham] Sumner did in three years." The testy Elkins added, "What folly to promise something in a platform to satisfy a minority—which if carried out will be a positive injury to the country."[37]

During the debate, everybody in the Senate and many outside that august body were well aware that Aldrich had control of the situation and had the means to obtain a sufficient number of votes. What they did not know was exactly how Aldrich would use his votes. An article on Aldrich, published in the *Providence Tribune*, June 6, began, "In this year's tariff legislation," Aldrich "is literally 'the whole thing.' The House, the Senate, the Administration, the Republican party itself, sink into comparative inconsequence beside him as he stands towering above the whole aggregation, dignified, patient, resourceful, seldom allowing his temper to be ruffled, looking down almost compassionately on the smaller men around him, steadily, unswervingly and successfully pursuing day by day his purpose of giving the American people precisely the tariff which in his confident self-sufficiency and his almost untrammelled power he has decided they must have."[38] Then, without pausing for his readers to digest such a large serving of Aldrich fare, the writer proceeded to describe the sources of the Rhode Islander's great power. He wrote of Aldrich's two decades of experience as a tariff legislator and his superior mind, and finally his special ability at handling "the intricacies and complications of tariff rates and schedules." The writer acknowledged that "In a discussion of abstract tariff theories Senator Aldrich might be equalled by many and surpassed by some," but theories were not a part of the 1909 debate. In

[37] January (n.d.), 1909, Reid Papers.
[38] 6 June 1909, clipping, Aldrich Papers.

1909, the newsman correctly concluded, "Neither the rebellious Republicans . . . nor even the Democrats themselves have undertaken seriously to assail the general doctrine of protection."[39]

Within the protectionist doctrine, Aldrich consistently demonstrated that he believed tariff rates should favor manufacturers, even at the expense of producers of raw materials. To him, the more refined the factory product, the more protection it needed and deserved. He preferred to have "the rates progressive from the crude products, the raw materials, to the finished product; progressive as to the amount of difference in the cost of production here and in competing countries, which means that if you put one duty on iron ore you must put a higher duty on pig iron, a higher duty still on steel rails, a higher duty still on watch-springs, progressive all through the scale."[40] Farmers, miners, and processors of crude products could therefore expect little or no assistance from Aldrich. Political, not economic, considerations were the only basis for workable agreements between them and Aldrich.

In the course of the debate, the question arose as to whether the bill should include provisions for a corporation tax, an income tax, and an inheritance tax. The House bill included an inheritance tax, which Taft had recommended in his inaugural address, but the Senate eliminated it. In its place Senate Insurgents and Democrats attempted to include a provision for a graduated income tax. Aldrich objected. Taft thereupon insisted, successfully, that Aldrich accept as a compromise a corporation tax provision and a resolution by Congress initiating an income tax amendment to the Constitution. Taft, always conscious of the courts, argued that it would be unwise for Congress to pass an income tax law and thereby confront the Supreme Court with the necessity of either reversing its 1895 decision or declaring the measure unconstitutional.[41]

During the negotiations on the Taft compromise, communications broke down between the president and the Insurgents. The fact that Taft negotiated only with Aldrich led the Insurgents to

[39] Ibid.
[40] Quoted in Nathaniel W. Stephenson, *Nelson W. Aldrich: A Leader in American Politics*, 481 n.
[41] Taft to Horace Taft, 27 June 1909, Taft Papers.

believe, mistakenly, that the two were conspiring to defeat the income tax. Taft then became furious when the Insurgents revealed their disappointment and anger. He expressed his frustration to his brother Horace. "I give them an opportunity to carry out these [Rooseveltean] reforms, or to make real progress, as for instance, in the proposition to amend the Constitution to provide for an income tax, and pass the corporation tax, they turn and oppose that because they say they will not accept anything which comes as a gift from Aldrich."[42]

The debate dragged on in the Senate until early July. Root had early predicted that "If we run much longer than that we will be saved from being torn limb from limb by an outraged public by the fact that death from exhaustion will supervene."[43] On July 8 the Senate passed the Payne-Aldrich bill. Ten Republican Insurgents and twenty-four Democrats voted against it, but the forty-five supporters constituted a comfortable majority for the cause of traditional Republicanism. The bill did not provide for a genuine downward revision of the Dingley Tariff, for it greatly favored high-protectionist manufacturers. A House-Senate conference committee then attempted to reconcile the differences between the House bill and the Senate bill.[44]

Both Aldrich and Cannon selected high-tariff members for the committee. It was natural that Aldrich should do so, but it was somewhat surprising that Cannon should appoint a majority of ultraprotectionists to represent the moderate House bill. Actually only Payne represented moderate protectionism. Clearly, unless Taft injected himself vigorously into the proceedings, the final bill would emerge as a distinct triumph for Aldrich.[45]

A week before the Senate passed its bill, Taft had begun to show definite signs of uneasiness, and he doubtless wondered if he had made a mistake in not injecting himself into the contest

[42] Ibid.; see also William S. Cowles to Whitelaw Reid, 18 June 1909, Reid Papers; Root to John A. Sleicher, 24 June 1909, Root Papers; George E. Mowry, *Theodore Roosevelt and the Progressive Movement*, 57–59; Solvick, "Taft and the Payne-Aldrich Tariff," 433–36.

[43] Root to Charles S. Francis (ambassador to Austria), 31 May 1909, Root Papers.

[44] Mowry, *Roosevelt and the Progressive Movement*, 61.

[45] Ibid., 62; Pringle, *Taft*, 1: 436; Taft to Mrs. Taft, 25 July 1909, and to Horace Taft, 11 August 1909, Taft Papers.

earlier, as Roosevelt had done in 1906 when he observed that the Hepburn bill fight was getting out of hand. On June 29, Taft wrote to an old friend that Aldrich "in order to maintain a majority" for his bill "has had to consent to a lot of things going into the bill that he does not expect to keep there in conference."[46]

Taft expressed his concern in frequent long family letters, most especially to his politically conscious wife, but also to his brother Horace. "Many charge Aldrich with being behind the tobacco trust," Taft mused. "It is not apparent," however, "for he has consented to an increase in the tobacco tax which takes millions out of the profits of the Trust. I have always found him fair. I sincerely hope he will continue to be."[47] On the day the bill passed the Senate, he reported to Mrs. Taft, "Root thinks Aldrich will help make a good bill on the tariff but I don't know." Taft confided that "If I had more technical knowledge I should feel more confident."[48]

Three days later he wrote another lengthy letter to Mrs. Taft in which he discussed the unpopularity with the public of the Senate version in contrast to that of the House bill. He believed that a few changes would make the Senate bill essentially as acceptable as the House bill, "that upon a good many of these schedules the real difference to the consumer is not great and is largely sentimental, and the real fear of the manufacturer is also unfounded and so is sentimental."[49]

Next day, Taft reported on an important visit he had had with Aldrich which confirmed his growing awareness that the situation was less flexible than he had earlier assumed would be the case. He was "inclined to think" that Aldrich would come over to his view, "but the difficulty is that he has Senators who have supported him who will be bitterly opposed to having some of the things which I am working for adopted, and which were in the House bill and are not in the Senate bill." But, Taft added, personally Aldrich "regards these things as sentimental." So Taft,

[46] Taft to J. D. Brannan, 29 June 1909, Taft Papers; see also Taft to Horace Taft, 27 June 1909, ibid.
[47] Taft to Mrs. Taft, 7 July 1909, ibid.
[48] 8 July 1909, ibid.
[49] 11 July 1909, ibid.

"with a view to making some of these people come over," told Aldrich he could use him as he pleased and that "I would threaten him if he wished me to."[50]

A few days later Taft indicated to his wife both optimism and skepticism as to his success on the tariff bill. "I do not know whether I am going to succeed in winning this tariff fight or not," he wrote. "I am dealing with very acute and expert politicians, and I am trusting a great many of them and I may be deceived; but on the whole I have the whip hand."[51]

As the conference committee deliberated, Taft considered the effect of a possible veto, which he knew would give him personal popularity but only at the expense of the party, and "would defeat a bill that has a great many good features . . . and would leave us with the Dingley bill." As a way out of the dilemma, he thought that securing tariff-free hides would give the "bill a character" that would prevent "its being known as the Aldrich Bill." In spite of intense opposition to free hides, Taft hoped "to carry it through."[52]

In the end, the conference committee and Congress made enough concessions to the president to allow him to claim a small measure of personal success, but he failed to achieve his goal of a bill that approximated the House bill in overall reduction of duties. The reductions from the Senate bill were relatively insignificant and were on items in which Aldrich personally felt no interest—raw materials and low-quality manufactured goods. Conspicuous among them were hides, iron ore, low-quality cotton goods, oil, leather, and shoes. Taft's pet provision for Philippine reciprocity remained in the bill as a concession to his ego. The bill passed on August 5. In the Senate only seven Insurgents voted against it; in the House twenty Republicans voted against it. The result was a distinct victory for Aldrich and high protection, but Taft managed to convince himself that the bill was a good one. The Taft-Aldrich-Cannon leadership remained intact.[53]

[50] Taft to Mrs. Taft, 12 July 1909, ibid.; see also Taft to Mrs. Taft, 13 July 1909, and to Albert J. Beveridge, 13 July 1909, ibid.; Clarence R. Edwards memorandum, box 50, Biographer's Notes, Aldrich Papers.
[51] 18 July 1909, Taft Papers; see also Taft to Mrs. Taft, 22 July 1909, ibid.
[52] Taft to John Warrington, 26 July 1909, ibid.
[53] Taft to Mrs. Taft, 27, 28, 30 July 1909, to Aldrich, 29 July 1909, to Elbert F. Baldwin, 29 July, 3 August 1909, to Charles P. Taft, 1 August 1909, to Horace

Aldrich wired the good news to J. P. Morgan, then relaxing on board his yacht, the *Corsair*. The message stated, "Bill passed this afternoon. Everything all right."[54]

The passage of the Payne-Aldrich Tariff severely threatened the vital East–Middle West alliance in the Republican party, for it pleased only the industrial East. Middle western voters, feeling that Aldrich had made Taft a captive of eastern manufacturers, were in a mood to turn in revolt to Insurgent leaders and Democrats.

Taft set out to convince the public of the virtues of the tariff and to "punish his enemies and reward his friends" for their particular voting record on the measure. He wrote a few letters of praise to selected party members, such as Senator Charles Curtis of Kansas,[55] and planned a speaking tour in September and October 1909 into and beyond the unhappy Middle West. His plan was to "get out and see the people and jolly them."[56] Taft seemed to believe that all he needed to do was to make an appearance and deliver some routine, casually-prepared speeches. He pointedly ignored the Insurgents, whom he disliked personally and resented for their vote on the tariff. He felt these visionaries were expendable.

Throughout his tour Taft demonstrated above all else his ineptitude as a conciliator. He brashly defended the Payne-Aldrich Tariff, showing more inclination to discipline the Republicans in Congress who had voted against it than to pacify them. In Wisconsin, where he made half a dozen speeches, he failed even to mention fellow Republican LaFollette.[57] At Winona, Minnesota, in one of the major political blunders of his career, he forthrightly took to task those Republicans who had voted against the tariff and praised House member James A. Tawney, a resident of Winona and the only member of the Minnesota delegation in Congress who had supported the bill.[58] He naively told his lis-

---

Taft, 11 August 1909—all in Taft Papers; Mowry, *Roosevelt and the Progressive Movement*, 63–64; Pringle, *Taft*, 438–39, 445–49; Solvick, "Taft and the Payne-Aldrich Tariff," 440–41; Hechler, *Insurgency*, 144–45.

[54] Aldrich to J. P. Morgan, 5 August 1909, copy in box 166, Beveridge Papers.

[55] 6 August 1909, Taft Papers.

[56] Taft to F. H. Gilbert, 13 September 1909, ibid.

[57] Pringle, *Taft*, 1: 452.

[58] Ibid., 1: 454–55; Mowry, *Roosevelt and the Progressive Movement*, 69–70.

teners, "On the whole, however, I am bound to say that I think the Payne bill is the best bill that the Republican party ever passed,"[59] without suggesting that in the future he intended to work with the Insurgents to obtain better rates. By making such statements, he further alienated great numbers of voters and their political leaders. That evening he telegraphed to his wife about his busy day in Wisconsin and Minnesota, and remarked of his Winona performance that the "Speech [was] hastily prepared, but I hope it may do some good."[60] Three days later he wired again, this time reporting "I breakfasted with Senator Cummins. There is still a hush over my Winona speech but I suppose it will break with renewed emphasis in a day or two. However, I said what I thought and there is that satisfaction."[61] Uncle Joe Cannon thought it was a good speech and that "Of course, the Bryan party . . . will denounce it, and those who claim to be Republicans but constantly seek to betray the party will, it seems to me, be driven to forsake their position heretofore taken or openly join the enemy."[62]

Taft remained defiant. Several weeks later he wrote to his wife from Oregon, "I see that Cummins and LaFollette and the rest of them propose to fight, but I anticipated this, and I am ready to stand with the party and see who comes out best."[63] The criticism aligned him more with Aldrich and at the same time he tried to minimize its seriousness, believing public sentiment was with him more than the newspapers indicated. The "great receptions everywhere" and the numerous "expressions of kindly feelings" led him to discount the avalanche of unfriendly newspaper comments on his Winona speech and to believe they were "lacking in sense." When his private secretary sent a "lot of clippings" from the New York Times and other papers, he requested that no more be sent because "they are of such a wild and infuriated nature."[64] In a letter two months later, he ques-

[59] Quoted in Pringle, Taft, 1: 454.
[60] 17 September 1908, Taft Papers. In the telegram he also said, "Leave tonight for Minneapolis where I shall spend Sunday and write you a good long letter." That promised letter is not in the Taft Papers.
[61] Taft to Mrs. Taft, 20 September 1909, Taft Papers.
[62] Cannon to James A. Tawney, 18 September 1909, quoted in Blair Bolles, Tyrant from Illinois: Uncle Joe Cannon's Experiment with Personal Power, 197.
[63] 3 October 1909, Taft Papers.

tioned the intelligence of newspaper correspondents. "When you tell the truth they are at sea."[65] Taft also felt newspaper publishers were angry because they had not gotten lower tariff rates on newsprint and because they held the general philosophy, especially in the East, of "free trade."[66]

At year's end, Root privately summarized the situation as he saw it in a letter to Ambassador Whitelaw Reid. "We are in a very disturbed condition here," he began. The core of the trouble, Root emphasized, was the intense dissatisfaction in the "Middle West and Northwest" with the Payne-Aldrich Tariff. The people in those areas were in favor of a theoretical tariff but were "opposed to any particular tariff." Their dissatisfaction, Root explained, "gives heart to a body of so-called Insurgents in the Senate and House," where "Aldrich is suspected of representing especially the large capitalists of the country" and Cannon "has become suddenly most extraordinarily unpopular as a representative of tyrannical machine methods."[67] Lodge too noted the decline in Cannon's popularity. In a letter to Roosevelt, who was then in Africa, he wrote, "I . . . saw Morgan in New York. . . . He confided to me that he was very much disappointed in Taft, and I do not think there is anybody in the country who is more anxious for Taft's success than Morgan."[68]

The leaders were clearly worried and disappointed, though not in a state of despair. Root concluded that the regular Republicans would sustain serious losses in the 1910 election. "This is the appearance of things today. It may all straighten out. We have both seen a good many worse situations straightened out by the extraordinary capacity of the Republican party to make itself effective." Meanwhile, Root added, "The people of the country" show that they miss the excitement . . . of Roosevelt's vigorous policies, and the mild and conservative methods of President Taft commend themselves more to the thinking people

---

[64] Taft to Mrs. Taft, 24 October 1909, ibid.; see also, Taft to Mabel Boardman, 11 October 1909, ibid.

[65] Taft to W. C. Brown, 5 January 1910, ibid.; see also Taft to Charles Nagel, 1 June 1908, ibid.

[66] Taft to Philander C. Knox, 24 October 1909, ibid.

[67] Root to Whitelaw Reid, 20 December 1909, Reid Papers.

[68] 30 November 1909, Henry Cabot Lodge, ed., *Selections from the Correspondence of Theodore Roosevelt and Henry Cabot Lodge, 1884–1918*, 354–55.

of the country than to the great crowd of people who like to have things whooped up."[69]

Toward the end of 1909, however, as Taft looked back over the events of the year, he gave no indication that he would strive to accommodate himself to progressivism, as many people now called the growing reform movement. He continued to feel dependent on Cannon and Aldrich, who were anathema to progressive reformers. In mid-November 1909, the president wrote to William D. Foulke, "The alliance between Mr. Cannon, Senator Aldrich and myself is one of the easy accusations to make; but as I am engaged in trying to lead a party to take up certain measures and pass them, which we have promised to do, I cannot avoid the charge of cooperation with those who are in leadership in each House."[70]

Before Congress convened, indications accumulated that the leadership was determined to discipline lesser party leaders and functionaries with Insurgent tendencies. Cannon provocatively flaunted his power by announcing his removal from House committee chairmanships of reform-minded Charles N. Fowler of New Jersey, Augustus P. Gardner of Massachusetts, and Henry A. Cooper of Wisconsin. Aldrich, meanwhile, ignored the mounting anger of Insurgent senators. Word also reached the public that Richard A. Ballinger, the Taft-appointed secretary of the interior, was mistreating Gifford Pinchot, conservationist and chief forester, and was unduly solicitous of Seattle businessmen who were attempting to deliver rich, government-owned coal lands in Alaska to the Morgan-Guggenheim Syndicate. Taft came to Ballinger's defense and the situation soon became a *cause célèbre* that deeply wounded the Taft regime.[71] The new leadership was off to a poor start.

[69] Root to Reid, 20 December 1909, Reid Papers.
[70] 18 November 1909, Taft Papers.
[71] Mowry, *Roosevelt and the Progressive Movement*, 67–68.

XIII

PARTY REGULARITY
DISINTEGRATES
1910

A F T E R 1909, the Taft-Aldrich-Cannon leadership continued to decline in popularity with the voters and at the same time lost its hold on Congress. Cannon lost much of his great power in the House; Aldrich became more amenable in the Senate; and under Insurgent attack Taft suffered humiliation in his role as party chief. The election results in the fall of 1910 graphically illustrated the failure of the party command.

Soon after passage of the Payne-Aldrich Tariff and Taft's attempt to "jolly the people" into endorsing the measure, he and some other public servants, especially Senate Insurgents, gave earnest attention to the widely recognized need for a new railroad rate law. Taft had an opportuniy to restore party harmony if he could find a way to induce the Insurgents to cooperate with him in a joint undertaking to improve administration of the Hepburn Act. Since both Taft and such leading Insurgents as LaFollette, Cummins, and Dolliver had earlier demonstrated a genuine interest in this sort of reform, it was logical to think such an effort was possible. It seemed to be up to the president to work closely with the Insurgents in order to avoid the appearance of too close identification with friends of the railroads. Taft, however, continued to lean on Cannon and Aldrich, which further aroused the indignation of the Insurgents. While Taft was not directly a captive of the railroad interests and had long been suspicious of them, he nevertheless felt politically dependent on powerful men identified in the public mind with the railroads, most notably Aldrich.[1] Louis T. Michener, an old-time professional politician who watched Taft's performance, despaired over the president's lack of political judgment and his inability to select satisfactory advisers. In January 1910 he wrote his friend James S. Clarkson, "I do wish the President had two or three good, level-headed political advisers in his cabinet, or even in his list of close personal friends, but there is not one in the whole lot." Michener exploded that "such a set of political amateurs I have never known in Washington." Consequently, "proposed official action is not sufficiently studied as to its ultimate result."[2]

On January 7, Taft sent a lengthy special message to Congress requesting a law to modify the Hepburn Act.[3] A few days later he submitted to Congress a draft of a bill. It was moderate in its treatment of both the railroads and the shippers. Suspicious reformers said it had loopholes, giving the railroads an opportunity to escape adequate control, and even declared that railroad interests had played a major role in formulating the measure. Senate Insurgents Cummins and Clapp found two provisions in the bill particularly offensive. They were Taft's inclusion of his pet scheme for a Court of Commerce to deal with rate disputes, and the overall emphasis on regulation rather than the prevention of monopoly. The bill did not strengthen the Sherman Antitrust Act. Though the measure did fall short of the advanced goals of progressivism, such as LaFollette's physical valuation of railroad properties, the Insurgents were unfair in their criticism. A substitute bill which Cummins introduced was also basically generous toward the railroads,[4] and this gave credence to the charge that politics provided the chief motivation for attacks on the Taft measure.

In the Senate, the Insurgents attempted to add several amend-

---

[1] On the railroad rate question, see George E. Mowry, *Theodore Roosevelt and the Progressive Movement*, 93–102; Kenneth W. Hechler, *Insurgency: Personalities and Politics of the Taft Era*, 163–77; Gabriel Kolko, *Railroads and Regulation, 1877–1916*, 177–207; James Holt, *Congressional Insurgents and the Party System, 1909–1916*, 34–35.

[2] 25 January 1910, Clarkson Papers.

[3] James D. Richardson, *A Compilation of the Messages and Papers of the Presidents*, 15: 7441–49.

[4] Kolko, *Railroads and Regulation*, 189.

ments to Taft's bill and around these efforts a bitter quarrel ensued, which drove Taft further into the Aldrich camp. The president believed the Senate Insurgents were sabotaging the bill in an effort to destroy him. To his brother Horace he expressed his hope that, "with the assistance of my wicked partners, Cannon and Aldrich," the railroad proposal would pass Congress. He then launched into a diatribe against Cummins, LaFollette, Dolliver, Clapp, and Bristow. Those five senators, he said, "are determined to be as bitter as they can against the administration, and to defeat everything that the administration seeks. Their method of defeat," he explained, "is to attempt to load down the legislation with measures so extremely radical that the sensible members of Congress won't vote for them, or that I shall have to veto them if they come to me. They are exceedingly malignant, and do not hesitate at times to say things right out against the administration," and hence, Taft asserted, if "I can beat them in the legislation that I am trying to get, I shall not be at all troubled that they have aligned themselves against me."[5] At about the same time, Lodge reported to Roosevelt, "The Insurgents, as they are called . . . set to work to make the bill as odious as possible, while professing a desire to pass it, to break down the Administration and discredit the party."[6]

Indeed, it did appear that the Insurgents were determined to rid the party of Taft and thus pave the road to the White House for the ambitious Cummins, or perhaps LaFollette. At the same time, several other anti-Taft individuals aided the Insurgents' cause by spreading the word of Taft's ineptitude. In late May, in the course of the debate in Congress, a Washington correspondent for the *Chicago Tribune* wrote to Roosevelt, "Taft despises the insurgents. He has had rows with all of them and denounces them in the severest language."[7]

In mid-May Taft took action to bring the railroad rate measure to final vote in the Senate. He asked Aldrich to call a conference of wavering Republican senators, "indeed everybody but LaFollette, Clapp, Cummins, Dolliver, and Beveridge." He be-

[5] 5 March 1910, Taft Papers.
[6] 30 April 1910, Roosevelt Papers; see also Lodge to Roosevelt, 3 September 1910, ibid.
[7] John Callan O'Laughlin (signed Cal) to Roosevelt, 30 May 1910, ibid.

lieved "that if you do this and have a full discussion you will be able to get two or three of these men to vote with you on party principles."[8]

Taft himself attended the conference, held on May 14. His aide, Archie Butt, saw the list of senators scheduled to attend and recorded that the president called them together "with a view of bringing a little peace into the distressed Republican ranks." Taft, he said, "pocketed his pride and asked men for whom he has no respect at all to join the conference." Butt wondered in particular what effect the meeting would have on western Senators William E. Borah of Idaho, Norris Brown of Nebraska, Coe Crawford of North Dakota, Elmer J. Burkett of Nebraska, and Samuel H. Piles of Washington.[9]

After two more weeks of effort, both the regular and the Insurgent Republicans agreed upon a measure and on June 3, by an overwhelming vote, they placed the Mann-Elkins Act on the statute books. Both the Republican regulars and the Insurgents claimed it as their handiwork. Actually both groups and the Democrats deserved a share of the credit. It was a superior measure, markedly improving the Interstate Commerce Commission procedures and expanding its authority to include the telegraph and telephone industries. The new act gave the commision the important power to initiate rate changes and to prevent rate changes from going into effect until the commission had passed upon their need. The law included, though with much less authority than Taft desired, provision for a Court of Commerce.[10]

The hassle over the railroad legislation had widened the split between the Taft regulars and the Senate Insurgents.[11] For a few weeks, nevertheless, Taft gained popularity with voters, who

[8] Taft to Aldrich, 12 May 1910, Aldrich Papers.

[9] Archie Butt, *Taft and Roosevelt: The Intimate Letters of Archie Butt, Military Aide,* 1: 349. Butt lists the other conferees as: Senators Elihu Root (New York), Joseph M. Dixon and Thomas H. Carter (Montana), Knute Nelson (Minnesota), Frank P. Flint (California), Wesley L. Jones (Washington), Frank B. Brandegee (Connecticut), Reed Smoot and George Sutherland (Utah), George S. Nixon (Nevada), Simon Guggenheim (Colorado), Weldon B. Heyburn (Idaho), W. Murray Crane (Massachusetts), Robert J. Gamble (South Dakota), and Nelson W. Aldrich (Rhode Island).

[10] Mowry, *Roosevelt and the Progressive Movement,* 101–02.

[11] George E. Roberts to James S. Clarkson, 5 December 1910, Clarkson Papers.

saw that his contribution to the enactment of the Mann-Elkins law indicated he was no mere tool of Aldrich and cynical business interests. Minnesota's Frank B. Kellogg wrote Taft that in his state the anti-Taft feeling was dying down, because of the Mann-Elkins Act. He warned, however, that it would be folly for Aldrich to invade the Middle West as the press rumored he was planning to do. "Aldrich would very greatly aid the insurgent cause" in the region.[12] But Taft's modest success with the voters was short-lived. They were more interested in the Ballinger-Pinchot controversy, the House fight on Cannon, and Roosevelt's return from Africa.

The failure of Taft and the Insurgents to cooperate in the movement for railroad regulation contributed more significantly to the Taft-Insurgent struggle for control of the party than it did to Taft's standing with the voters. Early in the debate in Congress on the Mann-Elkins bill, Taft and Aldrich had made plans to defeat the Insurgents in the 1910 primary elections and in state conventions. Aldrich promised to raise large sums of money in the East for the purpose. Also, a group of wealthy easterners pooled half a million dollars to establish a standpat newspaper in Des Moines, Iowa, and also early agreed to withhold patronage from Cummins, Dolliver, and Beveridge. The Insurgents retaliated with bitter criticism of Taft and his followers as a tool of special privilege. Their efforts were successful, for progressives made substantial gains against Taft regulars in the spring election and at state conventions.[13]

In the House, meanwhile, the influence of both Cannon and Taft deteriorated. A series of events increased the antagonism between them and House members. In early January a coalition of Republicans and Democrats caught Cannon off guard long enough to launch a congressional investigation of the Ballinger-Pinchot affair. Taft, at the same time and seemingly at the behest of Cannon, began to deny patronage to selected Insurgents. By mid-January, Taft had withdrawn patronage from Congressmen

[12] 15 August 1910, Taft Papers.
[13] James S. Clarkson to Grenville M. Dodge, 17 September 1909, 11 April 1909, Dodge Papers; George E. Roberts to Clarkson, 5 December 1910, Clarkson Papers; Clarkson memorandum, folder Q, box 4, ibid.; Butt, *Taft and Roosevelt*, 1: 301; Mowry, *Roosevelt and the Progressive Movement*, 106–19.

George Norris of Nebraska, Irvine Lenroot and William Cary of Wisconsin, and Clarence B. Miller of Minnesota. Before the month ended, other members reported patronage difficulties with the president.[14] Thus, as the work of the House got under way, neither the Insurgents nor the Taft-Cannon alliance was in a mood to seek reconciliation. The Insurgents made plans to reduce the power of Cannon, and Cannon made it clear that he regarded them as disloyal to the party. He felt confident that the Republican voters would sustain him.

On March 8, shortly before he anti-Cannon explosion in the House, Taft and Cannon had a most friendly visit. They took an automobile ride in the crisp spring air. Archie Butt, the president's aide, had his hands at the wheel and his ears cocked toward the conversation, which he recorded next day. On the journey to pick up Cannon, Taft remarked to Butt, "I am following to the letter the injunction to make friends of the mammon of unrighteousness, so that, when those who ought to be my friends fail me, I will have others to fall back upon."[15]

Taft and Cannon discussed the pending progressive-inpired Postal Savings bill. The speaker said he opposed it, but because the party platform had pledged its passage, he would support it. But, he added, "I am getting so damned tired, Mr. President, of this everlasting yielding to popular outcry against wealth that unless we put a check on it somewhere there is no telling where it will lead." To that, Taft replied, "Exactly, but those fellows in the Senate [the Insurgents] who are opposing this bill are not doing it for any reason which you have given, but merely to make trouble or else to freight it down with heavier populistic burdens." Cannon then said, "that is why I have such a contempt for those who are fighting you and am willing to give you my support."[16]

Then they discussed the matter that had really prompted Taft to invite Cannon for the ride. The president explained that in order to carry out one of the few promises he had made to Roosevelt, he would have to obtain authorization from Congress

[14] Richard Lowitt, *George W. Norris: The Making of a Progressive, 1861–1912,* 158–62.
[15] Butt, *Taft and Roosevelt,* 1: 301–02.
[16] Ibid., 302–03.

for at least two new battleships a year. In 1908 the House had gone out of its way to show its enmity toward Roosevelt by turning down his battleship request. Now Taft was eager to demonstrate his superior ability to obtain House cooperation. Much to his surprise, Cannon agreed to support the request. The Speaker remarked, according to Butt, that "Nothing illustrates better than this the difference between our last two Presidents. Roosevelt never wanted but two [battleships] at a time, and yet he always asked, even demanded, four a year, hoping thereby to get two. You, on the contrary, want two and ask for two."[17] Both men that day did well at their fence building.

In mid-March 1910, the Insurgents and the Democrats combined forces to effect reform in the House rules. Some annoyed regular Republicans joined them, and others indicated they were tempted but lacked the courage to do so. Under the leadership of Insurgent George W. Norris, a Republican-Democratic coalition successfully challenged Cannon's dictatorial control of the House. They used their power very sparingly, however, because the Republican members of the coalition feared the consequences of too close identity with the Democrats. Neither did they wish to enhance Democratic popularity. They merely reorganized the powerful Rules Committee depriving the Speaker of membership on the committee and providing that the House, rather than the Speaker, would henceforth select its members, the number of whom was increased.[18] Several Insurgents, however, voted with the Republican regulars against the Democrats' attempt to remove Cannon from the Speakership. They also permitted the regular Republicans to retain control of the newly formed Rules Committee. The Insurgent effort, though moderate, did provide publicity that fostered further revolt against the Republican leadership, the consequences of which exceeded their intention. It contributed more to Democratic strength than to their own.[19]

Actually the Republican leaders, those at the top and lesser

[17] Ibid., 303–04.
[18] Lowitt, *Norris*, 169–79; Hechler, *Insurgency*, 65–74; Holt, *Congressional Insurgents*, 14–19.
[19] Lowitt, *Norris*, 180–82; Hechler, *Insurgency*, 75–78; Holt, *Congressional Insurgents*, 19–28.

ones, served their party and the nation poorly in the Cannon affair. The Insurgents failed to remove Cannon from the Speakership and were too timid to use the opportunity to modernize House procedures. Taft failed to support them actively. Only the misguided, ridiculous Cannon showed the degree of spirit the situation called for, but he, regrettably, was on the wrong side. A few days after his removal from the Rules Committee, Cannon wrote an Iowa state party leader that he believed the Insurgents represented no more than 5 percent of the Republicans of the country, for "at least 95% of the Republicans in the U. S. have red blood in their veins. . . . We had better fight and fail standing by Republican policies than to fight and win and have victory, like the Dead Sea fruit, turn to ashes on our lips."[20]

Party chieftain Taft followed the House melee philosophically. He was actually not in Washington at the time, but upon reading the morning newspaper account of the contest as it approached its climax, Taft looked up, "laughed rather roguishly" and remarked to his aide, Archie Butt, "Well, Archie, I think they have got the old fox this time." He went on to muse that the action makes certain "that the old man has got to go and that he can never be elected to the Speakership again, if indeed he can retain his seat in Congress." Then Taft added, "But it is fine to see how he is fighting. That is the quality I admire most in Uncle Joe: he does put up a good fight."[21] On that same day, however, Taft wrote to his wife that if the move to oust Cannon from the Rules Committee succeeded, it might cause such a wide party rift that it would be impossible to "keep a Republican majority" in the House "sufficiently loyal and disciplined to pass the legislation which we promised." If that should happen, "Cannon would feel vindicated." Taft said that he rather hoped for a compromise that would retain Cannon in the Speakership for the remainder of the session even if he lost his membership on the Rules Committee.[22]

[20] Cannon to George D. Perkins, 22 March 1910, quoted in Ralph Mills Sayre, "Albert Baird Cummins and the Progressive Movement in Iowa" (Ph.D. dissertation, Columbia University, 1958), 368–69.
[21] Butt, *Taft and Roosevelt,* 1: 307–08.
[22] 19 March 1910, Taft Papers.

Cannon made the situation embarrassing for the party leaders by insisting that he expected to retain the Speakership if the Republicans still had a majority in the House after the 1910 election. Thus a vote for a Republican regular would in effect seem to be a vote for Cannon as Speaker. His refusal to retire threatened to induce hosts of Republican voters to go Democratic. Senator Charles Curtis of Kansas, whose views on the tariff and most matters were close to Uncle Joe's, wrote Aldrich in August that at the opening of the spring election campaign in his state, "it looked very much as if we would be successful. But, during the last week or ten days, I could see a decided change." This change "was noticeable after Mr. Cannon had made the announcement in one of his speeches, that if the House was again Republican, he would be a candidate for Speaker." He pointed out that the *Kansas City Star* and the *Topeka Daily Capital* used Cannon's announcement effectively. They "put it before the people in such a way as to make that the issue, rather than High Taxes, which I had been presenting to the people." The regular Republicans sustained a defeat in the Kansas election.[23]

In June 1910, Theodore Roosevelt returned from Africa and Europe and applied his considerable talents to reinvigorating and reuniting the Republican party. Gradually it became apparent that he was also attempting to redirect the party. The Taft regulars were uneasy. They could not be certain of the former president's intentions, either for the future leadership or for the future policies of the party. For the present, however, Roosevelt concentrated his major effort on modernizing party policy. In August he enunciated what he called the New Nationalism in speeches at Denver, Colorado, and Osawatomie, Kansas.[24] He was at his eloquent best and the speeches attracted wide attention. His effort was so popular with the voters that Warren G. Harding, candidate for governor of Ohio, for example, sent word to Roosevelt that if he would come there and speak on the Ohioan's behalf, he (Harding) in turn would

[23] 20 August 1910, Aldrich Papers; see also Frank B. Kellogg to Taft, 15 August 1910, Taft Papers.
[24] See William E. Leuchtenburg, ed., *Theodore Roosevelt: The New Nationalism*, 21–49.

announce that the Osawatomie speech was the platform on which he stood.[25]

The New Nationalism consisted of a call for positive action by the national government to preserve and advance for individuals the dream of equality of opportunity, justice, and security for person and property. It also recognized the value of large corporations when subject to the firm supervision of the national government. Roosevelt had voiced these views on previous occasions, but never before with such pointed logic and such effective rhetoric. His views differed somewhat from Taft's but not enough to precipitate a serious political cleavage. "The difference between them," Root wrote a friend, "is the natural difference between a man of a reflective cast of mind with the training of a lawyer and a judge, and a man of intense activity who has led a life of physical and literary adventure."[26]

At Osawatomie on August 31, Roosevelt reiterated the views expressed in his January 1908 special message to Congress. He called for increased federal power over the uses of property. "The man who wrongly holds," he asserted vigorously, "that every human right is secondary to his profit must now give way to the advocate of human welfare, who rightly maintains that every man holds his property subject to the general right of the community to regulate its use to whatever degree the public welfare may require it." He declared, "The true friend of property, the true conservative, is he who insists that property shall be the servant and not the master of the commonwealth; who insists that the creature of man's making shall be the servant and not the master of the man who made it." He said that the citizens of the nation "must effectively control the mighty commercial forces which they have themselves called into being" and reminded his audience, "there can be no effective control of corporations while their political activity remains," and "To put an end to it will be neither a short nor an easy task, but it can be done."[27]

Roosevelt also called for more control over the financial sys-

[25] Roosevelt to Lodge, 12 September 1910, Morison, *Letters*, 7: 122–23.
[26] Root to Edward W. Smith, (n.d.) September 1910, quoted in Philip C. Jessup, *Elihu Root*, 2: 164.
[27] Leuchtenburg, *New Nationalism*, 27, 33–34.

tem. After stating that the people of the United States "suffer from periodical financial panics to a degree substantially unknown among the other nations which approach us in financial strength," he declared, "There is no reason why we should suffer what they escape." Roosevelt insisted that "our financial system should be promptly investigated," and prophetically added that it should be "so thoroughly and effectively revised as to make it certain that hereafter our currency will no longer fail at critical times to meet our needs."[28] He failed to add, however, that Aldrich's Monetary Commission had yet to make its report, nor did he later commit himself on its 1912 proposal.

At Denver, on August 29, Roosevelt spoke out forthrightly against the record of the Supreme Court. He emphasized that through a series of decisions the Court had allowed a neutral zone of injustice to develop beyond the jurisdiction of either the state or the federal courts. He cited the famous Knight Sugar Trust case and the New York Bakeshop case to illustrate his charge that the Supreme Court had permitted neither the federal nor the state governments to legislate effectively against exploitative, greedy business interests.[29]

The Roosevelt speeches, carefully constructed to help Republican candidates, Insurgents and regulars alike, quickly became in the view of many people a call for a great surge of reform to smash the vested interests. Newspapers and partisans of various shades chose to place an extreme interpretation on his remarks concerning property and his criticism of the Supreme Court. Some leaders in the party, however, knew better. Both progressives and regular Republican leaders recognized that Roosevelt's New Nationalism was far from radical.

Taft and such old hands as Root and Lodge saw nothing really new in Roosevelt's New Nationalism. Root, in a letter to his law associate and friend Willard Bartlett, said, "What is the New Nationalism? I don't know. If it means having the Federal Government do the things which it can do better than the states and which are within the limits of its present constitutional power, I am for it. If it means more than that, I am

28 Ibid., 31.
29 Ibid., 42–44.

against it."[30] After all, as Republicans, and particularly as Republicans whose political activity had been mostly on the national stage, such men as Taft, Root, and Lodge were themselves basically nationalists. They prescribed a national approach, rather than a state and local government approach, to many problems.

The entire Taft administration was permeated with nationalists. For example, in 1910, he appointed as solicitor general a former Democrat, Frederick Lehmann, who had switched to the Republican party. A friend reported that Lehmann "views with distinct disfavor the State Rights views as to the regulation of corporations held by Democratic leaders. The theory advanced by Woodrow Wilson that the states rather than the Federal Government should deal with the problems of the time are not acceptable to him."[31]

The Insurgents, moreover, were more oriented to the state approach to public questions than were the regulars in the party. LaFollette and Cummins, who had served as governors, possessed great pride in their state governments, even though they were not, as were Democrats, doctrinaire states' righters. On one important subject, that of the income tax, Taft and Root at that time appeared to be even more nationalist than Roosevelt. They had endorsed a federal income tax, to be employed in times of national emergencies. Roosevelt, on the other hand, agreed with Lodge that while it was for the federal government to nationalize the inheritance tax, it would be well if the federal government refrained from taking over from the states the income tax as a source of revenue.[32] They apparently did not consider it feasible, at least politically, to advocate that both the states and the federal government simultaneously employ that form of taxation.

Root and Taft exchanged letters about the Osawatomie and Denver speeches and were in basic agreement on them. "So far as the New Nationalism goes," Root said, "the only real objec-

[30] 1 October 1910, Root Papers.
[31] George E. Roberts to James S. Clarkson, 5 December 1910, Clarkson Papers.
[32] Lodge to Roosevelt, 3 September 1910, Roosevelt Papers; Roosevelt to Lodge, 10 September 1910, Morison, *Letters*, 7: 122.

tion I see to it is calling it 'new.'" He remarked that Roosevelt "really proposes nothing more than we learned in the law school as being a matter of course." But Root's and Taft's cautious, legally-professional bent caused them to feel a little irritated at what they thought to be Roosevelt's bad manners in regard to the Supreme Court. "The difficulty about the speeches," Taft said, "is their tone, and the conditions under which they [were] delivered." They agreed that Roosevelt was correct in what he said about the Court's performance in the cases he cited but they were sorry he had said it to a western audience. Taft said, "The whole difficulty about the business is that there is throughout the West, and especially in the Insurgent ranks, to which Theodore was appealing, a bitterness of feeling against the Federal Courts that this attitude of his was calculated to stir up, and the regret which he certainly expressed that courts had the power to set aside statutes was an attack upon our system at the very point where I think it is the strongest." On the judicial review item, Root did not believe that Roosevelt really meant to advocate its removal from the Court's powers.[33] Roosevelt had indicated to Lodge that he meant it as a warning or reminder to the Court, and not as a proposal to alter its authority.[34]

Lodge viewed his friend Roosevelt's New Nationalism speeches mainly in the light of their effect on easterners, to whom he himself had to answer. The report he sent to Roosevelt on the eastern reaction was similar to his usual comments on his friends' speeches. Rather than discuss the legalistic aspects of the New Nationalism, he confined his observations to the rhetoric and the political implications. "I have told some people who have spoken to me," he said, "that the speech simply set forth the policies which you had advocated in messages and elsewhere for some time but the passage which alarmed them was what you said about property." But even some Roosevelt supporters continued to be upset. "I think," Lodge said, "the trouble really was with the word 'property.'" He observed, and his point was well taken and one which Roosevelt seemingly

[33] Root to Taft, 14 October 1910, and Taft to Root, 15 October 1910, Root Papers.
[34] Roosevelt to Lodge, 12 September 1910, Morison, *Letters*, 7: 123.

heeded, that the terms "capital" and "combinations" or "aggre-
gations of capital" and "corporations" carried meanings that
"are all understood and have certain natural limits but the word
property ranges from a Vanderbilt down to a man who has got
two hundred dollars in the savings bank or a house and farm
with a mortgage on it." Lodge observed that "the small property
owner is the backbone of this country" and that although "he is
not easily frightened he becomes more terrified than the man of
many millions because he feels that his little all is at stake and
his little all as a rule represents the fruit of savings and hard
earnings."[35]

The campaign and election of 1910 were a sad experience for
the Taft-Aldrich-Cannon leadership and for the Republican
party in general. As it approached, former Vice-President
Charles W. Fairbanks wrote Spooner, "The President is passing
through a rather unpleasant experience. He is receiving more
than his share of hyper-criticism and abuse." Moreover, Fairbanks added, "I rather think it is beginning to worry him
some."[36]

The results in the November balloting confirmed the suspi-
cions of Taft and everybody else that the party was in dire
trouble. The Democratic achievements were especially ominous.
They swept into control of the House, having gained fifty-nine
additional seats. They also made serious inroads into the Republican majority in the Senate. A Democrat even defeated
Indiana's Senator Beveridge.[37] Senator Shelby Cullom of Illinois,
an old-timer, wrote Aldrich after the election, "The darned
senate is pretty near busted by either the retirement or defeat
of our friends all over the country."[38]

The Republicans also suffered grave losses in local and state
contests. In Rhode Island, the power of boss Brayton suffered a
distinct decline.[39] In New Jersey, Princeton University president

[35] 3 September 1910, Roosevelt Papers.
[36] Fairbanks to Spooner (who sent it on to Whitelaw Reid), 23 August 1910,
Reid Papers.
[37] Holt, Congressional Insurgents, 41–43.
[38] 12 November 1910, Aldrich Papers.
[39] Erwin L. Levine, Theodore Francis Green: The Rhode Island Years, 1906–
1936, 46.

Woodrow Wilson, a Democrat, won the governorship. In some states where the Democratic organization was weak, Insurgent and progressive Republicans replaced Taft regulars in public offices. As Lodge reported to Roosevelt, "the tide was sweeping all over the country and nothing could stem it anywhere."[40]

[40] 13 November 1910, Roosevelt Papers; Holt, *Congressional Insurgents*, 40–41.

XIV

TAFT, TARIFF, AND TRUSTS
1911-1913

T HE REPUBLICAN LEADERSHIP during the final two
years of the Taft administration needed, above all else, to
formulate a sound and attractive party program. Party modernization had been an imperative need during the previous two
years and also during the final two years of the Roosevelt administration. The results of the 1910 election emphasized the
extent of the party's bankruptcy. By early 1911, it seemed apparent that the party was headed for almost certain defeat and
that little remained from the recent past from which to fashion
a new program more suitable to the times. The Taft administration failed to meet this critical need. Instead, the president
launched an intensive effort to commit the Republican organization to his own renomination. To achieve this goal, he called
upon already entrenched leaders in local and state Republican
organizations throughout the land to unite with him to turn back
the party Insurgents and the disaffected Roosevelt, who sought
to strengthen the voice of the people in the government and to
enhance governmental paternalism. Taft believed the elite
should rule and that they should rule through well-defined and
limited laws.

Taft seemed unable to use the basic historical strengths of the
Republican party. Traditionally the party had had a humanitarian mission, a positive economic policy, and a dream of great
national unity. Taft failed even to pretend that the party of
Lincoln should carry on the work "so nobly begun." He brushed
aside the crying need for political championship of the Negroes
and other underprivileged citizens. He was even less willing

than McKinley and Roosevelt to hand out patronage crumbs to Negroes.[1]

Two years after his election Taft stated in a letter to an equally cautious citizen that he was firm in the view on Negroes that he had earlier expressed. "In my inaugural address," he wrote William G. Brown of New York, "I attempted to foreshadow a policy of not making Southern appointments" from among the Negroes. "I based the principle on the proposition that public servants, the discharge of whose official functions aroused public prejudice necessarily interfered with the effectiveness of their work and so the public was deprived of that which it was entitled to—an efficient service." Now, he told Brown, he had still "another ground upon which this principle can be sustained," and he thought that maybe it "is a ground that is higher than the other." He reasoned that appointment of Negroes to positions in the South, "instead of helping the race from which they are made retards the growth of that race in its association with the whites and in the benefit that is to derive from the friendship and protection of the Southern whites."[2]

Taft showed no disapproval of the disfranchisement movement that had so effectively nullified the constitutional voting rights of Negroes. But he did express the qualified hope that "the vote will be restored to them . . . at a time when they should become really eligible under proper qualifications to exercise the franchise, in such small numbers, however, as not to threaten control by the better element of the community."[3] He failed either to observe or to care that disgusted Negroes in the North and the South were meanwhile drifting toward the Democratic party.[4]

In his failure to foster politically acceptable currency, tariff, and trust programs, Taft starkly revealed his lack of understanding of voter attitudes, his doctrinaire nineteenth-century

[1] Thomas Robert Cripps, "The Lily White Republicans: The Negro, the Party, and the South in the Progressive Era" (Ph.D. dissertation, University of Maryland, 1967), 331–36.

[2] 3 November 1910, Taft Papers.

[3] Ibid.

[4] Cripps, "Lily White Republicans," 332.

economic philosophy, and a temperament woefully unsuited for leadership. His performance on these economic issues confirmed the earlier doubts of observers that if he was the best his party could offer the nation as a leader, then it was time for citizens to look elsewhere.

On the currency question, Aldrich and his associates on the Monetary Commission virtually ignored Taft and Secretary of the Treasury Franklin MacVeagh in drafting a proposal for Congress. Nor did Taft even send a message to Congress on the need for currency reform.[5] Perhaps neither Taft nor Aldrich wished to be identified with the other lest a joint effort on currency reform end in a political debacle even greater than one they had helped create by working together on the tariff. The Insurgents and Democrats now constituted a bigger and more experienced force.

Early in 1911, however, Taft expressed to Aldrich his belief that it would be good politics if the senator "would formulate" his plan into a "definite bill backed by the Commission," after which "I can recommend it and present it with the arguments in its behalf to a Democratic Congress and in this way perhaps prepare the way for its being adopted as a plank of the next Republican platform."[6] By the end of the year, however, Taft had abandoned whatever hope he had previously entertained of making political use of Aldrich's labors on the currency question. In his December 1911 annual message to Congress, he presented the Aldrich point of view that Congress should approach the forthcoming recommendations of the Monetary Commission in the spirit of nonpartisanship.[7]

Meanwhile, Aldrich had retired from the Senate in 1911, feeling that his political power was in eclipse. Early in 1912, his bill for currency-banking reform reached Congress. The measure reflected Aldrich's conversion to assets currency and a more centralized bank structure but it also indicated his reluctance to

[5] A. Piatt Andrew memorandum, box 50, Biographer's Notes, Aldrich Papers; Nathaniel W. Stephenson, *Nelson W. Aldrich: A Leader in American Politics*, 399.
[6] 29 January 1911, Taft Papers.
[7] James D. Richardson, *A Compilation of the Messages and Papers of the Presidents*, 15: 7685.

accept strong governmental control over the world of finance. Aldrich and his Republican colleagues had avoided facing the problem ever since they obtained control of the government back in 1897. He now left that important issue for others to solve. Time had run out for him.

Taft and the Republican party found it convenient to accede to Aldrich's desire for a nonpartisan approach. This was reflected in the 1912 party platform[8] and in Taft's final annual message to Congress. In the latter, Taft outlined the Aldrich bill and then asserted, "I urgently invite the attention of Congress to the proposed plan and the report of the commission, with the hope that an earnest consideration may suggest amendments and changes within the general plan which will lead to its adoption for the benefit of the country."[9] It was a political gift to the next administration, if that new administration desired an opportunity to make a record of positive achievement.

Taft made a positive, albeit politically foolhardy, effort to modernize Republican tariff policy in two reform proposals. In his December 1910 message to Congress, he called for an adequately staffed Tariff Board to recommend rate changes on a "fact finding" basis.[10] In January 1911 he launched a drive for lower tariff rates through reciprocity, asking Congress to ratify a recently negotiated reciprocity treaty with Canada.[11]

Taft had told Sereno E. Payne in 1909 that a permanent "fact finding" tariff commission was a sound approach to the rate-making problem. "I should be the last," he had nevertheless insisted, "to advocate a commission with any power to fix rates."[12] Upon passage of the Payne-Aldrich bill, Taft audaciously made the most of a vaguely worded statement in that measure which read: "To secure information to assist the President in the discharge of the duties . . . in the administration of the customs laws, the President is hereby authorized to employ such

[8] Kirk H. Porter and Donald J. Johnson, *National Party Platforms, 1840–1956,* 185.
[9] Richardson, *Messages and Papers of the Presidents,* 15: 7793–95.
[10] Ibid., 7512–13.
[11] Ibid., 7581–86.
[12] 18 January 1909, Taft Papers; see also Taft to Henry Riesenberg, 18 January 1909, ibid.

persons as may be required."[13] Upon that authorization, he appointed what he called a Tariff Board.

His choice of members for the board greatly disturbed the standpat element. The editors of the protectionist *American Economist* looked upon the moderate chairman of the board, Henry C. Emery, professor of political economy at Yale University, as a "pronounced Free-Trader" from "a free-trade institution." Another member, Alvin H. Saunders, was the editor of the *Breeders' Gazette* and chairman of the American Reciprocal Tariff League. That organization, according to the *American Economist*, through its "pernicious but futile activity," had shown its desire "to trade away the protection of some industries for the benefit of others."[14] The third member, James B. Reynolds, an assistant secretary of the treasury and a one-time secretary of the Massachusetts Republican State Committee, was a protectionist, but, the *American Economist* feared, was tractable.[15]

With these able men forming a base, Taft worked assiduously toward making the Payne-Aldrich Tariff more acceptable to the public. In the course of his ill-fated Winona speech, the president said he intended to direct the Tariff Board to study the effect of the Payne-Aldrich Tariff on commerce and industry. His instructions to the Board were to study certain rates so that he could make recommendations to Congress for changes and have information available if he felt he needed to veto certain pressure group or partisan-inspired tariff bills.[16]

The tariff commission idea gained widespread popularity with the voters and in Congress, even though many people could not bring themselves to associate it or any other reform proposal with Taft, who was too closely identified in their thinking with Aldrich and Cannon. Taft urged fellow Republicans to crusade for the cause, stating that it was the most important issue in the nation.[17] In January 1911, Republican Congressman Nicholas

---

[13] Quoted in Joseph F. Kenkel, "Tariff Commission Movement: The Search for a Nonpartisan Solution of the Tariff Question" (Ph.D. dissertation, University of Maryland, 1962), 41.

[14] *American Economist*, 17 September 1909, quoted in ibid., 42–43.

[15] Ibid., 42–43.

[16] Ibid., 86–87; Richardson, *Messages and Papers of the Presidents*, 15: 7408–09.

Longworth of Ohio introduced a tariff commission bill. Lodge, hitherto not enthusiastic about it, introduced the proposal into the Senate at Taft's request.[18]

Prospects for the bill appeared to be most auspicious at the outset. It quickly passed the House by a margin of two to one. In the Senate, however, it confronted obstructionist tactics by standpatters and Democrats.[19] Aldrich, doubtless in part out of a desire to cooperate with Taft and in part because he recognized the undesirability of higher-than-necessary rates, raised no objections to the measure. He was at home ill at the time, but Taft wrote lengthily to him about the measure. "I long for your presence," he said. "I feel about you as Scott said of Roderick Dhu, 'A blast upon your bugle horn were worth a thousand men.'"[20] Genuine ultraprotectionists, such as Hale, made a futile effort to block the measure, but their opposition soon collapsed.[21]

Democrats, however, objected to the Longworth bill as a device to perpetuate high protectionism. Doubtless their real purpose was to prevent Republicans from gaining credit for a tariff reform measure. The Senate Democrats, nevertheless, despite a filibuster, failed to control the situation. The Taft forces and the Republican Insurgents, united on this particular issue, won easily when the final vote was taken on the day before Congress was scheduled to adjourn. With only one Republican joining the Democrats, the bill passed by a 56 to 23 vote.[22]

Upon the return of the bill to the House for acceptance of the Senate's minor changes, opponents surprised the friends of the measure, including Taft, by taking advantage of the state of confusion that usually marked the closing hours of a session. Democrat John J. Fitzgerald, congressman from Brooklyn, and

---

[17] Taft to Herbert S. Hadley, 7 February 1910, to John V. Farwell, 19 February 1910, to Otto T. Bannard, 19 February 1910, to J. W. Pierce, 14 April 1910, Taft Papers; Whitelaw Reid to Hart Lyman, 7 October 1910, Reid Papers.

[18] Kenkel, "Tariff Commission Movement," 63, 65; Taft to Roosevelt, 9 December 1910, and Lodge to Roosevelt, 15 February 1911, Roosevelt Papers.

[19] Kenkel, "Tariff Commission Movement," 72–73.

[20] 29 January 1911, Aldrich Papers; see also Taft to Aldrich, 14 January 1911, Taft Papers.

[21] Kenkel, "Tariff Commission Movement," 72–73.

[22] Ibid., 73–75.

the still powerful Speaker Cannon operated with perfect harmony to delay the final vote on the bill. Payne, perhaps aggrieved by the growing opinion in the country that politicians should not be entrusted with tariff-making, also contributed to the obstructionist maneuvers. In the course of a roll call, which Fitzgerald had unnecessarily called for and which Cannon had unnecessarily granted, Payne arose and announced that passage of the bill was impossible of achievement. Cannon then suspended the roll call, thus killing the bill. When next the House met, the Democrats were in control, and they left out of the next appropriation bill any provision to continue even the Tariff Board that Taft had put together on the basis of the vague authorization in the Payne-Aldrich bill.[23]

Tariff reciprocity with Canada interested Taft even more than the tariff commission measure. He believed the reciprocity issue afforded him a great political advantage, though he did recognize in it certain dangers. He saw it as an opportunity to promote international trade for the United States, which would, he thought, bring increased prosperity and lower living costs and at the same time expose his Insurgent Republican enemies as shallow and despicable frauds if they did not fall into line. By the same token, he hoped to enhance his own prospects in the 1912 election.

The movement for reciprocity with Canada grew out of the fears that had been mounting in recent years over the probability of a Canadian-American trade war. Roosevelt had entertained the idea of a reciprocity treaty with Canada that would not only remove that danger but also foster a mutual lowering of trade barriers through lowering of tariff duties on selected items. He failed, however, to push the matter. The idea gained momentum during the Taft administration, and in January 1911, the president submitted to Congress a treaty which Secretary of State Philander C. Knox had negotiated with Canada. The most conspicuous reductions proposed were on farm products and on raw materials that manufacturers purchased.[24] The measure, as the head of the *Chicago Tribune*'s Washington Bureau wrote to

<hr>

[23] Ibid., 75–80, 96.
[24] See George E. Mowry, *The Era of Theodore Roosevelt, 1900–1912,* 282–83.

Roosevelt, was "the vital legislative matter of the session." Taft, he added, "realizes the importance it will have upon the 1912 campaign, and is urging the Republican standpatters to get into line on the proposition." They were doing so, but "with wry faces."[25]

Shortly after submitting the treaty to Congress along with a message urging its passage,[26] Taft wrote a detailed letter to the ailing, about-to-retire Aldrich, who had earlier indicated his willingness to go along with the idea. The president told Aldrich that he wished the Senate leader were on hand "to lead the confused and dazed members of your body," and explained his reasons for being enthusiastic over the treaty. He recognized, he said, that certain farmers would be hurt by the new competition from Canadian products but argued that such dislocation would be temporary. Farmers, he pointed out, would quickly switch to other crops and thus share the general increased prosperity that the nation as a whole would experience. Taft also argued that instead of destroying the protective tariff system, this measure would save it. If Congress failed to pass the treaty, he believed the Democrats would win the 1912 election, and they "without restraint will play havoc with our industries and create chaos in business from which we shall be a long time recovering."[27]

In the absence of Aldrich, Taft himself played the most active role in pushing the measure through the Senate. He wrote to wavering senators and recruited their friends to pressure them to vote affirmatively. Taft pleaded successfully with Senator William O. Bradley of Kentucky, saying, "I regard this as the most important measure of my administration."[28] He also wrote friendly letters to newspapermen and made speeches.[29] But he greatly missed the helping hand of Aldrich, who during the fray

[25] John C. O'Laughlin to Roosevelt, 31 December 1910, Roosevelt Papers.
[26] Richardson, *Messages and Papers of the Presidents*, 15: 7581–88.
[27] Taft to Aldrich, 29 January 1911, Aldrich Papers.
[28] 27 February 1911, Taft Papers; see also Taft to J. C. Shaffer, 1 March, 22 July 1911, to Charles Hopkins Clark, 20 May 1911, to Robert Ives Gammell, 20, 27 May 1911, to Hoke Smith, 25 May 1911, to William Hoster, 2 June 1911—all in Taft Papers; Archie Butt, *Taft and Roosevelt: The Intimate Letters of Archie Butt, Military Aide*, 2: 701.
[29] Taft to J. M. Dickinson, 5 June 1911, and to H. V. Jones, 13 July 1911; and H. H. Kohlsaat to Taft, 17 June 1911, Taft Papers.

wrote to Taft with great cordiality but without committing himself on the specific treaty before the Senate. "I am inclined to think," he wrote, "it is more liberal in its concessions than I should have had the courage to make [it]." However, he added, "I do not and cannot know all the conditions and circumstances and therefore am not disposed to criticise." He added that he felt that "in view of my future influence on certain parties" he should not "be a partisan or announced as such. I think you will understand what I mean by this."[30]

No one else in the Senate stepped forward to help Taft. Senator Smoot, Aldrich's right-hand man, could not see why Taft had taken up the reciprocity movement in the first place, nor why Aldrich went along with him on the matter.[31] Taft complained to his brother Horace, "I labor under the very serious disadvantage" of having no "very earnest supporters to take the lead." Even Root, he said, was predicting "great political disaster to those who are supporting the bill, although he is going to support it." Taft told his brother that "some of my supporters disgust me more than I can say" and added, as an example, that "Lodge never misses an opportunity to say things that heap ridicule on the bill."[32]

Lodge was indeed disgruntled. He reported to Roosevelt that while he favored the policy and would do what he could to help Taft with it, the treaty was "making a great deal of trouble." Taft "has embarrassed us needlessly by keeping it until the last minute and by making a very poor agreement from the point of view of reciprocal benefits, so that the scheme is extremely vulnerable." Lodge, particularly concerned over the provisions regarding fishing, complained that the negotiations were carried on by men in the State Department "who refused to consult the tariff board and who knew nothing about the subject."[33]

Taft's supporters had good reason to be concerned over the possible consequences of the reciprocity contest, especially as it affected the party in the Middle West. It was all too apparent

[30] 17 February 1911, ibid.
[31] Reed Smoot memorandum, box 50, Biographer's Notes, Aldrich Papers.
[32] 25 May 1911, Taft Papers.
[33] 21 February 1911, Roosevelt Papers.

to them that Taft's stubborn insistence on passage of the measure was seriously alienating what little support he and those loyal to him retained in that agrarian segment of the Republican party. It might be sound economics for the government to lower tariff rates on agricultural products at the same time it reduced raw material costs for manufacturers, but it was manifestly suicidal politics when administered to large numbers of the Republican party who were not prepared to change their deeply ingrained economic views. Taft failed to find anybody in the Senate who believed with him that the Republican farmers would accept his economic philosophy.

The regular session of Congress refused to ratify the treaty, so the determined Taft made a deal with southern low-tariff Democrats and called a special session to carry it out. This session lasted throughout the hot summer of 1911 and ended with the Republican party badly shaken as Congress passed the reciprocity treaty. To his brother Charles, the victorious president wrote on July 22, "at half past one today, the reciprocity bill passed the Senate by a vote of 53 to 27. I am delighted because I believe it is going to be a great epoch in the history of our relations with Canada." As for the politics of it, "When I recommended reciprocity, I expected the insurgents not only to support the bill but to claim that I was only trailing after them, and coming to their view. Instead of which, they repudiated the bill, and have put themselves in the hole in which they find themselves."[34]

But it turned out otherwise. Canada, fearful of becoming a mere appendage of the United States, refused to ratify the treaty, and within the United States Taft lost indispensable voter support in the Middle West. The Republican farmers did not forget what they considered his failure to recognize their needs. In February 1912 the secretary of the Nebraska Farmers' Congress reported that farmers in his area were against "President Taft by reason of his position on the tariff as exemplified in his Winona speech and the Canadian reciprocity matter." He had failed to "stand close to the people" and "does not get down

[34] 22 July 1911, Taft Papers.

on the bottom rung of the ladder and look at matters from the view point of the common people."[35] Taft supporters in the region were discouraged. A sympathetic Chicago newsman, after interviewing Taft, concluded, "Lacking somewhat in vision, lacking somewhat in insight, distinctly lacking in skill, he recalls to mind that frontier musician who was doing the best he could."[36]

Taft, like his predecessor, gave serious attention to the trust problem. His approach, however, differed from Roosevelt's. Always the traditionalist, Taft contented himself largely with vigorous enforcement of the 1890 Sherman Act, which he considered to be in danger. He viewed the Sherman Act as the cornerstone of the nation's trust policy and insisted that it was important and sufficient to "preserve the law intact" against the attempts "concentrated wealth is making against the law itself."[37] He seemed largely unaware of the failure of the Sherman Act to meet the requirements of a large and complex economy and strongly disagreed with those who would tamper with or compromise it through the legalization of "reasonable" restraint of trade. He felt any such distinction was impracticable.[38] Taft nevertheless had no qualms about increased federal power as long as it remained within what he considered constitutional bounds. He favored an amendment to the Constitution allowing a federal income tax in time of war, supported stringent federal regulation of interstate commerce, and endorsed federal inheritance taxes, corporation taxes, and a federal incorporation law. He was not a "states' rights" Democrat.

Intent on being a trustbuster, Taft employed the services of his politically unseasoned Attorney General George W. Wickersham, whose broad and vigorous attack on the trusts frightened and incensed businessmen. The more they lamented, however, the more vigorous seemed to be the Taft-Wickersham crusade. Prominent Washington banker Charles C. Glover reported in mid-1910 that the financial world looked upon erstwhile Wall

[35] W. S. Delano to Roosevelt, 15 February 1912, Roosevelt Papers.
[36] Chicago Daily News, 1 December 1911, clipping, ibid.
[37] Taft to J. C. Hemphill, 16 November 1911, Taft Papers.
[38] Richardson, Messages and Papers of the Presidents, 15: 7449–54.

Street lawyer Wickersham as the greatest traitor since Benedict Arnold.[39] Henry L. Higginson no longer exuded the spirit of goodwill toward Wickersham that he had expressed to Lodge when the attorney general assumed office. Formerly, in the course of praising Taft's cabinet appointments, Higginson had written Lodge, "Wickersham is delightful, and is a partner in absolutely the highest-toned office in New York."[40] By early 1910, however, Lodge found it necessary to calm Higginson's fears regarding the administration's antitrust intentions.[41] News had spread that Wickersham had said in a public address that at least a hundred corporations would need to dissolve. Businessmen claimed that the general uneasiness was causing business to stagnate.[42] They were particularly worried as they awaited the outcome of the Standard Oil case.[43]

The May 1911 Supreme Court decision dissolving the Standard Oil Company compounded the frenzied state of mind of businessmen and caused political pressure to mount against Taft. It was now apparent that the Supreme Court, as well as the administration, remained loyal to the Sherman Act. The Court added on to its Standard Oil decision, moreover, the historic "rule of reason," which Taft had considered impractical. The "rule of reason" left unanswered the question of which trusts should be saved.

The Wickersham-Taft trustbusting effort, together with the Standard Oil decision, caused both friend and foe of the administration to press Taft for some action to calm the troubled waters. Some of his friends said the situation harmed his chances of being renominated in 1912. Some suggested that Wickersham "talked too much" and should relax his antitrust drive. Taft's close friend Otto Bannard feared a business depression. He suggested, "At some time in the near future it may

[39] Butt, *Taft and Roosevelt*, 1: 366.
[40] 5 March 1909, Lodge Papers.
[41] 21, 28 January, 3, 9 February 1910, Higginson Papers.
[42] H. H. Kohlsaat to Taft, 25 October 1911, Taft Papers.
[43] Root to N. T. Porter, 18 February 1910, and Henry L. Higginson to Root, 1 April 1910, Root Papers; W. Emlen Roosevelt to Roosevelt, 24 March 1910, Roosevelt Papers; Charles G. Dawes to Charles D. Norton (Taft's secretary), 23 March 1911, Taft Papers.

become good politics to stop 'knocking,' and to smile upon industrious endeavor approvingly."[44] Whitelaw Reid remarked that "It would be a pity" if Taft should lose his support among the moderates "through entry upon prosecutions of corporations which the responsible public would regard as persecutions."[45]

But the stubborn Taft and the equally stubborn Wickersham did not relax their attack. In fact, short of suddenly reversing their basic approach to the whole trust problem, there was not much they could do. Horace Taft mused, "The queer thing about the situation is that no business man has anything to suggest." The businessman "growls, but he can hardly be fool enough to think that the Sherman law can be repealed or modified in any way toward leniency. The only other suggestion possible is that the Administration refrain from enforcing the law, which, put bluntly, is rather a tough thing for them to urge."[46]

Although the Taft brothers and other traditionalists might feel that no businessman, or anybody else, could "be fool enough" to suggest repealing or modifying the Sherman Act, there certainly was a growing feeling among lawyers, business-men, economists, and eastern politicians that the administration should lead the nation in that direction. But Taft refused to entertain such a thought. When Henry L. Higginson wrote insistently to him that businessmen often were unable to judge whether or not they were violating the Sherman Act,[47] Taft replied just as insistently that "Every business man knows when he is violating the anti-trust law."[48] Amid the worried and angry furor in the business world, Taft wrote privately to his brother Charles, "The business men are fools, like some of the voters." At times "they don't see their real interest; they don't have the power of discrimination." They "only think of their

[44] Otto Bannard to Taft, 6 August 1911, Taft Papers.

[45] Reid to Hart Lyman, 18 August 1911, Reid Papers; see also: Max Pam to Taft, 16, 20 September 1911; H. L. Kramer to Taft, 6 October 1911; Horace Taft to Taft, 25 October 1911—all in Taft Papers.

[46] Horace Taft to Taft, 25 October 1911, Taft Papers; see also copy of Horace Taft to Julius Maltby, 17 October 1911, enclosed in above letter.

[47] 7 September 1911, ibid.

[48] 8 September 1911; see also: Taft to Higginson, 28, 31 July, 3 August 1911; Otto Bannard to Taft, 5 November 1911; *Chicago Daily News*, editorial, 30 October 1911, clipping—all in Taft Papers.

own particular interest," favoring "special privilege in the sense of having themselves favored and everybody else prosecuted." He cited in particular Elbert H. Gary, George W. Perkins, and T. Coleman du Pont.[49]

Although the Supreme Court's enunciation of the "rule of reason" was a blow to Taft's oversimplified trustbusting position, the president did not recognize the full extent of its implications. On the day after the Court declared its decision, Taft wrote to his wife, "It did not take exactly the line of distinction I have drawn but it certainly approximates it."[50] As a former judge, he tried valiantly to explain to himself and to the public that he and the Court were really in agreement in regard to "reasonableness" in restraint of trade.

In the course of a speech delivered in Detroit, Taft declared that his statement in his special message to Congress of January 1910 concerning "good trusts" and "bad trusts" was in harmony with the Court's "rule of reason."[51] But he had never really admitted there was such a thing as a good trust. He simply quoted a cumbersome paragraph from the 1910 message, and then in an *ex cathedra* manner dismissed the matter with one sentence: "Instead of being at variance," he said, that paragraph "is in exact accord with those decisions." One-time Attorney General Richard Olney, a Boston Democrat and railroad attorney, remarked in a sophisticated essay that Taft's statement was "a robust assertion but not exactly satisfying" and that it left "the impression that the task of reconciling the President's two utterances is very much like that of reconciling the supreme court's two versions of the anti-trust law." Olney himself adhered more to the Rooseveltian approach and was encouraging fellow Democrats to do likewise.[52] He told Democratic Senator Francis G. Newlands that his bill for the establishment of an "Interstate Trade Commission . . . proposes the only legislation from which the great industries of the country can expect any

---

[49] 2 June 1912, ibid.; see also Taft to Arthur R. Kimball, 21 November 1911, ibid.

[50] 16 May 1911, ibid.

[51] See Richardson, *Messages and Papers of the Presidents,* 15: 7454.

[52] Olney, "National Judiciary and Big Business," *Boston Herald,* Special Feature section, 24 September 1911, copy in Olney Papers.

relief from the war that is now being made upon them by the government under the provisions of the Sherman Anti-trust law."[53]

Certainly the day had passed when the Taft-Wickersham trustbusting approach might have been equal to the situation. It was ironical that Olney, an old-time Cleveland Bourbon Democrat, should demonstrate more sense on the trust problem than twentieth-century Taft. Olney pointed out Taft's illogic and the misfortune of having the problem left to the courts. Obviously Olney saw that the courts lacked the necessary technical and economic basis for such decisions. He scolded Congress and called upon it to modernize the government's trust policy, making it clear that he favored additional federal supervision of business. "In that connection," Olney stated, "it is to be noted that a large and growing volume of opinion among the most intelligent and influential men of the day favors the proposition that large industrial combinations may be regarded as in the same class with the public service corporations, and, by reason of their size and the resulting power, may require in their own interest as well as that of the public like supervision and regulation." To emphasize his point, Olney went on to say, "In short, the same causes and considerations which have brought into being and which justify an interstate commerce commission and an interstate commerce court, which make business men, whatever their past affiliations, hope for great results from the work of an expert and permanent tariff commission, these same causes and considerations forcibly suggest . . . that some similar agency be employed in the case of big industrial combinations."[54]

Some old-line trustbusters lauded the Taft-Wickersham crusade. Ironically, however, the most ardent trustbusters, including LaFollette, had become so angry at Taft over other matters that they left it to others to praise the administration. Railroad-oriented Grenville M. Dodge concluded that the Taft administration "has actually accomplished more in acts [actions] than any one that ever went before." Wise old Dodge, looking toward

[53] 17 November 1911, Olney Papers.
[54] Olney, "National Judiciary and Big Business."

the 1912 election, added, "Since this reform movement started, there is one thing that is absolutely certain that whoever is elected has got to come out with a well defined policy of protecting and making safe the big business of the country."[55] Hence, he and Olney were not far apart.

Taft and Wickersham continued to push forward their trust-busting, apparently without recognizing that not all trusts were a national evil. The administration's indictment of the U. S. Steel Corporation in October 1911 finally antagonized none other than Roosevelt. It hurt Taft in Wall Street, with Roosevelt followers, and with his own followers. It was one of the greatest political blunders of his career.

Politically, there was grave concern within the Taft camp, particularly in the East, when the inauguration of the U. S. Steel suit was announced. New Jersey leader Franklin Murphy expressed his concern in letters to Charles D. Hilles, soon to become chairman of the Republican National Committee and a political confidant of the president. Hilles slyly passed on to Taft Murphy's letters and those of some other persons. Murphy declared, "Great as my devotion is to President Taft and his welfare, and fully as I believe that he is the finest specimen of manhood that we have had in the Presidential chair since Lincoln, I cannot let my admiration for him prevent my speaking out when I think he is taking a course which is likely to plunge the country into disaster." Murphy was frightened when he learned of the Steel Corporation indictment "because," he said, "I knew that it would for the present take away from the President a large number of supporters, whose help he needs, and with whom some of us are sitting up nights to hold them fast."[56]

Taft's allies and friends initially tended to place the blame for what they considered his mistaken judgment in the U. S. Steel matter on his advisers, but later they blamed his own stubborn disposition. "The President ought to be properly advised," said Murphy in a letter that reached Taft, "before he

[55] Dodge to James S. Clarkson, 10 November 1911, Clarkson Papers.
[56] 2 October 1911; see also Murphy to Hilles, 11 October, 2 November 1911; H. H. Kohlsaat to Hilles, 30 October 1911, Taft Papers.

reaches a conclusion, for when he gets 'sot,' he is hopeless."[57] Otto Bannard pleaded with Taft to "Please talk these things over with some of your close advisers."[58] But Taft brushed aside their advice.[59]

Many of Taft's admirers felt that his trustbusting was not only politically foolhardy but economically unsound. A member of the Taft organization, newspaper publisher Charles F. Scott of Iola, Kansas, was worried upon his return from a two-week speaking tour in Massachusetts. "I never saw men in quite the mood that the 'big business' men of that State are now in," he informed Taft. "They are angry and alarmed and discouraged. They are angry because they think the Administration is needlessly aggressive and harsh in its prosecutions. They are alarmed because they don't know where the next bolt will fall. And they are discouraged because they don't see any prospect for relief from a situation which they declare is paralyzing enterprise." These people, Scott said, were pleading for the government to present some business guidelines as a means of obtaining reasonable insurance against possible prosecution. Scott's solution was simply the Rooseveltian approach of more federal supervision of business. "Personally," Scott asserted, "I have wondered if it might not be practicable to handle the trusts as we do the railroads. . . . This much is certain: The sentiment of the country is ripe now, as it has never been before, for legislation which shall recognize the fact that big corporations are a necessity and shall deal with them as great instruments of commerce, not as public enemies." The public, he insisted, has abandoned its "Down with Trusts" attitude, and "will give serious and respectful attention, I believe, to any recommendation that promises reasonable regulation with no danger of strangulation."[60] A few months earlier, another Kansas editor, William Allen White, writing to Taft, had mentioned favorably the "rule of reason." He explained that he believed "trusts and combinations are economic and industrial necessities and should be controlled rather than dismembered."[61]

[57] Murphy to Hilles, 2 November 1911, Taft Papers.
[58] 11 November 1911, Taft Papers.
[59] Taft to Bannard, 13 November 1911, Taft Papers.
[60] 13 November 1911, Taft Papers.

Some of Taft's friends wanted Wickersham fired as the one most to blame for the overzealous trustbusting activity. It was certainly true that Wickersham conducted the crusade as though possessed. Perhaps he wished to quell doubts concerning his conscientiousness which had been a subject of unfriendly public speculation at the time of his appointment as attorney general. Observers such as Henry Adams had questioned Taft's wisdom in placing an unknown Wall Street law partner of Henry Taft in that sensitive position.[62] And Wickersham disliked Roosevelt. In September 1910, Archie Butt had remarked that "Attorney General Wickersham literally grows frenzied when he talks of Roosevelt."[63]

In a less partisan, emotional atmosphere, more people might have observed that Wickersham was conducting his office in a manner to please legal purists and laissez faire economists. As his tenure in office approached the end, he expressed some revealing thoughts to an attorney general of an earlier era, Richard Olney. To that famed member of Cleveland's cabinet, who had broken up the Pullman strike of 1894, Wickersham wrote, "none here ever forget that you are entitled to the credit of having advised President Cleveland to take the effective steps which he did to remove the 'restraint on interstate commerce' caused by the strikers at Chicago; and, through the prosecutions of [Eugene] Debs and others, of having established the great principle that it is within the constitutional power of the Federal Government to remove any restraint on interstate commerce, whether caused—to use Mr. Knox's phrase in arguing the Northern Securities case— 'by a mob, a sandbank, or a conspiracy.'" Following that lengthy, one-sentence introduction, Wickersham made the point, "If I could feel, on leaving this office, that I had rendered as great a service to my country as you did in that matter, I should, indeed, be well satisfied."[64]

During the U. S. Steel Corporation suit, which eventually

---

[61] 20 June 1911, Taft Papers.

[62] Adams to Whitelaw Reid, 15 February 1909, Reid Papers; Horace Taft to Taft, 25 October 1911; Franklin Murphy to Charles D. Hilles, 27 October, 2 November 1911; Otto Bannard to Taft, 20 March 1912—all in Taft Papers.

[63] Butt, *Taft and Roosevelt*, 2: 538.

[64] 12 January 1912, Olney Papers.

ended in victory for the corporation, Wickersham's singleness of purpose and commitment to the Sherman Act, together with Taft's stubborn honesty and desire to be a consistent trustbuster, entrapped them in a most unfortunate situation with Roosevelt. The specific question at issue was whether U. S. Steel's 1907 acquisition of the Tennessee Coal and Iron Company had violated the Sherman Act. Roosevelt had consented to the acquisition when he and Wall Street leaders were working together to check the 1907 financial panic. Now, however, the federal government's indictment of U. S. Steel contained the charge that the 1907 action was illegal.[65]

When Taft decided to go along with the Justice Department's investigation of U. S. Steel, it was inevitable that the solicitor general's office would have to review the history of the Tennessee Coal and Iron Company acquisition. Otherwise critics might charge that politics had motivated the oversight. The government did include in its bill of equity the charge that that purchase was partly responsible for the creation of the monopoly, that "A desire to stop the panic was not the sole moving cause." The steel company was seeking also to absorb "a company that had recently assumed a position of potential competition."[66]

Roosevelt interpreted this as a personal criticism of him and believed that Taft had treated him shabbily.[67] Indignant at the implication that he had been a pawn of U. S. Steel, he stated privately, "Taft was a member of my cabinet when I took that action and he was enthusiastic in his praise of what was done. . . . It ill becomes him either by himself or through another afterwards to act as he is now acting."[68]

The U. S. Steel Corporation indictment gave Roosevelt a good

[65] Mowry, *Era of Theodore Roosevelt*, 288–89.

[66] Quoted in John A. Garraty, *Right-Hand Man: The Life of George W. Perkins*, 252.

[67] Several years later, Senator Robert A. Taft stated that of course his father had had to proceed with the case if he considered the steel combination illegal. But he criticized "the dragging in of T. R.'s name when the case could have been stated much less offensively to him." Senator Taft added, "I always blamed Wickersham for this—but it never occurred to me to question the justice of filing the case." Robert A. Taft to Henry Pringle, 31 August 1939, Henry F. Pringle Papers.

[68] Roosevelt to James R. Garfield, 31 October 1911, Morison, *Letters*, 7: 430–31; see also Garfield to Roosevelt, 27 October 1911, Roosevelt Papers.

chance to publicize his New Nationalism views on governmental regulation of business. In an article published in *Outlook* magazine, November 18, 1911, he examined the trust situation, pointing out what he considered to be the chaos in the Taft antitrust effort. At the same time he argued the merits of governmental regulation of trusts as a substitute for their dissolution. He called for a government regulatory body for industry similar in nature to the Interstate Commerce Commission. Such a body, he suggested, should have the authority to set prices on goods produced under monopolistic conditions.[69]

Roosevelt's article reflected his remarkable political agility. He used the indictment of U. S. Steel to attack Taft's trust policy without risking a public outcry that he was a friend of greedy trusts. U. S. Steel had maintained better relations with the public and with the government than had most other giant concerns, thanks to the efforts for several years of Elbert H. Gary and George W. Perkins. Roosevelt's article, moreover, appeared at a time when business interests showed great concern over what many of them considered to be the unreasonable, indiscriminate nature of the Taft-Wickersham trustbusting. Consequently, many business leaders publicly commended Roosevelt for his forthright article on the subject. Grenville M. Dodge, Andrew Carnegie, Elbert H. Gary, and Frank A. Vanderlip spoke out in favor of Roosevelt's regulatory plan.[70] But Taft continued to regard the Sherman Act as a cure-all and to believe the public would sustain him in that view. To his brother Horace he wrote, "Roosevelt's outburst has held the attention of the public for a time, but mark my words, the result of the suggestion" for a change in the Sherman law "is going to be nothing but a flash in the pan and a fizzle."[71] It was an understatement when Lodge reported to Higginson, "I do not believe I could persuade the President to do anything in regard to the Sherman law." But Lodge felt that the nation greatly needed "constructive legislation" on trusts, as Roosevelt had "pointed out in his article."[72]

[69] "The Trusts, the People, and the Square Deal," *Outlook* 99 (18 November 1911): 649–56.
[70] George E. Mowry, *Theodore Roosevelt and the Progressive Movement*, 192.
[71] 25 November 1911, Taft Papers.
[72] 8 December 1911, Higginson Papers.

Roosevelt's anger was understandable; but so was Taft's decision to proceed against U. S. Steel. The panic of 1907 had caught Roosevelt in an awkward predicament; the Taft-Wickersham trustbusting commitment caught Taft in a similar quandary. But by 1911, the relations between Taft and Roosevelt, which had become strained long before, had deteriorated to such a low point that neither of them was able to place the situation in retrievable perspective.

Taft's bid for renomination to the presidency reflected his adherence to elitism. Rather than appeal to the public, he sought the irrevocable endorsement of the many conventional, substantial, and cautious Republican regulars who for a long time had presided over local and state party organizations. These men would make up many of the slates of delegates to the national nominating convention. Early in 1911, Taft, with the able assistance of his energetic and strongly anti-Roosevelt private secretary, Charles D. Hilles, began assiduously to obtain the firm endorsement of these habitual, tradition-bound Republicans. Following the convention, Hilles became chairman of the Republican National Committee. Taft's preconvention campaign netted him a slim majority of thirty-seven delegates over all his opponents. His control of the National Committee assured him an advantage in the settlement of disputes over contested delegates. On the final vote in the convention, held in June, Taft received 561 votes and Roosevelt 107, while 349 were recorded as present but not committed, and 41 votes scattered. Roosevelt supporters then left to establish a more reform-oriented party, thereby leaving the Republican party firmly in the hands of men of great caution who were suspicious of the public and of paternalistic government.[73]

The 1912 election brought to an end a political era that had begun auspiciously a decade and a half earlier. In Republican terms the election was a sorry exhibition of confusion, obfuscation, and neglect. Republican leaders gave no vitality to the great issues that had shaped and sustained their party for so long—the Negro problem, the currency question, and the tariff

[73] Norman M. Wilensky, *Conservatives in the Progressive Era: The Taft Republicans of 1912*, 12–18, 37–48, 68.

and trust issues. Personality differences divided the Republicans, as Taft's regulars and Roosevelt's Progressives vilified each other. The campaign descended to a hassle over such relatively minor matters as Roosevelt's visionary court reform proposal. Nor did the revived Democratic party with Woodrow Wilson at the helm raise the level of public dialogue.

The election greatly reduced the political power of the surviving 1897–1912 top Republican leaders. Taft remained active in public affairs, however, and became chief justice of the Supreme Court in 1921. The Democrats carried on his crusade for a tariff commission and for reciprocity. Roosevelt forfeited his position of great power and influence when he left the Republican party to head the Progressive party. The Democrats adopted his nationalist approach to the trust problem and eventually picked up the Negro problem where he had left it. Uncle Joe Cannon, although defeated in his 1912 bid to return to the House, did return soon, serving from 1915 to 1923. He lived on until 1926, dying at the age of ninety. Unlike some of the others, however, he left nothing that the Democrats wanted to include in their New Freedom, New Deal, Fair Deal, or Great Society.

Clearly, in the course of the decade and a half between 1897 and 1913, the Republican party had lost its way. Looking ahead, no one could predict when or if the Grand Old Party would find adequate programs and new leadership sufficient to meet the demands of an ever expanding nation.

Bibliography of Works Cited

In addition to the works listed here, the authors used selected newspapers and documents; to list them here would be of little aid to the reader.

I. *Manuscript Collections*

Aldrich, Nelson W. Papers. Library of Congress. Part of this collection, boxes 46–52, consists primarily of the research notes of biographer Nathaniel W. Stephenson, which his able research assistant, Dr. Jeannette Nichols, obtained for him. In this collection of notes we found particularly valuable for our purpose the memorandums on interviews that Dr. Nichols had with acquaintances of Aldrich, and the occasional letters addressed to Aldrich during his career in the Senate. In the footnotes we have designated this portion of the collection as Biographer's Notes; because of its disorganized condition we have indicated the number of the box in which a particular item is located. The Biographer's Notes were not available to researchers before May 1967.

Allison, William B. Papers. Iowa State Department of History and Archives, Des Moines.

Beveridge, Albert J. Papers. Library of Congress.

Bonaparte, Charles J. Papers. Library of Congress.

Chandler, William E. Papers. Library of Congress.

Clarkson, James S. Papers. Library of Congress.

Cortelyou, George B. Papers. Library of Congress. Some of these are actually in the William McKinley Papers, also in the Library of Congress, listed as an addenda to that collection.

Cummins, Albert B. Papers. Iowa State Department of History and Archives, Des Moines.

Dodge, Grenville M. Papers. Iowa State Department of History and Archives, Des Moines.

Hamlin, Charles S. Papers. Library of Congress.

Higginson, Henry L. Papers. Baker Library, Harvard University, Cambridge, Mass.

Knox, Philander C. Papers. Library of Congress.
Lenroot, Irvine L. Papers. Library of Congress.
Lodge, Henry Cabot. Papers. Massachusetts Historical Society, Boston.
McKinley, William. Papers. Library of Congress.
Olney, Richard. Papers. Library of Congress.
Perkins, George W. Papers. Columbia University Library, New York.
Platt, Orville H. Papers. Connecticut State Library, Hartford.
Pringle, Henry F. Papers. Library of Congress.
Reid, Whitelaw. Papers. Library of Congress.
Roosevelt, Theodore. Papers. Library of Congress. In the footnotes we
    have cited this collection only for those items not printed in Elting
    E. Morison, ed., *The Letters of Theodore Roosevelt*, 8 vols. (Cam-
    bridge, Mass., 1951–1956); or in Henry Cabot Lodge, ed., *Selections
    from the Correspondence of Theodore Roosevelt and Henry Cabot
    Lodge, 1884–1918,* 2 vols. (New York, 1925).
Root, Elihu. Papers. Library of Congress.
Spooner, John C. Papers. Library of Congress.
Sullivan, Mark. Papers. Library of Congress.
Taft, William Howard. Papers. Library of Congress.
Washington, Booker T. Papers. Library of Congress.

II. *Unpublished Dissertations and Papers*

Barfield, Claude, Jr. "Theodore Roosevelt and Congressional Leader-
    ship: Trust Legislation in 1903." Paper presented at annual con-
    vention of the Organization of American Historians, 23 April 1965,
    Kansas City, Missouri.
Buchanan, William. "Theodore Roosevelt and the Business Com-
    munity." Master's thesis, University of Maryland, 1968.
Cripps, Thomas Robert. "The Lily White Republicans: The Negro,
    the Party, and the South in the Progressive Era." Ph.D. dissertation,
    University of Maryland, 1967.
Kenkel, Joseph F. "The Tariff Commission Movement: The Search for
    a Nonpartisan Solution of the Tariff Question." Ph.D. dissertation,
    University of Maryland, 1962.
Markowitz, Stanley. "The Aldrich-Vreeland Bill: Its Significance in the
    Struggle for Currency Reform, 1893–1908." Master's thesis, Univer-
    sity of Maryland, 1965.
Polster, Harvey. "Mark Hanna and the Republican Hierarchy, 1897–
    1904." Master's thesis, University of Maryland, 1964.
Rumble, Walker. "Rectitude and Reform: Charles J. Bonaparte and the

Politics of Gentility, 1851–1921." Ph.D. dissertation, University of Maryland, 1971.

Sayre, Ralph Mills. "Albert Baird Cummins and the Progressive Movement in Iowa." Ph.D. dissertation, Columbia University, 1958.

Wiseman, John B. "Dilemmas of a Party out of Power: The Democracy, 1904–1912." Ph.D. dissertation, University of Maryland, 1967.

III. *Books*

Barry, David S. *Forty Years in Washington.* Boston, 1924.

Bartholdt, Richard. *From Steerage to Congress.* Philadelphia, 1930.

Bishop, Joseph Bucklin. *Theodore Roosevelt and His Times, Shown in His Own Letters.* 2 vols. New York, 1920.

Blum, John M. *The Republican Roosevelt.* Cambridge, Mass., 1954.

Bolles, Blair. *Tyrant from Illinois: Uncle Joe Cannon's Experiment with Personal Power.* New York, 1951.

Bowers, Claude G. *Beveridge and the Progressive Era.* Cambridge, Mass., 1932.

Brownlow, Louis. *Passion for Politics: The Autobiography of Louis Brownlow.* 2 vols. Chicago, 1955–1958.

Busbey, L. White. *Uncle Joe Cannon: The Story of a Pioneer American.* New York, 1927.

Butt, Archie. *Taft and Roosevelt: The Initimate Letters of Archie Butt, Military Aide.* 2 vols. New York, 1930.

Chessman, G. Wallace. *Governor Theodore Roosevelt: The Albany Apprenticeship, 1898–1900.* Cambridge, Mass., 1965.

Clark, Champ. *My Quarter Century of American Politics.* New York, 1920.

Cole, Cyrenus. *I Remember, I Remember: A Book of Recollections.* Iowa City, 1936.

Coletta, Paolo E. *William Jennings Bryan: Political Evangelist, 1860–1908.* Lincoln, Neb., 1964.

Coolidge, Louis A. *An Old-Fashioned Senator: Orville H. Platt of Connecticut.* New York, 1910.

Crissey, Forrest. *Theodore E. Burton, American Statesman.* Cleveland, 1956.

Croly, Herbert D. *Marcus Alonzo Hanna: His Life and Work.* New York, 1912.

Current, Richard Nelson. *Pine Logs and Politics: A Life of Philetus Sawyer, 1816–1900.* Madison, Wis., 1950.

Dawes, Charles G. *A Journal of the McKinley Years.* Chicago, 1950.

Evans, Lawrence B. *Samuel W. McCall, Governor of Massachusetts.* Boston, 1916.

Faulkner, Harold U. *The Decline of Laissez Faire, 1897–1917.* Vol. 7 of *The Economic History of the United States.* New York, 1951.

———. *Politics, Reform and Expansion, 1890–1900.* New York, 1959.

Foraker, Joseph Benson. *Notes of a Busy Life.* 2 vols. Cincinnati, 1916.

Fowler, Dorothy Ganfield. *John Coit Spooner: Defender of Presidents.* New York, 1961.

Garraty, John A. *Henry Cabot Lodge: A Biography.* New York, 1953.

———. *Right-Hand Man: The Life of George W. Perkins.* New York, 1957.

Gompers, Samuel. *Seventy Years of Life and Labor: An Autobiography.* 2 vols. New York, 1925.

Gwinn, William Rea. *Uncle Joe Cannon, Archfoe of Insurgency: A History of the Rise and Fall of Cannonism.* New York, 1957.

Hagedorn, Hermann, ed. *The Works of Theodore Roosevelt.* National Edition. 20 vols. New York, 1926.

Harbaugh, William Henry. *Power and Responsibility: The Life and Times of Theodore Roosevelt.* New York, 1961.

Harvey, George. *Henry C. Frick.* New York, 1928.

Haynes, George H. *The Senate of the United States: Its History and practice.* 2 vols. Boston, 1938.

Heaton, John L. *The Story of a Page: Thirty Years of Public Service and Public Discussion in the Editorial Columns of the New York World.* New York, 1913.

Hechler, Kenneth W. *Insurgency: Personalities and Politics of the Taft Era.* New York, 1940.

Hirshson, Stanley P. *Farewell to the Bloody Shirt.* Bloomington, Ind., 1962.

Holt, James. *Congressional Insurgents and the Party System, 1909–1916.* Cambridge, Mass., 1967.

Jessup, Philip C. *Elihu Root.* 2 vols. New York, 1938.

Kolko, Gabriel. *Railroads and Regulation, 1877–1916.* Princeton, 1965.

———. *The Triumph of Conservatism: A Reinterpretation of American History, 1900–1916.* Glencoe, Ill., 1963.

LaFeber, Walter. *The New Empire: An Interpretation of American Expansion, 1860–1898.* Ithaca, N. Y., 1963.

LaFollette, Belle Case, and LaFollette, Fola. *Robert M. LaFollette.* 2 vols. New York, 1953.

LaFollette, Robert M. *Autobiography: A Personal Narrative of Political Experiences.* Madison, Wis., 1911.

LaFollette, Robert M., ed. *The Making of America.* 10 vols. Chicago, 1907.

Leech, Margaret. *In the Days of McKinley.* New York, 1959.

Leopold, Richard W. *Elihu Root and the Conservative Tradition.* Boston, 1954.

Leuchtenburg, William E., ed. *Theodore Roosevelt: The New Nationalism.* Englewood Cliffs, N. J., 1961.

Levine, Erwin L. *Theodore Francis Green: The Rhode Island Years, 1906–1936.* Providence, 1963.

Lodge, Henry Cabot, ed. *Selections from the Correspondence of Theodore Roosevelt and Henry Cabot Lodge, 1884–1918.* 2 vols. New York, 1925.

Longworth, Alice Roosevelt. *Crowded Hours: Reminiscences.* New York, 1932.

Lowitt, Richard. *George W. Norris: The Making of a Progressive, 1861–1912.* Syracuse, 1963.

Lowry, Edward G. *Washington Close-Ups: Intimate Views of Some Public Figures.* Boston, 1921.

MacNeil, Neil. *Forge of Democracy: The House of Representatives.* New York, 1963.

Manners, William. *TR and Will: A Friendship that Split the Republican Party.* New York, 1970.

Marden, Orison S., ed. *Little Visits with Great Americans.* New York, 1904.

Maxwell, Robert S. *LaFollette and the Rise of the Progressives in Wisconsin.* Madison, Wis., 1956.

Merrill, Horace Samuel. *Bourbon Democracy of the Middle West, 1865–1896.* Baton Rouge, La., 1953.

———. *William Freeman Vilas, Doctrinaire Democrat.* Madison, Wis., 1954.

Millis, Walter. *The Martial Spirit: A Study of Our War with Spain.* Boston, 1931.

Morgan, H. Wayne. *America's Road to Empire: The War with Spain and Overseas Expansion.* New York, 1965.

———. *William McKinley and His America.* Syracuse, 1963.

Morison, Elting E., ed. *The Letters of Theodore Roosevelt.* 8 vols. Cambridge, 1951–1956.

Mowry, George E. *The Era of Theodore Roosevelt, 1900–1912.* New York, 1958.

———. *Theodore Roosevelt and the Progressive Movement.* Madison, Wis., 1947.

Neilson, James W. *Shelby M. Cullom, Prairie State Republican*. Urbana, Ill., 1962.

Nye, Russel B. *Midwestern Progressive Politics: A Historical Study of Its Origins and Development, 1870–1958*. New York, 1965.

Orcutt, William Dana. *Burrows of Michigan and the Republican Party*. New York, 1917.

Perry, Bliss. *Life and Letters of Henry Lee Higginson*. Boston, 1921.

Phillips, David Graham. *The Treason of the Senate*. Edited and with an Introduction by George E. Mowry and Judson A. Grenier. Chicago, 1964. (Originally published serially in *Cosmopolitan Magazine*, February–November 1906.)

Porter, Kirk H., and Johnson, Donald J. *National Party Platforms, 1840–1956*. Urbana, Ill., 1956.

Pratt, Julius W. *Expansionists of 1898: The Acquisition of Hawaii and the Spanish Islands*. Baltimore, 1936.

Pringle, Henry F. *The Life and Times of William Howard Taft: A Biography*. 2 vols. New York, 1939.

Richardson, James D. *A Compilation of the Messages and Papers of the Presidents*. 20 vols. New York, 1897–1927.

Richardson, Leon Burr. *William E. Chandler, Republican*. New York, 1940.

Robinson, William A. *Thomas B. Reed, Parliamentarian*. New York, 1930.

Roosevelt, Theodore. *An Autobiography*. New York, 1913.

Ross, Thomas Richard. *Jonathan Prentiss Dolliver: A Study in Political Integrity and Independence*. Iowa City, Iowa, 1958.

Rothman, David J. *Politics and Power: The United States Senate, 1869–1901*. Cambridge, Mass., 1966.

Sage, Leland L. *William Boyd Allison: A Study in Practical Politics*. Iowa City, Iowa, 1956.

Shaw, Leslie M. *Current Issues*. New York, 1908.

Simkins, Francis. *Pitchfork Ben Tillman, South Carolinian*. Baton Rouge, La., 1944.

Stanwood, Edward. *American Tariff Controversies in the Nineteenth Century*. 2 vols. Boston, 1903.

Stealey, O. O. *130 Pen Pictures of Live Men*. Washington, D. C., 1910.
———. *Twenty Years in the Press Gallery*. New York, 1906.

Stephenson, Nathaniel W. *Nelson W. Aldrich: A Leader in American Politics*. New York, 1930.

Sullivan, Mark. *The Education of an American*. New York, 1938.
———. *Our Times: The United States, 1900–1925*. 8 vols. New York, 1926–1935.

Tarbell, Ida M. *The Life of Elbert H. Gary.* New York, 1925.

Taussig, Frank W. *Tariff History of the United States.* New York, 1931.

Thorelli, Hans B. *The Federal Antitrust Policy: Origination of an American Tradition.* Baltimore, 1955.

Watson, James E. *As I Knew Them: Memoirs of James E. Watson.* Indianapolis, 1936.

Weinstein, James. *The Corporate Ideal in the Liberal State: 1900–1918.* Boston, 1968.

Wiebe, Robert H. *Businessmen and Reform: A Study of the Progressive Movement.* Cambridge, Mass., 1962.

Wilensky, Norman M. *Conservatives in the Progressive Era: The Taft Republicans of 1912.* Gainesville, Fla., 1965.

Wise, John S. *Recollections of Thirteen Presidents.* New York, 1906.

Woodward, C. Vann. *Origins of the New South.* Baton Rouge, La., 1951.

IV. *Articles in Periodicals and Collective Works*

Braeman, John. "The Square Deal in Action: A Case Study in the Growth of the 'National Police Power.'" In Braeman, John; Bremner, Robert H.; and Walters, Everett, *Change and Continuity in Twentieth-Century America*, 42–80. Columbus, Ohio, 1964.

Buenker, John D. "The Urban Political Machine and the Seventeenth Amendment." *Journal of American History* 56 (September 1969): 305–22.

Coolidge, Louis A. "Senator Aldrich, the Most Influential Man in Congress." *Ainslee's Magazine* 8 (December 1901): 405–13.

Hadley, Arthur T. "The Formation and Control of Trusts." *Scribner's Magazine* 26 (November 1899): 604–10.

Hoing, Willard. "David B. Henderson: Speaker of the House." *Iowa Journal of History* 55 (January 1957): 5–21.

Holbo, Paul S. "Presidential Leadership in Foreign Affairs: William McKinley and the Turpie-Foraker Amendment." *American Historical Review* 72 (July 1967): 1321–35.

Johnson, Arthur M. "Antitrust Policy in Transition, 1908: Ideal and Reality." *Mississippi Valley Historical Review* 48 (December 1961): 415–34.

———. "Theodore Roosevelt and the Bureau of Corporations." *Mississippi Valley Historical Review* 45 (March 1959): 571–90.

Jones, Chester Lloyd. "The Rotten Boroughs of New England." *North American Review* 197 (April 1913): 486–98.

"Lincoln." *Boston Transcript*, reprinted in the *Providence Tribune*, 17 June 1909. Copy in Nelson W. Aldrich Papers, Library of Congress.

Lowitt, Richard. "George W. Norris, James J. Hill, and the Railroad Rate Bill." *Nebraska History* 40 (June 1959): 137–45.

Olney, Richard. "National Judiciary and Big Business." *Boston Herald*, Special Feature section, 24 September 1911. Copy in Richard Olney Papers, Library of Congress.

Potter, David M. "The Historical Development of Eastern-Southern Freight Rate Relationships." In Abrams, Richard M., and Levine, Lawrence W., eds. *The Shaping of Twentieth-Century America*, 24–61. Boston, 1965.

Roosevelt, Theodore. "The Trusts, the People, and the Square Deal." *Outlook* 99 (18 November 1911): 649–56.

Sherman, Sidney A. "Relation of State to Municipalities in Rhode Island." *Annals of the American Academy of Political and Social Science* 17 (May 1901): 472–74.

Solvick, Stanley D. "William Howard Taft and the Payne-Aldrich Tariff." *Mississippi Valley Historical Review* 50 (December 1963): 424–42.

Steffens, Lincoln. "Enemies of the Republic: Wisconsin." *McClure's Magazine* 23 (October 1904): 564–79.

———. "Rhode Island: A State for Sale." *McClure's Magazine* 24 (February 1905): 337–53.

Thornbrough, Emma Lou. "The Brownsville Episode and the Negro Vote." *Mississippi Valley Historical Review* 44 (December 1957): 469–93.

Wellman, Walter. "Spooner of Wisconsin: A Sketch of the Present Leader of the Senate." *Review of Reviews* 26 (August 1902): 167–70.

Wiebe, Robert H. "The Anthracite Strike of 1902: A Record of Confusion." *Mississippi Valley Historical Review* 48 (September 1961): 229–51.

———. "The House of Morgan and the Executive, 1905–1913." *American Historical Review* 65 (October 1959): 49–60.

Wiseman, John B. "Racism in Democratic Politics, 1904–1912." *Mid-America* 51 (January 1969): 38–58.

Index

Abbott, Lyman, 113, 178, 179, 238
Adams, Henry, 273, 331
Aldrich, Abby, 80
Aldrich, Nelson W.: as one of the Four, 4, 7, 19, 27; marries, 21; in Civil War, 21; business career of, 21–22, 188–91; in business-Republican partnership, 21–22, 300; connections with J. P. Morgan and Wall Street, 22, 255–56, 259, 261–62, 264–65, 266; and Rhode Island machine politics, 22–23; personal characteristics of, 22–26, 285, 290; political philosophy of, 24–25, 277; interest in currency and tariff issues compared, 26; relations with Democrats in Senate, 26–27; and Platt, 29; and Allison, 29, 104, 123, 284; and Spooner, 32, 33, 284; beliefs on good tariff laws, 36–37, 291; and enactment of Dingley Tariff, 44, 45, 46; and Spanish-American War, 50, 52, 54; and imperialism, 54; and currency reform efforts under McKinley, 61, 63, 64, 66; and railroad rate regulation issue in 1898–1900, 70; marriage of daughter, 80, 96–97; advises Roosevelt on first message to Congress, 97; at 1902 Oyster Bay conference, 117, 119; and 1902 Rhode Island election, 133; and creation of Bureau of Corporations, 139; and 1903 Wall Street crisis, 148, 151–54; in 1904 presidential election, 167; on tariff issue in 1904–1905, 167, 197, 198, 200, 201; in 1904 Rhode Island election, 184, 187–92; in 1904 Spooner-LaFollette dispute, 185–86; Lincoln Steffens attacks, 188, 206; and Catholics, 190–91; rumored resignation of, 190; and Thomas Lawson, 207; and David

Graham Phillips, 208; in contest over Hepburn bill, 216–20; and Roosevelt during 1906 railroad rate regulation contest, 216, 217, 243; and pure food, drug, and meat inspection acts, 221; Republican decline in 1906 Rhode Island election, 234; in Roosevelt-Aldrich-Cannon triumvirate, 1907–1908, 243; in 1908 enactment of Aldrich-Vreeland Act, 255–66; and Taft, 274, 275–76, 279, 296, 299–300; in 1908 election, 274, 275–76; in new Republican command of 1909, 277, 279, 298; as head of Monetary Commission, 277, 316–17; in tariff battle of 1909, 279, 281, 283, 287–95, 297; and railroad rate regulation in 1910, 301, 303; in 1910 election, 303; 1910 election in Rhode Island, 312; retires from Senate, 316; avoids debate on tariff commission bill, 319; on reciprocity with Canada, 321–22. See also Four, the; Republican command; Roosevelt-Aldrich-Cannon triumvirate; Taft-Aldrich-Cannon triumvirate
Alger, Russell A., 14, 15, 150
Allison, William B.: as one of the Four, 4, 17; and Iowa Idea, 6, 86; power over congressional committees, 18, 19, 29; and Aldrich, 25, 29, 104, 284; and Platt, 29, 104; personal characteristics of, 29–31; in Iowa Republican party, 29–31; in Civil War, 30; in business-Republican partnership, 30, 31; leader in currency legislation in pre-McKinley decades, 30–31; close connection with railroad interests, 30, 31–32, 68, 70; political philosophy and tactics of, 30–31,

345